D1796584

Palgrave Explorations in Workplace Stigma

Series editor
Julie Gedro
Empire State College
Rochester, New York, USA

This series is a call to action for organizations to not only recognize but accept and support employees of all walks of life, regardless of the social stigmas that separate them from their seemingly "normal" counterparts. It fills the gap in scholarship surrounding the difficult issues employees face based on their background, lifestyle, or past mistakes, including mental illness, alcohol and drug addiction, sexual minorities, ex-offender status, and military veterans.

Through rigorous research and contributions from the foremost scholars in human resources, books in the series will provide an in-depth treatment of each population and offer tactful solutions for HR scholars and practitioners to effectively navigate the delicate nature of these matters. The series speaks on behalf of anyone who has ever been affected – directly or indirectly – by discrimination from an employer, and promotes a positive, productive, and purposeful working environment for employees at all levels

More information about this series at
http://www.springer.com/series/15458

Valerie Caven • Stefanos Nachmias
Editors

Hidden Inequalities in the Workplace

A Guide to the Current Challenges, Issues and Business Solutions

palgrave
macmillan

Editors
Valerie Caven
Nottingham Business School
Nottingham Trent University
Nottingham, UK

Stefanos Nachmias
Nottingham Business School
Nottingham Trent University
Nottingham, UK

Palgrave Explorations in Workplace Stigma
ISBN 978-3-319-59685-3   ISBN 978-3-319-59686-0   (eBook)
https://doi.org/10.1007/978-3-319-59686-0

Library of Congress Control Number: 2017949294

© The Editor(s) (if applicable) and The Author(s) 2018
This work is subject to copyright. All rights are solely and exclusively licensed by the Publisher, whether the whole or part of the material is concerned, specifically the rights of translation, reprinting, reuse of illustrations, recitation, broadcasting, reproduction on microfilms or in any other physical way, and transmission or information storage and retrieval, electronic adaptation, computer software, or by similar or dissimilar methodology now known or hereafter developed.
The use of general descriptive names, registered names, trademarks, service marks, etc. in this publication does not imply, even in the absence of a specific statement, that such names are exempt from the relevant protective laws and regulations and therefore free for general use.
The publisher, the authors and the editors are safe to assume that the advice and information in this book are believed to be true and accurate at the date of publication. Neither the publisher nor the authors or the editors give a warranty, express or implied, with respect to the material contained herein or for any errors or omissions that may have been made. The publisher remains neutral with regard to jurisdictional claims in published maps and institutional affiliations.

Cover illustration: marcin jucha / Alamy Stock Photo

Printed on acid-free paper

This Palgrave Macmillan imprint is published by Springer Nature
The registered company is Springer International Publishing AG
The registered company address is: Gewerbestrasse 11, 6330 Cham, Switzerland

Preface

The past decade or so has witnessed a battle to address diversity and equality needs in the workplace. This battle provides a kind of leitmotif for this book. We note that recent changes in employment relations and working conditions underscore the increase in thinking around diversity and equality. Although organisational issues differ from nation to nation, current sociopolitical environment across the globe raises concern as to how organisations can achieve greater inclusion which promotes visible and non-visible differences. Various laws and legislations have somehow provided a legal framework to protect the rights of individuals and advance equality of opportunity for all. Nevertheless, changing workforce demographics has created a number of ongoing organisational and individual challenges, including gender bias, non-declared medical or physical conditions, voluntary and involuntary disclosure of difference, dietary requirements, lifestyle and organisational engagement. Many organisations have recognised those difficult challenges which could be a first step towards improving awareness. A plethora of academic tools and framework are available to support businesses; however, there is not a single blueprint for recasting organisational attitude and addressing social stigma, and discrimination in the workplace. We have the tendency to reduce things into tidy dichotomies and homogeneous groups, but as Lisa Burrell (2016) says, 'reality is a lot messier than that'.

We acknowledge that it is difficult to review all aspects of managing diversity and equality in the workplace. Our intention in assembling this collection of chapters has been to assess how organisations manage hidden inequalities and whether the current legislative framework addresses organisational realities. We note that this book title includes the term 'hidden' and was named as an explicit label to assess whether any form of organisational practice and function reinforces not readily unseen potential differences among individuals in the workplace. There is no doubt that managing individual differences and supporting people of all walks of life have attracted more visibility in media, academic community and public debate. Nevertheless, organisations need to accept and support employees who are experiencing any form of unseen social stigmas and inequalities in the workplace. This is in line with the scope of the *Palgrave Explorations in Workplace Stigma* series aiming to understand work-related stigmas and offer tactful solutions for Human Resource scholars and practitioners.

In essence, the chapters of this book act as a critical platform to unveil 'hidden' aspects of organisational reality, challenge individual abilities to informal personal and professional practices, enhance personal learning and support the development of positive working environment for all employees. Above all, the authorship composition provides a unique blend of scholar and professional experience putting at the front anyone who has been affected by social stigmas and discrimination in the workplace. Their ultimate goal is to provide new practical and strategic insights for practitioners, managers, students and policymakers, and delve into the strategic nature of policy intervention and thought-provoking dialogue. We hope that readers will appreciate the inclusive and positive arguments expressed in this book.

Nottingham, UK   Valerie Caven
                                                        Stefanos Nachmias

References

Burrell, L. 2016. We just can't handle diversity. https://hbr.org/2016/07/we-just-cant-handle-diversity. Accessed 9 Feb 2017.

Acknowledgements

The authors wish to thank all contributors for taking part in this book and sharing their personal stories, expertise and knowledge. We also wish to thank the team at Palgrave Publication and most importantly Julie Gedro and Joshua Collins for giving us the space to include our work in the *Palgrave Explorations in Workplace Stigma*. The reviewers are also thanked for their feedback and comments on making this book a good piece of reading. Finally, we would like to give our gratitude to our colleagues at Nottingham Trent University for their continued support throughout the journey of producing the book.

Contents

Editors and Contributors

About the Editors

Valerie Caven is a senior lecturer at Nottingham Trent University, Nottingham Business School, and academic fellow of the Chartered Institute of Personnel and Development with research interests of the transmission of diversity policy into practice, in particular how policy becomes ignored or corrupted during the transfer. She is experienced in conducting qualitative research and has a strong understanding of both cocliac disease and the lack of organisational knowledge surrounding the management of the condition.

Stefanos Nachmias is a senior lecturer at Nottingham Trent University and academic fellow of the Chartered Institute of Personnel and Development. His research lies within the area of employability and diversity issues, especially in relation to the business case for diversity and diversity education. He is experienced in developing and delivering diversity awareness educational programmes, and supporting organisations in addressing equality issues.

About the Contributors

Janet Astley is Lecturer in Human Resource Management (HRM) at Leeds Beckett University, Leeds Business School. With extensive public sector experience prior to becoming an academic, her research interests relate to policing in the UK. Her particular interests lie in diversity and gender issues, workplace policy and practice for police officers who fall outside of the normal UK employment legislation as they are Officers of the Crown and subject to Queen's regulations. She has an interest in the ethical deployment of female officers in a male-dominated environment and the influences that socially constructed society imposes upon them in their work and life choices.

Anne Cockayne is a senior lecturer teaching on a range of post-graduate programmes in the Human Resource Management (HRM) division of Nottingham Business School. She has spent most of her career within Human Resources, most recently within management learning and development, and as a qualified business coach, working with senior managers within and outside the university sector. In 2012, Cockayne's daughter was diagnosed with Asperger's syndrome, and this has prompted her interest in the challenges facing HR specialists in managing neurodiversity in the employment context, in particular career development and employment experiences for women with Asperger's syndrome.

Irene Hardill (FAcSS) is Professor of Public Policy and Director of the Northumbria Centre for Citizenship and Civil Society, Northumbria University. She has a particular expertise in volunteering and the voluntary and community sector, demography and ageing, and knowledge exchange and user engagement. Her recent books include *Enterprising Care: Unpaid Voluntary Action in the 21st Century for Policy Press* with Sue Baines (Manchester Metropolitan University [MMU], UK) and *Knowledge Mobilisation and the Social Sciences: Research Impact and Engagement* with Jon Bannister (MMU, UK).

Scott Lawley is a senior lecturer in the Department of Human Resource Management (HRM) in Nottingham Business School. His teaching and research interests are around post-structural approaches to organisation theory and their links with gender and diversity issues in organisations. With Daniel King, he is the co-author of the textbook *Organizational Behaviour* (King and Lawley 2016). He is also active in campaigns which promote advocacy and capacity building for LGBTI (lesbian, gay, bisexual, trans, and/or intersex) inclusion in sport, and as such is the academic and research lead for the international Football versus Homophobia campaign.

Chris Lawton is a senior research fellow in the Economics Division at Nottingham Business School, Nottingham Trent University. Recent projects explore the factors affecting graduate retention and perceptions of the quality of employment for young people in Nottingham: an assessment of the impact of European Union (EU) free movement on migration, employment and wages in the East Midlands for East Midlands Councils and the UK representation in the EU. Lawton writes widely on issues related to employment quality, skills matching and migration for *The Conversation* and the *Huffington Post*, and he has recently written a Q&A article for the BBC on skills shortages in the UK labour market.

Sarah Pass is a senior lecturer at Nottingham Trent University, Nottingham Business School and academic member of the Chartered Institute of Personnel and Development (CIPD) with research interests in health and social care, the implementation of research into practice and employee experiences of work. She has been conducting research (both qualitative and quantitative) on a number of funded health-related research collaborations for over 15 years.

Maranda Ridgway is a senior lecturer at Nottingham Trent University, Nottingham Business School, having gained extensive strategic and operational Human Resource (HR) experience from a range of diverse industries including aviation, engineering consultancy, fast-moving consumer goods (FMCG), financial services, hospitality and retail. As a commercially focussed HR practitioner, Ridgway has offered expertise encompassing HR management, project management and support of the entire employee life cycle. She spent five years in Abu Dhabi, United Arab Emirates (UAE), and during this time, she had management responsibility for HR activity in the Gulf Cooperation Council (GCC) region. Ridgway also has led numerous projects including acquisitions, new business creation, programme implementation, service centralisation and organisation restructures. Finally, she has represented HR at board-level meetings, coached and influenced senior executives and led multi-cultural and disciplinary teams based in different countries.

Simon Roberts is Senior Lecturer in Human Resource Management and Organisational Behaviour at Bournemouth University where he delivers both undergraduate and postgraduate programmes. His research interests include sexual minorities in the workplace, managing gay identities, and discrimination and inequalities at work.

Daniel Wheatley is Senior Lecturer in Economics in the Department of Business and Labour Economics at the University of Birmingham. He completed his PhD, titled 'Working 9 to 5? Complex Patterns of Time Allocation Among Dual Career Households' in 2009. His primary research interests centre on time-use, flexible working arrangements, the quality of work and subjective well-being. His work employs both quantitative and mixed method approaches. His work has been published in a range of academic journals, including *Cambridge Journal of Economics*; *Gender, Work & Organization*; *Industrial Relations Journal*; *New Technology, Work and Employment*; and *Work, Employment and Society*.

Zara Whysall is a Chartered Psychologist and senior lecturer at Nottingham Trent University, Nottingham Business School. She has over a decade of experience in HR research, consultancy and training in public and private sector organisations. Her previous experience includes a number of years in Occupational Health Management, where she provided training, research and consultancy services to a wide range of clients in areas such as managing presenteeism and work-related stress. Prior to this, she also spent some years in horizon scanning, using research and tools such as scenario planning to identify and understand the implications of emerging trends for managing future work-related risks to health and well-being.

Ning Wu is Senior Lecturer in Human Resource Management at Nottingham Trent University, Nottingham Business School. Having been developing research interests in high-performance work systems, employee well-being and work-life balance practice with a special focus on the setting of the private sector, Wu's work has been published in academic journals such as *The International Journal of Human Resource Management* and *Human Resource Management Journal*.

List of Figures

List of Tables

1

Introduction to 'Hidden' Inequalities in the Workplace

Stefanos Nachmias and Valerie Caven

1.1   Background to the Book

The purpose of this section is to introduce the reader to the main themes of the book. It seeks to outline the key context and concepts explored across the chapters and enable the reader to examine the importance of understanding 'hidden' inequalities in the workplace.

The idea of producing the book arose from the authors' personal experiences in dealing with the implementation of diversity policies and organisational capacity to train and educate individuals. Many organisations have developed various strategies to diversify the workforce and establish an inclusive working environment. A number of organisational policies and procedures have been adopted to assist individuals in establishing consistent practice and addressing attitude-related issues. This is

S. Nachmias (✉) • V. Caven
Department of Human Resource Management, Nottingham Business School, Nottingham Trent University, Nottingham, UK

© The Author(s) 2018
V. Caven, S. Nachmias (eds.), *Hidden Inequalities in the Workplace*,
Palgrave Explorations in Workplace Stigma,
DOI 10.1007/978-3-319-59686-0_1

partly supported through various training and developmental activities with the aim to address diversity challenges and to somehow enhance people's awareness of the need to recognise differences in the workplace. Although there is a growing academic literature on diversity and equality, discrimination and social-related stigmas, it is still a major organisational issue (CIPD 2012). Some organisations might offer instructional diversity training (awareness and enlightenment learning practices) to encourage individuals to challenge held assumptions and ultimately entrenched stereotypical beliefs (Kulik and Roberson 2008; Anderson 2004; Harris 2003). Other organisations might offer behavioural-based training to educate participants to take personalised and participatory action towards the development of behavioural-based skills and modify implicit and explicit biases in self-reported behaviour. Nevertheless, we still find it hard to deliver long-term changes in individual attitudes and behaviour within the workplace (Pendry et al. 2007; Celik et al. 2012). For example, a recent survey into sexism in the UK reveals that sexism in the workplace is increasing rather than decreasing, with 42% of 18–34-year-olds experiencing sexism compared to 26% of the baby-boom generation (CIPD 2012). This is critical as appropriate individual attitudes towards any organisational policy is a critical factor in achieving an inclusive working environment (Purcell and Hutchinson 2007).

At a personal level, we found it sometimes difficult to deal with the level of ignorance amongst individuals, but most importantly to understand existing management perceptions in addressing organisational diversity issues. We believe that addressing diversity and equality needs requires sufficient knowledge (both at individual and organisational level), effective leadership skills and appropriate assessment of the wider business environment. Some people might call this thinking 'naive' because theory is weaker than practice due to differences in the economic and organisational context. Nevertheless, there is now the expectation to address cultural intelligence failures and ensure diversity is part of the business model roots. The Chartered Institute of Personnel and Development (CIPD 2012) argued that most British organisations have developed a strategy, policy or guidelines to address diversity needs; however, most covered the legally protected individual requirements. We do not blame them as addressing diversity issues is almost as diverse as the subject itself, and this has made the interpretation of findings and experience highly judge-mental. The issue here is that there is a kind of a 'fore-feeding' attitude towards satisfying legal expectations and preventing discrimination in the workplace. As Sherbin and Rashid (2017) argued in the Harvard Business Review, *'diversity doesn't stick without inclusion'* as measuring diversity is easy, measuring feeling is dicey. This can be better explained by highlight-ing Ahonen et al. (2014, p. 278) argument that we are unable to break the *'cycle of production of knowledge about diversity'* that does not relinquish the benefits of diversity and protect an individual's different needs.

Of course, we do not agree that the legal framework is the one to blame. Decades of social and organisational science research point to a simple truth, *'you won't get individuals on board by blaming and shaming them with rules and rededications'* (Dobbin and Kalev 2016). As educa-tors, we felt the need to assess how to ease up on the control tactics and somehow take actions in understanding the behaviour and attitude of those people who have experienced discrimination and social exclusion. Thomas Roosevelt's work was particularly influential as he argued that affirmative action is essential to manage diversity challenges by learn-ing to understand and modify organisational and individual values. Therefore, we are very fortune as we have the ability to design curricu-lum interventions and activities aiming to educate individuals on how to manage effectively individual differences and address social stigmas in the workplace. Higher education can have a powerful effect upon improving future practices and developing appropriate management practices. This is not to assume that providing appropriate learning opportunities is one-size-fits-all solution to long-standing issues around diversity and equality. Nevertheless, we share some responsibility for the current organisational ineffectiveness on addressing 'hidden' inequalities and inability to support individuals in transferring appropriate knowledge back in the workplace.

We also felt the need to share our 'frustration' with the academic and professional community. Apart from scholarly activities, we delivered a conference stream entitled *'hidden inequalities in the workplace: dignity and well-being'* in the 2016 Equality, Diversity and Inclusion conference, Cyprus. Surprisingly, we found that other academics and practitioners shared similar perceptions around the subject. A key theme emerged from contributors is that diversity is a stepping stone in modern organisations;

however, organisational diversity practices reflect a more cosmetic rather than deep-rooted changes as to how diversity is supported by leaders. What is more positive is the fact that many individuals are very keen to discuss any challenges they face in the workplace and vent out their frustration with current thinking. This particular event acted as a motivation boost to produce this book. We recognise that organisational realities might be different in theory; nevertheless, personal development, resource allocation and skills capacity seem to contribute towards addressing workplace stigmas and discrimination, but most importantly in developing a progressive and productive workplace. Individual awareness is an important first step in enabling change to happen at both an individual and organisational level, with Celik et al. (2012) suggesting that establishment of awareness is followed by acceptance, adoption and adherence. Therefore, management of 'hidden' inequalities should be seen as a necessity, where individuals should be involved in a process of examining the operational and behavioural realities, leading to durable and relevant diversity work-based solutions.

1.2   Aims and Objectives

The book aims to understand further how organisations manage inequalities and whether the current legislative framework provides sufficient tools to support individuals. The book is part of the 'Palgrave Explorations in Workplace Stigma' series with the remit to action for organisations to accept and support employees with visible and non-visible needs and ensure that social stigmas are removed from the workplace. In line with the series ethos, the main objective of the book is to critically assess and evaluate any form of organisational practice and function that could reinforce 'hidden' systematic and potential remediable differences amongst individuals in the workplace. There is now a wider debate that individual diversity (differences in background, education and knowledge) is critical to sustain and improve economic performance by bringing different skills, experience, ideas and perspectives (Jayne and Dipboye 2004). Therefore, this book aims to continue to grow and stimulate academic and professional scholarship on the topic of equality and diversity through the lens of multi-disciplinary, evidence-based research and practice. We aim to encourage critical reflection of current debate areas on 'hidden' discrimination to support higher education students learning experience and provide useful learning resources to enrich knowledge on diversity and equality in business. To achieve that, we need to challenge current thinking and mobilise individual action towards developing positive working environments. As Lisa Burrell (2016) argued, *we just can't handle diversity*' as cognitive roadblocks keep getting in the way. Therefore, it is important to enable people who have been affected to express their perception and provide insightful arguments as to how key processes by which equality and diversity are ascribed to people and systems might reinforce workplace 'hidden' inequalities.

The hope is that the book provides students at various levels including undergraduate and postgraduate programmes with useful and positive learning resources around the subject. There are many diversity and equality books in the market; however, most of the publications focus on cultural diversity, legal requirements and formal discrimination cases in the workplace. The objective is to provide students with 'real case' scenarios and academic research needed to explain and assess current organisational realities. The book also provides organisations with opportunities to enrich knowledge on explaining and addressing 'hidden' aspects of diversity and equality in the workplace. All contributors have been tasked to provide a number of practical, operational and strategic recommendations needed to unseen diversity and equality issues.

1.3   Equal or Diverse?

Since the 1990s, authors have viewed diversity as a conventional approach to equal opportunities and legislation compliances enabling organisations to create a productive environment that promotes visible and non-visible differences. There is a growing debate about the emergence of the business case perspective for diversity, as opposed to the equal opportunities perceptive where emphasis has been paid on adopting sameness practices with an emphasis on moral concern for social justice (sameness reflects a uniform, group-focussed approach in addressing equality), (CIPD 2012;

Mavin and Girling 2000). The main goal is to achieve greater social justice from within a society through affirmative action that consists of government-mandated or voluntary programmes undertaken to support disadvantaged groups (Herring and Henderson 2015). Legislation has played a key role in delivering progress towards inclusivity and equality through tackling unfair discrimination (Harris 2003). However, the equal opportunity approach was perceived to have failed, that is, in the achievement of greater organisational inclusion. Evidence suggests that few organisations have taken proactive steps to enable the mainstreaming of diversity into the way people do their jobs or operational practices (CIPD 2007). As a result, a more neo-liberal perspective is being sought which moves away from the 'stick' of legal compliance (Mavin and Girling 2000). Diversity management is perceived as '...*the background of new thinking about the implications of a person being different*' (CIPD 2012, p. 14). This perspective has its origins in the USA with a growing interest about its strategic benefits worldwide. This diversity philosophy has a broader scope and perspective when compared to traditional and accepted ways of understanding diversity within business (Kirton and Greene 2010), and has been influenced by rapidly changing workforce demographics and social mobility which led many businesses to re-evaluate organisational values and belief systems (CIPD 2012). A fundamental value of diversity management is the need to managing people strategically through the adoption of Human Resources practices (Foster and Harris 2005). Embracing diversity is not only a moral imperative but also has a sound business case with an explicit strategic approach to valuing individual differences (van Dijk et al. 2012). The real benefit assigned to diversity management is gaining competitive advantage and enhance performance through human capital (Kochan et al. 2003; Mavin and Girling 2000). This lends supports from Cox's (2001) findings that organisations that are actively seeking and managing a diverse workforce are able to meet complex business and organisational problems.

However, the challenge is how to best enhance the opportunities that diversity has identified. Organisational studies literature highlights that diverse groups outperform homogeneous groups (Cox 2001; Kumra and Manfredi 2012), and there are recognised difficulties in managing these teams. These include cultural differences in communication and performance (Watson et al. 1993). From a social perspective, social identity theory emphasises that diversity management creates ingroup-outgroup distinctions generating negative social processes that influence group performance (Turner 1987). Group members establish a positive identity by favouring characteristics of the ingroup and developing negative identities by behaving towards the outgroup in a belligerent way. This is not surprising as finding a way to break free from the status quo is a hard task to achieve. Nevertheless, fostering awareness, value and acceptance of individual differences through the deployment of key talents in an environment of trust (Kumra and Manfredi 2012) requires resources and most importantly people's commitment to change. Failure to achieve this leads to performance loss (Ely 2004), prevents effective management decision-making regarding team performance (Kumra and Manfredi 2012) and reinforces social stigmas in the workplace. Other studies have identified that a lack of diversity policy and positive management action could result in high labour turnover and loss of talented individuals, consequently damaging publicity through employment tribunals (CIPD 2012).

Some others have been critical with regard to diversity management paradigm (Kumra and Manfredi 2012). Foster and Harris (2005) suggest, however, that the diversity management approach is not something distinctively different or new, it is just a repackaging of equal opportunities. Kumra and Manfredi (2012) support this consideration suggesting that the new diversity approach is focussing on the quality of the opportunity supporting and justifying equality initiatives which are still based in promoting 'sameness' rather than 'difference'. Greene and Kirton (2011, p. 65) from an organisational perspective raise concerns over the place of diversity within strategic planning suggesting that although it 'is *not entirely absent from the approach, it is not central'*. Therefore, the achievement of organisational goals then becomes the ultimate guiding principle and explanatory device for people in organisations (Kumra and Manfredi 2012), rather than educating a truly diverse organisation. Nevertheless, the narrative of equal opportunities creates a culture of silent acceptance with limited focus on the individual aspects of diversity (Mavin and Girling 2000). This culture may be generated through a discourse which promotes diversity as a prerequisite for company success (CIPD 2012), without providing a uniform managerial solution. It has been identified that uniform solutions seek the identification of 'sameness' developing in and out groups (Celik et al. 2012), which does not release the new insights into organisational culture that individual differences can bring (Argote et al. 2001). Seeking to identify 'difference' creates a complex challenge for managers through the demand of identifying a plurality of interventions to *'diminish effects of social categorization processes without relinquishing the benefits of diversity'* (Ely 2004, p. 756).

Managing diversity is therefore perceived as a unitarist managerial concept (matching individual differences) rather than diversifying. Implementation of diversity management is context specific and varies significantly across organisations (Janssens and Zanoni 2014). Nonetheless, providing flexible practices, supporting employee well-being and developing key talents are prerequisites in establishing a truly inclusive and diverse workforce. Different organisations can promote diversity for the sake of satisfying numbers (ticking the box), but diversity along with appropriate inclusive practices often leads to a diversity backlash. As Verna Myers (2017) suggests, *'diversity is being invited to the party. Inclusion is being asked to dance'*. In other words, understanding individual needs leads to a positive, productive and purposeful working environment for employees at all levels.

1.4   The Legal Framework and Expectations

Over the last four decades, policymakers have been actively addressing a number of equality and diversity problems that arise with the implementation of national legal initiatives against discriminative practices. In the UK, the Equality Act 2010 legally protects people from discrimination in the workplace and in wider society. It replaced previous anti-discrimination laws with a single Act, making the law easier to understand and strengthening protection in some situations. The European Union (EU) Member States have also empowered it to take appropriate action to combat discrimination through the introduction of two EU directives on anti-discrimination and racial equality. This is similar to the United States Equality Act of 2015 which amends the Civil Rights Act of 1964 to include protections that ban discrimination on the basis of sexual orientation, gender identity and sex. In fact, the USA and the EU are the most powerful players in a number of international regulatory hard and soft regimes. Legal positivists refer to hard law as legal obligations of a formally binding nature including key protecting characteristics and formal areas that prohibit discrimination in employment. While soft law refers to those that are not formally binding but may nonetheless lead to binding hard law (Shaffer and Pollack 2010) including individual attitude and behaviour in the workplace. Rationalists, in contrast, argue that hard and soft law have distinct attributes due to different contexts. Regardless of the perspective, both hard and soft laws mutually support anti-discrimination. The book's aim is not to adjudicate the weaknesses and strengths of hard and soft laws, but to focus on understanding individuals and their perceptions on 'hidden' social stigmas and discriminatory practices in the workplace.

In a recent survey, the Government Equalities Office (2016) found that there is a widespread organisational engagement with equality legislation through the use of written policies. Interestingly, compliance and external image has been mainly seen as a key organisational concern with workplace equality legislation. Evidence suggests that practice can be influenced by legislation and create a sense of moral and social responsibility. Nevertheless, the workplace is still not succeeding in reducing issues of racism and sexism (Tomlinson and Schwabenland 2010), for example, the accusation of institutionalised racism within the London Metropolitan Police 15 years after the first allegation (Dodd and Evans 2014). There are also reports to provide tougher restrictions over workplace dress code and sexist language ('get along with the boys') as the legal framework might be inadequate to protect women, people of colour and LGBT+ individuals from being directly and indirectly discriminated. In a recent survey conducted by the European Commission, only one-third of people in Europe know that they are protected by EU anti-discrimination law. They also found that 15% of respondents have suffered discrimination or harassment in last 12 months, and 29% have witnessed discrimination (European Commission 2016). A longitudinal study of over 700 US companies found little positive effect of training to individual attitude towards gender and ethnicity; in fact, they found that there is a decreased representation of black workers (Hewlett et al. 2008). Also, recent events in the UK and USA political arena have brought into the surface infamous, offensive behaviours around immigration, social mobility and gender equality.

Given the complexity of the current business environment, organisations may struggle to balance compliance with affirmative action and find appropriate management practices in addressing individual needs. Indeed, as Klarsfeld et al. (2012, p. 312) assert, neither hard nor soft approaches are effective, in that *control rules are not as binding as they appear...[and] voluntary practices are not as deliberate as they seem*. They go further on to explain how these rules are subverted in order to portray compliance. There are also concerns over the feasibility and efficiency of diversity strategy (Greene and Kirton 2011; Foster and Harris 2005) and whether organisations have the appropriate capacity to address diversity policy needs (Mavin and Girling 2000). Evidence shows that there are 'grey' areas which may not specifically be legislated for, but when used to identify an individual as 'other' can serve as an exclusionary mechanism and impact upon individuals' dignity and well-being. At the same time, organisations place less strategic emphasis in managing those 'hidden' inequalities due to poor leadership commitment (Tomlinson and Schwabenland 2010) and limited allocation of budget and resources for addressing diversity issues in the work (CIPD 2012). Of course, it would not be productive to regulate every aspect of organisational life. Nevertheless, poor recognition of 'hidden' inequalities could have a detrimental effect upon individual behaviour including turnover and psychological withdrawal and performance issues (Parzefall and Coyle-Shapiro 2011). In other words, the extent and nature of individual discretionary behaviour in the workplace is influenced by the level of organisational support and workplace norms (Ehrke et al. 2014).

1.5   Book Context

Regardless the academic perspective, there is no doubt that policymakers, organisations and individuals need to gain a new insight into workplace diversity. Current uncertainties around the globe reinforce the argument that addressing diversity and equality issues can have a powerful positive impact upon organisational life. Failure to fully understand and most importantly explain diversity and equality-related matters is most likely to negatively influence organisations' ability to address the changing employment relationships. Highlighting key issues without actions reflects a more cosmetic rather than deep-rooted changes as to how diversity is understood. There is no denial that organisations need to meet their legal duties. Nonetheless, organisations should provide learning opportunities to support management for driving progress, which is not limited to specialist understanding of diversity issues, but extends to an understanding of the broader business case arguments for diversity and develop knowledge and expertise in changing individual attitudes. We hope that the book's chapters can generate a positive action in enabling managers to understand and support employees who are experiencing any form of unseen social stigma and inequality in the workplace. Building management commitment and accountability is key in any successful diversity policy implementation. Reflecting the issues briefly outlined above, the book is structured into 13 insightful chapters considering various aspects of work arrangements, social integration and individual capabilities. Contributors have used a number of different tools to assess key issues through primary research, experiential assessment, vignettes and case studies. Maintaining respondent confidentiality while protecting the identities of the individuals who participated in the book is critical. Hence, we have used pseudonyms for any individual names across all chapters.

This chapter provides an introductory assessment of the book's key dimensions and offers an insight into the key themes on 'hidden' inequality in the workplace. The chapter allows the reader to get an overview of the context and access the key objectives of the book.

Chapter 2 offers an insight evaluation on the levels of awareness existing amongst employers and human resource professionals with regard to coeliac disease. It seeks to assess whether employees with coeliac disease experience discriminatory practices which impact on their equal opportunities and dignity within the workplace. The chapter presents a qualitative, phenomenological approach to explore individual's accounts, perception and insights and unveils any 'hidden' aspects of their working life as coeliac sufferers.

Chapter 3 presents the findings from an investigation exploring the 'hidden' inequalities that employees with Asperger syndrome (AS) experience within the workplace. This chapter aims to provide new knowledge for those concerned with diversity and inclusion planning. In particular, the voices of AS employees and line managers have been assessed to understand the differences that surface in the workplace and expose how they also connect to employment inequalities.

Chapter 4 examines the challenges faced by female police officers in England, Wales and Northern Ireland, focussing on assessing whether organisational culture, customs and practice; and policies, systems and processes can negatively impact upon the opportunities for development and progression based upon gender. A liberal, qualitative, feminist approach has been used to assess individual perceptions and the role of specific language and behaviours that empower discrimination.

Chapter 5 presents and assesses the patterns of employment and reports on the variable quality of work amongst older adults in the UK using the Annual Population Survey, Labour Force Survey and Understanding Society data. In the light of recent economic and welfare policy changes, this chapter seeks to shed light into the experiences of older adults in the UK who continue to engage in paid work and assess current challenges related to lack of career development and/or training opportunities, the presence of health conditions, the negative perceptions of co-workers and employers, and a number of other factors which can lead to low-quality work being encountered by older workers.

Chapter 6 reviews studies in the area of flexibility and examines 'hidden' inequalities associated with gender, class location, career advancement and family status in relation to the practice of work flexibility in workplaces. It seeks to assess current flexible-working arrangements and support organisations in recognising and addressing any 'hidden' discrimination against those who use them and protect employees from retaliatory treatment.

Chapter 7 explores the organisational and cultural reasons for the marginalisation and exclusion of LGBT++ participants in sports. This chapter adopts a critical angle into the role of heterogeneous 'culture' in creating marginalisation and exclusion issues amongst LGBT+ participants in various sports groups, and how space can create discriminatory practices.

It seeks to inform current thinking around organisational design and promotion of fairness in sports.

Chapter 8 aims to assess current gender differences in paid and unpaid work by assessing various patterns of paid work and the growth of flexibility in the employment market. To achieve that a life-course approach has been adopted to encompass the role of chronological age as well as the experiences throughout the life course including specific milestones and transitions. Such analysis is critical in understanding contemporary advanced society and inform future policymaking.

Chapter 9 opens up the debate on implicit bias in recruitment, selection and promotion by assessing the risk of subconscious discrimination over decision-making. It seeks to expand current literature on the impact of stereotyping in the modern workplace by assessing current practices on screening of resumes, ingroup bias in interviews, the impact of stereotype threat on candidate performance and interviewer confirmation bias.

Chapter 10 focuses on sexual minorities and identity amongst gay men in the workplace. It seeks to explore the way gay men manage their identity in the workplace since the introduction of anti-discrimination legislation. This chapter provides the reader the opportunity to assess key challenges gay men negotiate and conform in the two-way process of managing their identities. The adoption of a qualitative method, coupled with in-depth interviews, has resulted in a chapter that gives a voice to the key participants, the gay men themselves. The chapter also extends our understanding amongst individuals whose sexual identity, orientation or practices differ from the majority of the surrounding society.

Chapter 11 explores the wider issues around employee engagement and whether organisational practices create 'hidden' inequalities amongst employees. A critical analysis of the current literature has been undertaken to explore the positive links between employee engagement and organisational outcomes and the factors that lead to disengagement in the workplace through the lens of exclusion, equality and diversity thinking.

Chapter 12 offers an insight into the world of the expatriate workforce, and the challenges they face in dealing with diverse culture and different legislative frameworks. The chapter provides a number of unique real-life case (vignettes) examples from organisations operating in the Gulf Cooperation Council (GCC) by exploring how the protected characteristics, detailed in the Equality Act 2010, become 'hidden' inequalities in an expatriate context.

Chapter 13 provides room for concluding remarks, highlights key findings and identifies a number of implications for individuals, policymakers and organisations. It seeks to identify areas for exploration and give the space for further debate and evaluation.

References

Ahonen, P., J. Tienari, S. Merilanlnen, and A. Pullen. 2014. Hidden contexts and invisible power relations: A Foucauldian reading of diversity research. *Human Relations* 67: 263–286.

Anderson, K.L. 2004. Teaching cultural competence using an exemplar from literary journalism. *The Journal of Nursing Education* 43: 253–259.

Argote, L., D. Gruenfeld, and C. Naquin. 2001. Group learning in organizations. In *Groups at work: Theory and research*, ed. P. Turner, 369–412. New York: Erlbaum.

Bezrukova, K., K. Jehn, and C. Spell. 2012. Reviewing diversity training: Where we have been and where we should go. *Academy of Management Learning and Education* 11: 207–227.

Burrell, L. 2016. We just can't handle diversity. https://hbr.org/2016/07/we-just-cant-handle-diversity. Accessed 9 Feb 2017.

Celik, H., T. Abma, I. Klinge, and A. Widder. 2012. Process evaluation of a diversity training program: The method strategy. *Evaluation and Programme Planning* 35: 54–65.

Charted Institute of Personnel and Development. 2007. *Diversity in business: A focus for progress*. London: CIPD.

Chartered Institute of Personnel and Development. 2012. *Managing diversity: Linking theory and practice to business performance*. London: Chartered Institute of Personnel and Development.

Cox, T. 2001. *Cultural diversity in organizations: Theory, research and practice*. San Francisco: Berrett-Koehler.

Dobbin, Frank, and A. Kalev. 2016. Why diversity programs fail. https://hbr.org/2016/07/why-diversity-programs-fail. Accessed 9 Feb 2017.

Dodd, V., and R. Evans. 2014. Lawrence revelations: Admit institutional racism, Met chief told. https://www.theguardian.com/uk-news/2014/mar/07/lawrence-revelations-institutional-racism-met-police. Accessed 9 Feb 2017.

Ehrke, F., A. Berthold, and M.C. Steffens. 2014. How diversity training can change attitudes: Increasing perceived complexity of superordinate groups to improve intergroup relations. *Journal of Experimental Social Psychology* 53: 193–206.

Ely, R. 2004. A field study of group diversity, participation in diversity education programs, and performance. *Journal of Organizational Behaviour* 25: 755–780.

European Commission. 2016. *Discrimination in European Union in 2015.* http://ec.europa.eu/COMMFrontOffice/publicopinion/index.cfm/Survey/getSurveyDetail/instruments/SPECIAL/surveyKy/2077. Accessed 9 Feb 2017.

Foster, C., and L. Harris. 2005. Easy to say, difficult to do: Diversity management in retail. *Human Resource Management Journal* 15: 4–17.

Greene, A.-M., and B. Kirton. 2011. *The dynamics of managing diversity.* 3rd ed. London: Routledge.

Harris, T.M. 2003. Impacting student perceptions of and attitudes toward race in the interracial communication course. *Communication Education* 52: 311–317.

Herring, C., and L. Henderson. 2015. *Diversity in organizations: A critical examination.* London: Routledge.

Hewlett, S.A., C.B. Luce, L.J. Servon, L. Sherbin, P. Shiller, and E. Sosnovich. 2008. The Athena factor: Reversing the brain drain in science, engineering, and technology. Harvard Business Review Research Report, Boston.

Janssens, M., and P. Zanoni. 2014. Alternative diversity management: Organizational practices fostering ethnic equality at work. *Scandinavian Journal of Management* 30: 317–331.

Jayne, M., and R. Dipboye. 2004. Leveraging diversity to improve business performance: Research findings and recommendations for organizations. *Human Resources Management* 43: 409–424.

Kirton, G., and A. Greene. 2010. *The dynamics of managing diversity: A critical approach.* London: Elsevier.

Klarsfeld, A., E. Ng, and A. Tatli. 2012. Social regulation and diversity management: A comparative study of France, Canada and the UK. *European Journal of Industrial Relations* 18: 309–327.

Kochan, A., K. Bezrukova, R. Ely, L. Jackson, A. Joshi, K. Jehn, J. Leonard, D. Levine, and D. Thomas. 2003. The effect of diversity on business performance: Report of the diversity research network. *Human Resources Management* 42: 3–21.

Kulik, C., and L. Roberson. 2008. Common goals and golden opportunities: Evaluations of diversity education in academic and organizational settings. *Academy of Management Learning and Education* 7: 309–331.

Kumra, S., and S. Manfredi. 2012. *Managing equality and diversity: Theory and practice*. Oxford: Oxford University Press.

Mavin, S., and G. Girling. 2000. What is managing diversity and why does it matter? *Human Resource Development International* 3: 419–433.

Myers, V. 2017. *Diversity doesn't stick without inclusion*. https://hbr.org/2017/02/diversity-doesnt-stick-withoutinclusion. Accessed 9 Feb 2017.

Parzefall, R.M., and M. Coyle-Shapiro. 2011. Making sense of psychological contract breach. *Journal of Managerial Psychology* 26: 12–27.

Pendry, L.F., D.M. Driscoll, and C.T. Field. 2007. Diversity training: Putting theory into practice. *Journal of Occupational and Organizational Psychology* 80: 227–250.

Purcell, J., and S. Hutchinson. 2007. Front-line managers as agents in the HRM–performance causal chain: Theory, analysis and evidence. *Human Resource Management Journal* 17: 3–20.

Shaffer, G., and M. Pollack. 2010. Hard vs. soft law: Alternatives, complements and antagonists in international governance. *Minnesota Law Review* 94: 706–799.

Sherbin, L., and R. Rashid. 2017. Diversity doesn't stick without inclusion. https://hbr.org/2017/02/diversity-doesnt-stick-without-inclusion. Accessed 9 Feb 2017.

Tomlinson, F., and C. Schwabenland. 2010. Reconciling competing discourses of diversity? The UK non-profit sector between social justice and the business case. *Organization* 17: 101–121.

Turner, I. 1987. *Rediscovering the social group. A social categorisation theory*. Oxford: Blackwell.

Van Dijk, H., M. Engen, and J. Paauwe. 2012. Reframing the business case: A values and virtues perspective. *Journal of Business Ethics* 111: 73–84.

Watson, W.E., K. Kumar, and L.K. Michaelson. 1993. Cultural diversity's impact on interaction process and performance: Comparing homogeneous and diverse task groups. *Academy of Management Journal* 36: 590–602.

2

The Challenges and Social Impact of Coeliac Disease in the Workplace

Valerie Caven and Stefanos Nachmias

2.1 Identifying, Stating and Justifying the 'Problem'

Coeliac disease (CD) is a life-long chronic condition where the gut reacts to gluten-containing foods. Sufferers account for around 1% of the population worldwide (Coeliac UK 2014; Araújo and Araújo 2012), although it is estimated that there are many more who have not received a diagnosis. Left untreated, it can raise an individual's risk of bowel cancer, cause growth problems, contribute to infertility and/or miscarriage, and there are connections to mental health issues (Mendoza and McGough 2005). The only 'cure' is strict adherence to a gluten-free diet which, if maintained, results in full remission (Hall et al. 2013).

V. Caven (✉) • S. Nachmias
Department of Human Resource Management, Nottingham Business School, Nottingham Trent University, Nottingham, UK

© The Author(s) 2018
V. Caven, S. Nachmias (eds.), *Hidden Inequalities in the Workplace*,
Palgrave Explorations in Workplace Stigma,
DOI 10.1007/978-3-319-59686-0_2

While the physical and emotional effects of CD and their impact on the sufferer have to some extent been documented in terms of the psychosocial aspects (Ford et al. 2012), little is known about how CD sufferers manage in the workplace. Many sufferers have expressed feelings of anxiety and depression as a result of perceived stigma (Goffman 1963) and exclusion from social settings due to formal diagnosis (Black and Orfila 2011). However, research has failed to explore the emotional impact of diagnosis on sufferers' working lives including the social context. For example, food plays a significant role in organisational culture; it is used as a morale booster, a form of reward or celebration, a means to build team working and to network (Thomson and Hassenkamp 2008). For CD sufferers, these food rituals have the potential to result in isolation and exclusion. The Equality Act 2010 provides the legal framework to promote equality of practices and enhance diverse activities within organisations. Despite the legal expectations, organisations also have a moral obligation to accommodate individual needs and ensure key policy providing guidance to individuals (Black and Orfila 2011). Awareness of dietary requirements, especially on religion grounds, is on the increase; however, we suggest that there is a lack of knowledge and understanding on the part of employers about both the 'actual' condition and their role in supporting the sufferer in its management.

The issue is compounded by the fact that CD is not specifically considered a disability or 'chronic long term condition' under the UK Equality Act (2010) which would require employers to make 'reasonable adjustments' to accommodate the sufferer. As the disease is managed via adherence to the gluten-free diet, for which 60% of coeliac sufferers (CSs) report, they experience some difficulty in maintaining (Araújo and Araújo 2012). There are evident difficulties in workplace provision whether through lack of facilities to buy or store home-prepared food. However, organisational support for CSs should go beyond the practical availability of food. It is important to consider the emotional and perceptual implications of being excluded from social events where food has a social, psychological and symbolic dimension (Holtzman 2006). There is a grey area as to what, if any, are the employers' obligations and what may be reasonable for employees to expect in terms of equal treatment and consideration for their dignity at work. It is also important to explore whether there is any responsibility on the part of the employers towards the coeliac employee.

The emphasis in the UK of the employee having to 'prove' they have been treated unfairly in the eyes of the law is not an effective means of addressing the problem. Issues of stigmatisation, mistreatment and financial implications might prevent individuals disclosing any discriminatory activities. Organisations and individuals should not ignore the social and emotional aspects of unfair treatment and act to address any 'hidden' inequalities in the workplace. Existing research in the field is vague, and thus employers might not have the knowledge or awareness through which to develop policies or codes of practice to address any deficiency.

This chapter is timely as there is a growing attention around employers' 'duty of care'. Organisations are expected to support the health and wellbeing of their employees. A survey by Coeliac UK (2007) found that pre-diagnosed sufferers took an average of 21.4 days sick (with this dropping by 3.6 days after diagnosis). By providing organisational support for sufferers, the number of sick days could be dramatically reduced. In addition, research has highlighted that employees who perceive that their organisation values their contribution and supports their wellbeing are more likely to display positive employee attitudes and behaviours (Eisenberger et al. 1986; Dulac et al. 2008; Rich et al. 2010). Employees who perceive their organisation provides a lack of social support are more likely to become disengaged with their work (Demerouti et al. 2001) and create the sense of unfairness in the workplace (Griffiths 2008). Although it is discriminatory for an employer to treat a coeliac employee differently from other employees in the UK, the onus is on the employee to prove that they have been treated unfairly and are left to pursue it via an employment tribunal (Griffiths 2008). This is costly in both financial and emotional terms, and the reality is likely to be that employees tend not to take actions in addressing any discriminatory behaviours.

Therefore, the chapter assesses current issues faced by CD sufferers and unveil any 'hidden' inequalities in the way organisations accommodate their individual needs. Some might argue that the proportion of CD sufferers is disproportional across the labour market. Nevertheless, the emotional and social dimensions of any unfair treatment should be addressed by employers and ensure that they make reasonable adjustments to address specific personal and work-related needs. It is also important to understand the way organisations design and introduce key practices that aim to support employee wellbeing and health in the workplace. Most importantly, the study allows the in-depth exploration of individual stories and their perceptions on current practices, a powerful tool to share ideas widely.

2.2   The Impact of CD on Working Life

Literature highlights a number of psychological, behavioural and cognitive issues related to CD working life. As Lee et al. (2012) argued in their longitudinal quality of life study of living with CD, while the impact on family, dining out and travel diminishes as time following diagnosis passes, the effect on work remains the same whether the diagnosis is recent or more than 10 years prior. This is in line with Black and Orfila's (2011) findings which reported feelings of anxiety and depression due to exclusion in social settings (difficulty of adhering to the gluten-free (GF) diet), lack of awareness of the CD and its effects as well as management's unwillingness to educate individuals. Most interesting is the ignorance or lack of understanding by non-coeliac employees, which might cause unintentional and indirect discrimination. This is further compounded by silence or resentment by the 'involved' party. Evidence of indirect discrimination occurs if a 'provision, criterion or practice' is imposed which members of one group are much less likely to be able to comply with, and which is not justified by the requirements of the job.

Despite the above evidence, the practical aspects of managing the condition in the workplace have been overlooked. No exploration of any obligations on the part of the employer has been carried out and most importantly what a coeliac employee can reasonably expect in terms of support from their employers. In fact, the Advisory, Conciliation and Arbitration Service (2017) argues that employers are not expected to provide religion-specific food (non-specific comments about food requirement upon health grounds) at work-related meetings '*if it is not proportionate to do so*'. Nevertheless, they highlight that organisations (when possible) should provide some alternative food available for employees. This is also compounded by the fact that CD is not specifically covered by the Equality Act 2010 which refers to conditions such as depression, diabetes and the like followed by the clause '...*and any other long-term chronic condition*' (Equality Act 2010). Until this is tested in case law, it will remain outside the specific provision of the Act. Where employers' obligation to their employees with CD has been the subject of legal action, it has been because the employee has had a specific protected characteristic covered by the Equality Act 2010, and CD has been considered as 'an attendant condition'. For example, in the case of Duckworth v British Airways, a member of cabin crew working on long-haul flights, who was both diabetic (covered by the Equality Act 2010) and coeliac, became ill as a result of his in-flight meal containing gluten which exacerbated his diabetes and he was hospitalised. On his return to work, Mr. Duckworth applied for a transfer to short-haul flights to help manage his disability better. The case arose as his application was at first declined and then delayed unreasonably by British Airways. However, while recourse to law is not necessarily the solution, sometimes organisations feel more 'encouraged' to support diversity if there are legal rather than just moral requirements (CIPD 2012).

CD sufferers are prevented from joining the Police Service or Armed Forces due to the difficulty of maintaining a GF diet while on deployment (www.gov.uk accessed 20/12/2016 AFCO form 5); however, those who are diagnosed once in the military are offered alternative positions or, in some cases, a medical discharge dependent upon their job role and suitability for redeployment. This leads to questions about the time of diagnosis—whether it is prior to or post joining an organisation—and can add a further dimension of complexity. If an employee is diagnosed prior to taking their employment, they are likely to understand what adjustments are needed or will know how to manage their condition. They are not required to disclose any information to a potential employer. However, if the diagnosis comes after accepting the employment, there can be additional difficulties. As previous research shows that the first year or so after diagnosis presents specific challenges in adapting to the radical change in dietary lifestyle required with quality of life scores initially improving but then declining for as long as four years following diagnosis (Lee et al. 2012). Employers have a moral responsibility to take actions to accommodate their needs and support CD sufferers' wellbeing. There are not specific legal requirements for employers to comply.

2.3   Socialising, Catering and Marginalisation

Anecdotal evidence also leads us to believe there is discrimination against CD sufferers in the workplace in being excluded from joining in corporate hospitality. This is due to lack of GF options, the condition being referred to as an 'eating disorder' or being told to take their own food as they were considered 'too difficult' to cater for and the like. This could be a real source of establishing 'hidden' inequalities and highlighting the organisation's inability to accommodate individual needs. Food and eating are symbolic in the workplace as they represent celebrations of success, cement team 'togetherness' and cohesiveness (Ortlieb and Sieben 2011), and other organisational 'rituals' (Flores-Pereira et al. 2008). Rosen (1985) was among the first to acknowledge the symbolism of organisational celebrations featuring eating. Nevertheless, social exclusion diminishes the value of socialisation and create a sense of stigmatisation and marginalisation amongst colleagues. As Sturdy et al. (2006, p. 907) argued, business dinner is a *'liminal space between work and private spheres'* thus providing us with a linkage between an employers' obligations to the coeliac employee.

Cunha et al. (2008) go a step further and conceptualise food within organisations in four ways: food as need, social interaction, culture and as a metaphor. This provides us with a framework to examine the needs of the coeliac employee in the workplace. Firstly, food as need refers to meal breaks and the availability of GF food or the facilities to safely store and reheat food from home. Secondly, food as social interaction whether it be business-related entertaining, networking opportunities or the exchange of news and knowledge at the coffee machine. Thirdly, the cultural aspects of food at work in terms of cakes for celebrations, birthdays, for example, or food to symbolise religious festivals, or food as reward; food as metaphor is used by Cunha et al. (2008) in a number of ways—to explain the organisation as a consumer of worker flesh or to reflect the organisation's 'health' whether it be anorexic or over-weight to name two.

Taking the theme of the organisation (employer) as a consumer of worker flesh then that highlights the need for the worker to be healthy—hence our argument for the need for employers to consider the needs of their CD sufferers. In order to determine what is known about the management of the condition in the workplace, we conducted a search of the academic literature via library and other databases using a range of keyword terms including 'coeliac', celiac (in order to ascertain if work had been carried out in the USA) and 'employment' which yielded no results; likewise a search of the fact-sheets, reports and on-line discussion/advice forums offered by the Chartered Institute for Personnel and Development (the professional body for human resource managers in the UK), again produced no results. While Coeliac UK provides a wide and informative range of guidance and advice covering school meals, eating out and holidaying abroad, once more, there is no formal guidance for either the coeliac employee or his/her employer. Further to that, the lack of resources could be an indication that any forms of food or mental disorder are not covered by the legal framework. These are seen as less important items on the organisational agenda. This might be seen a 'bold' statement; however, organisations have the moral imperative to valuing individual differences (van Dijk et al. 2012).

2.4 Blurring of the Boundaries Between 'Public' and 'Private'

While personal health and wellbeing may be considered a private sphere and an area which individuals are unwilling to discuss publicly, for example, in the workplace, there may be occasions where the public and the private collide. Those who have not yet received a diagnosis and who are suffering from 'tummy troubles' may be taking periods of sick leave thus drawing attention to their ill health. Those who are newly diagnosed may be struggling with the major adjustment to their diet and lifestyle that accompanies a diagnosis of CD. While evidence clearly shows an improvement in quality of life following a diagnosis (Kurppa et al. 2014; Gray and Papanicolas 2010), there is additional evidence which indicates that the adjustment period may cause psychological distress, regret at being diagnosed, feeling isolated and stigmatised, reduced enjoyment of food and, in some cases, avoidance of social occasions which involve eating (Whitaker et al. 2009).

The blurring of the boundaries between the public spheres and private spheres can lead to stigmatisation (Goffman 1963, p. 9), defined as the *'situation of the individual who is disqualified from full social acceptance'*, in other words, as we argue in this chapter, the coeliac who feels excluded from organisational functions in some way because of their dietary requirements. Goffman goes on to add that the bearer (of the stigma) must have a concern for what others think about their condition and thus *'internalise the social norms to which they fail to conform'* (Perez 2014, p. 1) highlighting both the psychological and sociological aspects of stigmatisation. Perez (2014, p. 2) critiques Goffman's focus on emphasising the stigmatised rather than those who are stigmatisers, *'framing individuals as victims and stripping them of agency rather than drawing attention to the broader structural concerns that lead to stigmatisation'*. However, we feel that Goffman's definition is emblematic of its time, and it is from this as a starting point we can start to build a case for improved organisational awareness of CD and its management.

2.5   The Need to Acknowledge Social Stigmas and Exclusion

Despite the shift in thinking, the current legislative framework has achieved little change in improving organisational justice (Ahmed 2007). Legislation plays a key role in tackling unfair discrimination and delivers the progress that is needed to create an inclusive society (Özbilgin et al. 2008). Physical and emotional effects have not been fully addressed at organisational level. Anecdotal evidence leads to the argument that current management practices (appraisal, performance management, wellbeing) are not in line with the principles and perspectives of diversity. Of course, large organisations might be more proactive in establishing appropriate practices; however, there is a lack of a generic framework to provide guidance and actions for different organisations. This is interesting as organisations have now been encouraged to effectively address their moral and strategic obligations through the development of explicit strategies to valuing individual differences at organisational level (CIPD 2012).

In examining the theoretical and conceptual developments, understanding individual' specific needs contribute towards creating a 'positive' culture that promotes efficiency and organisational justice (Niederle and Vesterlund 2013). In theory, managing diversity means enabling every member of the organisation to perform work tasks by satisfying specific needs including CSs' needs. In practice, there is no single approach that organisations can adopt to eradicate discrimination (Kumra and Manfredi 2012), especially in relation to 'hidden' inequality and social stigmas. To achieve that, changing organisational knowledge and awareness is essential in addressing discrimination and leveraging employee differences to benefit the organisation. This is because 83% of organisations in the UK had an articulated diversity strategy; however, most covered only the basic legal requirements and had not implemented improvement actions (CIPD 2012). Factors like organisational size, individual capabilities, time, resources and knowledge might prevent many organisations from identifying and addressing any discriminatory practices amongst individuals, especially where there are no specific legal requirements.

Diversity actions to the management of the condition in the workplace should be able to address 'hidden' assumptions and ignorance barriers moving away from a 'box ticking' exercise (Greene and Kirton 2011). Awareness of employee 'special' needs is now a strategic imperative in contemporary organisations (Bezrukova et al. 2012) with the capability to respond more effectively to the increasing numbers of CSs and the need to conform to social norms and avoid stigmatisation. It is not a legal requirement or a moral obligation to understand the changing workforce, but a requisite for any successful work strategy (Kumra and Manfredi 2012). This reinforces the need to explore current management practices and assess CSs' perceptions and emotions with regard to current workplace practices. There is a disconnect between the legal expectations and moral obligations. Evidence, as detailed above, suggests that there is a lack of knowledge that leads to instances of bullying, stigmatisation and social exclusion, and that these run counter to policies and practice of ensuring dignity for all at work.

Reflecting on the current knowledge gap, this chapter seeks to further understand individuals' perception of the CD and the real impact in the workplace. It is important to understand what is the level of organisational knowledge and awareness regarding the condition on the part of line managers, employers and HR professionals who have responsibility and ultimately a 'duty of care' towards their employees' health and wellbeing. This provides an opportunity to evaluate the basic requirements of the CS in the workplace and examine whether there are any areas of discriminatory practice in organisations. Such knowledge is critical in identifying examples of good practice that help in managing the condition, and most importantly eliminating discriminatory behaviours. While the study is UK-based, we argue that similar types of food disorder and difficulties will exist in countries due to the increase in exploring the role of employee welfare upon organisational success. In such a rapidly changing business environment, an improved understanding of the factors and issues of CSs in the workplace is critical to organisations and policymakers alike.

2.6   Methodological Considerations

The study adopted a qualitative, phenomenological approach to explore participants' accounts, perceptions and insights. The aim was to bring to the fore the experiences and perceptions of individuals aiming to unveil any 'hidden' aspects of their working life as CSs. The world is constructed with meanings and that explaining a phenomenon must be done through the participants' own perspectives. This is in line with Hayles (1996, p. 106) who argues that exploring diversity issues requires three distinctive competencies: '*head (knowledge), hand (behaviour and skills) and heart (feedings and attitudes)*'. Therefore, the study uses individual knowledge and understanding of the issue as a powerful tool to gain insight into personal motivation, actions and challenges (Blamey and Mackenzie 2007) and to consider the emotional and perceptual implications of being CS in the workplace.

A group of 25 CSs were invited to participate in the study. They were chosen purposefully against criteria of having been diagnosed as CS and currently in employment. Participants had a strong interest in diversity and equality, and its role in promoting individual fairness. To attract individuals, permission was obtained from an online CD forum. Overall, a group of five individuals took part in the study by using an 'on-line focus group' approach, which is broadly similar to a separate private discussion thread restricted to those who had agreed to participate. Participants were asked to identify areas of discriminatory and/or best practices they have experienced with regard to the management of their condition. They were encouraged to recount their experiences of how they manage their specific dietary requirements at work; what (if any) adjustments have been made by their employers. There were no significant differences in terms of age, education and gender amongst participants.

An initial discussion took place to discuss the experiences of key participants at work in relation to their management of the condition. Emphasis was paid to encourage on-line 'chat' amongst the key participants to explore the specific theme of being a CS in the workplace. Such a technique allowed the probing or challenging of individuals by other group members and enabled us to elicit a wide variety of views as these types of group discussions encouraged members to explore issues in greater depth. All participants had been previously exposed to on-line discussions through an existing CD's online community, which eliminated any risk of using modern technology to collect the data. An experienced and credentialed facilitator aiming to provoke debate and discussions around key topical issues and assess participants' emotional and perceptual behaviour in the workplace facilitated the online discussion forum. The facilitator was a non-CS to prevent any data bias and to provide a more objective line of questioning on key issues.

A thematic synthesis has been adopted to analyse participant perceptions and experiences around the issues highlighted in this chapter. Such an approach is essential to summarise key individual behaviours and provide an insightful meaning to individuals' perceptions. Key participants' quotations have been included in the analysis to provide them with a voice and allow the readers to get a real sense of participants' personal journeys. Arguably, there are a multitude of facets that could be discussed around the research questions; we draw on the most prominent to emerge from the data. The analysis is structured using pseudonyms to preserve anonymity and confidentiality.

2.7   The Public Realm of Eating Versus the Private Domain of Digestion

The findings have brought to the surface some interesting arguments around the public versus private eating practices. While the condition is relatively easily managed by strict adherence to the GF diet, accidental (or otherwise) ingestion of gluten results in unpleasant and potentially humiliating effects of vomiting, diarrhoea, intestinal pain, joint pain and mental health issues. The impact of the vomiting and diarrhoea is serious and violent as the body seeks to expel what it considers to be 'poison'. The amount of gluten required to provoke such a reaction is minimal, for example, current guidance as to whether food can be labelled as GF in the UK and Europe is below 20 parts per million (Coeliac UK 2017); in Australia, the level is zero parts per million. While the intestinal consequences of ingestion are severe and unpleasant, they are short-lived lasting for a few days; however, the longer-term damage to the gut is much more serious and can take several weeks or even months to recover from an attack. Long-term gluten damage can result in a higher risk of intestinal cancers and other serious conditions (Mendoza and McGough 2005). Despite this, Hall et al. (2013) found significant variance in the levels of adherence to the GF diet; however, their survey did not probe far enough as to the causes of non-compliance, as to whether it was accidental, from cross-contamination or otherwise.

Hence, cross-contamination of food is a serious concern for CSs, whether this is in the cooking/preparation stages or by contact with gluten-containing food during serving; for example, buffets are particularly problematic with the potential for bread or pastry crumbs being scattered over what would ordinarily be GF food such as salad or potatoes. All focus-group participants had informed their employers or co-workers about their condition although there is no formal or legal requirement to disclose nor is the employer obliged to make any reasonable adjustments in response. Goffman (1963) refers to 'information control' in relation to stigma and CD presents a dilemma of whether to disclose or not for fear of being stigmatised but also for the desire not to emphasise the 'visibility' of the condition because of the impact on social and personal identity. Jim was unsure what to do when going through the selection process for his current job: '*I had to have a medical as part of the job offer, I did tell the nurse that I was coeliac but I really was in two minds whether to say anything or not for fear of not getting the job*'. Here, he demonstrates a concern that disclosure of his health condition over the selection process (as discussed in Chap. 9 about implicit bias) may prevent him from taking the post. Chloe was diagnosed during her present employment after a long period of being unwell; following the diagnosis, her employer consistently and publicly referred to it as her 'eating disorder'. Sally was reassured to find that '*[at] the interview I found out that one of the other ladies has Coeliac disease and a lady that left not long before also had it...It did not influence my choice to take the job but on my first day it was reassuring that I was not the only one with dietary requirement*'.

Levels of support from employers were variable, perhaps in keeping with the public/private blurring of boundaries highlighted earlier. Jim mentions that he *had no support from work other than sympathy*. A further two mentioned the uncertainty of not knowing if they would be catered for at work-related events:

Occasionally I am catered for in the kitchen or for someone's birthday but 80% I am not. I've got a buffet lunch today and will be the only one who won't be catered for on the whole; without going on about it...easier to bring my own in as usual (Julie).

Sally also made an interesting point:

When it does become difficult is when we have buffet lunches on special occasions.

On a day-to-day basis, all participants said they usually took their own lunches to work either because they cannot rely on their canteens providing a GF option or to feel secure in the knowledge that their food will be GF:

Home-made soup, everyday ... (Naomi).

I generally bring my own lunch to work and ensure it is kept separate from others. And I always use my own cutlery and such like…however I do envy those that can eat lovely warm meal from the canteen and have variety every day (Sally).

The restaurant at work makes really nice food, occasionally there might be a gluten free option but [I] can't rely on something every day so I always take a packed lunch (Jim).

Have been 'glutened' too many times by the canteen … (Chloe).

That Jim and Sally mention their canteens making good food, yet not being able to join their colleagues to eat together emphasises the 'hidden' nature of the inequality. They felt unable to socialise creating the stigma of being 'socially' unapproachable. Julie went a step further and argued that:

What can be difficult is if I forget my packed lunch as even the food in the vending machines isn't usually gluten free, been known to drive out to a fast food restaurant for lunch. If I forget my dinner I have to go to the local mini market and get a rice pot.

There is a sense of irony that it is possible to depend on finding GF options in convenience stores and fast food restaurants rather than in professional catering establishments. The theme of exclusion by employers was emphasised by Julie who provided her own sausages and gravy for the Christmas lunch and Jim who now refuses to attend company celebration events:

The company I work for have award nights held at a hotel for length of service. A gluten free option is supplied on request but it is usually the same main course but without gravy or sauces and the pudding is fresh fruit salad where others have a really nice sweet. I stopped going as the food was disappointing and I always fear cross contamination/being given the wrong food when places are catering for groups of 50+ people (Jim).

Overall, they experienced much more support and equal treatment from their co-workers, having GF cakes and treats provided for them at workplace birthday celebrations, for example, although colleagues frequently commented on the cost of providing GF treats. Despite feeling excluded by their employers, there is a marked reluctance to request equal treatment with all participants playing down their obvious hurt feelings, which Goffman refers to as 'acceptance' of the stigma and its impact upon their social identity. Comments of 'I don't mind' or 'I don't want to make a fuss', 'I felt I was moaning and ungrateful' and 'it's generally not a problem' were commonplace when referring to their situation. Jim commented that his company could do anything they liked, as they did not recognise trade unions, which indicates a feeling of helplessness and powerlessness. As discussed earlier, recourse to hard law is not always appropriate, and this is perhaps where soft law (as mentioned in Chap. 1) can make a difference by encouraging organisations to adopt voluntary practices. This is an area where Coeliac UK and the Chartered Institute of Personnel and Development could make an impact by supporting organisations and managers (human resource managers and line managers) in becoming more open and receptive to individual difference and dignity at work, in line with the theme of this edited collection and the messages delivered by the other chapters. In particular, Chap. 3 (Considerations of Asperger's syndrome for HR specialists) addresses similar issues, where disclosure of a condition is not mandatory but where acceptance and inclusion reflect the portrayal of positive values by the organisation with its attendant impact on improved productivity and higher engagement with organisational values.

The current study shows that there is an internalising of reactions of participants towards their organisations and the exclusionary mechanisms which may be inadvertent but which clearly exist. While two of the focus-group members felt it was their duty to 'educate' their managers and co-workers (Chloe and Julie), Jim's response was more of a resigned acceptance, while Naomi and Julie felt their organisations had no obligation to provide any support. The differences in responses suggest there is a lack of knowledge about whether it is realistic to expect any support from employers and highlights a lack of existing research in this area. This shows the power of education and awareness in the organisation. Some participants expressed their concerns in an apologetic way taking responsibility for their own exclusion and stigmatisation.

2.8   Conclusion and Implications

The primary goal was to assess the emotional and perceptual implications of being a CS in the workplace. The study shows that within the workplace it is not possible to rely on being offered a GF option either in a designated canteen or at work-related function even when requested or if it is an organisational obligation to attend. These findings reinforce Goffman's (1963) argument that disqualification from full social acceptance creates a sense of stigmatisation and exclusion. Of course, the main point participants highlighted was not the actual lack of food provision, but the inappropriate 'social norms' which perpetuate discrimination and feelings of exclusion and a failure to support individuals reinforcing Perez's (2014) point that emphasis should be mainly paid on stigmatisers rather than drawing attention to the broader structural concerns that lead to stigmatisation.

We also aimed to assess the level of organisational knowledge and awareness regarding CD on the part of managers, employers and HR professionals who have a 'duty of care' towards the health and wellbeing of their employees. Sadly, the response was very much as we expected—a lack of knowledge except where there had been previous personal experience which had 'paved the way' for those who followed. There was evidence of policies being in place regarding people's dignity at work, but these existed only as formal policies and were not adhered to. As mentioned before, personal health and wellbeing may be considered a private sphere; nevertheless, a lack of social support creates a high sense of disengagement in their work (Demerouti et al. 2001) and generates the sense of unfairness in the workplace (Griffiths 2008). Symptomatic of many organisations, there was a reluctance to acknowledge difference and accept diversity. Surprisingly, analysis shows that participants have internalised their feelings and reactions to be able to cope with being coeliac at work. Taking part in the study was used as a tool to 'let' their frustration out. This was partly because there was a surprising reluctance to challenge management and superiors for fear of being labelled as 'difficult', and there was an overwhelming sense of 'just putting up with it'. This does reflect our earlier discussion on the collision of public and private spheres and the blurring of the boundaries between the two but also emphasises the stigmatisation of someone who is not fully able to become 'socially accepted' because of their dietary requirements. In other words, participants displayed a negative attitude and behaviour due to poor levels of wellbeing, contribution and support (Eisenberger et al. 1986; Dulac et al. 2008; Rich et al. 2010).

Next, we turn to our second research question of what are the basic requirements of the CSs in the workplace, and here we found that our participants relied heavily on preparing their own food to take to work as canteen and/or vending machine options were either limited or non-existent. Cross-contamination was a key concern where food was provided or even where computer equipment was shared in an environment where people had to eat at their desks. For special occasions, it was apparent that some attempts were made at providing a GF menu option but by special request only. There is still a long way to go before GF eating becomes accepted as mainstream in the same way that vegetarian options are now routinely provided. None of our participants mentioned facilities to store food under refrigeration or be able to heat food they had prepared for themselves; instead, they spoke of needing to find places where they could buy a suitable GF option for the occasions when they had forgotten their lunch. We argue that the basic requirements of the CS in the workplace should be facilities for the safe storage of food and for basic heating facilities; however, these should be available to all workers as a matter of course. We are constantly warned of both the hygiene implications of eating at our workstations and decline in productivity because of not taking a proper meal break (Hitchcock 2013), so basic provision could benefit all staff.

Our third research question aimed to identify any areas of discriminatory practice within the workplace. Perhaps the overwhelming finding here was that of stigmatisation of the coeliac individual. They were overlooked at celebratory events, felt they were being difficult for raising concerns about provision of GF options, suffered comments about the cost of providing GF food for them and so tended to internalise their condition and emotions. What is important here is that participants have been exposed to more implicit than explicit discrimination and so highlight the effects of the 'hidden' element of inequality. This confirms Black and Orfila's (2011) findings that social exclusion creates feelings of anxiety and depression; hence, management willingness to educate individuals and create an exclusive working environment is of a great importance. As mentioned before, ignorance or lack of understanding by the non-coeliac might cause an unintentional and indirect discrimination compounded by silence or resentment by the 'involved' party (Araújo and Araújo 2012).

We also asked what examples are there of good practice towards helping the management of the condition in the workplace. This question remains unanswered. Participants were unable to provide any examples of good practices within their organisations. Of course, there are those organisations that have developed a distinctive set of wellbeing practices supporting all individual needs. Nevertheless, participants highlight the need to establish three best practices: understanding, support and recognition. These are all behavioural qualities and attributes supporting the literature that appropriate behaviour increases awareness of dietary requirements (Holtzman 2006). There appears to be apathy on the part of management which then acts as an inhibitor of change and reluctance to accommodate workers' needs. The sense of lack of understanding on the part of management, compounded by treating CD as a 'problem', creates divisions at work by differentiating between those who can eat and those who cannot which is not a good way to support people and be inclusive to all. This reinforces the arguments around food and eating as being important symbols in the workplace (Ortlieb and Sieben 2011). Poor access to celebrations of success, cementing of team 'togetherness' and cohesiveness and other organisational 'rituals' (Flores-Pereira et al. 2008) creates the sense of stigmatisation and marginalisation amongst colleagues confirming Sturdy et al.'s (2006, p. 907) argument that the business dinner is *a liminal space between work and private spheres*. Thus, it provides a linkage between an employer's obligation to coeliac employees to enable them to carry out their work duties safely and without incurring personal harm.

Consequently, the study shows that there is a strong connection between CD and social exclusion. A feeling of guilt and not wanting to appear as being difficult prevents CSs from expressing their concerns. Participants demonstrated that the psychological aspects of the disease are ignored by managers and employers, probably because they lack understanding of the condition. Much is made in the literature of the psychological impact of the disease, and it is significant yet it focusses on the internal aspects rather than being made to feel 'difficult' or ignored by colleagues, managers and employers. There is no denial that the legal protection afforded by the Equality Act 2010 is important to protect individuals in the workplace. Nevertheless, organisations have a moral obligation to protect employees' psychological needs and accommodate any 'special' needs. We believe that we should not 'force' individuals to change their behaviour around CSs without providing appropriate learning opportunities. Organisations like Coeliac UK, Coeliac Support Associate and other support association are providing useful resources to enhance awareness across the workplace. It is important to continue offering educational opportunities to allow individuals to understand CD, and most importantly take actions in addressing any discriminatory behaviours in the workplace. Knowledge, awareness, inclusion and management actions are essential dimensions to satisfy individual needs.

References

Advisory, Conciliation and Arbitration Service. 2017. Help and advice. http://www.acas.org.uk/index.aspx?articleid=5920. Accessed 5 Feb 2017.

Ahmed, S. 2007. The language of diversity. *Ethnic and Racial Studies* 30: 235–256.

Araújo, H., and W. Araújo. 2012. Coeliac disease: Eating habits and quality of life. *British Food Journal* 114: 1297–1309.

Bezrukova, K., K. Jehn, and C.S. Spell. 2012. Reviewing diversity training: Where we have been and where we should go. *Academy of Management Learning and Education* 11: 207–227.

Black, J.L., and C. Orfila. 2011. Impact of coeliac disease on dietary habits and quality of life. *Journal of Human Nutrition and Dietetics* 24: 582–587.

Blamey, A., and M. Mackenzie. 2007. Theories of change and realistic evaluation: Peas in a pod or apples and oranges? *Evaluation* 13: 439–455.

Chartered Institute of Personnel and Development. 2012. Diversity management. http://www.cipd.co.uk/binaries/diversity-and-inclusion_2012-fringe-or-fundamental.pdf. Accessed 17 Aug 2016.

Coeliac UK. 2007. *Coeliac disease.* https://www.publications.parliament.uk/pa/cm200607/cmhansrd/cm070221/debtext/70221-0022.htm. Accessed 8 Feb 2017.

———. 2014. Key facts on coeliac disease. https://www.coeliac.org.uk/document.../coeliac-uk-fact-sheet-2014.pdf. Accessed 12 Jan 2017.

———. 2017. *Gluten-free and the law.* https://www.coeliac.org.uk/food-industry-professionals/gluten-freeand-the-law/. Accessed 8 Feb 2017.

Cunha, M.P., C. Cabral-Cardoso, and S. Clegg. 2008. Manna from heaven: The exuberance of food as a topic for research in management and organization. *Human Relations* 61: 935–963.

Demerouti, E., A.B. Bakker, F. Nachreiner, and W.B. Schaufeli. 2001. The job demands-resources model of burnout. *Journal of Applied Psychology* 86: 499–512.

Dulac, T., J. Coyle-Shapiro, D.J. Henderson, and S. Wayne. 2008. Not all responses to breach are the same. The interconnection of social exchange and psychological contract processes in organizations. *Academy of Management Journal* 51: 1079–1098.

Eisenberger, R., R. Huntington, S. Hutchison, and D. Sowa. 1986. Perceived organizational support. *Journal of Applied Psychology* 71: 500–507.

Equality Act. 2010 (2017). Equality Act 2010 breakdown. http://www.legislation.gov.uk/ukpga/2010/15/contents. Accessed 3 Feb 2017.

Flores-Pereira, M.T., E. Davel, and N.R. Cavedon. 2008. Drinking beer and understanding organizational culture embodiment. *Human Relations* 61: 1007–1026.

Ford, S., R. Howard, and J. Oyebode. 2012. Psychosocial aspects of coeliac disease: A cross-sectional survey of a UK population. *British Journal of Health Psychology* 17: 743–757.

Goffman, E. 1963. *Stigma: Notes on the management of spoiled identity.* Englewood: Prentice-Hall.

Gray, A.M., and I. Papanicolas. 2010. Impact of symptoms on quality of life before and after diagnosis of coeliac disease: Results from a UK population survey. *BMC Health Services Research* 10: 1–7.

Greene, A., and G. Kirton. 2011. Diversity management meets downsizing: The case of a government department. *Employee Relations* 33: 22–39.

Griffiths, H. 2008. *Coeliac disease: Nursing care and management.* Chichester: Wiley.

Hall, J., G. Rubin, and A. Charnock. 2013. Intentional and inadvertent non-adherence in adult coeliac disease. A cross-sectional survey. *Appetite* 68: 56–62.

Hayles, V.R. 1996. *Diversity training and development. The ASTD training and development handbook.* New York: McGraw Hill.

Hitchcock, H. 2013. Government health minister says eating at desks is 'disgusting', but should it be banned? www.bmmagazine.co.uk/in-business/legal/government-health-minister-says-eating-at-desks-is-disgusting-but-should-it-be-banned/. Accessed 12 Jan 2017.

Holtzman, J.D. 2006. Food and memory. *Annual Review of Anthropology* 35: 361–378.

Kumra, S., and S. Manfredi. 2012. *Managing equality and diversity: Theory and practice.* Oxford: Oxford University Press.

Kurppa, K., P. Collin, M. Mäki, and K. Kaukinen. 2014. Celiac disease and health-related quality of life. *Expert Review of Gastroenterology & Hepatology* 5: 83–90.

Lee, A.R., D.L. Ng, B. Diamond, E.J. Ciaccio, and P. Green. 2012. Living with coeliac disease: Survey results from the USA. *Journal of Human Nutrition and Dietics* 25: 233–238.

Mendoza, N., and P. McGough. 2005. Coeliac disease: An overview. *Nutrition & Food Science* 35: 156–162.

Niederle, M., and L. Vesterlund. 2013. How costly is diversity? Affirmative action in light of gender differences. *Management Science* 59: 1–16.

Ortlieb, R., and B. Sieben. 2011. Christmas parties and other social events in organisations: A hotbed for the (re)production of gender regimes. Workshop WK Organisation VHB, Freie Universitat, Berlin.

Ozbilgin, M., G. Mulholland, A. Tatli, and D. Worman. 2008. *Managing diversity and the business case.* London: Chartered Institute of Personnel and Development.

Perez, C. 2014. Revisiting Erving Goffman's stigma: Notes on the management of spoiled identity. Blog post from Social Analysis of Health Network. University of Cambridge. https://sahncambridge.wordpress.com/2014/07/01/revisiting-erving-goffmans-stigma-notes-on-the-management-of-spoiled-identity-by-cristina-perez/. Accessed 16 Jan 2017.

Rich, B.L., J.A. LePine, and E.R. Crawford. 2010. Job engagement. Antecedents and effects on job performance. *Academy of Management Journal* 53: 617–635.

Rosen, M. 1985. Breakfast at Spiro's: Dramaturgy and dominance. *Journal of Management* 11: 31–48.

Sturdy, A.J., M. Schwartz, and A. Spicer. 2006. Guess who's coming to dinner? Structures and uses of liminality in strategic management consultancy. *Human Relations* 59: 929–960.

Thomson, D., and A. Hassenkamp. 2008. The social meaning and function of food rituals in healthcare practice: An ethnography. *Human Relations* 61: 1775–1802.

van Dijk, H., M.L. van Engen, and J. Paauwe. 2012. Reframing the business case for diversity: A values and virtues perspective. *Journal of Business Ethics* 111: 73–84.

Whitaker, J.K., J. West, G.K. Holmes, and R.F. Logan. 2009. Patient perceptions of the burden of coeliac disease and its treatment in the UK. *Alimentary Pharmacology and Therapeutics* 29: 1131–1136.

3

The 'A' Word in Employment: Considerations of Asperger's Syndrome for HR Specialists

Anne Cockayne

3.1 Introduction

Asperger syndrome (AS) is a neurodiverse condition lying on the autistic spectrum which for many years was classified distinctly from autism but is now subsumed under a more general classification and recognised in the American Psychiatric Association's *Diagnostic and Statistical Manual of Mental Disorders (DSM-5:2013)*. It is characterised by difficulties in social interaction, rigidity in thinking and over- or undersensitisation to surrounding sounds, lights and textures, and these have placed AS as a 'hidden' disability protected under the Equality Act (2010). AS people are frequently troubled by loud noises and feelings of being different from their peers, which have created adverse impacts upon job satisfaction, earnings and securing meaningful employment (Haertl et al. 2013; Krieger et al. 2012).

A. Cockayne (✉)
Department of Human Resource Management, Nottingham Business School, Nottingham Trent University, Nottingham, UK

© The Author(s) 2018
V. Caven, S. Nachmias (eds.), *Hidden Inequalities in the Workplace*,
Palgrave Explorations in Workplace Stigma,
DOI 10.1007/978-3-319-59686-0_3

In theory, AS people are less likely to experience employment difficulties than others with spectrum conditions as they have higher than average levels of intelligence quotient (IQ) (Baron-Cohen et al. 2003; Assouline et al. 2012; Chiang et al. 2014), but despite this, they are less likely to be employed than non-disabled adults and up to four times more likely to be unemployed than other adults with a more recognised disability (Riddell et al. 2010; NAS 2016). Once employed AS individuals struggle disproportionately to maintain secure employment (Richards 2012, 2015) and suffer mal-employment as a result of skills being underutilised (Baldwin et al. 2014; Baldwin and Costley 2015).

An alternative perspective on neurodiversity views autism as a strength due to similar neurological conditions, which create valid and different pathways within human diversity. This area has been overlooked in the employment context, despite clinical studies which identify that AS people possess talents and special abilities, including intense concentration, independence in thought, affinity with computers and other technology, good writing skills, attention to detail and precision (Frith and Happe 2001; Happe and Vital 2009), original ideas, reliable meeting of deadlines (Griffin and Pollak 2009) and capacity to gather and store expert knowledge (Friedrichs and Shaughnessy 2015). All of these have the potential to be of interest to employers, and indeed some companies have deliberately recruited AS individuals for technology-related roles on account of these skills and preferences (Grant 2015; Warnick 2015; Wang 2014). In more targeted employment-based studies, AS employees are considered trustworthy, reliable and capable of achieving high work output (Parr and Hunter 2014) more so than comparable non-AS employees (Hagner and Cooney 2005; Hiller et al. 2007). Neurodiversity advocates (Silberman 2015; Goldstein 2014) have been much readier to confer strengths upon AS individuals and go further, rating them as superior to the neurotypical population who are the non-autistic and 'normal' majority (Owren 2013, p. 35). In a somewhat 'tongue in cheek' comparison, Ortega (2009, p. 432) suggests that neurotypical people are disadvantaged as they are *characterised by preoccupation with social concerns, delusions of superiority and obsession with conformity* alluding to the irritation that two distinct groups can experience when dealing and working with each other.

3.2   Duality

This duality in the AS condition means that AS people can experience both problematic *disability* in the workplace and possess strengths from these *diverse* skills, and is what has inspired me to find out more about AS. My intention here is to report the views and opinions of those in the study, who like me share a commitment to finding out much more about the AS condition in the workplace to increase the scope for using diverse skills as well as to reduce the inequalities from the problematic employment outcomes outlined. In beginning to research this topic, a colleague thoughtfully remarked to me that it was surely impossible for anyone working in HR or related disciplines *not* to view this as an interesting topic to study, reflective perhaps of the low levels of knowledge and understanding about AS in the employment context as well as some of the mystique that surrounds conditions which are unseen and therefore open to stigmatisation and stereotyping. Readers should bear in mind that my interests have also introduced some bias into this discussion.

3.3   Academic and Methodological Considerations

Those familiar with critical diversity and disability studies will note that more is known about physical disabilities than less visible disabilities such as autism and AS, and that ableist norms permeate both (Williams and Mavin 2012; Van Knippemberg et al. 2004). Diversity studies similarly focus upon the differences between people, which can be seen, such as race, gender, ethnicity and functional background, driven in the main by the belief that there is a strong business case for diversity (Pelled et al. 1999; Jackson and Joshi 2004; Economist Intelligence Unit 2009, p. 16; Bunderson and Sutcliffe 2002). Overall, disability has been put aside in diversity studies (Procknow and Rocco 2016), and for 'hidden' disabilities like AS, this is even more the case. Another difficulty researchers like myself have faced is that while approximately 1 in 200 people are diagnosed as AS each year with the numbers increasing (Brugha et al. 2012), far fewer go on to disclose their condition as a result of various disclosure barriers and individual sensitivities which have hindered research (Morris et al. 2015). Additionally, many people remain unaware of their condition as diagnosis is often missed, confused with personality disorders, particularly in women (Bargiela et al. 2016), or not received until late adulthood.

Most organisations therefore will have a small minority of AS individuals who have chosen not to disclose, which taken together with the non-visible nature of AS makes it difficult, if not impossible, to know easily who 'is' or 'has' AS. This created ontological and epistemological challenges, in that there was a need to study a condition that positivist approaches have identified as having distinctive attributes and capacities, but which at the same time is surrounded by concepts which are very much socially constructed. *Skill* is a problematic and value-laden construct, noted in gendered and cultured studies (Grugulis and Vincent 2009; Shan 2013), and can mean virtually anything that employers want it to be (Payne 2000). Clinical studies have treated AS as *disability* and impairment, as does employment legislation which recognises that disability arises from society's perceptions and reactions, not the condition itself. Ability and strength are underexplored even though knowledge of the condition in the clinical domain has connected these with particular talents, and it is this paradox that makes considering how AS characteristics come to enable, disable or create inequalities that make it interesting and challenging to study. *Diversity* is also socially constructed, in part, because categorisation of difference depends very much on the 'others' who label differences, the norms against these differences are being identified and from which the term 'neurodiverse' has emerged.

Given that diversity, disability and skill are all socially constructed concepts, readers will be unsurprised that positivism was rejected as the most appropriate way of investigating how perceptions of this very real condition are filtered through these concepts, necessary for developing understanding of how people relate to each other within the workplace. Social life is activity dependent, but the outcomes of that activity, such as clinical diagnoses, then become an important and 'real' part of new rounds of social action, which have effects in the world, albeit these are refracted through the perceptions of actors. This can be termed 'weak' social constructionism (Burr 1998; Cohen et al. 2004) and guided the investigation of how key actors, line managers and HR specialists operate in their dealings with AS individuals and how they vary in the ways they and their organisations construct disability, diversity and skills. This investigation also benefitted from the more objective exploration valued by critical realism (Porpora 2015). This has enabled me to confront the reality that relatively far fewer AS people disclose than would be predicted by prevalence estimates both in the population as a whole and in the organisations involved in this study informing the current discussion about disclosure.

Interviews with line managers from six organisations of varying size and sector aimed to reveal if or how they used the skills of their AS employees, what might enable or constrain them in doing so and what AS people talked about in terms of their own employment experiences. I wanted to know how these managers formed their conceptualisations about AS, and following Smith's (2010) call for researchers to value sheer description, I used prompt cards each with a word or short phrase derived from the literature review to help them recall scenarios and events. Care was taken that managers compared these with their other team members, as it was the *differences* which AS individuals exhibit versus the neurotypical population which were being explored. The way in which these differences affected the immediate team as well as how the role and context within which AS employees worked was also considered, given how significant these are for AS employees (Baldwin et al. 2014; Baldwin and Costley 2015; Richards 2012, 2015). Mindful of the heterogeneous nature of AS and the need to avoid stereotypes, respondents were asked if they had encountered any surprises in dealings with AS employees. Throughout this chapter, the voices of the 14 AS employees and the 12 line managers who took part in the study show how these really interesting differences surface in the workplace and at the same time expose how they also connect to employment inequalities. AS employees worked in roles across varying skill levels: administrative officers working in call centres and data input roles, technical specialists, nurses, engineers and team managers. Disability or identity first language (an 'AS individual') is used throughout, consistent with the notion of neurodiversity (Robison 2011). This views AS as an integral to individual identity rather than person's first language ('an individual with AS') which separates a person's autism from their identity. This can undermine its positive characteristics, implying that something is 'wrong' with the person or that difficulties come from being 'broken' in some way.

3.4   Findings and Discussion

3.4.1   Disclosing

Knowing that disclosure sensitivities exist (Blockmans 2015), it is also important to step back and consider what AS employees talked about when describing their experiences and thoughts about disclosure. More than half of the employees interviewed mentioned in detail the tensions they had experienced in disclosing, worrying that if they *announce it to the whole office I would be labelled*; *'I've never discussed with anyone, don't want to admit I've got anything, even to my wife'*. All bar one AS employee linked the existence of powerful media stereotypes as a major influence upon the perceptions that their colleagues and managers held about AS and autism, which in the main they viewed as negative. Examples cited were of 'The Undateables' and 'Rainman' with one employee talking about 'The Big Bang' TV show as giving the impression that *'Aspies are: rude, arrogant, self-absorbed, socially inept and, perhaps worst of all, very hard to be friends with'*. Stereotypes were described by AS individuals as *'mixed and inaccurate, patronising in the extreme'*. It is unsurprising that these fears about stereotyping which are present right from the outset of someone's employment experience can be a strong disincentive to disclose, thereby reducing still further the chance that someone will ask for and receive the support they are entitled to.

Despite these tensions and feelings of being perceived as less or perhaps unequal to their colleagues, some people do disclose, particularly once they have 'made it' into reasonably secure employment, which made it possible to find out directly from managers how this population operate distinct from their neurotypical colleagues. The following section describes the characteristics that managers noticed about their AS employees which cluster into seven broad areas: having a high work ethic, a higher than average IQ, strong attention to detail, honesty and directness, inflexibility, social interaction and hypersensitivities. These were conceptualised variously as strength and as weakness, and the varying conceptualisations created a powerful incentive to explore further how and why they have come to be placed as such, and with an eye to contemporary HR practice to explore how best to utilise these strengths. Doing so also provides an opportunity to consider how 'hidden' inequalities may arise where managers decide that these same characteristics are problematic. Space does not permit expansion of all the characteristics noted, but given my aim of stimulating thinking about how differences between neurodiverse and neurotypical employees play out in a typical workplace, there is a particular focus upon the strengths reported by managers as high IQ and work ethic.

Also interesting are the examples managers provided when asked about hypersensitivities and working with others as these created conceptualisations that can be constructed as either strength or weakness representing something of the duality that is fascinating to me. Neurodiversity advocates would connect this duality to neurotypical notions of what constitutes a 'normal' working environment. At this point, it is worth noting such an assessment is fairly meaningless, being very much a matter of who decides it to be so, *and* by what norms they refer to in deciding that someone is somehow lesser or unequal in their capacities. This AS employee, pausing to consider her condition, vividly illustrates that perceptions of any condition really do depend on who is doing the labelling:

> What if AS is really not a thing and it's just how some of us are? Why has it got to be said that's it's a thing that **I am**, not a thing like **you** are.

3.4.2 Working Hard: Better, Different or Exploitative?

The majority of the managers acknowledged work ethic as a key strength for AS employees compared to non-AS employees. This manager reports how work ethic is reflected in this employee's obsession with finishing a task:

> If he's given a task to do he has to do it and it has to get done. He will do it until he has finished it.

Almost every line manager reported that their AS employees were willing to perform tasks that others did not want to do often on account of their repetitive nature. For example, this employee who willingly volunteered to sort out basic filing despite being employed as a highly skilled technical specialist:

I could tell her to do filing and she wouldn't mind. She did a really boring data hunting job for me the other day.

Similarly, an administrative officer working in a lower-skilled role volunteered to organise car parking:

He just wants to be busy he will take anything on. He helps me out quite a lot. For example, he sorted out the car park rota for me.

Findings indicate that AS employees are often willing to perform tasks that are frequently unattractive or low profile:

Sometimes there are accidents in the restaurant, children's sickness or worse – that kind of thing he would literally be absolutely fine. Doesn't matter what the situation was or how bad that was. He would just say yes OK. Not many people would like to do that.

Another participant argued that:

We had a new box to put the keys in for the filing cabinets. It takes ages to number all the cabinets and the keys and then write on hooks. She took her time over it enjoyed doing it. I knew I couldn't give it to another person-it's those jobs that don't belong to anybody.

Employees were noted as being willing to work hard on a consistent basis, over and above what might be reasonably expected, in comparison to others in the team, as these managers noted in their employees who worked as administrative officers:

He was very happy with whatever we wanted him to do will do what you ask him to do. Others would say 'I don't want to do that'. His mindset is that if he's been asked to do something then he will do. He usually never says no.

In transferring this administrative officer from one department to another:

You won't have any trouble – he is low maintenance and you'll get a large proportion of work out of him.

Reporting high levels of output, a manager describes his administrative assistant as a:

Model employee – he does the work of 2 people, covered for an absent manager, carried on doing the data handler as well as the management job. He had taken on 2 roles during the summer holidays. He just sucked it up.

Higher levels of output were reported directly through focussed and determined efforts at a particular task, or simply by keeping focussed when others want to socialise.

People from that team were incredibly impressed by how and how quickly she had turned it around; others in the same cohort would take days if not weeks. Trainees normally don't turn it out as such a polished finished product.

Talking about this highly skilled engineer:

I think he is very focused on trying to complete and move on. It's not overly obsessive, just very focused. The strengths side of obsession.

While for these two less-skilled administrative officers:

It's just the fact that a lot of it is really strong, it's just the speed, accuracy and quality that comes back is above her pay grade. I think it's a strength – it's really big. He doesn't let himself get distracted. He is one of the people I go to when I have a complex task that I need to know that it will get done.

From a line manager's perspective, having a team member who works hard and is happy to take on routine or unpopular tasks, which others in the teams avoid, can be extremely useful. Further to that findings show that line managers feeling pleased and relieved that they do not have to ask or coerce other team members to pick them up. Managers' accounts of people working hard are expansive, describing people who work hard in a number of different ways and reflecting how work ethic itself has been viewed, as reliability, trustworthiness, timekeeping or as professionalism (Jackson 2009; Branine 2008; McQuaid and Lindsay 2005). In considering the effects of working hard, it is known that someone with a disability may or may not choose to work harder than their colleagues, implicitly accepting ableist norms around productivity (Mik-Meyer 2016; Jammaers et al. 2016). It is likely that the 'hidden' nature of AS predisposes this 'working hard' reaction more so than someone who has a more visible disability. This is a difficult area for those who manage AS employees to intervene, as they may not know the person 'is' AS, and so may be tempted to leave things as they are, allowing these exceptional levels of output and hard work to continue perhaps secretly wishing others in the team would do the same. Or perhaps they simply accept this as someone's preferred way of working even if they view it as a little odd. In light of exposure to new knowledge about AS, another choice is to understand that these patterns are likely to come from the condition itself and then adopt a more reflexive stance, seeking to intervene in ways that constraints around the role and environment allow. Where someone has disclosed managers are a little more likely to recognise these adverse effects are connected to the condition as this manager did: *'I want to highlight that I can see this is someone who is trying their hardest on a daily basis; there is nothing worse than this'*.

3.4.3 'Hidden' Talents: Amazing, Gifted and Exceptional Employees

Given how important IQ is in many selection decisions, I wanted to see what managers noticed about how their AS employees operate when it came to the aspect of IQ equated with ability in handling complex systems and data, as well as the notion of 'raw' IQ itself. Not only were AS employees noted by their managers as being really hard working across a variety of roles, the majority also rated their employees as being more intelligent than others. These two employees both working in administrative roles were viewed as:

always being able to get his head around complex systems and data. Always gets to the bottom of things; definitely the highest IQ in the team – she'll look behind the result, not just take it at face value.

Managers connect positive outcomes of high IQs for these more highly skilled AS employees, working as a data specialist and engineer respectively:

She [a financial data specialist] has a higher IQ than the rest of the team. She is exceptional. ... I would say gifted; works more quickly, makes less mistakes, generates higher levels of output than all of her more experienced colleagues, and has a more creative approach to solving problems.

He [engineer] has skills in connecting complex data – an ability to draw connections that other people just don't. This is definitely strength. I've a really bright lady in my team, she's doing similar work ... but he is at a completely different level – it comes naturally to him, not to others – they are at 80/20, with him it's 95/5. It's the extra piece, it's natural, not being asked to do.

AS employees gave another perspective on IQ which came from the connection between having a special interest which drove them to develop expertise in a particular topic similar to those identified by Friedrichs and Shaughnessy (2015) in their work with AS student populations. This employee, working as a restaurant manager, was noted by his more senior manager as someone seeking out additional responsibilities, in this case connected to his particular interests in environmental matters:

I doubt that there will ever be anybody at his level that would be able to take on that additional level of responsibility – he has an absolute passion for environmental management systems ... you could joke about it and say it was almost an obsession because he is so into it that he writes a leaflet off his own back. He's done that for 7 years. It's amazing.

Words like 'gifted', 'exceptional' and 'amazing' describe how managers notice that their employees have unusual abilities which stand out from the crowd; the engineer is seen as not just being better but somehow having different abilities, the 'extra piece', special by virtue of the facts that others 'just don't' and is analogous to the abilities first noted by Asperger ([1944] 1991). The restaurant manager is viewed as unusual for so readily acquiring vast amounts of knowledge which has nothing to do with his day-to-day responsibilities. Either way, this kind of exceptional ability appears to be something that is rare and that for those who have not yet come across it hard to understand and conceptualise. Clearly organisations are not vehicles for indulging anyone with their special interest or passions, but talent specialists could be more aware that at all levels and grades in their organisations there are people with exceptional talents that may be underused. At the day-to-day job level, discussions with managers indicate that there is some scope for enhancing roles through crafting jobs (Wrzesniewski and Dutton 2001) rather than simply making adjustments required by law to accommodate perceived disability, although in this study, these examples were limited, partly due to structural factors which will constrain the extent to which roles can be shaped to suit individual characteristics, as this example of an employee working in heavily standardised role in a call centre shows:

> This is like a production line, calls are like widgets produced – the idea is to have good quality calls time after time. This is not a creative environment.

3.4.4   Hypersensitivities

AS employee noted the discomfort experienced from noise and open plan offices:

> I don't like very loud noise; especially people talking, when voices start to get raised. (Administrative officer, complaints handling). In an open plan office, she [his co-worker] gets a lot of people coming to her desk and stays chatting 15 minutes at a time, I'm trying to concentrate and it's disruptive. I've had no discussion with anyone, I just told my manager, that was it. No one has suggested anything.

This manager describes the problems experienced by this customer service advisor working in an open plan call centre where about 1000 people work:

He can't cope because of the noise, so what I've done is moved desks about so he's next to someone who is very quiet and away from the noisy ones. He just can't function if desk lighting is too bright. He is the only one in building wearing a hat, as no one else is allowed to. I can't move these teams about. These are national procedures; we can't change it for him.

Another manager describes what this staff nurse who had to work night shifts found hard:

It is hard because the lights are usually on. Night lights aren't the greatest when you're working night shifts. I asked if we could just turn off alternate lights at night. As an organisation they said, no it's all on one system; it would be too much to rewire the whole system. I would say it's OK just take a bulb out!

The difficulties these managers' report from moving desks in the large open plan call centre and changing light bulbs in a hospital corridor were both experienced in large, heavily regulated and bureaucratic organisations—one being a government agency and the other a health trust—and shows how even where legislation dictates adjustments have to be made, organisational constraints are likely to play a part in the ease that managers can secure them. In the government agency as well as moving desks to a quieter space, adjustments were made for the call centre employee to take more frequent breaks. He also chose to wear a hat to further reduce the noise disruption, and both these accommodations are really difficult to hide from the rest of the team. Wearing the hat marks him out *only* because no one else is allowed to and some organisations would find such restrictions puzzling illustrating just how subjective this concept of 'reasonable' is and which are likely related to many factors including organisational climate, culture, sector and size and the pervasive belief that 'ideal' workers exist (Foster and Wass 2012) who will readily slot into working arrangements that the majority have accepted. Such accommodations also represent something of a double-edged sword for AS employees as on one hand they help redress inequalities simply by reducing noise or other sensory problems, but at the same time marking people out either as needing special attention and treatment, or being perceived as awkward. AS employees then become prone to experience the trap of the social model (Procknow and Rocco 2016), for example, consider the reactions from other team members if the quietest part of the office also happens to be the most attractive, perhaps next to a window with good views and natural light. No wonder then that some employees do not pursue this, perhaps considering the reactions this may create as did this data specialist when asked if he had asked for headphones or desk partitions to help manage noise disruption: *'No. I have tried to cope with it without asking. In fact, I've tried to get on with it and just "man up".*

When putting in place such adjustments, managers are frequently pressurised to maintain team performance, an area on which the legislation is silent. Someone with reduced productivity from taking breaks that are more frequent will affect upon the team's performance in environments like a call centre where performance is measured at both team and individual level and so unless the presence of an individual with impairment in the team is adjusted for at *both* levels, the potential for resentment and subsequent unfavourable treatment of that person by the team exists, something which legislation alone cannot protect the employee from. This manager is well aware of the tensions that follow the adjustments: *'I'm really looking to Occupational Health for evidence so I can help him and so I can adjust the targets'.*

In juggling these new working arrangements, managers then often have no choice but to make adjustments 'off line' with the individual, for example, by changing targets underperformance management systems and which even if these are not seen by the rest of the team have the potential to contribute to growing feelings of inadequacy, common to these experienced by many employees with disabilities. For AS employees, regardless of whether they have disclosed or not, these feelings are exacerbated immensely by the fact that their condition is not visible as this manager describes:

I feel there is a lot more support and understanding placed upon someone who has a disability that you can see rather than someone who had different brain chemistry. He isn't unique in this. I had someone who had a [hand] disfigurement. So it is really obvious to all around that there is a disability. Not like K, he drives a car!

3.4.5   Being 'Social': Team Working or Team Contribution?

The previous discussion has revealed how talented and hard-working AS people are, and on the surface this makes the employment inequalities they experience somewhat puzzling. Talking to AS employees and their managers about the differences they see in how AS people work with others offers some insight but also requires some reflection upon the norms which govern the way many people in most workplaces interact with each other. Writing about their own employment experiences, AS individuals have cited prolonged social interaction and noisy environments as problematic (Muller et al. 2008), and most of the AS employees in this study also found these aspects troubling:

The biggest drawback for someone with AS, more than anything else is the interaction with people – it's what limits me most in the workplace.

Social interaction is superfluous to doing the job – so when I come into work I can shut down. I don't want to be rude, am trying to accommodate it, focusing on getting prepared for the next call. Sometimes it's horrible, as I want to be a team member, a valued member of the team but I just can't handle the team in this environment.

People are needlessly complex and extremely draining.

Every manager interviewed also noted that their AS employees had some difficulties with the interactions they have at work with others:

Sometimes he mixes with them if we are in a group, but he doesn't choose to mix. He is part of the team. But I wouldn't say he is the best at team working, not a natural team worker. The team take a long time to get used to L because of the way she interacts in class – She definitely has a strong desire to help in the case team. Will help other trainees if they have another issue with a particular subject but not in a sort of comradely way. It's about getting the job done and passing on knowledge. When she is in chatty mood, she chats a lot, that's nice to have that engagement. But more often than not she doesn't want to chat gets on with work. I don't see that as a problem. Good at working within a team in terms of understanding the role that they and others play, but not good at work-ing a team in terms of day-to-day interactions. Not engaging really in normal conversations and chit chat. That kind of thing that may or not add value to the job in hand but I think is largely beneficial.

Managers seem to be assessing there is a 'natural' way of working in a team, and that some 'ways' of interacting with others exist that others may find hard to warm to. In considering how they see teamwork, it seems they are likely to make value judgements as to what is normal and natural; 'comradely' is an implied norm as are preferences for team members to engage in the team in a particular manner by labelling these as 'nice' and 'normal'. Managers noted also how much their AS employees wanted to be part of the team:

He definitely wants to work in a team … isn't a loner, far from it; certainly wasn't a loner, within the team I think she was quite well liked.

This manager expands on the type of relationships she observed in this recent graduate IT systems engineer:

He didn't have difficulty in making friends, he would often start a conversation with people. At team meetings he would happily and openly share what he had been doing at the weekend, certainly work relationships were ok.

Across different organisations and different roles, these observations counter stereotypical knowledge derived from media portrayals and clinical literature as these descriptions of 'loner' most definitely do not fit the AS employees these managers know, who instead note how much they want to contribute to the team. Managers suggest there are some aspects of the way teams operate though that make it much more difficult for an AS employee to feel comfortable; for example, this manager describes how wanting to be a part of the team is being weighed up against the amount of perceived disruption from others talking as they work.

He is not a loner – he wants to be part of the team, as long as not too many people are talking at once.

This manager highlights how these preferences for standing back from office gossip may be beneficial to herself in managing this team member who works in an administrative role, handling customer complaints and where the volume of output is key:

Always sits on own when having lunch. In a way this is better you get more work out of the person. He doesn't chat to anyone.

Turning now to the differential effects experienced by AS employees, this employee feels it is obvious that working environments need to be quiet and that noise is distracting:

Only adjustment [that I want] is that people should use their common sense, and take their discussion into a room so it's quieter.

Is it 'common sense' that a good working environment is quiet? In many workplaces, sociability is valued and assumptions made that such an atmosphere is good for productivity, where people are engaging with each other and seemingly appearing to enjoy their work rather than working in a more isolated way. However, conflicting views of what common sense actually is exist and may explain how hard it can be for different people to agree on what constitutes an acceptable working environment, illustrated again by this manager describing an occasion which his AS employee working as a restaurant manager found difficult:

His role meant that all of a sudden he needed to have contact with General Managers and their deputies. They go for meals every night when they are at work, socialising, and going out for dinner. He found that very, very difficult and had to ask for some more time, it was hard for him to adjust.

It is unclear whether these difficulties for AS people are connected directly to the social interaction itself, perhaps from working out complex social meanings, an effect noticed in both clinical- (Frith 2008; Vermeulen 2011) and employment-based studies (Müller et al. 2003; Hurlbutt and Chalmers 2004), including specific problems with getting 'jokes' (Richards 2015, p. 11). Or they could come from the direct effects of noise and lighting levels which characterise the particular environment as have been discussed prior.

In this study, HRM polices emerged as a contributory factor in exclusionary employment experiences for AS employees, particularly the explicit requirement for team working in competency frameworks reflecting near universal positive valuations of these 'soft' skills, particularly in career progression (Giusti 2008, p. 2; Wolosky 2008; Nilsson 2010; Marks and Scholarios 2008). HR specialists noted that, *'leadership skills are definitely high on the priority list, especially networking'*; *'people skills—without these none of the above can be delivered effectively'*; *'hard skills can only carry you up till a point'*.

Using a blunt and direct style was another area that the majority of the managers in this study construed as a strength, commenting positively that their AS employees were willing to highlight problems, decisions or processes that others would simply keep quiet about: *his honesty is refreshing; her directness is brilliant.* However it is not hard to see how this same directness can also create problems for managers.

I have had issues when he sent emails that were too blunt and upset one member of staff. It did cause me a real problem, I don't think that the recipient will ever really understand they don't know about the condition. (senior manager of restaurant manager)

Another participant added:

There were some things ... what I would class as embarrassing. She would be very honest and open in front of colleagues. That would have an impact on how they would react. Some would say 'I didn't want to hear that'. Others would go to the point where they might laugh at her. I found that having to manage that situation was really quite uncomfortable. I had to manage it and say to her that you can't be like that. (manager of nursing assistant)

Looking now at the employees' perspective, it is also not hard to imagine that these same qualities could act as a barrier in negotiating progression pathways which typically demand a degree of political and tactful consideration and which AS people will, in general, find more difficult to navigate than their neurotypical counterparts. Such differences in communications style can set someone apart from others making them potentially a riskier choice in key appointments and can suppress the many talents and capacity for hard work that have been noted prior.

Given that this is an area difficult for AS people, there is potential for these differences to be a major source of 'hidden' inequalities for AS employees in both career progression and simply the day-to-day efforts involved in holding down a job. Case law shows employers disregard differences in communication styles, viewing them instead as rudeness or inappropriate behaviours (Wallis 2012), which in turn make employment problematic and in some instances results in someone's eventual dismissal. Where employers have lost cases, they have failed to understand that these differences in how people work, and in their communications styles are 'real' and serious enough to matter. This reflects Richards' (2015) assertion that this is a major cause of exclusionary employment outcomes for AS people. Returning to the preferences noted for routine tasks across different skill levels, managers might face tensions when they actively want their employees to expand their skills for their own development:

> *How can I have a conversation with [employee-data specialist] about career development when I know that he loves doing this type of repetitive work?.*

Thinking back to the previous discussion on page six of just how different neurotypical and neurodiverse people may see the world, from an AS employee's perspective doing repetitive work, is not inevitably problematic, and it may be the case that one person's liking for sameness can be welcomed rather than worried about.

> *Repetition is boring, but if you are an Aspie you tend to think it is perfectly OK. I am not very good at grey areas and lateral thinking. I like a routine setting where I know what I am doing, that OK. A neurotypical might do this for a week; I could go happily at this routine task for months on end.*

Managers could therefore 'weigh up' not just the contents of a particular role but the length of time in which an employee feels comfortable performing that role. In relation to higher skills roles, where this liking for repetition may play out as wanting to stay in the same or similar role, it may be that those tasked with promoting and developing technical specialists into leadership positions need to recognise the possibility that AS employees will have different timescales on their career trajectories, and reconcile this with organisational career systems which frequently prescribe development through varied career experiences.

3.5   Conclusions and Implications

These discussions have shown that AS employees have strengths, and I hope that shining a light upon these innate differences has built confidence that these can be utilised more productively. However, it is true that by itself the nature of the AS condition can create outcomes which may be exclusionary. For example, where AS employees become trapped in low-skilled, uninteresting or unpleasant roles on account of their preference for detail and routine, just like the AS employees in this study who worked mostly in semi-skilled roles involving repetitious tasks. Some may have freely chosen to do, but, for others, this is likely to have been from a more considered decision to deliberately offset the difficult working environments that have been highlighted. Viewed more critically, these 'choices' create exclusionary outcomes where demanding ways of working and misunderstanding of what is 'normal' for AS people result in disparities in pay and status between AS people and their non-AS counterparts and which must not be accepted as simply a different yet valid interpretation of a good work experience. A further cause of concern is the adverse outcomes, which are possible for AS people who naturally work hard over sustained period. Such behaviour might tempt employers particularly in low-skilled sectors to favour those with strong 'work ethics' (people who are willing to work long hours with little reward and who readily comply with managerial directives) rather than the more positive interpretations of professionalism and reliability that AS people have.

It is very difficult to 'know' categorically that someone 'has' or 'is' AS. It is an unseen condition and one that many chose not to disclose nor may even be aware of, and employers could therefore be mindful that performance issues connected to different ways of working or working in particular environments may not be a fault of the employee but related directly to the AS condition. Doing so may help them avoid problematic legal situations, which in turn yield negative outcomes for both employees and organisations. Better understanding of the significance of social demands and the physical constraints of some working environments should also enable AS individuals to be directed towards roles, which play to strengths rather than exacerbate known impairments.

In addition to improving knowledge of the condition itself, practitioners could also rethink what are 'normal' ways of working and how they value 'soft' skills. Managing someone who may not want to be quite as 'social' as their colleagues is a challenge, as apart from regular team meetings, there are many other workplace activities with even higher social content such as celebratory occasions, Christmas parties and team away days. Many of these are unlikely to fit easily with the ways that feel comfortable to AS employees, and so imposing a requirement to attend such events can create 'hidden' inequalities by making participation difficult in these aspects of working life which many people take for granted, and indeed often see as fun or as a reward from their day-to-day responsibilities. Managers could actively consider just how much AS employees need to be involved in these kinds of activities setting this against the recognised benefits they bring in building team cohesion and learning, by rethinking how team meetings can be organised and managed differently. In relation to the soft skills that can be genuinely difficult for AS employees in relation to their neurotypical counterparts, key questions for employers to ask are whether positive valuations of these skills are always appropriate as well as to more precisely specify the attributes or skills that are actually required. For example, what attributes or ways of working do count as team working; is team integration a more inclusive term than team working; and when and where different levels of directness could be deployed? Employers and recruiters could also reflect upon the assumptions that are made about what is a desirable and comfortable working environment.

Recognising the duality of the AS condition means that practitioners are better placed to challenge what is meant by the terms strength and weakness and instead note that these are arbitrary classifications created by each person's own notions of disability, skill and diversity. For AS people, these are particularly shaped by the role someone works in, and the surrounding norms, which govern how skills are valued, specified and interpreted. Acquiring a balanced appreciation of both strengths and difficulties means that HR specialists are more likely to notice that an AS person may be struggling simply because they are trying to fit into norms imposed by the majority as well as spotting where their strengths could be better utilised. In combination, this means they are better equipped to achieve the '*better contemporary term of inclusion*' (Syed and Ozbilgin 2009, p. 2440) rather than simply satisfying equality and diversity interventions, which protect and recognise difference. Reconciling the demands of a neurotypical majority with this AS minority is a substantial challenge and requires knowledge not just of how to recognise difference and avoid legislative sanctions but how to appreciate the subtleties of what creates differences and for AS, what might contribute to disclosure tensions and 'hidden' inequalities. This will involve examining and challenging the 'tools' used by HR specialists, for example, competency frameworks, person specifications and job descriptions to minimise the application of neurotypical norms resulting in unintentional discrimination.

This chapter has scratched the surface of the possible inequalities that all AS people face in finding and maintaining meaningful employment and opened up many more areas about AS to explore. In particular, the views that AS is a 'male' condition suggest that the experiences of AS women are underresearched, reflecting the lack of intersectionality approaches in disability and diversity studies. Another gap in knowledge is the experiences of AS people working in roles outside those stereotypically associated with technology.

As knowledge about AS increases, everyone in the workplace will have more choice in deciding how they respond to someone whose behaviours and ways of working differ from their own; employers can choose to adapt their established policies and practices, managers can seek to harness these differences in a productive manner and colleagues can treat AS people with admiration, tolerance or irritation; curiosity, apathy or disdain. It is also possible that applicants and employees will be more willing to declare their diagnosis and so HR specialists need to consider carefully how they create and promote information about AS. I hope that this chapter has stimulated readers to invest some time and effort into revisiting how the norms governing ways of working and the policies and practices by which individuals come to be noticed, selected and developed in organisations.

References

American Psychiatric Association. 2013. *Diagnostic and statistical manual of mental disorders–5 (DSM-5)*. Washington, DC: American Psychiatric Association.

Asperger, H. 1991. Autistic psychopathy in childhood. In *Autism and Asperger syndrome*, ed. U. Frith, 37–92. Cambridge: Cambridge University Press.

Assouline, S.G., N.M. Foley, and L. Dockery. 2012. Predicting the academic achievement of gifted students with autism spectrum disorder. *Journal of Autism and Developmental Disorders* 42: 1781–1799.

Baldwin, S., and D. Costley. 2015. The experiences and needs of female adults with high-functioning autism spectrum disorder. *Autism* 20: 483–495. June 25.

Baldwin, S., D. Costley, and A. Warren. 2014. Employment activities and experiences of adults with high-functioning autism and Asperger's disorder. *Journal of Autism and Developmental Disorders* 44: 2440–2449.

Bargiela, S., R. Steward, and M. Williams. 2016. The experiences of late-diagnosed women with autism spectrum conditions: An investigation of the female autism phenotype. *Journal of Autism and Developmental Disorders* 46: 1573–3432.

Baron-Cohen, S., J. Richler, D. Bisarya, N. Gurunatha, and S. Wheelwright. 2003. The systemising quotient (SQ): An investigation of adults with asperger syndrome or high functioning autism and normal sex differences. *Philosophical Transactions of the Royal Society B* 358: 361–374.

Blockmans, I.G.E. 2015. "Not wishing to be the white rhino in the crowd": Disability-disclosure at university. *Journal of Language and Social Psychology* 34: 158–180.

Branine, M. 2008. Graduate recruitment and selection in the UK: A study of the recent changes in methods and expectations. *Career Development International* 13: 497–513.

Brugha, T., S.A. Cooper, S. McManus, S. Purdon, J. Smith, F.J. Scott, N. Spiers, and F. Tyrer. 2012. *Estimating the prevalence of autism spectrum conditions in adults: Extending the 2007 adult psychiatric morbidity survey*. Leeds: NHS Information Centre for Health and Social Care.

Bunderson, J.S., and K.M. Sutcliffe. 2002. Comparing alternative conceptualizations of functional diversity in management teams: Process and performance effects. *Academy of Management Journal* 45: 875–893.

Burr, V. 1998. Overview: Realism, relativism, social constructionism and discourse. In *Social constructionism, discourse and realism*, ed. I. Parker, 13–26. London: Sage Publishing.

Chiang, H.M., L.Y. Tsai, and Y.K. Cheung. 2014. Meta-analysis of differences in IQ profiles between individuals with Asperger's disorder and high-functioning autism. *Journal of Autism and Developmental Disorders* 44: 1577–1596.

Cohen, L., J. Duberley, and M. Mallon. 2004. Social constructionism in the study of career: Accessing the parts that other approaches cannot reach. *Journal of Vocational Behavior* 64: 407–422.

Economist Intelligence Unit. 2009. *Global diversity and inclusion, perceptions, practices and attitudes*. Alexandria: Society for Human Resource Management.

Foster, D., and V. Wass. 2012. Disability in the labour market: An exploration of concepts of the ideal worker and organisational fit that disadvantage employees with impairments. *Sociology* 47: 705–721.

Friedrichs, T.P., and M.F. Shaughnessy. 2015. A reflective conversation with Terry Friedrichs on teaching academics to gifted students with Asperger syndrome. *Gifted Education International* 31: 41–53.

Frith, U. 2008. *Autism: A very short introduction*. Oxford: Oxford University Press.

Frith, U., and F. Happe. 2001. Exploring the cognitive phenotype of autism: Weak "central coherence" in parents and siblings of children with autism: I. Experimental tests. *Journal of Child Psychology and Psychiatry* 42: 299–307.

Giusti, G. 2008. *Soft skills for lawyers*. London: Chelsea Publishing.

Goldstein, H.M. 2014. Just another Aspie/NT love story: A narrative inquiry into neurologically-mixed romantic relationships. *Interpersona: An International Journal on Personal Relationships* 8: 70–84.

Grant, T. 2015. Working wisdom: How workers with disabilities give companies an edge. *Globe and Mail*, February 27.

Griffin, E., and D. Pollak. 2009. Student experiences of neurodiversity in higher education: Insights from the BRAINHE project. *Dyslexia* 15: 23–41.

Grugulis, I., and S. Vincent. 2009. Whose skill is it anyway?: 'Soft' skills and polarization. *Work, Employment and Society* 23: 597–615.

Haertl, K., D. Callahan, J. Markovics, and S.S. Sheppard. 2013. Perspectives of adults living with autism spectrum disorder: Psychosocial and occupational implications. *Occupational Therapy in Mental Health* 29: 27–41.

Hagner, D., and B.F. Cooney. 2005. I do that for everybody': Supervising employees with autism. *Focus on Autism and Other Developmental Disabilities* 20: 91–97.

Happe, F., and P. Vital. 2009. What aspects of autism predispose to talent? *Philosophical Transactions of the Royal Society Biological Sciences* 364: 1369–1375.

Hiller, A., H. Campbell, K. Mastrianni, M. Vreeburg Izzo, A.K. Kool-Tucker, L. Cherry, and D.O. Beversdorf. 2007. Two year evaluation of a vocational support programme for adults with autism. *Career Development for Exceptional Individuals* 30: 25–47.

Hurlbutt, Karen, and Lynne Chalmers. 2004. Employment and adults with asperger syndrome. *Focus on Autism and Other Developmental Disabilities* 19 (4): 215–222.

Jackson, D. 2009. An international profile of industry-relevant competencies and skill gaps in modern graduates. *International Journal of Management Education* 8: 29–58.

Jackson, S.E., and A. Joshi. 2004. Diversity in social context: A multi-attribute, multilevel analysis of team diversity and sales performance. *Journal of Organisational Behavior* 25: 675–702.

Jammaers, E., P. Zanoni, and S. Hardonk. 2016. Constructing positive identities in ableist workplaces: Disabled employees' discursive practices engaging with the discourse of lower productivity. *Human Relations* 69: 1365–1386.

Krieger, B., A. Kinebanian, B. Prodinger, and F. Heigl. 2012. Becoming a member of the work force: Perceptions of adults with Asperger syndrome. *Work* 43: 141–157.

Marks, A., and D. Scholarios. 2008. Choreographing a system: Skill and employability in software work. *Economic and Industrial Democracy* 29: 96–124.

McQuaid, R., and C. Lindsay. 2005. The concept of employability. *Urban Studies* 42: 197–219.

Mik-Meyer, N. 2016. Othering, ableism and disability: A discursive analysis of co-workers' construction of colleagues with visible impairments. *Human Relations* 69: 1341–1363.

Morris, M.R., A. Begel, and B. Wiedermann. 2015. Understanding the challenges faced by neurodiverse software engineering employees: Towards a more inclusive and productive technical workforce. ASSETS 2015 – Proceedings of the 17th international ACM SIGACCESS conference on computers and accessibility.

Müller, E., A. Schuler, B.A. Burton, and G.B. Yates. 2003. Meeting the vocational support needs of individuals with asperger syndrome and other autism spectrum disabilities. *Journal of Vocational Rehabilitation* 18: 163–175.

64   A. Cockayne

Muller, E., A. Schuler, and G.B. Yates. 2008. Social challenges and supports from the perspective of individuals with Asperger syndrome and other autism spectrum disabilities. *Autism* 12: 173–190.

National Autistic Society. 2016. *Autism facts and history.* National Autistic Society. Available from http://www.autism.org.uk/about/what-is/myths-facts-stats.aspx. Accessed 05 Apr.

Nilsson, Staffan. 2010. Enhancing individual employability: The perspective of engineering graduates. *Education + Training* 52 (6): 540–551.

Ortega, F. 2009. The cerebral subject and the challenge of neurodiversity. *BioSocieties* 4: 425–445.

Owren, T. 2013. Neurodiversity: Accepting autistic difference. *Learning Disability Practice* 16: 32–37.

Parr, A.D., and S.T. Hunter. 2014. Enhancing work outcomes of employees with autism spectrum disorder through leadership: Leadership for employees with autism spectrum disorder. *Autism* 18: 545–554.

Payne, J. 2000. The unbearable lightness of skill: The changing meaning of skill in UK policy discourse and some implications for education and training. *Journal of Education Policy* 15: 353–369.

Pelled, L.H., K.M. Eisenhardt, and K.R. Xin. 1999. Exploring the black box: An analysis of work group diversity, conflict, and performance. *Administrative Science Quarterly* 44: 1–28.

Porpora, D. 2015. *Reconstructing sociology: The critical realist approach.* Cambridge: Cambridge University Press.

Procknow, G., and T.S. Rocco. 2016. The unheard, unseen, and often forgotten: An examination of disability in the human resource development literature. *Human Resource Development Review* 15: 379–403.

Richards, J. 2012. Examining the exclusion of employees with Asperger syndrome from the workplace. *Personnel Review* 41: 630–646.

Riddell, S., S. Edward, E. Weedon, and L. Ahlgren. 2010. *Disability, skills and employment: A review of recent statistics and literature on policy and initiatives* (Research report 59). Manchester: Equality and Human Rights Commission.

Robison, J.E. 2011. *An emerging voice of autism.* Autism Key. Available from http://www.autismkey.com/john-e-robison-an-emerging-voice-of-autism/. Accessed 08 Apr 2013.

Shan, H. 2013. Skill as a relational construct: Hiring practices from the standpoint of Chinese immigrant engineers in Canada. *Work, Employment and Society* 27: 915–931.

Silberman, S. 2015. *Neurotribes: The legacy of autism and the future of neurodiversity.* London: Penguin Publishing Group.

Smith, C. 2010. *What is a person? Rethinking humanity social life and the moral good from the person up*. London: Cambridge University press.

Syed, J., and M. Ozbilgin. 2009. A relational framework for international transfer of diversity management practices. *International Journal of Human Resource Management* 20 (12): 2435–2453.

Van Knippernberg, D., C. De Dreu, and A. Homan. 2004. Work group diversity and group performance: An integrative model and research agenda. *Journal of Applied Psychology* 8: 1008–1022.

Vermeulen, P. 2011. Autism: From mind blindness to context blindness. http://www.faaas.org/assets/autism-from-mind-blindness-to-context-blindness.pdf. Accessed 3 Dec 2016.

Wallis, L. 2012. They said I was rude. *Nursing Standard* 26: 24–25.

Wang, S. 2014. How autism can help you land a job. https://www.wsj.com/articles/SB10001424052702304418404579465561364868556. Accessed 27 Mar 2016.

Warnick, J. 2015. *Microsoft hiring program opens more doors to people with autism*. Microsoft. Available from https://blogs.microsoft.com/blog/2016/02/09/microsoft-hiring-programopens-more-doors-to-people-with-autism/#sm.00 1o6w5d416muep2zjy2hws21mbj5

Warnick, J. 2016. Microsoft hiring program opens more doors to people with autism. https://blogs.microsoft.com/blog/2016/02/09/microsoft-hiring-program-opens-more-doors-to-people-with-autism/#sm.00 1o6w5d416muep2zjy2hws21mbj5. Accessed 4 Feb 2017.

Williams, J., and S. Mavin. 2012. Disability as constructed difference: A literature review and research agenda for management and organization studies. *International Journal of Management Reviews* 14: 159–179.

Wolosky, H.W. 2008. Closing the soft skills gap: The focus is on making soft skills part of the firm's psyche. *Practical Accountant* 41: 16–21.

Wrzesniewski, A., and J.E. Dutton. 2001. Crafting a job: Revisioning employees as active crafters of their work. *The Academy of Management Review* 26: 179–201.

4

Conflicts and Challenges of Gender in the Workplace: The Police Service in England, Wales and Northern Ireland

Janet Astley

4.1   Introduction

Workplace gender equality has been a subject of discussion in a range of industrial sectors by many eminent authors for decades, and this chapter focuses particularly upon the conflicts and challenges of gender within the police service of England, Wales and Northern Ireland.[1] There are 43 individual forces within England, Wales and Northern Ireland each with its own unique identity and culture. Each force operates under the same national guidelines as defined by the Home Secretary and Parliament, but how those guidelines are interpreted and implemented differs on a force-by-force basis. No two forces are the same. Each force is shaped by the characteristics of the senior management team and particularly influenced by the Chief Constable. Gender equality tends

J. Astley (✉)
Leadership, Governance and People Management, Leeds Business School, Leeds Beckett University, Leeds, UK

© The Author(s) 2018
V. Caven, S. Nachmias (eds.), *Hidden Inequalities in the Workplace*, Palgrave Explorations in Workplace Stigma, DOI 10.1007/978-3-319-59686-0_4

to evoke passionate discourses relating to pay and conditions, policies, systems processes and the implementation of local customs and practices, but the subtleties of establishing strong networks and mentors enabling individuals to gain greater access to more equal opportunity in terms of career progression can prove significant. Where organisations adopt a more androgynous approach to their workforce identity, by the adoption of similar dress codes, uniforms, titles and 'apparent' equality of opportunity, the lines can become blurred and discriminatory behaviours and practices fall below a veil of superficial acceptance of a gender-neutral society. The police service falls into this category. From its militaristic origins, male dominance and cult of 'hegemonic masculinity' (Connell 1987, p. 183), the culture of the police has overtly shifted, with the demise of what Waddington (1999), Brown (2000) and other scholars describe as 'canteen culture', to a seemingly gender-blind or gender-neutral organisation where gender equality is visibly promoted in principle. There has been an emasculation of both male and female officers by the service identifying both males and females as 'officers'. Previously, females had been identified as women police officers (WPCs), although this fell into decline with the term officer being used to refer to both genders in more recent times. In some instances, there appears to be positive discrimination towards underrepresented groups, such as women, resulting in the prevalence of, in the case of women, female tokens (Archbold et al. 2008) being strategically placed within senior or high-profile roles. This phenomenon is explored further within this chapter.

However, despite the efforts of the service to promote gender equality, there remains disparity between career development opportunities and promotion for females as opposed to males. Males appear to have greater opportunity to progress their careers more easily, providing they fall into the category of being dominant and manly. Females, particularly black and minority ethnic (BME) females, face a more challenging career trajectory, and some of those factors that inhibit female progression also affect some male officers' progression, particularly those who do not fall into the cultural norms of masculinity, those who may be single parents, carers or openly homosexual. The continued existence of male nepotism in the guise of '*old boy's networks*' (Linehan 2001) remains an aspect of society generally, and this is equally the case within the police service.

4.2 Methodology

This chapter emanates from field research conducted in 2009 where senior female officers in the ranks from Inspector to Deputy Chief Constable participated in semi-structured, individual life-history narrative interviews. Quotations from officers who participated in the research are reproduced throughout the chapter. However, the identity of the officer and the force within which they served is not identified due to agreement between the author and research subjects with regard to confidentiality and anonymity. Senior ranking females can be easily identified within individual forces due the fact that they are few in number. By being assured of complete confidentiality and anonymity in relation to their rank and force, officers who participated offered rich and insightful data with complete honesty in recounting their experiences throughout their career.

Positioned within the feminist criminology framework shaped by Heidensohn (1985) and Walklate (2004), the relationships are explored between feminist and gendered criminology research utilising discourse analysis to identify key challenges to women in policing. Women tended to lack identity within the criminal justice system (Heidensohn 1985), rendering those who did enter it as deviant. Walklate (2004, p. 48) comments that '*the kind of work done by feminists in criminology are to be seen as both a heuristic device and as an issue of contention*'. Thus women in policing are the ultimate challenge to male dominance. As the number of women entering the service continues to grow, their status can no longer be regarded as 'token'; therefore, a significant shift in societal and organisational culture is already in progress.

Walklate (2004) endorses the importance of empirical research defining liberal feminism as the beginning of the framework where non-discrimination and equity exist for women. She further positions radical feminism as the next logical step challenging the traditional notion of

Table 4.1 Rank profile of one-to-one in-depth interview subjects

Inspector	3
Chief inspector	14
Detective chief inspector	4
Superintendent	10
Detective superintendent	2
Chief superintendent	0
ACPO	2
Total	**35**

Adapted from Astley (2011, p. 169)

female subservience to males. Yet postmodern feminism appears to reflect more closely the position of female police officers as they are positioned outside the socially constructed paradigms relating to gender in the workplace where the majority of those within it are male, as is evident across the criminal justice system in the UK.

Silverman (2004) comments upon the need for a flexible approach towards data collection when considering human and social activity allowing the exploration of meaning and perception of attitudes and opinions of the research participants. Miles and Huberman (1994) in relation to data analysis, interpretivist approaches to social and anthropological or collaborative research previously suggested the necessity for flexibility when collecting data and its subsequent analysis. Eight forces participated across England, Wales and Northern Ireland with 35 senior female officers being interviewed (see Table 4.1).

Officers were invited to relate their experiences throughout their careers from point of recruitment to their current situation, identifying both barriers and opportunities to their career progression and to consider the influence their gender had upon their career trajectories. Each interview lasted 1–2 hours and was digitally recorded, transcribed and coded. Analysis using discourse analysis resulted in five clear discourses relating to difference, performance and development, networking, family life and flexibility, and Queen Bees and bitches. This chapter focuses upon the discourse of networking. Baxter (2003) considers discourse analysis as an appropriate method of analysing empirical research suggesting it is linked to feminist poststructural methodology. As such, she considers the links between socially constructed feminism, and language analysis enables real insight to be gained especially in relation to power relationships. She identifies this as Feminist Poststructuralist Discourse

Analysis (FPDA). Baxter suggests that elite females will utilise specific language and behaviours that will either empower or disempower them.

4.3 Women in Male-Dominated Environments

Martin's (1979) ground-breaking study was the first to focus upon gender in policing followed by her subsequent study (1991) which led to authors such as Walklate (1995, 2004), Martin and Jurik (1996), Brown (1997, 1998, 2000), Brown and Heidensohn (2000), Metcalfe and Dick (2000), Dick and Cassell (2002), Silvestri (2003) (2007) and Astley (2011) to continue exploring the ongoing challenges for women in policing within the UK. Many studies had been predominantly conducted within Australia or the USA with little focus upon the UK. Cultural differences meant that while some parallels could be drawn from these international studies, they presented a view through different lenses due to the socially constructed norms that exist within these differing continents. As such, they cannot be considered representative of the situation within the UK.

There is a plethora of academic evidence (Meyerson and Fletcher 2000; Vinnecombe and Singh 2002; Cornelius and Skinner 2005), indicating that women in male-dominated environments have more challenges in terms of career development, status, acceptance and authority. The conflicts and challenges in policing are exacerbated by the militaristic origins of the service and the perpetuation of the public perception that the role is 'male'. This is further endorsed by the notion that criminology and all aspects relating to the criminal justice system are predominantly male. *'It is a male power base ... where men shape and define the interactions that occur in the workplace'* (Astley 2011, p. 67). Eagly and Carli (2007) comment that agentic (male) behaviour is considered to be *'effective leadership'* (p. 66) yet they similarly identify that women who display such behaviours are ostracised by both genders rendering women into a complex *'double bind'* (p. 66) as their biological identity is female yet the identity associated with leadership is male. Patterson (2010) concurs commenting that society considers the concepts of masculinity and leadership have become '*so deeply intertwined that the language of leadership and language of masculinity have become synonymous*' (p. 58). Consequently, public perception towards women officers remains parochial in relation to them attaining rank and authority, particularly in rural, white middle-class society. British society tends to impose the narrow ideal upon women, that they are predominantly mothers, carers and home makers. Wilson (2003) identifies the notion of stereotypical job roles, which was clearly reflected by one female officer's comment:

> *The general public would say the male is superior to the female and the dark haired female is superior to the blonde. If you have dark hair and wear glasses and you are female, you might be bright.*

Thomas and Davies (2002) comment that despite the efforts by the service to rebrand and restructure during the 1980s and 1990s the accepted policing norms in relation to a long-hours culture, the notion of commitment to the role/organisation (so the concept of part-time working or job sharing is an anathema) and the sense of duty to public service to the detriment of private life perpetuates. Both male and female officers accept this as 'normal' for policing and even though the increase in civilian and female staff have positively impacted upon the gender ratio of the workforce, it seems that there is a cultural reluctance to shift from this entrenched male stance. However, demographic changes in British society suggest that the dominance of senior male officers is likely to be challenged and senior ranking females should be considered 'normal'. Brown (1997, p. 15) suggested that this could be measured by a figure of 25% representation of women in the service which was exceeded in 2009. By 2016 the number of female officers has increased year on year from 23.3% in 2006 to 28.6% (Hargreaves et al. 2016). Although the majority of these female officers are represented at the lower ranks, there is a general shift in the numbers of females rising through the ranks with a total of 22.9% achieving the ranks of Chief Officers in 2016 as opposed to the 15% identified in 2010. The apparent 10% increase in senior female officers over the past six years suggests that either females are managing to overcome perceived conflicts and challenges in their career progression or women have achieved a critical mass within the service resulting in them gaining greater access to promotion opportunities due to a dearth of appropriately qualified males.

In 2015, Home Secretary Theresa May commented that individual forces' attempts to increase the recruitment of females had reaped benefits and was a necessity in order to respond to the changing nature of criminal activity (UK Government 2015). Recent attempts to increase workforce diversity include the Direct Entry scheme and the establishment in 2016 of Police Now, an independent social enterprise (Policenow 2016). The aim of Police Now is to widen participation in police recruiting including women and BME communities by sourcing graduates with leadership potential and complementing the established probationer recruitment schemes within forces. Coincidentally, the reformation of the College of Policing and the establishment of the police effectiveness, efficiency and legitimacy programme overseen by Her Majesties Inspectorate of Policing have seen positive moves towards challenging the status quo. Although any intervention to encourage improvements in the opportunities for the recruitment of women into the service is welcome, there is no doubt that these relatively recent changes will take time to take effect. Organisations and societies are notoriously slow to effect cultural change. The challenges remain within individual forces and their early adoption of changes in policy relating to increasing diversity and inclusion and a change in attitudes of those senior ranking officers that are currently in post.

However, what the majority of these interventions fail to address is the development and career progression of existing women in the service as all of these concentrate on recruitment into the service rather than managing the existent talent within it. Frequently senior teams are male dominated; therefore, although the rhetoric suggests change is desirable, the reality is that often forces continue to repress female promotion by not enabling them to have access to the mechanisms they need, such as effective mentoring and networks. Therefore the perpetuation of 'hidden' inequalities persists due to a public expression by the service that it appears to be embracing the challenges of creating a more diverse workplace, yet by its actions maintains its masculine culture by covertly impeding women's career progression through inactivity for existing serving officers. Until the service provides a structured and sustainable networking and mentoring scheme for women, the likelihood is that the policy makers will fail in their attempts to diminish the conflicts and challenges they face when attempting to gain rank.

4.4   Gender Neutral or Gender Blind?

According to Wood and Lindorf (2001), women fail to interpret organisational politics and power sufficiently, thus inhibiting their potential for advancement. In task-focussed organisations, such as the police, Grisoni and Beeby (2007) suggest that organisations become gender blind or gender neutral which enables women to shift the focus of their power relationships by achievements that are recognised by others within the organisation as being measurable. This could link to skills such as high-speed and pursuit driving, dog handling, firearms, public order and other such activities in which women can and do excel. This raises their profile within the organisation enabling them to gain recognition and to an extent, 'belonging' and acceptance by their male counterparts and to an extent by the general public. By proving themselves to be skilled in specific tasks, they shift the focus from the necessity to be politically astute to one of acceptance as '*one of the boys*'. However, this can produce further challenges to women as those who are perceived by society as adopting a 'masculine expression' (Sumner 1990) may be considered troublesome or deviant. Deviance from socially constructed paradigms in society's perception as to what women should or could do was highlighted by Butler (1990, 2004) who narrates that women become targets of criticism, scepticism and vilification, particularly when placed in situations of significant public exposure, as senior female officers frequently are. The media does not treat senior female officers well, particularly in situations where decisions have been taken that have been publicly perceived to have been mishaps or failures. Similarly in police fiction, females are frequently represented as being the underdog or portrayed as making significant errors of judgement that impact upon their ability to make decisions in serious or life-threatening situations. Rodgers et al. (2016, p. 185) comment '*media focus on dress, femininity and appearance and looking the part played to and against women's career expectations*' further identifying how powerful women are considered to be '*a bitch*' (p. 185). Although they identify that dramatic representations of female police officers have improved and that to an extent society is influenced by such media representations. However, the tensions relating to gendered stereotypes remain firmly embedded within the service and wider society.

There is no doubt that the unique culture within policing attracts a particular type of individual with specific personality traits, strong values and beliefs in relation to public service and upholding the law. This is frequently reflected in specific language, gestures and behaviours which superficially may appear masculine. One senior officer commented:

> *I think many women emulate their male counterparts, think they have got to be like male managers. They are often feminine in appearance, but I think that femininity belies a very masculine style of leadership. They are bullies and hard, prickly and treat people in an awful way. They are male characteristics.*

However, there is no doubt that some women in policing recognise that they do bring a different, more feminine approach to police activities. Their skills lie in what is perceived as the 'softer' skills of negotiation, communication, arbitration and problem solving. During one of the in-depth life-history narrative interviews one officer commented:

> *I am a woman and it needs to be recognised, because I have skills as a woman that a man hasn't got and vice versa. I don't want to be recognised as equal, I want to be recognised for what I am and we are almost going too far the other way. They have made us all PCs and you can't recognise if it is a man or a woman coming to see you because they have changed our numbers. Maybe I'm old fashioned.*

From this statement, it can be deduced that females recognise that they bring different qualities to the role of policing and that both males and females have unique contributions to make to the service they provide based upon their experiences and gender.

Male traits include physical fitness, strength and a more combative approach to dealing with problems and issues. The challenge is for the service to recognise that both genders bring equally valuable yet different qualities to the complex situations faced by front-line officers and to value their contribution regardless of gender. Morgan (1981) identifies males as behaving competitively in relation to their masculine skills, which fuel the discrimination against and exclusion of women. Women police officers are merely tolerated rather than valued for the work that they do; to claw their way up the promotional ladder it seems they are required to adopt some male traits and use power bases. Thus, gaining the reputation of being masculine in their approach affects derision from both sexes. One senior officer commented:

There are some (women) who are self-focussed and nothing else matters, but there are ACPO men like it as well. It is not peculiar to gender.

But, she goes on to state:

There are some ACPO women who say it was hard for me so it should be hard for you. They pull the ladder up.

While another commented:

Some senior women shy away from being approachable, the bitches from hell. They think I've had it tough and hard and so will you.

Marvin (2006) describes such behaviour as '*Queen Bee*' (p. 349) syndrome where those who have gone before '*pull up the ladder(s)*' (p. 352) behind them. For those that do attempt to progress their careers, Marvin identifies that this comes at an emotional cost and women need to make life style choices often prohibiting them to achieve their true potential, thus sacrificing their careers. This sacrificing by women is frequently evidenced in both wider society and the police service; the influence of societal and organisational culture offers a significantly influencing factor when making such choices.

4.5   Culture

Traditionalists deem a degree of normality in relation to gendered career choices, whereas feminists identify women who challenge this notion as gender champions. It seems that few women who enter the service are unsupported by their immediate family. This challenges Yim and Bond's (2002) suggestion that gender difference is influenced right from early childhood, throughout early and secondary education into adulthood, yet society's perception about women's career choices continues to regard male-dominated organisations as a peculiar choice for women. This reinforces Hymowitz and Schellhardt's (1986) phraseology relating to the so-called glass ceiling which remains firmly embedded in literature relating to obstruction to female career progression. However, Schein's (1973, 1975) research already began to identify a narrowing of the demarcated differences between the genders because of increasingly androgynous stereotyping relating to managers.

Perhaps the first challenge for women is the physical, emotional and psychological stresses mentioned by Patterson (2010) and Messerschmidt (2009) identified in police probationer training where for two years body and mind are pushed to the limits to test all aspects of an individual's personality to establish if they are the 'right type' to become a police officer. Haar (2005) identified that recruit dropout rates frequently relate to gender, including the exposure to sexual harassment, a misalignment of personal and organisation values, and the understanding of the true nature of the role. Sims et al. (2003) find that females who have partners in the service tend to fare better due to having a greater understanding of what is expected, and therefore the culture shock is reduced. Burke and Mikkelson's (2005, p. 425) '*macho*' image of policing suggests that this is perpetuated throughout the ranks and a degree of resilience is required for females to progress successfully. Powell and Butterfield (2003) identified that women aspiring to senior roles tended to display significantly greater 'masculine' traits forcing them into a discriminatory position from the outset by requiring them to disassociate with their biological gender. They further suggested that in some cases women opt out of the challenge or accept their lowly position in male-dominated organisations by choosing to measure success differently and placing greater emphasis on non-work-related activity.

There is no doubt that the long-hours culture plays a significant part in challenging women and in many cases men. In 2009 the Fawcett Society commissioned a report into the criminal justice sector, including policing, endorsing the view that this promoted inequity particularly in relation to promotion prospects, largely due to the stereotyping of female roles. The lack of response by the service to the needs of individuals in relation to either child or elder care roles, which frequently fall to women in society, and poor practices in return to work from maternity leave were specific issues. The report identified a lack of education within the service in relation to flexible working practices in relation to both male and female officers. Astley's (2011) study highlighted the negative influence the managers of duty rota teams can have upon individuals who either work on a part-time basis, are returning to work or seek to job share. Her study identified that application of force policies and practices relies on the localised interpretation of individual managers (frequently male senior ranking officers) in relation to shift patterns and workload delegation. In some cases, this varies within individual forces; different divisional commanders may interpret the same policy and practice in differing ways and that is reliant upon their societal and cultural beliefs. He et al.'s (2002) earlier study along with Tomlinson (2006) identified the complexity of managing shift patterns and work flow and how the concept of full-time working and commitment are interlinked resulting in a lack of understanding and engagement with modern flexible working practices. This is despite the need to offer a 365 day per year 24/7 service to the public. It seems that outdated application of policies and practices results in barriers preventing a flexible approach to working that does negatively affect (some) women and occasionally, men. Individuals within the duty teams that create the shift work patterns (which vary from force to force) have been found to have negative attitudes towards expectant mothers, those who request part-time working and returns to work following maternity/paternity leave. Subtle obstructive behaviours, such as not advising officers of their shift patterns or place of work in sufficient time to enable them to organise any work/life balance issues, such as child or elder care, until the day they return to work can be disruptive.

Martin's (1979) seminal work identified how during the 1970s women themselves created conflicts between themselves by some police women feeling the need to outperform their male counterparts, adopting male traits and behaviours resulting in the de-feminisation and aversion to those females who chose to retain their natural femininity. It seems that in Martin's study some women contributed to the vilification and criticism of other women, thus reinforcing the proliferation of the male-dominant culture. This resulted in derogatory language being applied to women who seemed not to fit with the ideals of policing held by those who wanted to '*fit in with the boys*'. The nature of police work reinforces the notion of hard work and hard play which results in a predominantly heterosexual and drinking culture that is by its very nature exclusionary to women. One officer commented:

> *There is still a 'jobs for the boy's culture' and if as a woman you do not join the drinking, socialising, it can seem that you are overlooked, despite your skill and experience.*

Over time, as the representation of women in the service has increased, the prevalence of such behaviours and cultural norms has declined with a more gender-aware culture being proliferated and appearing to becoming more accepted by both the service and society at large. The UK itself tends to adopt a patriarchal approach to society norms, with expressions of control being reinforced by male power in parental relationships, and father figures continue to be the representation of authority within wider society.

Brown's (2000) account of the prevalence of '*canteen culture*' (p. 105) and the existence of the '*old boy's network*' (p. 105) identifies the challenges women have in their development. In order to establish an equitable career progression route, the cultural definitions that define femininity and masculinity need to be resolved. In an attempt to achieve this, the concept of the androgynous police officer has been created, which in turn affects some women's self-efficacy. An officer commented:

> *Confidence – I think it's a female thing. I find that women to need a little shove; you need permission to go for the next rank. … You kind of need someone to sit you down and say you are ready now. Women need permission. Women won't give themselves permission until they are 110%. Men have better self-belief.*

Lord and Friday (2003) comment that women entering non-traditional gender occupations often see that in itself being a barrier, and with the addition of shift work and anti-social hours this is further compounded. An additional factor can also be those roles that the public perceive to be not fit for women according to socially constructed paradigms relating to gender stereotyping. As a result, Walklate (2004) identifies that there are fewer women in the higher ranks due to the vertical and horizontal segregation linked to specific specialist roles which again is frequently linked to gender stereotyping, such as domestic violence, rape and sexual assault. Popular media programmes depicting women officers engaging in such stereotypical activities further endorse this notion of specific roles for women.

4.6   Challenges to Progressing Careers

The degrees of challenge in relation to career progression seem to increase in conjunction with the rank and career mobility. Those forces that occupy large geographical areas hinder promotion prospects for females as the need to relocate causes mobility issues for women with family responsibilities. Kelan (2009) and Marvin (2001) both comment that mobility affects women's life choices more fundamentally than those of males due to societal norms and biology which frequently renders them outside the promotion ladders. Despite several national and in-force initiatives to encourage women to progress their careers, it seems that there is some reluctance for women to engage with such initiatives. Although there is evidence to suggest women outperform men in the early promotional exams, they fail to take up promotion for various reasons. It seems that women who choose to remain single, or those whose partners will embrace a role-reversal (males becoming the predominant carer of children, elderly and household duties), can succeed. Others rebuff the positive interventions the service has embraced in order to offer women a 'leg up the ladder' with comments like:

> It has actually made things more difficult. When females do get these positions there can be whispers of 'she only got that because she is a woman'. Makes you wonder why you worked so hard to get it. Also, it knocks your confidence.

For those who do choose to attempt to climb the promotion ladder, the first real hurdle appears at the rank of Inspector (and above). Promotion from this rank onwards is by competence-based interviews before a panel of senior officers. Candidates selected have to evidence their capability for the role by recounting examples of their experiences within the service. A major difficulty occurs, for both genders when trying to gain promotion in a different specialist area to the one they currently work in. For example, to move from a road policing-based role to CID would require the candidate to evidence the skills and competences required by the new role, resulting in a de-skilling of existing skills. Women's approach to such interviews according to the accounts given by the research participants differs to that of men. Women tend to under-sell their skills, abilities and experiences whereas men overtly promote themselves. An example offered by one officer was:

Getting promoted is very competitive. They (men) do bullshit more than women. There needs to be a change in culture, but it will take years.

In recounting a promotion board experience one officer highlighted this phenomenon as follows:

I didn't want to be boastful. Officer X (male) talks about it as if he's done it. I was gob-smacked!

It seems that a lack of self-efficacy underpins many women's inability to gain promotion. Once they have been unsuccessful in the promotion stakes, they tend to recoil from further attempts choosing to place greater emphasis on those things they can do well. This may well be their existing role, as women tend to gain lateral rather than vertical promotion, or they concentrate on activities outside the workplace, such as family. Another officer commented:

Once women have got the knock-back they are not as tenacious, it's a confidence issue. They think, I can't do this. … I've got the kids, home life, I can't put up with this every year.

4.7   Networks and Mentors

There is no doubt that networking plays a significant role in the promotion stakes. Females frequently cite feeling isolated (Rutherford 2001, Jackson 2001, and Archbold and Moses Schulz 2008) despite the existence of internal and external, formal and informal networks. Nationwide networks such as the British Association of Women in Policing (BAWiP) plus individual force women's networks attempt to address these feelings of isolation with varied results. Some officers highly valued the inclusion within a network, while others shunned them. Wood and Lindorf (2001) and Metcalfe and Dick (2002) all comment upon the importance and necessity of networking within the police service, particularly for women. However, not all officers shared this view. Where in-force networks related to social activity, several women commented that in their opinion this undermined the developmental and professional aspects of networking, choosing to disassociate themselves. One officer was aghast that as a female officer she was automatically included in the in-force female network, citing that she felt it was an imposition and that individuals have the right to decide whether they were included in such networks. She stated:

> The in-force network and BAWiP are useful for those who need it. Not everyone wants to take part in them.

It seems that women's perceptions of the value of networks differ to those of males. Women seem to fear that the inclusion of female social activity may appear detrimental and a sign of weakness, rather than feminine power, strength and solidarity. Some women saw networking as a detrimental activity that highlights gender and focuses attention upon it, thus attracting hostility from males and females alike. Cortis and Cassar (2005) suggest that increased scrutiny because of highlighting networking may well subject women to increased vilification rather than offering the support and developmental opportunities that networking should offer. Male networking tends to occur and focus upon masculine and frequently sporting activity, which promulgates the notion of the 'old boys clubs' from which women are excluded. This exclusion combined with familial responsibility precludes women from engaging in networking activity, which frequently occurs at the end of a long working day. Women consider networking to provide support and encouragement within work-related activity, but that social activity is not necessarily helpful. On the other hand, the most senior officers appeared to value their networking opportunities identifying that support and encouragement from others in a similar position, alongside the capacity to influence policy and strategy at both a local and national level was beneficial. The difficulty for senior women to engage in networks again lies with their workload commitments and responsibilities. The downside to this is that the lower ranking female officers perceive the lack of networking by senior women to be due to inaction and apathy rather than fully understanding the constraints within which they have to perform their roles.

One positive intervention that appears to assist women's career trajectories in the service is the acquisition of a prominent and respected mentor. However, evidence suggests (Archbold et al. 2008) that male officers control networking and mentoring. They argue that those with access to senior ranking mentors, particularly male mentors, are more likely to be successful. Similarly, females frequently express a desire to be mentored by other females, who, due to their limited numbers, are less available than those demanded by aspiring officers. A female officer commented:

> *Overwhelmingly having a female role model is good. ... I think what might be useful is if female officers had a female officer of higher rank. It gives you a kick up the bum sometimes.*

Ramaswami et al. (2010) highlight the importance of mentors, placing little emphasis on gender. Aspiring women officers perceive senior ranking women as the key to their future success with those in traditionally male-dominated roles, such as firearms, public order and road policing as being particularly valued. Women who have achieved success in these areas are viewed as prized mentors due to their high-profile role, their apparent confidence and thus inspiration for those who seek to follow them. The difficulty lies in the nature of mentoring itself. Mentoring requires dedicated time to which both mentor and mentee can commit.

The long-hours, high-workload culture does not lend itself to such activity. As one officer commented:

In recent years one of the ACCs has offered to be a mentor but often cancels.

And another states:

I've been helped enormously by Superintendents. Chief Officer mentors are important.

However, many female officers feel that the attainment of a credible and respected mentor is pivotal in their ability to develop their careers. They seek not only guidance and expertise from such mentors but also 'permission' to progress to the next level. This seems to be dichotomous when consideration is given to the self-confident and in-control image the public sees when officers attend incidents. It seems that self-confidence in the role occurs as women ensure that they more than satisfy the role criteria and as previously stated, outperform their male counterparts. The difference between men and women appears to lie in that males tend to ensure that they develop a portfolio of evidence of their achievements, even if their part in the activity was minimal, whereas women seem to make improvements to working practices and conditions in order to benefit colleagues. There is no doubt this links to self-efficacy, authenticity and integrity.

Senior officers acknowledge the pivotal role mentoring plays in any officer's career and many have a desire to mentor aspirational officers. The issue lies in the burden of workload that senior ranks have placed upon them and the lack of recognition of the service that investment in such activity is a necessity, rather than a luxury.

4.8   Conclusion and Implications

There is no doubt that the task of serving in the police service at any level is challenging for either gender. The requirement to provide a service to the public, a service that is not appreciated by those who receive the service (offenders), 24/7 and 365 days per year puts immense strain on any workforce. Shift working naturally plays a part in making engagement in networking and mentoring more complicated, although at senior ranks the requirement to work shifts diminishes to an extent. It does appear that the challenges for females are greater for a variety of reasons. There is no doubt that the underrepresentation of females at senior ranks places those that do achieve the higher ranks in a precarious position, as tokens, open to scrutiny by both fellow officers and the public alike. This in itself places women on the back foot from the outset as at the point that they enter the service they do so knowing that if they choose to pursue a career, they are likely to be thrust into a world where they have to defend and justify every action they take. As both society and the service still regard senior female police officers as 'unusual' rather than the norm, they are deemed suspicious from the outset as to their reasons for wanting to pursue a career as a police officer, regarded by many as a distinctly male occupation. They are also scrutinised closely in the way they pursue their career options. Despite recent positive representations of female officers in the media, Thomas and Davies (2002) suggest that the public subconsciously and subversively continue to fuel the notion that women are less able to operate at senior levels in policing. Lord and Friday (2003) and Rabe-Hemp (2009) share also this view as they conclude that wider society continues to perceive that policing is intrinsically a male occupation. This calls into question the relevance and legitimacy of female networks as the socially constructed values and beliefs of wider society in relation to female senior officers remain negative. Until there is a critical mass of senior women, they will continue to be viewed as deviant.

The cultures and sub-cultures that exist in policing are well documented by authors such as Martin (1979, 1991), Brown (1997, 2000), Brown and Heidensohn (2000) and Walklate (1995, 2004). Their work focuses upon organisational culture and leadership and alludes to the difficulties faced by women in the service. Where forces have a visible presence of senior women it seems that the barriers to female progression are reduced, although not eradicated. Where there is a male-dominant senior team, the likelihood of women attaining the senior ranks is minimalised due to males closing rank and for deals being done informally within the sanctity of the male networks that exist either internally to individual forces or across the wider family of forces. There is no doubt that from the rank of Inspector upwards the importance of attaining a respected mentor or champion is pivotal to success. The recommendation and endorsement from another officer of rank, being of either sex, appear to be essential, with greater emphasis in the literature being placed upon the recommendation by a male. However, it seems that serving female officers prize the opportunity to be mentored by another female. By not being able to access male networks, it seems that some females are merely passed by as much of the informal business takes place within such male networks commonly referred to as old 'boys clubs'. Until the prevalence of such informal male networks is reduced, it seems unlikely that women will have an equitable experience in the promotion stakes.

The long hours and heavy workload also contribute negatively in relation to women's career progression. The emphasis women place on their careers varies according to their circumstances, whether they are single, in a relationship, have children or have a partner who is a serving officer. All of these factors contribute to women's career choices and so affect the numerical representation of women at senior levels. The police service is an excellent response service and strategic planner, particularly in relation to major incidents and work-related activity. A command and control, task-focussed organisation's weakness lies in its inability to recognise human capability, skills and differences between its male and female officers. By failing to encourage aspiring women and reducing their self-efficacy, the lack of appropriate female networks and mentors, the service contributes to the continuance of women opting out of the promotion stakes by making informed choices about their lives. Senior women in particular lack the time to engage in networking and mentoring activity, rendering themselves isolated from potential support leaving them to tread a high-profile, but lonely path. For many women in policing, this path fails to be attractive. As a result, many competent and capable women either remain in the lower ranks sacrificing their careers, or they leave the service altogether. This lack of parity and equity needs to be addressed in order for the service to more accurately represent the society it serves, but also to reduce the drain of human and financial resources. Policy makers need to undertake a review of the promotion systems currently in place and to establish sustainable networking and mentoring schemes for women that will enable them to carve their careers with the same opportunities as their male counterparts. The rhetoric needs to change to reality with more positive interventions to develop the existing talent within and not to just concentrate on recruiting to the lower ranks.

Notes

1. The police service in Scotland operates under different regulations, therefore does not fall into the same category as England Wales and Northern Ireland and as such is excluded from this study.

References

Archbold, C.A., and D. Moses Schulz. 2008. Making rank. The lingering effects of Tokenism on female police officers' promotion aspirations. *Police Quarterly* 11 (1): 50–73.

Astley, J. 2011. Women in police service: Why do so few achieve the ACPO ranks? PhD thesis, Liverpool University.

Baxter, J. 2003. *Positioning gender in discourse: A feminist methodology.* Basingstoke: Palgrave Macmillan.

Brown, J. 1997. European policewomen: A comparative research perspective. *International Journal of the Sociology of Law* 125: 1–19.

Brown, J.M. 1998. Aspects of discriminatory treatment of women police officers serving in forces in England and Wales. *British Journal of Criminology* 38: 265–282.

Brown, J. 2000. Discriminatory experiences of women police. A comparison of officers serving in England and Wales, Scotland, Northern Ireland and the Republic of Ireland. *International Journal of the Sociology of Law* 28: 91–111.

Brown, J., and F. Heidensohn. 2000. *Gender and policing; comparative perspectives.* New York: St. Martin's Press.

Burke, R.J., and A. Mikkelsen. 2005. Gender differences in policing: Signs of progress? *Employee Relations* 27: 425–436.

Butler, J. 1990. *Gender trouble: Feminism and the subversion of identity.* Abingdon: Routledge.

———. 2004. *Undoing gender.* Abingdon: Routledge.

Connell, R. 1987. *Gender and power.* Cambridge: Polity.

Cornelius, N., and D. Skinner. 2005. An alternative view through the glass ceiling. *Women in Management Review* 20: 595–609.

Cortis, R., and V. Cassar. 2005. Perceptions about women as managers: Investigating job involvement, self-esteem and attitudes. *Women in Management Review* 20: 149–164.

Dick, P., and C. Cassell. 2002. Barriers to managing diversity in a UK constabulary: The role of discourse. *Journal of Management Studies* 39: 953–976.

Eagly, A.H., and L. Carli. 2007. Women and the labyrinth of leadership. *Harvard Business Review* 85: 62–71.

Fawcett Society. 2009. Engendering justice – From policy to practice. http://www.fawcettsociety.org.uk/engendering-justice-from-policy-to-practice-2/. Accessed 18 Nov 2016.

Government UK. 2015. Women in policing. https://www.gov.uk/government/speeches/women-in-policing. Accessed 22 Feb 2017.

Grisoni, L., and M. Beeby. 2007. Leadership, gender and sense-making. *Gender, Work and Organization* 14: 191–209.

Haar, R.N. 2005. Factors affecting the decision of police recruits to "drop-out" of police work. *Police Quarterly* 8: 431–453.

Hargreaves, J., J. Cooper, E. Woods, and C. McKee. 2016. *Police workforce, England and Wales.* London: Home Office. https://www.gov.uk/government/uploads/system/uploads/attachment_data/file/544849/hosb0516-police-workforce.pdf. Accessed 03 Nov 2016.

He, N., J. Zhao, and C. Archbold. 2002. Gender and police stress. The convergent and divergent impact of work environment, work family conflict, and stress coping mechanisms of female and male police officers. *Policing: An International Journal of Police* 25: 687–708.

Heidensohn, F. 1985. *Women and crime.* Basingstoke: Macmillan.

https://www.policenow.org.uk/about/who-we-are/#influence-for-generations. Accessed 22 Feb 2017.

Hymowitz, C., and T. Schellhardt. 1986. Cracking the glass ceiling. https://www.wsj.com/articles/the-phrase-glass-ceiling-stretches-back-decades-1428089010. Accessed 9 Nov 2016.

Jackson, J.C. 2001. Women middle managers' perception of the glass ceiling. *Women in Management Review* 16 (1): 30–41.

Kelan, E. 2009. Gender, logic and (un)doing gender at work. *Gender, Work and Organization* 17 (2): 174–194.

Linehan, M. 2001. Networking for female managers' career development. *Journal of Management Development* 20: 823–829.

Lord, V., and P.C. Friday. 2003. Choosing a career in police work: A comparative study between applicants for employment with a large police department and public high school students. *Police Practice and Research* 4: 63–78.

Martin, S.E. 1979. POLICEwomen and policeWOMEN: Occupational role dilemmas and choices of female officers. *Journal of Police Science and Administration* 17: 314–322.

———. 1991. The effectiveness of affirmative action: The case of women in policing. *Justice Quarterly* 8: 489–503.

Martin, S.E., and N.C. Jurik. 1996. *Doing justice doing gender; Women in law and criminal justice occupations*. Thousand Oaks: Sage.

Marvin, S. 2001. Women's career in theory and practice: Time for change? *Women in Management Review* 16: 183–192.

———. 2006. Venus Envy 2: Sisterhood, queen bees and female misogyny in management. *Women in Management Review* 21: 349–364.

Messerschmidt, J.W. 2009. Doing gender: The impact and future of a salient sociological concept. *Gender and Society* 23: 85–88.

Metcalfe, B., and P. Dick. 2000. Is the force still with you? Measuring police commitment. *Journal of Managerial Psychology* 15: 812–832.

Metcalfe, B., and G. Dick. 2002. Is the force still with her? Gender and commitment in the police. *Women in Management Review* 17: 392–403.

Meyerson, D.E., and J.K. Fletcher. 2000. A modest manifesto for shattering the glass ceiling. https://hbr.org/2000/01/a-modest-manifesto-for-shattering--the-glass-ceiling. Accessed 26 Jan 2017.

Miles, M., and M.A. Huberman. 1994. *An expanded sourcebook; Qualitative data analysis*. London: Sage.

Morgan, G. 1981. The schismatic metaphor and its implications for organisational analysis. *Organisation Studies* 2: 23–44.

Patterson, N. 2010. Leader and follower perspectives of entrepreneurial leadership: How is gender experienced in small firms? PhD thesis, Newcastle Business School, Northumbria University.

Powell, G.N., and D.A. Butterfield. 2003. Gender, gender identity, and aspirations to top management. *Women in Management Review* 18: 88–96.

Rabe-Hemp, C.E. 2009. POLICEwomen or policeWOMEN? Doing gender and police work. *Feminist Criminology* 4: 114–129.

Ramaswami, A., G.F. Dreher, R. Bretz, and C. Weithoff. 2010. Gender, mentoring and career success: The importance of organizational context. *Women in Management Review* 63: 385–405.

Rodgers, H., L. Yeomans, and S. Halliday. 2016. An interdiscursive analysis of television representations and professional femininities: The "Gogglebox". In *Gender, media and organization: Challenging mis(s)representations of women leaders and managers*, ed. C. Elliott, V. Stead, S. Mavin, and J. Williams. Charlotte: IAP, Information Age Publishing.

Rutherford, S. 2001. Organisational cultures, women managers and exclusion. *Women in Management Review* 16: 371–382.

Schein, V.E. 1973. The relationship between sex role stereotypes and requisite management characteristics. *Journal of Applied Psychology* 57: 95–100.

———. 1975. The relationship between sex role stereotypes and requisite management characteristics among female managers. *Journal of Applied Psychology* 60: 340–344.

Silverman, D. 2004. *Doing qualitative research: Theory, method and practice.* London: Sage.

Silvestri, M. 2003. *Women in charge: Policing, gender and leadership.* Cullompton: Willan Publishing.

———. 2007. Doing police leadership: Enter the new smart macho. *Policing and Society* 17: 38–68.

Sims, B., K.E. Scarborough, and J. Ahmad. 2003. The relationship between police officers' attitude toward women and perceptions of police models. *Police Quarterly* 6: 278–297.

Sumner, C. 1990. Foucault, gender and the censure of deviance. In *Feminist perspectives in criminology*, ed. L. Gelsthorpe and A. Morris, 33–48. Buckingham: Open University Press.

Thomas, R., and A. Davies. 2002. Restructuring the "Old Bill": Policing identities and commitment. *Women in Management Review* 17: 180–189.

Tomlinson, J. 2006. Routes to part-time management in UK service sector organizations: Implications for women's skills, flexibility and progression. *Gender, Work and Organization* 13: 585–605.

Vinnecombe, S., and V. Singh. 2002. Sex role stereotyping and requisites of successful top managers. *Women in Management Review* 17: 120–130.

Waddington, P. 1999. Police (canteen) culture; An appreciation. *British Journal of Criminology* 39: 287–309.

Walklate, S. 1995. Equal opportunities and the future of policing. In *Core issues in policing*, ed. F. Leishman, B. Loveday, and S. Savage. London: Longman.

———. 2004. *Gender, crime and criminal justice.* 2nd ed. Cullompton: Willan Publishing.

Wilson, F.M. 2003. *Organisational behaviour and gender.* 2nd ed. Aldershot: Ashgate Publishing Ltd..

Wood, G., and M. Lindorff. 2001. Sex differences in explanations for career progress. *Women in Management Review* 16: 152–162.

Yim, P.C., and M.H. Bond. 2002. Gender stereotyping of managers and the self-concept of business students across their undergraduate education. *Women in Management Review* 18: 364–372.

5

The Quality of Work Among Older Workers

Christopher Lawton and Daniel Wheatley

5.1 Introduction

The lives of older adults are undergoing significant economic and social change prompted by a growing awareness of the challenges associated with ageing populations in advanced societies (Understanding Society 2014; Wellard 2011). Public and societal discourse is increasingly focused on extending the working lives of older adults (Felstead 2010, p. 1294), defined in this chapter as individuals aged 50 and over.[1] Due to a combination of increasing life expectancies and the spikes in birth rates immediately after the Second World War, and the subsequent 'baby

C. Lawton (✉)
Department of Economics, Nottingham Business School, Nottingham Trent University, Nottingham, UK

D. Wheatley
Department of Business and Labour Economics, Birmingham Business School, University of Birmingham, Birmingham, UK

© The Author(s) 2018
V. Caven, S. Nachmias (eds.), *Hidden Inequalities in the Workplace*,
Palgrave Explorations in Workplace Stigma,
DOI 10.1007/978-3-319-59686-0_5

boom' of the 1960s, the UK population aged 50 and over has grown and is expected to continue to rise in proceeding decades. Demographic factors alone do not account for the increase in older workers. The changing nature of work, including the shift towards employment in the service sector and decline in manual and physically demanding roles, wider cultural shifts and a changing legislative context all mean that working into later life has been recognised internationally as important to the continued progress of advanced societies. For over a decade, EU policymakers have promoted the concept of an 'active old age', in which older individuals remain in paid or voluntary work (European Commission 2003), while working into older age was also highlighted in the OECD's *Live Longer, Work Longer* (OECD 2006). Within the UK, the government has adopted strategies including *Opportunity Age*, launched in 2005 (DWP 2005), while a focus on older workers has recently returned to the policy forefront following the publication of '*A new vision for older workers: retain, retrain, recruit*' in 2015 (Altman 2015). In legislative terms, the Statutory (or Default) Retirement Age was abolished in 2011, while the State Pension Age is set to increase through a number of planned increments in the first half of the twenty-first century.

Extending the working lives of older adults does, however, present a number of challenges, creating uncertainty for these individuals during the latter part of the working lives. Within the broadly defined category of older adults aged 50 and over, there is considerable diversity in regard to economic, social and personal characteristics which can act as facilitators or barriers to continued engagement in paid work, for example financial position and health problems (Siegrist et al. 2006; Humphrey et al. 2003). Nevertheless, in 2015, almost 70 % of those aged 50–64 reported paid employment, just 4 percentage points lower than the total working age employment rate (compared to an 8 percentage point difference in 2005). Meanwhile, the number of older adults working beyond current State Pension Age is increasing: in 2015 there were approximately 1.2 million people in employment who were aged 65 and over in the UK, an increase of 592,800 on the same period ten years earlier (ONS 2016). While more older adults may be extending their working lives, organisational and co-worker misconceptions of older workers can result in a range of negative implications for the worker including, for example, reduced access to training (Hedge et al. 2006; Posthuma and Campion 2009; Ng and Feldman 2012). These issues, in turn, may result in inequalities in the experiences of paid work for older adults including the quality of work. Drawing on data from the *Annual Population Survey, Labour Force Survey*, and wave 4 (2012–2013) of *Understanding Society*, this chapter considers the experiences of older adults in the UK who continue to engage in paid work shedding light into this underexplored area of the labour market.[2] Specifically, the chapter explores patterns of work among older adults and reflects, in particular, on the quality of work encountered by older workers.

5.2   Extending Working Lives: The Policy Context

Policymakers in advanced economies are increasingly promoting the continued employment of older workers, sometimes referred to as 'extended working life' (EWL) (Smeaton and White 2016, p. 369). Public policy emphasises the importance of longer working lives against the backdrop of ageing populations. This contrasts starkly with the 'lump-of-labour' concept which shaped policymaking in the UK in the late 1970s (Laczko and Phillipson 1991), which argued that only a limited number of jobs are available and that the continued employment of one group of workers comes at the opportunity cost to the employment of other workers (Walker 2007). Under these assumptions a reduction in the labour supply of older workers could, therefore, help mitigate unemployment among others including young workers. The introduction of the *Job Release Scheme* (JRS) in the UK in 1977 acted as an incentive for older workers to retire, and required employers to provide a job to an individual from the unemployment register as a replacement for the retiring older worker. Evidence, at that time and since, continues to show that there exists no relationship between the number of older workers employed and levels of youth employment (Banks et al. 2010; OECD 2013, p. 52). The UK government has, in recent decades, implemented a raft of policy, summarised in Table 5.1, with a primary focus on extending the working lives of older adults, driven in particular by concerns surrounding the rising cost of state pensions and the welfare system.

Table 5.1 UK extending working lives policies

Policy area	Details
Employment	The *Equality Act 2010*, implemented in October 2012, prohibits the direct or indirect discrimination of workers on the basis of certain characteristics including age (see Gov.uk 2013)
Employment support	The *Work Programme*, introduced in 2011 to replace the *Future Jobs Fund*, focuses on provision of funding for private and voluntary sectors to help the long-term unemployed back into work. While not focused on specific age groups, it provides support, work experience and training for individuals for up to two years (DWP 2012a)
Welfare	In 2008 the *Employment and Support Allowance* (ESA) replaced, for new claimants, *Incapacity Benefit/Severe Disablement Allowance* and any *Income Support* received for incapacity, as the welfare payment for persons unable to work due to short-term or long-term illness
	Implementation of the 'fit note' provides doctors with ability to provide information and advice to patients regarding how their condition impacts ability to work, and to offer help in getting patients back into paid work. It also allows employers to take a more active role in the process
State pension	The *Pensions Act 1995* increased state pension age to 65 for both men and women, implemented through staged increase for women from 2010 to 2018
	The *Pensions Act 2014* outlined further increases to 66 by 2020, and 67 by 2028
	Increases to 68 by 2044–2046 were also outlined under the earlier *Pensions Act 2007* (see Gov.uk 2014)
	The *New State Pension* introduced in April 2016, providing single-tier system for anyone retiring after this date, with a weekly pension payment of £155.65 (at 2016 prices), although some older adults will receive less dependent on *National Insurance* (social security) contributions
Retirement	Statutory (or default) retirement age abolished through *The Employment Equality (Repeal of Retirement Age Provisions) Regulations 2011 (No. 1069)* as part of the UK Government's *Age Positive* (DWP 2012b)

At the same time as public policy has sought to actively encourage extended working lives, a number of challenges have been created by economic austerity measures implemented following the 2007–2009 global economic crisis. Funding cuts, including to care-related services, have adversely affected the ability of some older adults to remain in paid employment, with profound implications. Older adults devote time caring for family and non-kin, as grandparents and/or carers of elderly relatives (Understanding Society 2014; Wellard 2011). The value of this care to the economy is considerable. For example, it was estimated in 2011 that grandparenting had a value to the UK economy of £119bn (Carers UK 2011). Some support is offered to carers. For example, the *Work Programme* offers *Work Preparation Support for Carers*, which provides access to training and advice as well as potentially covering care costs while training is being undertaken. However, the challenges for carers in combining paid and unpaid work are significant, as considered in a later chapter in this book. In addition, older adults are some of those most engaged in voluntary acts of care, either formally through voluntary and community sector organisations (VSCOs) or informally often in domestic settings involving other household members, kin or neighbours. Retirement often acts a trigger for engagement in volunteering, especially among men, which in some cases is undertaken as a way of providing focus and structure in the absence of paid employment (see Hardill and Wheatley 2017). Volunteering also has a considerable value to society, estimated in the UK in 2012 as £23.9 billion (Foster 2013). This evidence suggests that it is likely that EWL policies will have important wider impacts on the propensity of older adults to provide care and engage in voluntary work.

5.3 Employment Options Among Older Workers

Retirement has historically been considered as a single event occurring at the end of a linearly structured career, often defined by reaching a specific age, for example 65 (Beehr 2014, p. 1093). Older workers increasingly engage in phased or partial retirement as they near the end of their working lives, sometimes involving use of bridge employment (see Table 5.2). Bridge employment can follow a similar form to phased or partial retirement, for example part-time work in the career occupation, but may equally involve a movement out of the career occupation and even industry (see Beehr and Bennett 2015 for a taxonomy of 'bridge jobs'). In the

Table 5.2 Employment options for older workers

Employment option	Definition
Phased retirement	Non-standard work arrangement in which an employee remains in their existing employment while reducing their work contribution, often gradually, in terms of both working hours and effort (Hutchens 2010)
Partial retirement	Usually used to describe a reduction in work effort outside of the career job (Gustman and Steinmeier 1984a)
Gradual retirement	General term used in reference to reduced work effort during the final years of work (Hutchens 2010)
Bridge employment	'Bridge job' (paid work) that is taken by an older worker, usually after career employment has ended, in order to span the gap between a career job and retirement (Beehr 2014, p. 1102; Hedge et al. 2006, p. 126)

latter case, this can result in employment in lower skilled occupations. In more highly skilled occupations workers may be able to negotiate individualised bridge employment, in part driven by employers seeking to ensure they do not face skill gaps and loss of knowledge stock as their senior workforce retires (Shultz 2003).

Phased retirement schemes have been implemented across Europe for a number of years with varying degrees of take-up and success, including in Denmark and Finland since 1987, France since 1988, Germany since 1992, Spain since the 1960s and Sweden since 1976 (Belloni et al. 2006, pp. 12–14). Many UK employers offer phased or flexible retirement, while most are also willing to negotiate reductions in working hours with older employees on an informal or case-by-case basis (Hedge et al. 2006, p. 127; Hutchens 2003; Loretto and White 2006, p. 323). Evidence indicates, though, that use of phased (and partial) retirement can be limited by incentives, which do not successfully engage older workers in this route to retirement. Inclusion of the phased retirement years in calculating pension or social security benefits has historically acted as one significant barrier (Gustman and Steinmeier 1984b), although working after State Pension Age in the UK does not have this effect (Altman 2015, 16). Those who do take partial retirement may, further, be unable to remain in their previous role, affecting income (Latulippe and Turner 2000). Phased retirement is more common among white-collar occupations, with availability and take-up greatest among more highly skilled employees who require little supervision and put in significant work effort (Hutchens 2010, p. 1018; Radl 2012, p. 767).

The use of flexible working arrangements, for example flexi-time, part-time and job share, is often associated with working into later life including phased or partial retirement (Hedge et al. 2006, pp. 123–125). Enabled through formal policy implemented in the UK in the *Flexible Working Regulations*, workers have the right to request a flexible working arrangement, albeit these requests must be granted by employers who make allowance decisions which often centre on meeting 'business need' (Wheatley 2017).[3] It has been suggested that use of non-standard work arrangements of this variety may not only provide a more satisfying path to full retirement (including retention of cognitive skills in old age), but also enable employers to preserve human capital and consequently enhance labour productivity (Hutchens 2010, p. 1010). Evidence further suggests that the presence of flexible working arrangements increases opportunities for phased retirement (Hutchens and Grace-Martin 2006), producing positive outcomes for older workers (Loretto and White 2006). However, flexible working options do not always deliver positive outcomes. Part-time work, in particular, is in some cases poor quality, reflected in negative impacts on job satisfaction (Fagan et al. 2012; Wheatley 2017). Part-time work also represents a constraint for some workers, evident in the proportions reporting part-time work due to a lack of a full-time alternative. Estimates from the April–June UK *Labour Force Survey* show that 15 % of those aged 50–59 reported this involuntary part-time working in 2015 (ONS 2015a). While few older adults may express preferences for full-time work as they enter their last years in the labour market—less than 6 % of those aged 60 and over reported part-time work due to a lack of a full-time alternative—this nevertheless is further indication of some of the difficulties faced in extending the labour market participation of older adults.

Self-employment offers a further route for extending the working lives of older adults. It is often undertaken as a form of bridge employment. While a potentially high-risk option given the lack of guaranteed income, it can be desirable to those who have had previous experience of self-employment, those who are educated, in good health (Zissimopoulos and Karoly 2007), and those who have some form of guaranteed retirement income, for example pension from previous employer (Beehr 2014, p. 1104). Consistent with part-time work, though, self-employment can reflect involuntary employment among older workers who may be pushed into 'trading down' from secure employment into insecure self-employment because of redundancy or other exit from employment, and is particularly prominent among men (TUC 2014). In these cases self-employment can involve 'gig' work (see Friedman 2014) defined as work performed for a firm to complete a particular task or for a defined period of time as an independent contractor or consultant, which often involves 'undertaking small and discrete parcels of work through digital technologies that connect providers and customers' (The Work Foundation 2016). Examples include activities such as delivery driving, selling goods online and performing 'odd jobs', referred to in the UK context as 'the rise of the odd jobbers' (TUC 2014). The existing evidence pertaining to both the employed and self-employed suggests a potential division among older workers into those who continue to engage in paid work on a more voluntary basis, and those who end their working lives in unskilled low-quality employment or self-employment (Smeaton and White 2016, p. 372).

5.4   Older Workers: Preconceptions, Skills and Knowledge Stock

Older workers are often undervalued as members of the working population, resulting in over-representation in lower quality jobs and among the long-term unemployed (Phillipson and Smith 2006). Older workers are subject to a number of negative preconceptions within the workplace. These have been summarised by Posthuma and Campion (2009, pp. 161–165) and Ng and Feldman (2012, pp. 821–822) to include: (1) poor performance; (2) resistance to change; (3) inability to learn and expectations of short tenure limiting benefits of training and development; (4) high costs associated with expectations of high wages; (5) lack of motivation; (6) aversion to training and development; (7) a lack of trust; (8) poor health; and (9) being more likely to encounter work–family conflict. These preconceptions act as barriers to successful EWL, negatively affecting recruitment decisions, the quality of work experienced by older workers, and training and career development opportunities (Hedge et al. 2006, p. 37). Moreover, there is limited evidence of any of these preconceptions being consistent with the reality of employing older workers. For example, Ng and Feldman (2012) investigated whether six common stereotypes associated with older workers (less motivated, generally less willing to participate in training and career development, more resistant and less willing to change, less trusting, less healthy and more vulnerable to work–family conflict) could be substantiated. They found limited evidence to support these preconceptions with the exception of older workers being more averse to training and career development.

Retention of knowledge represents an increasing challenge as the baby boomer generation reaches retirement (DeLong 2004; Levy 2011). The permanent exit of this knowledge stock from the labour market poses a specific problem for both organisations and society more broadly, due to the numbers of workers retiring who have remained in the same organisation, and even role in some cases, for extended parts of their career (Levy 2011, p. 583). Ensuring the knowledge held by these workers is transferred prior to retirement is, therefore, important to organisations and the broader human capital stock, and can be seen as an organisational-level driver for promoting longer working lives among older adults (Altman 2015, p. 18). International concerns surrounding the impact of an ageing population have resulted in the development of policies aimed at challenging social misconceptions of older workers, including diminishing productivity levels and commitment, in order to create favourable conditions for individuals to age successfully (Katz 2002). Policymakers' attempts to promote an 'active old age', however, face certain barriers. Slow-changing social attitudes, specifically occupational and gender norms, among some groups of workers result in some men, for example male skilled manual workers, and many women taking early retirement (Radl 2012). Research based on US data suggests that workers who are heavily reliant on certain forms of firm-specific training undertaken early in their careers may retire earlier than workers with more transferable skills (Montizaan et al.

2013). Designing effective workplace policies, which facilitate retention of older workers, is difficult. Research has shown that older workers do value policies which are designed to enhance their working lives, but that they perceive much workplace policy as preserving negative preconceptions and low status among this group of workers (Hennekam and Herrbach 2015). Work, though, represents a significant contributor to the well-being of older adults (Cameron and Waldegrave 2009). Against the policy backdrop promoting EWL, enhancing the working lives of older adults is highly important at both organisational and societal level.

5.5   Decisions to Leave or Remain in Paid Work: Economic Necessity, Health and the Quality of Work

Three main factors have been identified in previous research as primary drivers among older workers of the intention to remain in, or leave, paid work: (1) health status; (2) financial incentives including economic pressure from employers and government, pensions and alternative income sources; and (3) the quality of work (Altman 2015; Humphrey et al. 2003; Siegrist et al. 2006). Health is an important factor, which influences the ability of older adults to remain in paid work. Ill health, which can accompany ageing, renders paid work more difficult, increasing the attractiveness of retirement for those in a financial position to pursue this route (Beehr 2014). Special analysis of the 2015 *Annual Population Survey* (which combines two successive waves of *Labour Force Survey* data) investigated the reasons given by respondents for continuing in paid work beyond State Pension Age. This data broadly supports the idea that the majority of those who continue to work aged 65 and over do so out of choice, but a significant minority may remain in paid work because of economic imperatives. Although 52 % stated that their main reason was that they were simply 'not ready' to stop work, the next most frequently cited reason was 'to pay for essential items (such as bills)' (accounting for 15 % of respondents). Women were more likely to give the latter reason than men (18 % compared to 12 %), while men were more likely to state their main reason was that their employer 'needs [their] experience or [they] are needed in the family business' (8 % of men compared to 6 % of women) (ONS 2016). Economic necessity, though, is likely to become more of a prominent driver for remaining in paid work among older adults following changes to state pensions and the welfare system. This could result in involuntary employment among some older workers who will face little choice but to remain in paid work into later life, and further reflects a growing polarisation in employment among older workers.

The careers of older workers are becoming polarised into those with 'low' and those with 'high' career capital, where career capital refers to the range of assets owned by the worker including skills, networks and work identity which act as a foundation for career success (Tempest and Coupland 2016).[4] Older workers with high career capital are likely to remain in secure employment in their career occupation and/or industry, making use of phased or partial retirement arrangements, while those with low career capital may find themselves working, involuntarily, in precarious temporary, flexible or 'gig' low-pay, low-quality jobs. The quality of work refers to the degree to which work exhibits characteristics which provide benefits or otherwise to the worker, including to physical and psychological well-being (Green 2006). The quality of work, sometimes referred to as job quality, has been categorised in a number of different forms, although broadly paid work can be considered to be either: (1) low-quality 'low-commitment'; or (2) high-quality 'high-commitment' (see Holman 2013, pp. 477–478). In this categorisation, low-quality work exhibits characteristics of Taylorist work organisation including low autonomy, skill, pay, training, security, and is often associated with employer-driven flexibility, for example zero hour contracts and agency working (Gregory and Milner 2009, p. 123).[5] The latter category, in contrast, provides autonomy, variety, skill, training and development, better pay and security, and opportunities to use flexible working arrangements. Other research has expanded these broad categories, as summarised in Table 5.3. It should be noted, though, that even high-quality jobs can exhibit a number of negative characteristics including work–family conflict and intense working routines (Kalleberg 2012, p. 433). It has been argued that the quality of work is subject to influences from outside of the paid work sphere (Cooke et al. 2013). Considering the case of adults

Table 5.3 Taxonomy's job quality

	Job quality categories	Key features
Karasek and Theorell (1990)	(1) Active jobs	High autonomy, high demand
	(2) High-strain jobs	Low autonomy, high demand
	(3) Passive jobs	Low autonomy, low demand
	(4) Low-strain jobs	High autonomy, low demand
Holman (2013, pp. 477–478)	(1) Active	High autonomy, social support, complexity, security, and moderate pay and workloads
	(2) Saturated	High demands, long hours, high pay
	(3) Team-based	High autonomy, high demand, frequent team-working, high security
	(4) Passive-independent	Low demand, low autonomy, infrequent team-working
	(5) Insecure	Temporary employment, low demand, low pay
	(6) High-strain	Low autonomy, high demand

Source: Wheatley 2017

aged 40 and over, Cooke et al. (2013) argue that choices and constraints present in the home, for example, influence how individuals perceive the quality of work. This presents a significant challenge in attempts to develop policy and understanding with respect to the quality of work as it suggests policies will need to be tailored to the individual. However, consistent in 'good' jobs in the different taxonomies of the quality of work presented in Table 5.3 are task discretion and autonomy, and opportunities for training and development (Bartling et al. 2012), highlighting the relevance of these aspects to the quality of work, and in turn EWL.

Working into later life can bring benefits to the: (1) individual including greater choice over when and how to retire, and physical and psychological well-being; (2) organisation including retention of experience, loyalty, mentoring and interpersonal skills; and (3) society including higher national output, lower unemployment, lower welfare expenditure and reduced health spending (Altman 2015). For example, a study focusing on older workers in Singapore reported higher retention of cognitive function among older adults who continue in paid work or engage in volunteering, as well as higher levels of psychological well-being

(Schwingel et al. 2009). Older workers also remain under less pressure in their jobs than their younger counterparts (Felstead 2010, p. 1311). A range of previous research, reported in Kooij et al. (2008, p. 368), further evidences that job satisfaction among older workers is more often associated with intrinsic benefits, that is utility/well-being benefits, than extrinsic benefits, for example human capital development. UK evidence, however, suggests that exposure to high-strain (high demand, low autonomy) jobs increased among older workers between 1992 and 2006 (Felstead 2010, p. 1304).

Lack of autonomy, repetitive working conditions often associated with Taylorist work organisation and demanding physical working environments have been shown to reduce the quality of work among older workers, potentially leading to earlier exit from the labour market (Blekesaune and Solem 2005). Poor quality of work is a significant factor in driving the intention to retire from work (Siegrist et al. 2006, p. 64), especially among women (Schnalzenberger et al. 2014, p. 157). Other factors outlined in the existing literature affecting the motivation to continue working in later life include feelings of redundancy associated with reaching statutory age milestones, poor physical health, increased preferences for leisure time in later life and lack of opportunities for training and career development associated with age norms and stereotypes (Kooij et al. 2008, p. 383). It should be noted in the latter case, though, that it has also been reported that older workers are often more averse to taking on new tasks or skills, for example ICT skills, especially as they near retirement age (Friedberg 2003; Kooij et al. 2008; Ng and Feldman 2012). Older workers continue to show greater dissatisfaction with work, evidencing some of the concerns over job quality for EWL. Drawing on cross-sectional UK data from 1992, 2006 and 2012, Smeaton and White (2016, pp. 380–381) found that older workers reported growing dissatisfaction with the quality of work in a number of areas including the nature of work tasks, working hours, required work effort, the level of insecurity and occupational benefits, for example pensions. The relative importance of each of these aspects of work varied, though, throughout the period analysed. The quality of work appears important to experiences of paid work among older adults, while evidence also suggests considerable variation may be present in the quality of work encountered, which may have important implications given the EWL discourse and changing patterns of employment among older workers.

5.6   Patterns of Employment Among Older Workers in the UK

Data is extracted from a number of UK sources in this section, including the *Annual Population Survey, Labour Force Survey* and *Understanding Society*, to provide an empirical exploration of patterns of work and the relative quality of work encountered by older workers. As noted earlier, the proportion of the UK population aged 50 and over has increased. In 1995 this age group numbered 18.3 million, equivalent to 32 % of the total resident population. By 2015, it had reached 23.6 million, accounting for 36 % of the total population (NOMIS 2016a). The UK *Office for National Statistics* expects this trend to accelerate. Their 2014-based projections to 2039 suggest that the proportion of the population of working age will remain broadly similar. However, the number and proportion of those at or over *State Pension Age* will increase markedly from 12.4 million to 16.5 million (19–22 % of the population), reflecting a 33 % increase by 2039 (ONS 2015b).[6] In exploring the impact of these population changes on paid work, it is important first to establish the patterns of occupational change in the UK workforce as a whole and some general themes affecting the quality of individuals' experience of employment. These wider changes fundamentally relate to the shift in advanced societies from employment in production sectors to the services, with an associated move from occupations requiring manual skills towards those requiring cognitive and interpersonal skills. The *Standard Occupational Classification* (SOC) used in UK labour market statistics categorises jobs by *skill level* and *skill specialisation* and is, therefore, hierarchical. SOC groups 1–3 (managers, professionals and associate professionals) are associated with higher level cognitive skills, equivalent to higher education. SOC groups 4–7 (clerical and administrative, skilled trades, customer services and personal service) are associated with a mix of manual and interpersonal skills at an intermediate level. Finally, SOC groups 8–9 (process, plant and machine operatives, and elementary occupations) are associated with little training or formal qualification and describe activities that are often manual in nature.

As the structure of the UK economy has changed, particularly since the 1970s, analysts have described a 'hollowing out of the middle' of the occupational hierarchy, where new jobs in the services have tended to be either highly skilled or relatively unskilled, while traditional 'trades' requiring intermediate manual skills have declined (Wilson et al. 2016). With the expansion of participation in UK higher education since the 1970s (which increased particularly steeply after 1992 and 2006 with the increase in the number of universities and the adoption of the 50 % target for young people entering higher education respectively), these changes would be expected to disproportionately benefit younger workers who are more likely to be highly qualified. However, recent *Labour Force Survey* data shows a more complex picture. Managers, professionals and associate professionals are occupations where employment has grown strongly, with numbers employed in these SOC groups increasing by a total of 20 % between 2005 and 2015 (compared to just 1 % for intermediate-skilled SOC groups 4–7 and low-skilled SOC groups 8–9). However, within the intermediate-skilled occupations there have been significant differences. As automation has reduced the demand for clerical and administrative roles, employment in these occupations has declined by 10 % over the period, while skilled trades have continued their long-term decline (falling by 2 % since 2005). However, employment in caring, leisure and other service occupations, has increased very strongly, by 25 % over the decade. Moreover, the recent strong growth is itself closely associated with the ageing UK population, with jobs related to care growing fastest within this occupation group (ONS 2016).

Changes in the occupational structure of all employment (inclusive of self-employment) have coincided with a strong increase in the participation of older workers. Figure 5.1 illustrates the increasing employment rates of people aged over 50 (but under State Pension Age) over the last 20 years. At the start of the period (in the 3 months to December 1995), the employment rate of those aged 50–64 was significantly lower than the average for all working age UK residents, at 57.4 % compared to 69.9 %. Employment rates have increased for all age groups over 25 during the period (with employment falling for those aged 16–24 prin-

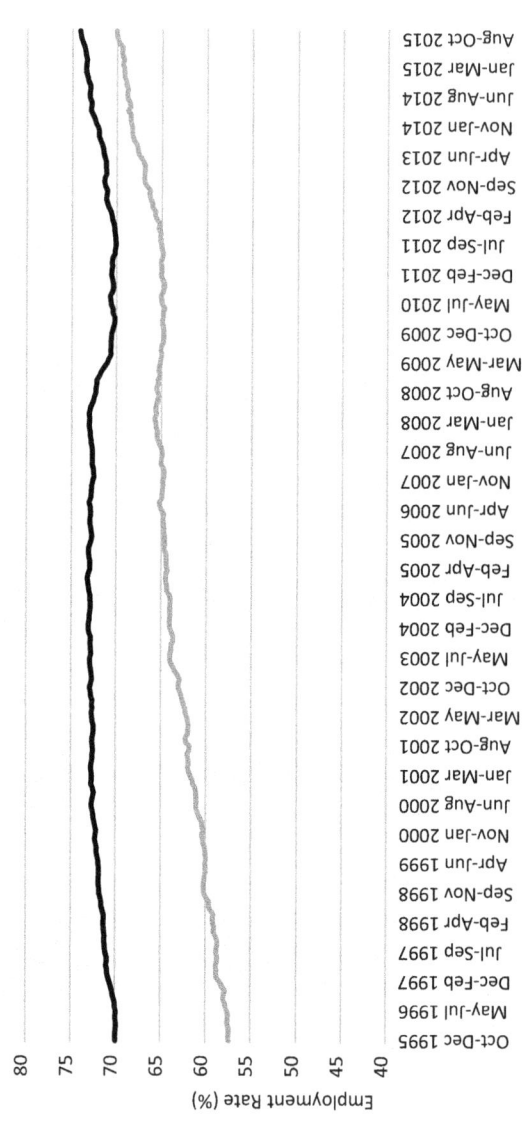

Fig. 5.1 Employment rate of people aged 50–64 and all working age (16–64) (Source: Adapted from data from the Office for National Statistics licenced under the Open Government Licence v.3.0—'Table A05 NSA: Employment, unemployment and economic activity by age group (not seasonally adjusted)', 2016 [accessed on 27 October 2016])

cipally because of the expansion of participation in further and higher education). However, they have increased particularly markedly for older workers—meaning that the 12.6 percentage point difference between the average working age employment rate and that of 50–64-year-olds at the start of the period had fallen to just 4 percentage points by the three months to December 2015 (ONS 2016). By 2015 approximately 8.4 million UK residents aged 50–64 reported some form of paid employment. This number has grown by 22 % over 10 years and 61 % over 20 years, compared to increases of 9 % and 21 % respectively for the entire employed workforce aged over 16. Although the number of workers aged 65 and over is much smaller, and the employment rates much lower, the increases over time have been even more notable. In the three months to December 1995, there were 433,000 adults over 65 in some form of paid work in the UK, an employment rate of 4.9 %. This number has increased by 177 % over two decades to 1.2 million, an employment rate of 10.6 %. Both the growth in the number of older adults and their increasing participation in the workforce have altered the age structure of UK employment. In 1995 older adults aged 50–64 accounted for just 20.2 % of all in employment (aged 16 and over), while those aged 65 and over accounted for only 1.7 % of the total employed workforce. Twenty years later, in the three months to December 2015, those aged 50–64 accounted for 26.7 %, and older adults aged 65 and over 3.8 % of the total employed workforce (ONS 2016).

In addition to considering the numbers of older adults extending their working lives, it is also important to reflect on the types of work in which they are engaged. *Labour Force Survey* data for those employed full-time compared to part-time reveals that over the last decade the proportion of older workers working full-time and part-time has remained relatively stable, at around 68 % and 32 % respectively, although it should be noted that older women, consistent with the rest of the working population, remain more likely to work part-time. Compared to the working age population as a whole, the proportion of older workers in full-time work is lower and part-time work is higher. However, this reflects a change across the UK labour market as the overall share of the working age population working full-time has fallen slightly (from 75 % to 74 %). This is primarily due to the significant fall in full-time employment among younger workers (aged 16–19 and 20–24) and corresponding increase in the proportion working part-time, driven by the expansion of participation in further and higher education, as well as the growth in flexibilised employment (Gregory and Milner 2009). However, in terms of absolute change, the numbers of older workers working part-time have increased more compared to those working full-time (by 32 % between 2004 and 2015 compared to 27 %) (NOMIS 2016b).

Self-employment becomes more common as individuals age.[7] Data from the *Labour Force Survey* reveals that self-employment is higher as a proportion of all in employment for those aged 70 and over: it is reported by over 30 % of those aged 70 and over compared to around 17 % among those aged 50–64. Among those reporting self-employment, around 17 % of older adults report 'running their own business or professional practice', while the bulk of those in self-employment report 'working for themselves' consistent with general patterns among all workers. Around 20 % of those aged 60 and over, and a quarter of those aged 70 and over, report self-employment in managerial and senior roles. A further 20 % of the self-employed aged 60 and over, and 18 % of those aged 70 and over, report professional occupations. The proportions in managerial occupations are also considerably higher than the average for all age groups (16.8 %). The majority of the remaining self-employed older adults work in skilled trade occupations (approximately a quarter), while there are also notable proportions, around 5 %, who report working in unskilled elementary occupations, especially in their 50s and early 60s, likely reflecting incidence of bridge self-employment including 'gig' work.

Data from the UK *Labour Force Survey* also provides useful insight into occupational patterns among employed older adults. Around 10 % of older workers report managerial and senior roles, a little over the average for all age groups. However, working in professional occupations appears to become less common among older adults, as only around 15 % of those aged 60 and over, and less than 14 % of those aged 70 and over, report employment in professional occupations. Interestingly, older adults are also over-represented in employment in elementary occupations, which accounts for around 11 % of employment among all age groups. This pattern is particularly prominent among those employed later in the life-course: around 11 % of those aged 55–59 and 60–64 and 12 % of those aged 65–69 report elementary occupations, but around 17 % of those 70 and over report employment in these unskilled occupations. This is likely to reflect bridge employment in a number of cases as older adults continue in paid work either voluntarily or involuntarily as they progress into older age (Beehr 2014; Beehr and Bennett 2015).

Turning to earnings, Fig. 5.2 shows the median real hourly earnings (adjusted to 2013 prices) by age for 16–64-year-olds in the UK, evidencing that as average wages have increased for all age groups between 1975 and 2009, the extent of the differences between age groups has widened. In 2009, average hourly wages peaked at £15 an hour at age 34 (on average, men's earnings peak in the 40s whilst women's earnings peak at least a decade earlier), £9.30 an hour higher than the median earnings for 16-year-olds, and £4.06 higher than the median for 64-year-olds. This compares to 1975, when 16-year-olds earned £3.90 less an hour than 34-year-olds and 64-year-olds earned £1.10 less. However, with the recession that started in 2008 and subsequent recovery in employment and earnings from 2011, Fig. 5.2 shows that median earnings in 2013 and

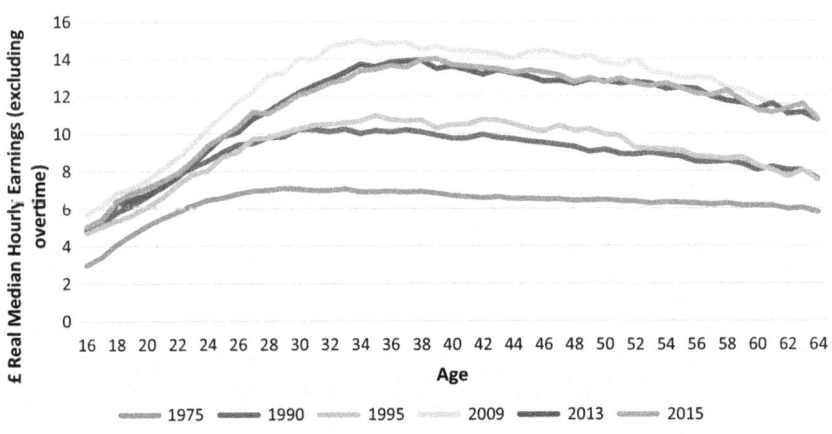

Fig. 5.2 Trends in real median hourly earnings (2013 prices, excluding overtime) by age (16–64) (Source: Adapted from data from the Office for National Statistics licenced under the Open Government Licence v.3.0—'Statistical Bulletin: Annual Survey of Hours and Earnings, 2015—Table 17: Real median hourly earnings (excluding overtime) by age', 2016 [accessed on 7 November 2016])

2015 both remained below 2009 for almost all age groups, and the gaps between the mid-career peak earnings and the earnings of older workers have narrowed. This is because the mid-career 'peak' in real earnings is lower (£14 an hour at age 39 in 2015), and the subsequent tail-off in later career has become less significant (with 64-year-olds earning £3.30 less an hour than 39-year-olds).

Offering some initial insight into the relative quality of work, reported levels of autonomy are summarised by age group in Fig. 5.3 using data from wave 4 (2012–2013) of *Understanding Society*. Patterns of autonomy are consistent with the presence of a division among older workers between those who are employed or self-employed in jobs exhibiting higher quality characteristics and those in low-quality work (Smeaton and White 2016). Older workers report some of the greatest levels of autonomy, reflected in proportions reporting 'a lot' of autonomy over various aspects of their job (autonomy over job tasks, pace of work, manner of work and order of tasks). However, a notable portion of older workers report low levels of autonomy, likely associated with low or unskilled bridge employment. In this respect, older workers are over-represented in comparison to all but young workers in the 16–24 age category. In

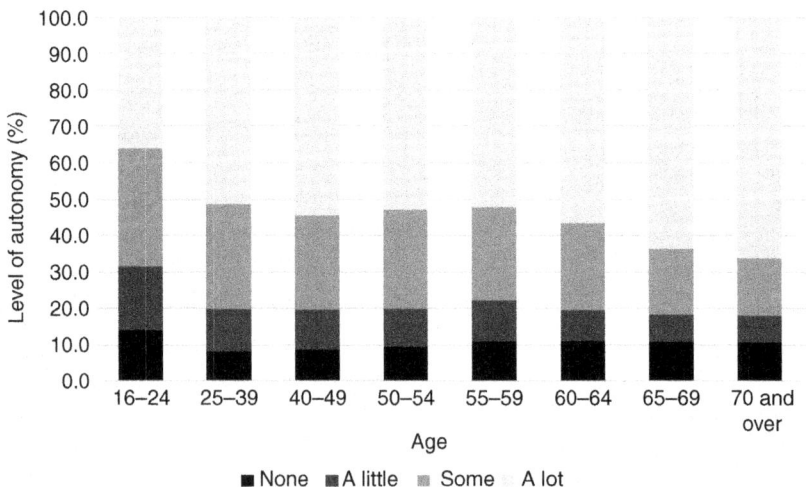

Fig. 5.3 Reported levels of autonomy in paid work by age (Source: Adapted from Understanding Society, wave 4 (2012–2013))

respect to other aspects of job quality, while around 5–6 % of younger and middle-aged workers report negative feelings about work (depressed, gloomy, uneasy, tense, worried), older workers report fewer negative feelings, as only around 4 % of those aged 50–59, 3 % of those 60–69 and less than 2 % of those aged 70 and over report negative feelings associated with work. This is likely to relate to the wider quality of work encountered by older workers, but to some degree may also reflect the relatively short tenure remaining for those in the later stages of their working lives reducing concerns surrounding paid work.

5.6.1   Two-Step Cluster Analysis

In order to gain a greater insight into the nature of paid work among older adults, two-step cluster analysis is performed using data extracted from wave 4 (2012–2013) of *Understanding Society*. Cluster analysis groups cases into homogeneous groups or clusters, differing from many other research techniques as it does not require any prior assumptions about the distribution of the data making it particularly suitable to exploratory analysis as employed in this chapter. It is chosen as it can be performed using large data-sets, unlike hierarchical cluster analysis, it allows the analysis of both continuous and categorical variables, and fits the data to the most appropriate number of clusters rather than requiring the number of clusters to be specified (Norušis 2012, pp. 394–395). The analysis explores the reported patterns and quality of work among older workers, incorporating those who report themselves as employed or self-employed in their main job. A range of variables is included comprising measures of relevant demographics, occupation details and variables pertaining to the quality of work. Table 5.4 summarises the results of the cluster analysis.

The analysis generates five clusters, which evidence the diversity of experiences of paid work among older workers. Cluster 1 is comprised of a greater proportion of older workers in their 50s, and it is evenly split between men and women. Members of this cluster report high-quality, high-commitment jobs (Holman 2013, pp. 477–478) evident in reported full-time hours, high levels of overtime, high skill levels (based

Table 5.4 Two-step cluster analysis

	Cluster				
	1 $n = 1296$	2 $n = 847$	3 $n = 1105$	4 $n = 1234$	5 $n = 506$
Demographic variables					
Age (mean)	57.1	59.4	57.7	55.5	55.4
Gender (% male)	52.6	65.6	41.9	39.1	39.3
Marital status (%)	74.5 (married/civil partnership)	72.1 (married/civil partnership)	63.3 (married/civil partnership)	63.8 (married/civil partnership)	65.0 (married/civil partnership)
Highest qualification (%)	45.7 (higher education)	46.5 (higher education)	35.7 (secondary education)	45.8 (higher education)	36.8 (higher education)
Disability/long-term illness (% 'yes')	30.9	33.8	34.3	38.7	44.7
Time-use variables (per week)					
Working hours (mean)	31.9	32.8	28.6	33.2	33.6
Overtime hours (mean)	3.4	3.0	1.8	3.6	3.6
Housework hours (mean)	8.6	8.3	9.9	10.1	10.2
Care (ill/elderly) hours (mean)	1.5	1.8	1.7	5.6	2.1
Volunteering hours (mean)	2.2	5.2	1.7	1.6	1.2
Occupation variables					
Employee (%)	100.0	4.3	96.9	95.5	89.7

(continued)

Table 5.4 (continued)

	Cluster				
	1 n = 1296	2 n = 847	3 n = 1105	4 n = 1234	5 n = 506
Major occupation group (SOC) (%)	26.2 (managers)	23.8 (skilled trades)	17.5 (elementary occupations)	18.1 (associate professional)	15.8 (associate professional)
Annual personal income (mean £,000 s)	36.7	29.5	21.8	27.8	26.7
Quality of work variables					
Autonomy over job tasks (%)	77.5 (a lot)	88.1 (a lot)	37.6 (some)	37.0 (some)	32.0 (a lot)
Autonomy over work pace (%)	83.3 (a lot)	88.0 (a lot)	41.0 (some)	36.5 (a lot)	33.4 (a lot)
Autonomy over work manner (%)	94.4 (a lot)	96.0 (a lot)	44.9 (some)	46.7 (a lot)	45.3 (a lot)
Autonomy over work task order (%)	90.8 (a lot)	89.6 (a lot)	41.8 (some)	48.8 (a lot)	44.5 (a lot)
Autonomy over working hours (%)	48.5 (a lot)	78.5 (a lot)	62.7 (none)	39.9 (none)	52.0 (none)
Informal flexibility (%)	71.6 (yes)	99.3 (some)	52.9 (no)	46.8 (yes)	46.6 (no)
Would like training (% 'yes')	30.3	18.5	29.4	43.5	37.7
Would like new job with different employer (% 'yes')	7.9	8.6	16.5	32.3	53.4

(continued)

Table 5.4 (continued)

	Cluster				
	1 n = 1296	2 n = 847	3 n = 1105	4 n = 1234	5 n = 506
Would like to start own business (% 'yes')	9.4	15.6	7.3	18.5	24.7
Would like to stop paid work (% 'yes')	35.4	23.8	36.1	50.6	60.5
Tense about job (%)	38.0 (never)	43.2 (occasionally)	42.8 (never)	51.1 (some of the time)	39.1 (most of the time)
Uneasy about job (%)	72.6 (never)	61.3 (never)	79.1 (never)	45.1 (occasionally)	41.9 (some of the time)
Worried about job (%)	70.9 (never)	57.3 (never)	83.3 (never)	48.1 (occasionally)	35.4 (some of the time)
Depressed about job (%)	94.9 (never)	86.2 (never)	96.5 (never)	51.1 (never)	48.4 (some of the time)
Gloomy about job (%)	88.0 (never)	79.6 (never)	92.6 (never)	58.2 (occasionally)	55.9 (some of the time)
Miserable about job (%)	93.8 (never)	88.7 (never)	94.4 (never)	49.5 (occasionally)	49.8 (some of the time)

Subjective well-being variables

(continued)

Table 5.4 (continued)

	Cluster				
	1 n = 1296	2 n = 847	3 n = 1105	4 n = 1234	5 n = 506
Satisfaction with job (mean)	6.0	5.9	5.7	4.9	3.5
Satisfaction with income (mean)	5.1	4.7	4.5	4.2	3.7
Subjective financial status (%)	51.4 (living comfortably)	43.3 (living comfortably)	36.6 (doing alright)	32.2 (doing alright)	29.4 (just about getting by)
Satisfaction with amount of leisure time (mean)	5.0	4.8	4.7	4.1	3.6
Satisfaction with life overall (mean)	5.6	5.3	5.3	4.8	4.1

Source: Understanding Society, wave 4 (2012–2013)
Notes: Table shows means or most frequent responses
Missing values for overtime hours for self-employed entered at the mean
Questions regarding autonomy levels have four possible responses: 'a lot', 'some', 'a little', and 'none'
Questions regarding preferences for changes in paid work, for example 'would like training', have two possible responses: 'yes' and 'no'
Questions regarding negative perceptions of paid work, for example 'tense about job', have five possible responses: 'all of the time', 'most of the time', 'some of the time', 'occasionally', and 'never'
The question regarding the presence of informal flexibility has three possible responses: 'yes', 'some' and 'none'
Subjective financial status has five possible responses: 'living comfortably', 'doing alright', 'just about getting by', 'finding it quite difficult', and 'finding it very difficult'
Satisfaction with job, income, leisure and life is measured on a 7-point Likert scale, where 1 = completely unsatisfied, 4 = neither satisfied or unsatisfied and 7 = completely satisfied

on education), and managerial and professional occupations. They report employment in good-quality jobs, reflected in the highest income, high levels of autonomy and informal flexibility in all aspects of work, few negative feelings around work, and around two-thirds report preferences to continue paid work. They are the most financially secure of all clusters, with just over half reporting 'living comfortably'. Older adults in this cluster exhibit the highest levels of satisfaction with paid work and other aspects of their lives, and this cluster also reports some of the greatest engagement in volunteering. This cluster likely represents those who engage in paid work through choice as they near the end of their working lives, and in some cases may involve partial or phased retirement. Cluster 2 is almost entirely comprised of self-employed older workers. This is the oldest cluster, averaging just under 60 years old, and is two-thirds men. Members of this cluster are engaged in either highly skilled managerial and professional occupations or skilled trades. They report some of the highest degrees of autonomy and flexibility in paid work and are the least likely to show preferences to stop paid work. They report some of the highest levels of satisfaction with work and other aspects of their lives, and are more often in comfortable financial positions. Engagement in paid work is also often accompanied by volunteering among members of this cluster. Paid work, and unpaid voluntary work, is likely to reflect activity undertaken voluntarily by members of both clusters 1 and 2 as they seek to remain active and use their skills during later life.

Cluster 3 reflects those older workers employed in low-skilled occupations and is likely to include those who have taken bridge employment. Members of this cluster are more likely to work part-time hours and report lower earnings in low-skilled occupations, especially elementary occupations. Despite their low earnings, and other reported characteristics of low job quality reflected in low levels of autonomy, these older workers predominantly report a reasonable financial position (36.6 % report their financial status as 'doing alright'), and few negative feelings towards work. They are generally satisfied with work and other aspects of life, which is consistent with a number of these older adults taking on these roles as a short-term bridge activity towards the end of their working lives (Beehr 2014; Hedge et al. 2006). Members of cluster 4 have some consistent characteristics to members of cluster 1, but in contrast more often work in associate professional, administrative, and caring, leisure and other service occupations. Those in cluster 4 report the greatest household contribution, alongside cluster 5, and report the greatest care commitments for ill/elderly relatives or friends. Paid work among this cluster has some characteristics of lower quality work, evident in the negative feelings expressed towards work, and around half of this cluster report a preference to stop paid work. The majority report reasonable financial security: 29.7 % report 'living comfortably' and 32.2 % report 'doing alright'. Members of this cluster generally report satisfaction with paid work and other aspects of their lives, but less so with the amount of leisure time, evidencing the trade-offs present where paid work is undertaken alongside significant household responsibilities (Drinkwater 2015).

Finally, cluster 5 is comprised of those who report low quality of work. Members of this cluster are younger, averaging 55 years old, and are predominately women (60.7 %). They are also over-represented in the divorced or separated category for marital status (23.5 % of this cluster report being divorced or separated), and are those most likely to report a long-term illness or disability. Those in cluster 5 are mainly employed full-time (reporting the lengthiest mean working hours), but also spend a significant amount of their time engaged in unpaid work, housework and providing care for ill/elderly relatives or friends. They are, however, the least likely to volunteer perhaps reflecting the trade-off present between time available for paid work and different forms of unpaid work (Hardill and Wheatley 2017). They work in a range of occupations, but are over-represented in caring, leisure and other service, and sales and customer service occupations. Despite this being the smallest cluster, accounting for only 10.1 % of the total sample of older workers, members of cluster 5 account for 12.5 % and 15.6 % respectively of all older workers in the sample reporting these occupations. Low job quality is evident in cluster 5 in reported levels of flexibility, as this cluster has some of the highest proportions reporting no flexibility in hours or informal flexibility in their job. They also report dissatisfaction with the conditions of work, reflected in over half of the cluster reporting a preference for moving to a new job with a different employer, and three-fifths reporting a preference to stop paid work. This cluster also reports the most negative feelings towards work, especially feeling tense and worried about their job. They report low job satisfaction and the lowest levels of satisfaction with other aspects of life. Financial constraints appear to be a primary diver for continued engagement in paid work alongside the significant unpaid work reported. Members of this cluster are highly over-represented among those reporting 'finding it very difficult', accounting for 35 % of all responses given in this category across the sample of older workers, and 23.4 % of all older workers reporting that they are 'finding it quite difficult'.

5.7   Discussion and Summary

Within advanced societies including the UK, older adults form a considerable and growing portion of the workforce—both 50–64 and post-65—due to both demographic factors (population ageing) and the changing structure and nature of paid work. Paid work is a significant, and increasingly common, feature of the lives of many older adults. Evidence in the existing literature highlights the potential benefits of paid work for older adults, and more broadly to advanced societies. However, there is also a number of challenges related to lack of career development and/or training opportunities, the presence of health conditions, the negative perceptions of co-workers and employers, and a number of other factors, which can lead to low-quality work being encountered by older workers. Consistent with evidence in the existing literature, though, the exploratory empirical analysis reported in this chapter suggests that the main driver of continued engagement in paid work is choice, as many older workers feel they are not ready to retire. In the aftermath of the 2007–2009 global economic crisis, there is little evidence to suggest a greater push into involuntary part-time work among older adults overall, certainly not when compared to young adults.

Paid work is an activity, which many older workers engage with voluntarily and this is reflected in reported levels of well-being associated with work and other aspects of life, including among those engaging in paid work as part of a partial or phased retirement, which may involve use of bridge employment. The quality of work varies among older workers, and while some report continued employment or self-employment in work, which has a number of good characteristics, others do report low-quality jobs. The evidence in this chapter suggests that, at least among some older workers, engaging in low-quality work may not have broader negative impacts. This may be especially the case where paid work is viewed as short-term bridge employment at the end of the working life. However, while paid work remains a choice among the majority, the evidence presented in this chapter does suggests that an important minority continue to engage in paid work including precarious and 'gig' work, which is often low quality, primarily due to financial insecurity. Moreover, these older workers are also those who more often report considerable unpaid work (housework, care) and ill health. Paid work for these older adults is involuntary, but a financial necessity, which has been exacerbated by changes to retirement and pension legislation and through reductions in welfare funding, including for care and related services.

These findings have important implications for organisations including those seeking to recruit, or already employing, older workers. Negative perceptions of older workers can limit opportunities and have other implications, which may result in older workers more often encountering low job quality. However, these perceptions are largely unsubstantiated as evident in the existing literature. Alongside other challenges faced by at least some older workers, as reported in this chapter, including financial insecurity and high levels of unpaid work, the presence of misconceptions within organisations may result in inequality in the experiences of paid work for older workers in comparison both to their younger counterparts and with other older workers. Some older workers do report good job quality. Organisations should focus on improving the quality of work among other older workers, and draw on the strengths of older workers and the range of benefits that they can bring to colleagues and their employer, rather than viewing these workers as a flexibilised source of short-term labour. Extending the working lives of older workers, additionally, has broader societal implications for both the provision of care and volunteering. Currently non-marketised care, including grandparenting, accounts for a substantive level of activity in many advanced societies including the UK. Meanwhile, volunteering is more prominent among older adults, especially among men where retirement often acts as a trigger for engagement. Given the evidence presented here, and in other studies (Drinkwater 2015; Hardill and Wheatley 2017), which show the trade-offs present between paid work, unpaid care and volunteering, it is likely that extending the working lives of older adults could result in significant reductions in the availability of non-marketised care for parents, currently provided by grandparents, and levels of engagement in volunteering. Reducing the ability of older adults to undertake these forms of unpaid activity could, therefore, have significant implications for advanced societies, putting further pressure on already squeezed public sector budgets and reducing the ability of some parents, especially mothers, to remain engaged in paid work. While extended working lives offer a number of benefits to older adults, organisations and advanced societies, the challenges are associated with not only direct concerns over the quality of work encountered by older workers and the involuntary nature of continued engagement in paid work among some older adults. Identifying ways of effectively balancing the benefits of extended working lives and these potentially negative impacts is essential for the continued progress of advanced societies.

Notes

1. In past research definitions of 'older adults' or 'older workers' vary considerably, from those aged over 40 to those aged over 75 (Bourne 1982; Warr 2000). However, increasingly it is accepted that older workers most appropriately refers to individuals aged 50 and over (Kooij et al. 2008, p. 365). It is also acknowledged that chronological age provides an imperfect measure of ageing, as it ignores the variations present in physical and psychological well-being and other demographic and occupational factors (Kooij et al. 2008, p. 365). Nevertheless, the policy context remains focused around chronological age in the absence of an alternative method of categorising individuals with respect to ageing.
2. The most recently available dataset at the time the research was conducted, wave 5 (2013–14) of *Understanding Society*, did not include the module containing relevant questions pertaining to the quality of work including levels of autonomy, and so was not used in this research.
3. The Flexible Working (Procedural Requirements) Regulations, SI 2002/3207 and the Flexible Working (Eligibility, Complaints and Remedies) SI 2002/3236 are amendments to the Employment Act 2002, s47, consolidated in the Employment Rights Act 1996, ss80F–80I. Initial policy was applied to parents of young and disabled children. It was extended to include carers of certain adults and parents of older children in 2007. Employees with parental responsibility for children under 16

were included from 2009. From June 2014, the 'right to request' a flexible working arrangement became available to every employee after 26 weeks' employment service.

4. Career capital comprises three core elements: knowing-how (competencies and skills), knowing-whom (professional intra- and inter-firm networks), and knowing-why (balancing the individual's identity and career choices).

5. Taylorist work organisation is named after Frederick W. Taylor whose scientific management approach emphasised increases in productivity through reducing inefficiency including that caused by malfeasance by standardising processes, monitoring workers (including use of time and motion studies), and high degrees of task sub-division (Taylor 1967). Taylorism has been criticised for removing initiative from the worker and emphasising managerial control over labour, resulting in low levels of discretion and the demotivation of workers (Choi et al. 2008, p. 423; Figart 2001, p. 408).

6. The definition of 'pensionable age' in the ONS projections takes into account the changing State Pension Age set out in the 2014 Pension Act (increasing to 66 for both men and women by 2020 and to 67 between 2026 and 2028), but does not reflect proposed further changes to 68 or beyond.

7. Data is from the March–June 2015 Labour Force Survey for self-reported employment status with 'Government scheme' and 'unpaid family worker' responses removed.

References

Altman, R. 2015. A new vision for older workers: Retain, retrain, recruit. https://www.gov.uk/government/uploads/system/uploads/attachment_data/file/411420/a-new-vision-for-older-workers.pdf. Accessed 12 Feb 2017.

Banks, J., R. Blundell, A. Bozio, and C. Emmerson. 2010. Releasing jobs for the young? Early retirement and youth unemployment in the United Kingdom. In *Social security programs and retirement around the world: The relationship to youth employment*, ed. J. Gruber and D. Wise, 319–344. Chicago: University of Chicago Press.

Bartling, B., E. Fehr, and K. Schmidt. 2012. Screening, competition, and job design: Economic origins of good jobs. *The American Economic Review* 102: 834–864.

Beehr, T.A. 2014. To retire or not to retire: That is not the question. *Journal of Organisational Behavior* 35: 1093–1108.

Beehr, T.A., and M. Bennett. 2015. Working after retirement: Features of bridge employment and research directions. *Work, Aging and Retirement* 1: 112–128.

Belloni, M., C. Monticone, and S. Trucchi. 2006. *Flexibility in retirement. A framework for the analysis and a survey of European countries.* Turin: Centre for Research on Pensions and Welfare Policies (CeRP).

Blekesaune, M., and P.E. Solem. 2005. Working conditions and early retirement: A prospective study of retirement behavior. *Research on Aging* 27: 3–30.

Bourne, B. 1982. Effects of aging on work satisfaction, performance and motivation. *Aging and Work* 5: 37–47.

Cameron, M., and C. Waldegrave. 2009. Work, retirement and wellbeing among older New Zealanders. In *Enhancing wellbeing in an ageing society*, ed. P. Koopman-Boyden and C. Waldegrave, 67–81. Hamilton/Lower Hutt: Family Centre Social Policy Research Unit, University of Waikato.

Carers UK and the University of Leeds. 2011. Valuing carers 2011: Calculating the value of carers' support. CIRCLE. http://circle.leeds.ac.uk/files/2012/08/110512-circle-carers-uk-valuing-carers.pdf. Accessed 19 Feb 2017.

Choi, S., J. Leiter, and D. Tomaskovic-Devey. 2008. Contingent autonomy technology, bureaucracy, and relative power in the labor process. *Work and Occupations* 35: 422–455.

Cooke, G.B., J. Donaghey, and I.U. Zeytinoglu. 2013. The nuanced nature of work quality: Evidence from rural Newfoundland and Ireland. *Human Relations* 66: 503–528.

DeLong, D. 2004. *Lost knowledge: Confronting the threat of an aging workforce.* New York: Oxford University Press.

Department for Work and Pensions (DWP). 2005. *Opportunity age-meeting the challenges of ageing in the 21st century.* Norwich: The Stationery Office.

———. 2012a. The work programme. https://www.gov.uk/government/uploads/system/uploads/attachment_data/file/49884/the-work-programme.pdf. Accessed 19 Feb 2017.

———. 2012b. Age positive: Managing without a fixed retirement age. http://www.dwp.gov.uk/policy/ageing-society/managing-without-fixed-retirement/. Accessed 19 Feb 2017.

Drinkwater, S. 2015. Informal caring and labour markets outcomes within England and Wales. *Regional Studies* 49: 273–286.

European Commission. 2003. *Adequate and sustainable pensions.* Luxembourg: Publications Office.

Fagan, C., C. Lyonette, M. Smith, and A. Saldaña-Tejeda. 2012. *The influence of working time arrangements on work-life integration or 'balance': A review of the international evidence*, Conditions of work and employment No. 32. Geneva: International Labour Organisation.

Felstead, A. 2010. Closing the age gap? Age, skills and the experience of work in Great Britain. *Ageing and Society* 30: 1293–1314.

Figart, D. 2001. Wage-setting under Fordism: The rise of job evaluation and the ideology of equal pay. *Review of Political Economy* 13: 405–425.

Foster, R. 2013. Household satellite accounts – Valuing voluntary activity in the UK. http://www.ons.gov.uk/ons/dcp171766_345918.pdf. Accessed 19 Feb 2017.

Friedberg, L. 2003. The impact of technological change on older workers: Evidence from data on computer usage. *Industrial and Labor Relations Review* 56: 511–529.

Friedman, G. 2014. Workers without employers: Shadow corporations and the rise of the gig economy. *Review of Keynesian Economics* 4: 171–188.

Gov.uk. 2013. Equality Act 2010 guidance. https://www.gov.uk/guidance/equality-act-2010-guidance#age-discrimination. Accessed 19 Feb 2017.

———. 2014. Pensions Act 2014. https://www.gov.uk/government/collections/pensions-bill. Accessed 19 Feb 2017.

Green, F. 2006. *Demanding work. The paradox of job quality in the affluent society.* Princeton: Princeton University Press.

Gregory, A., and S. Milner. 2009. Trade unions and work-life balance: Changing times in France and the UK? *British Journal of Industrial Relations* 47: 122–146.

Gustman, A., and T.L. Steinmeier. 1984a. Modelling the retirement process for policy evaluation and research. *Monthly Labor Review* 107: 26–33.

Gustman, A., and T.L. Steinmeier. 1984b. Partial retirement and the analysis of retirement behavior. *Industrial and Labor Relations Review* 37: 403–415.

Hardill, I., and D. Wheatley. 2017. Care and volunteering: The feel good Samaritan? In *Time well spent: Subjective well-being and the work-life balance,* ed. D. Wheatley. London: Rowman and Littlefield International.

Hedge, J.W., W.C. Borman, and S.E. Lammlein. 2006. *The aging workforce: Realities, myths, and implications for organisations.* Washington, DC: American Psychological Association.

Hennekam, S., and O. Herrbach. 2015. The influence of age-awareness versus general HRM practices on the retirement decision of older workers. *Personnel Review* 44: 3–21.

Holman, D. 2013. Job types and job quality in Europe. *Human Relations* 66: 475–502.

Humphrey, A., P. Costigan, K. Pickering, N. Stratford, and M. Barnes. 2003. *Factors affecting the labour market participation of older workers,* Research Report No 200. London: Department of Work and Pensions.

Hutchens, R. 2003. *The Cornell study of employer phased retirement policies: A report on key findings.* Ithaca: School of Industrial and Labor Relations, Cornell University.

————. 2010. Worker characteristics, job characteristics, and opportunities for phased retirement. *Labour Economics* 17: 1010–1021.

Hutchens, R., and K. Grace-Martin. 2006. Willingness to permit phased retirement: Why are some more willing than others? *Industrial and Labor Relations Review* 59: 525–546.

Kalleberg, A.L. 2012. Job quality and precarious work: Clarifications, controversies, and challenges. *Work and Occupations* 39: 427–448.

Karasek, R.A., and T. Theorell. 1990. *Healthy work: Stress, productivity, and the reconstruction of working life*. New York: Basic Books.

Katz, S. 2002. Growing older without ageing? Positive ageing, anti-ageism, and anti-ageing. *Generations* 25: 27–32.

Kooij, D., A. deLange, P. Jansen, and J. Dikkers. 2008. Older workers' motivation to continue to work: Five meanings of age, a conceptual review. *Journal of Managerial Psychology* 23: 364–394.

Laczko, F., and C. Phillipson. 1991. Great Britain: The contradictions of early exit. In *Time for retirement: Comparative studies of early exit from the labor force*, ed. M. Kohli, M. Rein, A. Guillemard, and H. van Gunsteren, 222–251. Cambridge: Cambridge University Press.

Latulippe, D., and J. Turner. 2000. Partial retirement and pension policy in industrialized countries. *International Labour Review* 139: 179–195.

Levy, M. 2011. Knowledge retention: Minimizing organisational business loss. *Journal of Knowledge Management* 15: 582–600.

Loretto, W., and P. White. 2006. Employers' attitudes, practices and policies towards older workers. *Human Resource Management Journal* 16: 36–53.

Montizaan, R., F. Cörvers, and A. de Grip. 2013. Training and retirement patterns. *Applied Economics* 45: 1991–1999.

Ng, Thomas W.H., and Daniel C. Feldman. 2012. Evaluating six common stereotypes about older workers with meta-analytical data. *Personnel Psychology* 65 (4): 821–858.

NOMIS. 2013. Annual population survey: Economic activity and unemployment rates, October 2011–September 2012. Office for National Statistics (ONS). http://www.nomisweb.co.uk. Accessed 12 Jan 2017.

————. 2016a. Mid-year population estimates, 2015. http://www.nomisweb.co.uk. Accessed 12 Jan 2017.

————. 2016b. Annual population survey 2015: Economic activity and unemployment rates. http://www.nomisweb.co.uk. Accessed 12 Jan 2017.

Norušis, M. 2012. *IBM SPSS statistics 19 statistical procedures companion*. Upper Saddle River: Prentice Hall.

OECD. 2006. *Live longer, work longer*. Paris: OECD Publishing.

———. 2013. All in it together? The experience of different labour market groups following the crisis. In *Employment outlook 2013*. http://dx.doi.org/10.1787/empl_outlook-2013-en. Accessed 27 Oct 2016.

Office for National Statistics (ONS). 2015a. *Quarterly labour force survey*, January–March, 2015, statistical bulletin. https://doi.org/10.5255/UKDA-SN-7725-1. Accessed 27 Oct 2016.

Office for National Statistics (ONS). 2015b. National population projections: 2014-based, statistical bulletin. http://www.ons.gov.uk/peoplepopulationand-community/populationandmigration/populationprojections/bulletins/national-populationprojections/2015-10-29. Accessed 7 Nov 2016.

Office for National Statistics (ONS). 2016. *Table A05 NSA: Employment, unemployment and economic activity by age group (not seasonally adjusted)*. https://www.ons.gov.uk/employmentandlabourmarket/peopleinwork/employmentandemployeetypes/datasets/employmentunemploymentandeconomicinactivitybyagegroupnotseasonallyadjusteda05nsa. Accessed 27 Oct 2016.

Phillipson, C., and A. Smith. 2006. *Extending working life: A review of the research literature*. Research report 299. London: Department of Work and Pensions.

Posthuma, R.A., and M.A. Campion. 2009. Age stereotypes in the workplace: Common stereotypes, moderators, and future research directions. *Journal of Management* 35: 158–188.

Radl, J. 2012. Too old to work, or too young to retire? The pervasiveness of age norms in Western Europe. *Work, Employment and Society* 26: 755–771.

Schnalzenberger, M., N. Schneeweis, R. Winter-Ebmer, and M. Zweimüller. 2014. Job quality and employment of older people in Europe. *Labour* 28: 141–162.

Schwingel, A., M. Niti, C. Tang, and T.P. Ng. 2009. Continued work employment and volunteerism and mental well-being of older adults: Singapore longitudinal ageing studies. *Age and Ageing* 38: 531–537.

Shultz, K.S. 2003. Bridge employment: Work after retirement. In *Retirement: Reasons processes, and results*, ed. G.A. Adams and A. Beehr, 214–241. New York: Springer.

Siegrist, J., M. Wahrendorf, O. von dem Knesebeck, H. Jürges, and A. Börsch-Supan. 2006. Quality of work, well-being, and intended early retirement of older employees – Baseline results from the SHARE Study. *European Journal of Public Health* 17: 62–68.

Smeaton, Deborah, and Michael White. 2016. The growing discontents of older British employees: Extended working life at risk from quality of working life. *Social Policy and Society* 15 (03): 369–385.

Taylor, F. 1967. *The principles of scientific management*. London: Norton.

Tempest, S., and C. Coupland. 2016. Lost in time and space: Temporal and spatial challenges facing older workers in a global economy from a career capital perspective. *The International Journal of Human Resource Management.* https://doi.org/10.1080/09585192.2015.1128455.

The Work Foundation. 2016. In search of the gig economy. http://www.theworkfoundation.com/wp-content/uploads/2016/11/407_In-search-of-the-gig-economy_June2016.pdf. Accessed 12 Jan 2017.

Trade Union Congress (TUC). 2014. More than two in five new jobs created since mid-2010 have been self-employed. https://www.tuc.org.uk/economic-issues/economic-analysis/labour-market/labour-market-and-economic-reports/more-two-five-new. Accessed 15 Nov 2016.

Understanding Society. 2014. *Understanding society insights 2014.* https://www.understandingsociety.ac.uk/d/140/Insights_-_2014.pdf?1414660258. Accessed 15 Nov 2016.

University of Essex. 2015. Institute for Social and Economic Research and NatCen Social Research, Understanding Society: Waves 1–5, 2009–2014. Colchester: UK Data Archive. SN: 6614. http://dx.doi.org/10.5255/UKDA-SN-6614-7

Walker, T. 2007. Why economists dislike a lump of labor. *Review of Social Economy* 65: 279–291.

Warr, P. 2000. Job performance and the ageing workforce. In *Introduction to work and organisational psychology: A European perspective*, ed. N. Chmiel, 407–423. Oxford: Blackwell.

Wellard, S. 2011. Doing it all? Grandparents, childcare and employment: An analysis of British social attitudes survey data from 1998 and 2009. http://www.grandparentsplus.org.uk/wp-content/uploads/2011/03/Doing-it-all__Online.pdf. Accessed 15 Nov 2016.

Wheatley, D. 2017. Work-time, the quality of work and well-being. In *Time well spent: Subjective well-being and the work-life balance*, ed. D. Wheatley. London: Rowman and Littlefield International.

Wilson, R., N. Sofroniou, R. Beaven, M. May-Gillings, S. Perkins, M. Lee, P. Glover, H. Limmer, and A. Leach. 2016. *Working futures 2014–2020, evidence report 100.* The UK Commission for Employment and Skills. London: UKCES.

Zissimopoulos, J.M., and L.A. Karoly. 2007. Transitions to self-employment at older ages: The role of wealth, health, health insurance and other factors. *Labour Economics* 14: 269–295.

6

Flexible Working: Are We Ready for This?

Ning Wu

6.1 Introduction

Flexible working is a way of working that suits an employee's needs (ACAS 2014). Formal flexible working arrangements comprise work patterns that focus on arrangement of work time (flexi-time, shift work, compressed hours), reducing work time (job share, part-time working, term-time work) and location (homeworking, mobile working) (ACAS 2015). Such arrangements extend the statutory right of requesting flexible working arrangements to any individual who has been continuously employed for a period of at least 26 weeks and wishes to improve their work-life balance by working flexibly, as stated in the Flexible Working Regulations 2014 in Britain. This shift-away from an early focus mainly on parents or carers who have childcare or adult care responsibilities (Lewis 2001),

N. Wu (✉)
Department of Human Resource Management, Nottingham Business School,
Nottingham Trent University, Nottingham, UK

© The Author(s) 2018   **127**
V. Caven, S. Nachmias (eds.), *Hidden Inequalities in the Workplace*,
Palgrave Explorations in Workplace Stigma,
DOI 10.1007/978-3-319-59686-0_6

as declared in Employment Rights Act 1996, undoubtedly indicates that flexibility management starts to become embedded into a broader diversity management agenda through equal opportunity (Kossek et al. 2010).

While it is laudable to see the increasingly widespread work flexibility across workplaces in countries such as Britain and the USA, prior studies nevertheless show that the presence of such policies and practices addressing work-life balance on paper does not mean workers have actually been comfortably using various work patterns to optimally benefit their experience between these two spheres (Blair-Loy et al. 2011). This could, in part, explain the mismatch between the equality that flexibility agenda sets out and biases stemmed from how flexibility is actually implemented in workplaces. In Britain, for example, 9% of employees actually worked in 'reduced hours' in 2011, while 56% of workplaces say they had such policy in place (Van Wanrooy et al. 2013). A similar picture is mirrored in the USA where, for example, 79% of companies claim they allow some of their employees to access their flexible working programmes, but only 11% of the full-time workers had a formal agreement with their employers to change their work hours (Williams et al. 2013). The proportion of employees who were using or had used flexible work policies is nonetheless generally low; the ratio of an overall usage rounds up to 26% when different flexibilities are considered together (Blair-Loy and Wharton 2002). The significantly low rates of the actual usage among employees compared to the proportion of workplaces with such policies or practices in place appear to suggest: (a) employees' fear of negative career repercussions for using such policies or practices hinders a much wider use among the labour force (Blair-Loy and Wharton 2002); (b) access to the flexible work programmes is restricted to specific group of employees, in particular those prestigious groups that have already been advantageous as a result of prior policies or special treatments, which is often related to their occupation or class status (Williams et al. 2013).

Although the overall adoption of flexible working practices has become much more widespread than before, a nationally representative study in Britain, Workplace Employment Relations Survey (WERS), reports that the changing patterns vary greatly among these flexibility arrangements (Van Wanrooy et al. 2013). While the proportion of workplaces where some employees were able to work from home or work compressed hours increased from 26% and 11% in 2004 to 30% and 19% in 2011 respectively, the proportion of workplaces with job sharing or reduced hours fell from 25% and 62% in 2004 to 17% and 55% in 2011 separately. Only the proportion of workplaces with flexi-time remains largely unchanged between 2004 (35%) and 2011 (34%). Compared with the proportion of workplaces adopting management practices such as employee training, team briefing, employee consultation, performance appraisals, which were all above 80% between 2004 and 2011, the usage rate of the most popular work pattern, namely reduced hours, is apparently low. There could be some resilient problems that have been long established, developed and redeveloped in employment relations that hinder the prevalence of flexibility. A compelling explanation suggests that the flexibility agenda violates the ideal worker norms that emphasise work devotion (Blair-Loy 2003), whilst request for flexible schedule signals caregiving responsibilities impinge on his/her job (Allen 2001; Coltrane et al. 2013). Hence, individuals engaging flexibility are viewed as incompetent, low commitment, unprofessional and thus disposable labour who are likely to face career penalties (Epstein et al. 1999; Kalleberg et al. 2000). Beyond the flexibility stigma associated with ideal worker stereotypes, there are other reasons that can explain such slow and uneven changes in the direction of flexibility. These are concerned with gender stereotypes, class status, social and economic penalties, and family status when it comes to who needs such changes, who have access to such benefits, and what are the consequences of using such work patterns. Directly or indirectly, these reasons all point to variable 'hidden' inequalities in the way of how flexibility is actually implemented in workplaces. The following sections are dedicated to each of these factors and discuss the extent to which engaging flexibility results in unequal treatment.

6.2   Gender Stereotypes

Various flexible working arrangements are practised and researched from different national contexts. Institutional factors are among the most researched areas with respect to the prevalence of such practice at workplaces. Government regulation and legislation over workplace flexibility is one of such factors that has shown a significant impact on such use (Kossek et al. 2010; Lewis 2001). In the USA, there is not yet any comprehensive national scheme addressing flexible working arrangements. Flexible working arrangements in workplaces are mainly driven by business necessity and legal compliance with policies against gender discrimination. Although not directly referring to flexible working arrangements, any negative employment actions taken on the basis of gender stereotypes are deemed illegal under existing federal antidiscrimination law (Title VII of the Civil Rights Act of 1964) (Bornstein 2013). With more women joining the labour force at higher rates, the stereotype of women being the caretakers has been changing when women are increasingly playing the role of breadwinners in household (Vandello et al. 2013).

However, it has long been established that the meaning of work and the importance of employment for men and women are different in respect of gender identity (Prentice and Carranza 2002). While feminine identity stresses a caretaker role, masculine identity views breadwinning as a central role (Pleck 1995; Thébaud 2010). This gender stereotype attached to identity has not changed much since female workers started to enter the labour force (Brescoll et al. 2013). Hence much of the debate on flexible working is from the perspectives of women, addressing the importance of accommodating women's family responsibilities in work plans so that happy workers with high performance can be mutually achieved. Within the increasingly popular field of work-life balance study, scholars consistently challenge the structure of contemporary organisations that build around the myth of an ideal worker who is expected to offer unlimited availability to work with no family conflicts (Blair-Loy 2003). The ideal worker norm also helps the organisation of production and reproduction that shape gender relations between ideal men and women (Mintz and Kellog 1988). Indeed, changes in men's domestic activities have been much slower compared to huge transformation in labour force as a result of fast increase of women's participation rates (Vandello et al. 2013). However, profound shifts in the ways of how housework and child care are divided in contemporary families simply suggest that men engage more in family responsibilities and the time, for example, American men spend on housework and child care, between 1965 and 2003, doubled (Bianchi et al. 2006).

In stark contrast with the gendered nature of flexible working primarily emphasising women's dual roles between work and family spheres, there is limited research challenging a gender bias towards men at work who also have a role in family care but reluctant to apply for flexibility at work at all (Coltrane et al. 2013). Reluctance can be reflected via the low rate of men's participation in such schemes compared to women. It could be argued that flexible working was initially designed to support women whose disproportionate domestic role dwarfs the significance of a similar role men can actually play, and thus flexible working continues to be considered to be a women's issue (Atkinson and Hall 2009). Gender congruence theories further the perception that women who take time off are conforming to gender expectations at home whereas men actually engage with counter-normative behaviours (Wayne and Cordiero 2003). Building upon backlash literature, any request for flexible schedules from a man who cites family responsibilities as the reason would be deemed as unmanly (Brescoll 2011; Vandello et al. 2013; Coltrane et al. 2013). Consequently, men taking time off from work for family reasons will confront greater degree of stigmatisation than women because this is against gender norms (Allen and Russell 1999; Brescoll et al. 2011). The ideal worker image, as discussed above, further reinforces the gender stereotype in the division of labour of a man's role at work. Emerging research starts to challenge the moral equality underpinning flexible working arrangements when fathers are disadvantaged in adopting paternal leave to share childcare at home (Coltrane et al. 2013).

Despite research showing individual and organisational benefits from flexible working arrangements, these arrangements are still under-used especially by men (Vandello et al. 2013). In addition to flexibility stigma stemmed from gender-incongruent behaviours, the low take-up of flexibility among men, in part, is resultant from employers and co-workers' negative attitudes towards work flexibility such as paternity leave, and thus viewing men who take advantage of such policies as unmasculine (Pleck 1993). Reducing work time to accommodate family obligations, men could be subject to stereotyping and negative judgements about their character and potentially be seen as 'not serious' about their work (Rudman and Mescher 2013; Vandello et al. 2013). Notwithstanding a high agreement in valuing work flexibility and work-life balance, men were significantly less likely than women to report intentions to actually 'ask' for such flexibility in their future employment. This suggests what men most value deep in their heart may well clash with their perceived external expectations (Vandello et al. 2013). Men are likely to suppress their intention to make a request for flexible working arrangement if they perceive such an 'ask' would erode their masculine identity, in particular for those who work in an organisation that has unwritten norms against men engaging work flexibility (Pleck 1993). Contrastingly, viewing work flexibility would enhance feminine prescriptive attributes, women were more likely to express their intention to request work flexibility.

It is worth noting that neither the under-utilisation of flexible working scheme nor the suppressed intention to apply for such work patterns among men should be viewed as men being less likely to have work-life conflicts as women do (Hyde et al. 1993) or lack interests in greater childcare or taking on house work (Hood 1993). Early research of fathers' work-life conflicts suggests there is no significant gender difference in the strength of such conflicts (Frone et al. 1992). In circumstances that they do need flexible schedules, the main difference between working fathers and working mothers is that fathers are much less likely than mothers to admit that their need is family related (Gerson 1985). It is evidenced that men often request flexibility due to career development reasons while women request due to family reasons (Coltrane et al. 2013; Galinsky et al. 1996). Gender conformity theories provide reasonable explanation for the reluctance of such usage, particularly among men. Using a global corporate sample of working fathers from 48 countries (N = 7692), for example, Hill et al. (2003) compared working fathers to working mothers and found that fathers had less family-to-work conflict than mothers, but equal amounts of work-to-family conflict. This seems to suggest fathers struggled as much as mothers to minimise negative spill-overs from work to family. To cope with work-to-family conflict, fathers tended to choose options that provided flexibility in when and where work was done (Hill et al. 2003) albeit the overall use of flexibility arrangements among men at work, such as paternity leave and reduced hours, was rarer compared to mothers. The avoidance of engaging more flexible work patterns that are perceived to derogate masculine traits simply lends support to gender congruence theories mainstreamed in gender discrimination literature.

6.3   Class Status

While mainstream studies of gendered organisations stress the important role gender stereotyping plays in understanding 'hidden' inequalities associated with employees' requests for flexible schedules, recent research suggests that there is significantly unequal distribution of flexible working arrangements among the workforce when individuals' class status within an organisation is under consideration (Coltrane et al. 2013). It has been widely acknowledged that, within organisations that provide flexible working options, access to flexible scheduling is by no means universal across occupational spectrum (Osterman 1995). Flexible schedules are reported to be more commonly available to workers in high-status positions of authority and in managerial and professional job categories (Glass and Fujimoto 1995; Golden 2001), and mostly support the needs of middle- to upper-class parents (Williams 2010). While typically useful to upper-tier salaried workers, flexibility often works against part-time or hourly paid employees (Lambert 2009). In general, low-wage jobs provide no flexibility; low-status women in particular have no access to flexibility (Dodson 2013). It is therefore clear that rather than viewing class status as a stand-alone factor that predicts inequalities associated with the practice of flexibility, the work-life balance scholarship acknowledges the importance and complication captured by the gendered flexibility scheme when class status interacts with gender difference.

In Britain, an analysis of Labour Force Survey in the UK suggests that about 90% of teleworkers are managers, professionals, associate professionals or skilled workers (Blyton 2010). In the USA, professionals in larger organisations and in the public sector have more access to work-family benefits than other workers (Secret 2000). The privilege enjoyed by the already powerful social groups allows them to access variable flexibility to improve work-life balance. Like many other fringe benefits, flexible working arrangements are often found in high-performance organisations that employ large proportions of professional and technical workers (Deitch and Huffman 2001). Consequently, these power groups accrue further benefits to strengthen their advantage and thus further exacerbate existing hierarchies of seniority and social class. The development of the vicious cycle polarises individuals' experience in flexibility arrangements and reinforces the degree of inequalities associated with such practice. For example, homeworking is often related to 'highly qualified white collar workers with high autonomy and where knowledge is a significant value-added aspect of their job' (Tregaskis 2000, p. 14). The correlation between remote working and occupational status has also been widely evidenced in extant literature (Felstead et al. 2002; Ruiz and Walling 2005), reflecting strong bargaining power among key workers and managers (Clear and Dickson, 2005, p. 230), which advances the privilege they have already enjoyed and exacerbates the divide between the power groups and the powerless groups with regard to accessing new ways of working.

The manifest inequalities associated with the privilege individuals of high-class status have compared to their counterparts become more complex when gender is also included in the equation, that is, high-status men are compared with high-status women in workplaces. Although men in high-status roles are more privileged than their female counterparts and less likely to be accorded with flexibility stigma or workplace penalties, they are more likely to encounter resistance for request due to family caregiving than career development reasons (Brescoll et al. 2013). This is because managers tend to view men in high status more competitive than women in similar positions (Eagly and Steffan 1984). Using career development as the reason for flexible scheduling, high-status men would be more likely to gather respect and support than high-status women doing the same. Hence, requesting flexibility for career progression, high-status men reinforce a gender hierarchy in gendered organisations—an advantage men already have in their initial status and greater power compared to women, whereas women are more likely to be granted flexibility for family care than career development regardless of their class status since they start performing gender-congruent behaviours when they engage flexibility due to family care responsibilities (Brescoll et al. 2013). Deprived of an equal opportunity to obtain additional training and skill development, high-status women would eventually lose their battle for fair treatment in seeking organisation's support to advance their career or enhance their class status.

6.4 Social and Economic Penalties

The 'hidden' inequality and its manifestation through workplace penalties lead to bias avoidance (Drago et al. 2006) regardless of gender or social status difference; that is, individuals suppress their intention to request flexibility to avoid potential social and/or economic penalties resulting from the use of flexible working arrangements. Professionals, men or women, were found to either hide their attempts to work part-time or flexibly to avoid discrimination or negative character judgement at workplaces (Stone and Hernandez 2013) or simply to quit their current jobs (Bornstein 2013). Inequalities associated with negative impact on an individual's work experience as a result of using flexible working arrangements can be reflected in three ways: first, work-related penalties; second, interpersonal and character stigma; and third, add-up effect on co-workers.

The so-called gender gap in the average wages of employed women and men (Budig and England 2001) starts to narrow when mothers and married women without children are compared with similarly situated men. Arguably, the reduction in the gender gap is due to women more and more acting like men and adopting more masculine attributes (Maupin and Lehman 1994). Nonetheless, the gap tends to be greater when women with children are compared to men with equivalent qualifications, with the former earning only roughly one half as much as the latter (Glass 2004). The gap has been explained as mothers' decision to reduce working hours or experience more frequent career interruptions to accommodate child bearing and child care (Williams et al. 2013). The wage penalty of mothers' first child and later children is placed at 7% per child (Budig and England 2001). These work flexibility and career interruptions certainly violate the ideal worker norm traditionally ingrained in a masculine workforce. In a study of managerial and professional women workers, the number of months spent working from home or working fewer than 30 hours per week showed a large and consistent negative impact on wages (Glass 2004). Wage penalties are also found to be associated with other specific type of flexible work: reduced hours or 'part-time' work (Budig and England 2001; Stone 2007).

For most employers, women taking on flexible schedules have the least instant availability when a crisis situation occurs, thereby any negative experience associated with flexible working arrangements is likely to be overly generalised and would inform managers' decision to train or promote those employees who never used flexible working arrangements (Fried 1998; Hochschild 1997). Similar to gender stereotype theories that men's engagement with flexible schedules is deemed as gender-incongruent behaviour and unprofessional, research examining both men and women taking on flexible schedules shows that men suffer similar pattern of wage penalties as women in the same situation (Blair-Loy and Wharton 2004). This again confirms the norms that contemporary organisations only prize single-minded commitment and a work-devoted identity (Blair-Loy 2003).

Participation in flexible work arrangement programmes is also found to be career damaging. A study of 107 seniors and managers of one multinational accounting firm in the USA indicates that individuals using flexible work arrangements were perceived as not pulling their weights and thus less likely to advance to partnership, compared to those not participating in flexible work arrangements (Cohen and Single 2001). Poor performance evaluations were also reported among managers and professionals who used organisational flexible working arrangements (Wharton et al. 2008). The work devotion framework would render managers engaging flexible work schedules as a deficit of work devotion. Since a single-minded professional identity is embedded in organisational *practices of evaluation, compensation, and advancement* (Blair-Loy 2003, p. 21), the traditional design of organisation structure optimises performance assessment based on visibility, close monitor and tight control. It is therefore not surprising when managers who have used flexible working arrangements are rated low in relation to performance.

Flexibility stigma associated with career progression is equally evidenced between women and men who ever took advantage of employers' policy of flexible working arrangements. Both male and female employees who requested part-time work after child birth were less likely to be recommended for promotion, leadership roles or a pay raise (Vandello et al. 2013). Caregiving men were therefore penalised for violating gender stereotypes of masculinity and breadwinner role while caregiving women are viewed as uncommitted and incompetent (Coltrane et al. 2013). Managers tended to give poor performance ratings and low reward recommendations (quarterly bonuses) to male workers who engaged flexibility for family caring responsibilities compared to men who did not experience such conflict (Butler and Skattebo 2004), whereas women's ratings were unaffected regardless of any work-family conflicts. Similarly, men who took a six-month parental leave of absence were less likely to be recommended for organisational rewards than men who did not engage such flexibility (Allen and Russell 1999). Not only individuals who engage in gender-atypical behaviours tend to experience social and economic penalties (Coltrane et al. 2013; Vandello et al. 2013), but men who cite family responsibilities as the reason why they want flexible work arrangements were less likely to have their request granted either due to their engagement in gender-unconformist behaviours (Brescoll and Uhlmann 2005).

Accommodating various flexible work modes does not only pose challenge to traditional management practices based on face-to-face supervision, but also potential unequal treatment between flexible working user group and non-user group as a result of different approaches to managing these two groups of workforce. Consistent with equity concerns, an apparent approach to managing employees on different work modes would be to treat them the same regardless of whether they are on a flexible work pattern or not (Dimitrova 2003). A study of teleworking management suggests the adoption of teleworking may indicate variable supervision practices and could lead to inequitable treatment, in particular between the teleworking and non-teleworking workers. A supervisor's behaviour that benefits telecommuters may harm non-telecommuters and trigger resentment from non-telecommuters (Collins 2005; Lautsch et al. 2009). For example, a supervisor's style favouring a separation of work and life for telecommuters in order to reduce their work-life conflict and improve their productivity also reduces telecommuters' helping behaviours towards their co-workers and thus intensifies non-telecommuters' work-life conflicts (Lautsch et al. 2009). Non-telecommuters tend to attribute any workload increase in office to telecommuters not working hard enough and question the privileges telecommuters are given. This raises issues of equity and justice between organisational members seeking particular 'benefits' through accessing specific work patterns and those who do not but whose work adds up because of the former.

Despite increasing debate on equity concerns over flexible working arrangements designed to improve individuals' work and life balance, unexpected co-worker backlash against flexible working innovations is evident in day-to-day management. Compared to the social and economic penalties flexible work users reportedly confront, the extent to which non-flexible work users are disadvantaged in front of those practices is still under-studied.

6.5   Family Status

Childless workers' entitlement for requesting flexible work modes has only recently been recognised since the issue of Flexible Working Regulation 2014 in Britain. This suggests that flexible working arrangements are no longer a privilege for parents with young children. Indeed, workplace demands more agility than ever since technology continues to blur the boundary between work and home. Hence employers need to open up their business mindset to adopt flexible working and attract a much bigger talent pool of qualified people who either cannot or choose not to work traditional hours. This is particularly the work pattern that most millennials view their jobs. As a generation, millennial typically refers to those who were born between 1982 and 2000 (DeFraine et al. 2014), and forms the largest age group since the baby boom generation who are predicted to comprise 75% of the global workforce by 2025 (Deloitte 2014). This generation differs from their previous generations in attitudes, values, preferences about the nature of the workplace and particularly, the optimal level of work-life balance (Deal et al. 2010; Twenge 2010). They view flexible working as a way of working that empowers individuals to choose where to work and when can be the most productive to work (Hope 2016). The millennial generation rejects the nine-to-five working model and they prefer *intertwined professional and personal lives within collaborative and flexible work environments* (DeFraine et al. 2014, p. 2).

Interestingly, the group that talks most about work-life balance today is childless people in their 20s (Twenge and Campbell 2009). Many believed this would be the driving force behind future legislative change very soon (Hope 2016).

An urge for broadening the access to flexible working benefits to every employee, in particular single adults without children, resides in a demographic change in global labour force. While the USA has been alerted that they are on the verge of becoming a nation of singletons (Conlin 2003; DePaulo 2006), the proportion of singles (47%) appears to outweigh married people (40%) in Britain (Office for National Statistics 2010). A more disproportionate demographic map depicts the Swedish labour force, with singles accounting for 61% and the childless singles accounting for 51% of the nation's households (Korsell 2008). Given a significant proportion of today's labour force comprising of groups such as singles or couples without children, it is critical to assess the perceptions of different treatment among the work force.

Complaints against employers for unfair treatment from childless employees have increased in the past two decades. Consistent with traditional family norms (i.e. married couples with 1.4 children), caring centres upon the work-family focus and so do the family friendly programmes in workplaces (Eikhof et al. 2007). Single adults without dependent children are '*less socially valued than those of married people or people with children*' (Young 1996, pp. 208–209) and their needs are different from those of traditional family employees (Casper et al. 2007). Having been perceived to have fewer responsibilities and more time available (Reilly 1996), childless single adults are expected to be flexible to work in unsocial hours, work on weekends and holidays, and cover for co-workers when childcare issues arise (Young 1996). Hence the childless often feel being taken for granted by employers and exploited by married and childrearing co-workers (Wells 2007). Perceived inequities are reported between employees with children and those without when it comes to the question whose work-life balance should be prioritised. For example, '*people with children have too many options or benefits compared to employees without children*' (Hewlett and Vite-León 2002, p. 9).

6.6   Methodological Considerations

Critiques about studies relying upon work-life balance policies and practices reported by managers have witnessed increasing number of research adopting a research design focusing on employees' experience in utilising such practices (Dex and Scheibl 2001). This is particularly the case for studies of inequalities associated with the operation of flexible working arrangements, either those who have ever engaged with such workplace amenities, or those who were co-workers but have never used these themselves. Researching the actual use of various work arrangements appears to become the mainstream approach to revealing a fragmented application of work-life balance ideology in workplaces and identifying barriers that prohibit either an individual or a business entity from achieving equity when accommodating employees' needs between their work and life.

Existing research of unequal treatment and discriminations against individuals' request for flexible working arrangements draws their data from various sources, arguably a majority of which has an Anglo-Saxon origin. Often constrained by small samples, researchers reported their concerns about the homogeneity in their small-sized data collection irrespective of their sample's geographical diversity (Stone and Hernandez 2013). Analysing about 50 college-educated upper middle class married mothers (consisting primarily of white non-Hispanic women) in the USA who had experience in professional or executive roles, for example, Stone and Hernandez (2013) acknowledged the limitation of any attempt to generalise the findings and cautioned over applying such findings to other ethnicity groups and suggested even married mothers in low-ranked jobs would reveal aspects of inequalities different from high-status women.

There is also an emergent call for research design to accurately reflect the fast-changing structure in global labour force. Much of the existing literature is predominantly published with data collected from a questionnaire ingrained with gender stereotype, class status inequalities and parenthood bias. Coltrane et al. (2013) used large sample surveys, National Longitudinal Survey of Youth (NLSY) in the USA, with data from multiple years and investigated reasons for individuals' current employment status or for changes in their work mode. Driven by understanding whether such changes fall into different patterns between women and men, researchers found the national surveys do not have questions asking men about their share of housework or caring responsibilities. The NLSY began in 1979 when 12,686 respondents between the ages of 14 and 21 were surveyed, with follow-up surveys once every year till 1994 and subsequently every other year. When constructing their own panel data, Coltrane et al. (2013) found that *'norms of male breadwinning are so pervasive that even this comprehensive survey is biased in that child care and parenting questions were often only addressed to women'* (p. 284). This undoubtedly compromised their research design and eventually rendered restricting their analysis to only five years of the NLSY survey data (namely, 1984, 1988, 1994, 1998 and 2006) since these are the only years with questions asking men to specify reasons for modifying work behaviours. Since men are increasingly recognised for their participation in a wide range of family-related behaviours, the sample size of men needs to be expanded to reflect such a change as well. This equally applies to the millennial generation in relation to the challenges employers face in relation to work-life balance policies and flexible work arrangements in workplaces (DeFraine et al. 2014; Hope 2016). To capture factors that explain inequalities in practising work flexibility, future studies in particular those adopting a longitudinal design need to ensure full information about men's family commitments and caring obligations, as well as the work and life behaviours of the single and childless employees. Currently, most work-life balance research still primarily collects full labour force and employment scheduling information from employed women. As new flexible working regulations in particular in Britain embrace not only gender-neutral assumptions about men and women as workers, but also parenthood-neutral assumptions about workers with or without dependent children, research instruments should enable us to ask more questions about men's parenting, the childless work-life balance in order to assess whether individuals are discriminated against gender, class location or family status in the workplace.

Given that a fast-growing number of organisations are starting to embed their diversity management strategy within a broader equal opportunity management agenda, the lack of appropriate data reflecting an increasingly diverse workforce can cause further 'hidden' inequality in the workplace. Predominantly focusing on gender stereotypes, class location and family status, this chapter's review of extant studies on the practice of flexible working reveals the reality of unequal treatment individuals experienced under various organisational management strategies targeting enhanced work-life quality for individual employees. Other areas in diversity management, relatively under-researched, such as age, ethnicity, religion and sex orientation equally deserve academic attention. Future research in these areas could provide more insights into the extent to which inequalities might have been 'hidden' underneath the gloss of equal opportunity policies alongside the implementation of flexibility at the workplace.

6.7   Findings and Discussion

Research of 'hidden' inequalities associated with flexible working practice has been developing fast particularly in the past two decades. Initially aiming to enable employees with caring responsibilities to achieve a good balance between work and family spheres, the shift of focus to enhance the wellbeing of all employees across various activity spheres undoubtedly challenges the original scope of such practices. The divide between the flexibility user groups and non-user groups has escalated due to new ways of working mainly with target 'disadvantaged' group who have family care responsibilities. In practice, flexibility remains a benefit for certain 'privileged' employees in specific class location or a fashionable way of working restricted to professional occupations. Increasing numbers of research also suggest that single and childless adults are extremely disadvantaged in workplaces exercising flexibility due to the underpinning logic of caring needs mainly, in spite of an ongoing management agenda of embracing diversity across various hierarchical levels. These 'hidden' inequalities pose challenges for contemporary organisations should they wish to harvest from an increasingly diversified workforce.

With respect to who are more likely to make request for flexible working schedules, studies adopting gender stereotype theories accord the differences in engaging such flexibility between men and women to flexibility stigma. Research also indicates men are no less likely than women to face flexibility stigma, albeit the mechanism of stigmatisation differs between genders (Coltrane et al. 2013). While women applying for flexible working are very much acting in conformity with their feminine identity in which caring plays a central role, it nevertheless violates the ideal worker norms that stress single-minded commitment and complete devotion unencumbered by family responsibilities (Blair-Loy 2003). Hence, motherhood often acts as a status characteristic that invokes negative stereotypes about competency, productivity and commitment in the workplace (Correll et al. 2007). Although men report similar level of work-life conflicts as women do (Hill et al. 2003), in spite of their entitlement for working flexibly to maintain a work-life balance, they are much less likely to ask for flexible work. A big hurdle for men to make such requests has been explained as fear of endangering their masculine identity (Coltrane et al. 2013). Men's engagement with flexible working arrangements in particular for family reasons is viewed as gender-incongruent behaviour, unprofessional and not trustworthy (Kossek et al. 2005). Albeit little evidence suggests the use of flexible working is more punishing for men than for women, men tend to face harsher character judgements than women as they are viewed as gender deviants (Vandello et al. 2013). It is therefore clear that, irrespective of the widespread recognition of work-life balance, the low uptake of flexible working arrangements seems to be undermined by employees engaging in bias avoidance (Bornstein 2013).

Inequalities associated with the diffusion of flexible working benefits among different class locations become more complicated when gender stereotype enters the equation. While employees in high-paid roles such as managers and professionals are more likely to access flexible working arrangements, salaried male workers in high-status position are more likely to be granted flexibility in their work schedules to advance their careers (specifically coupled with reasoning consistent with organisational priorities and management goals) than women in similar positions (Brescoll et al. 2013). This advantage may contribute partly to these men's more rapid career advancement relative to women. In contrast, neither women paid on an hourly basis nor those in high-status position would be granted with leeway in their choice of work patterns; in circumstances that women do apply for flexible work patterns, they often end up with withdrawing at some point in the future (Bornstein 2013). High-status women who requested flexibility for the reason of career development might still be viewed as less deserving of the chance to gain further training to advance their career. Inequalities in the practice of flexible working arrangements become more salient when social status interacts with gender. Contrary to a common sense that female-dominated workplaces are more likely to offer flexible schedules, in particular to women, it is the male-dominated occupations where flexibility is more frequently practiced (Glass and Camarigg 1992; Golden 2001). On one hand, this is because women are more likely to be biased by motherhood status in employment decision making with regard to flexible work scheduling, regardless of their high job status or a career development justification. On another hand, female-dominated jobs in retail and clerical settings, and even many professional and semiprofessional jobs such as teacher or social worker, are often structured as support positions or client-focused positions so that scheduling flexibility appears impossible to implement (Williams et al. 2013).

Employees working flexibly also face career penalties, poor character judgements and economic losses. This stream of research appears to suggest the social and economic damages one could face as a result of having actually worked flexibly mainly for family caring are gender neutral (Coltrane et al. 2013). This is in stark contrast to some of the class status literature that high-status men are likely to get promoted faster with high salaries if they have been granted flexible working mode for career development (Eagly and Steffan 1984). These contrasting findings simply suggest that flexibility stigma is always there if changing time schedules deviates from a single-minded hard working commitment norm. Given the foundation that contemporary organisations build upon continuously emphasises work devotion without work-family conflicts, any attempts or interventions aiming to accommodate work-family interactions are likely to be temporal, ad hoc and operated in a piecemeal manner. All in all, inequalities associated with flexible work practice due to class status simply mirror the traditionally masculine job design.

Compared to studies addressing inequalities in the exercise of flexible working programmes in relation to gender, class status, social and economic penalties, the impact of practising flexible working on single and childless employees is under-researched. This is partly because family care dominates early family friendly programmes and therefore only employees with family responsibilities are entitled to such requests. Exclusion of those who are single and childless at early stages of a flexible working exercise has also been explained by the high value many cultures place on marriage and children (Cain 2001; Reilly 1996), whereas the former clearly violates a society's commonly held view in relation to what a 'normal' life should entail (De Janasz et al. 2013). However, the demography of labour force has been changing fast in the past decade and the numbers of the singles and the childless have been increasing dramatically in history ever, in particular younger workers born between 1980 and 2000. These millennials are not motivated by the same factors as their predecessors; they value a good work-life interaction and a sense of purpose beyond financial success (Hope 2016). It is therefore important to develop new inclusive policies and practices to safeguard fair treatment and equal opportunities in workplaces and optimise individuals' work experience regardless of their family status (Ryan and Kossek 2008).

6.8   Conclusion and Implications

Overall, in light of dramatic changes in everyday organisation of time between work and life specifically enabled by technology advancement, it is reasonable to assume that ideal worker norms might change, although the magnitude of such changes is very much dependent upon how much the work devotion norms that contemporary organisations build upon are about to change. Apparently, this conventional view of ideal worker has been increasingly facing challenges. The so-claimed flexibility stigma is rooted in the conceptualisation that family care is a competing interest that absorbs workers' time and energy (Brescoll et al. 2013; Budig and England 2001). While a pessimistic view would assume gender discrimination, class status inequalities and non-parenthood discrimination to persist despite modest policy changes in flexible working arrangements, a more optimistic prediction would see flexibility stigma associated with gender is likely to fade away as labour force starts to be dominated by the millennials who prioritise work-life balance instead of financial success. However, the extent to which contemporary organisations are ready to fully embrace flexibility to accommodate employees' often changeable preferences and negotiate new arrangements is under-researched. While improved job satisfaction (Wheatley in press) as the result of flexible working is reported in workplaces, a few studies nonetheless argue, in addition to administration, supervision and management cost ensued, greater flexibility runs counter to the effective control and rationalisations that contemporary organisations rely upon (Blyton 1985; Todd and Binns 2013). This at least provides part of the explanation behind the slow and uneven implementation of various flexible working arrangements. Employers' resistance has also been manifested through unwritten rules against these new ways of working (Pleck 1993) as well as a lack of formal and transparent procedures of guiding employees to engage in such practices (Todd and Binns 2013).

The findings in this chapter hold important implications for managers and HR practitioners. Perhaps the most obvious implication is that organisations offering flexible working arrangements must recognise and address 'hidden' inequalities and discriminations against those who use them and those whose requests are perceived unlikely to be granted and thus never attempted to ask. New policies aiming to enhance a more widespread take-up of flexible work schedules should recognise bias avoidance associated with flexibility requests and install effective bias control measures (Dobbin and Kelly 2007; Kelly and Kalev 2006) when flexibility policies are introduced; otherwise, their policies risk being under-used. Employers could take measures to ensure greater enforcement of equal opportunity laws that prohibit gender discrimination in accessing work facilities such as flexi-time, work at home, job sharing, reduced work hours and work in compressed hours. At minimum, protecting individuals from retaliatory treatment as a result of requesting schedule flexibility could substantially increase the number of employees, both men and women, in need to ask for variable work modes (Coltrane et al. 2013). Managers can also develop new approaches attuned to the needs of workers in new flexible arrangements, such as increased information sharing, consultation and inclusive management, while at the same time maintain sustainable and equitable inter-group monitoring.

To ensure fair treatment in relation to who have access to what flexible schedules, managers need to develop and install operational rules and procedures around individual work patterns. The diversity of individuals' needs for a balanced work and life interaction also implies close observation and understanding of such needs associated with lifestyle fulfilment. Given considerable social unevenness in the distribution of various flexible working opportunities, procedures and outcomes of applications for flexible work patterns are likely to be influenced by dominant groups in a position, often through informal channels. Since departmental managers and supervisors play key 'gatekeeper' roles in deciding who have the access to specific organisational policies and resources (Poelmans and Beham 2008), it is important to set out clear rules and policies to safeguard the operation of flexible working arrangements and maintain high transparency, consistency and fair treatment.

The implication for HRM study is that flexible working arrangements should no longer be viewed as a human resource tactic at workplaces mainly for a disadvantaged workforce (Kossek et al. 2010). Flexible working may well be another managerial approach that could potentially shape the foundations upon which modern organisations are built (Wood et al. 2003). Beyond the employer-led flexibility mainly addressing operational needs or employee-led flexibility primarily satisfying individual needs specifically those with caring responsibilities ('disadvantaged' workforce) (Gregory and Milner 2009), employers need to explore management initiatives in particular targeting organisational structure and culture change in order to fully embrace the work-life balance value and facilitate its operation across the workforce regardless of differences in ranks, occupations or care responsibilities (Kossek et al. 2010). Changes include flexible working methods linked with the growing use of continued technology innovation ranging from work at home assisted by teleworking to flexi-time working enabled by job redesign. Since supervisors play a key role in the effectiveness of WLB policies and programmes (Perlow 1995; Thompson et al. 1999), further training and support should be given to line managers with respect to demographic changes in labour force landscape and diversity in individuals' request for work-life balance so that they are equipped with updated knowledge and tools to provide employees with assistance in boundary management.

References

ACAS. 2014. *The right to request flexible working: An ACAS guide.* London: ACAS.
———. 2015. *Flexible working and work-life balance.* London: ACAS.
Allen, T.D. 2001. Family-supportive work environments: The role of organisational perceptions. *Journal of Vocational Behaviour* 58: 414–435.
Allen, T.D., and J. Russell. 1999. Parental leave of absence: Some not so family friendly implications. *Journal of Applied Social Psychology* 29: 166–191.
Atkinson, C., and L. Hall. 2009. The role of gender in varying forms of flexible working, gender. *Work and Organisation* 16: 650–666.
Bianchi, S.M., J.P. Robinson, and M.A. Milkie. 2006. *Changing rhythms of American family life.* New York: Russell Sage Foundation.
Blair-Loy, M. 2003. *Competing devotions: Career and family among women executives.* Cambridge, MA: Harvard University Press.
Blair-Loy, M., and A.S. Wharton. 2002. Employees' use of family-responsive policies and the workplace social context. *Social Forces* 80: 813–845.
———. 2004. Mothers in finance: Surviving and thriving. *Annals of the American Academy of Political and Social Science* 596: 151–171.
Blair-Loy, M., A.S. Wharton, and J. Goodstein. 2011. Exploring the relationship between mission statements and work–life practices in organisations. *Organisation Studies* 32: 427–450.
Blyton, P. 1985. *Changes in working time.* New York: St. Martin's Press.
———. 2010. Working time, work–life balance and inequality. In *Reassessing the employment relationship*, ed. P. Blyton, E. Heery, and P. Turnbull, 299–317. Basingstoke: Palgrave Macmillan.
Bornstein, S. 2013. The legal and policy implications of the "flexibility stigma". *Journal of Social Issues* 69: 389–405.
Brescoll, V.L. 2011. Who takes the floor and why? Gender, power, and volubility in organisations. *Administrative Science Quarterly* 56: 622–641.
Brescoll, V.L., and E.L. Uhlmann. 2005. Attitudes toward traditional and nontraditional parents. *Psychology of Women Quarterly* 29: 436–445.
Brescoll, V.L., L. Sarnell, and C. Moss-Rascusin. 2011. Masculinity, status, and subordination: Why working for a gender stereotype violator causes men to lose status. *Journal of Experimental Social Psychology* 48: 354–357.
Brescoll, V.L., J. Glass, and A. Sedlovskaya. 2013. Ask and ye shall receive? The dynamics of employer provided flexible work options and the need for public policy. *Journal of Social Issues* 69: 367–388.

Budig, M.J., and P. England. 2001. The wage penalty for motherhood. *American Sociological Review* 66: 204–225.

Butler, A., and A. Skattebo. 2004. What is acceptable for women may not be for men: The effect of family conflicts with work on job-performance ratings. *Journal of Occupational and Organisational Psychology* 77: 553–564.

Cain, M. 2001. *The childless revolution: What it means to be childless today.* Cambridge, MA: Perseus Publishing.

Casper, W.J., D. Weltman, and E. Kwesiga. 2007. Beyond family-friendly: The construct and measurement of singles friendly work culture. *Journal of Vocational Behaviour* 70: 478–501.

Clear, F., and K. Dickson. 2005. Teleworking practices in small and medium-sized firms: Management style and actor autonomy. *New Technology, Work and Employment* 20: 218–233.

Cohen, J.R., and L.E. Single. 2001. An examination of the perceived impact of flexible work arrangements on professional opportunities in public accounting. *Journal of Business Ethics* 32: 317–328.

Collins, M. 2005. The (not so simple) case for teleworking: A study at Lloyd's of London. *New Technology, Work and Employment* 20: 115–132.

Coltrane, S., E.C. Miller, T. DeHaan, and L. Stewart. 2013. Fathers and flexibility stigma. *Journal of Social Issues* 69: 279–302.

Conlin, M. 2003. Unmarried America. *Business Week*, October 20, 106–116.

Correll, S.J., S. Benard, and I. Paik. 2007. Getting a job: Is there a motherhood penalty? *American Journal of Sociology* 112: 1297–1338.

de Janasz, S., M. Forret, D. Haack, and K. Jonsen. 2013. Family status and work attitudes: An investigation in a professional services firm. *British Journal of Management* 24: 191–210.

Deal, J.J., D.G. Altman, and S.G. Rogelberg. 2010. Millennials at work: What we know and we need to do (if anything). *Journal of Business Psychology* 25: 191–199.

DeFraine, W.C., W.M. Williams, and S.J. Ceci. 2014. Attracting STEM talent: Do STEM students prefer traditional or work/life-interaction labs? *PLoS ONE* 9: e89801.

Deitch, C.H., and M.L. Huffman. 2001. Family responsive benefits and the two-tiered labor market. In *Work and family: Today's vision, tomorrow's realities*, ed. R. Hertz and N. Marshall, 103–130. Berkeley: University of California Press.

Deloitte. 2014. Big demands and high expectations: What generation Y wants from business, government, and the future workplace. https://www2.deloitte.com/uk/en/pages/press-releases/articles/big-demands-and-high-expectations-what-generation-y-wants.html. Accessed 18 Jan 2017.

DePaulo, B. 2006. *Singled out: How singles are stereotyped, stigmatized, and ignored, and still live happily ever after*. New York: St Martin's Press.

Dex, S., and F. Scheibl. 2001. Family friendly and flexible-working arrangements in UK based SMEs: Business cases. *British Journal of Industrial Relations* 39: 411–431.

Dimitrova, D. 2003. Controlling teleworkers: Supervisions and flexibility revisited. *New Technology, Work, and Employment* 18: 181–195.

Dobbin, F., and E.L. Kelly. 2007. How to stop harassment: Professional construction of legal compliance in organisations. *American Journal of Sociology* 112: 1203–1243.

Dodson, L. 2013. Stereotyping low-wage mothers who have work and family conflicts. *Journal of Social Issues* 69: 257–278.

Drago, R., C.L. Colbeck, K.D. Stauffer, A. Pirretti, K. Burkum, J. Fazioli, G. Lazzaro, and T. Habasevich. 2006. The avoidance of bias against caregiving: The case of academic faculty. *American Behavioural Scientist* 49: 1222–1247.

Eagly, A.H., and V.J. Steffen. 1984. Gender stereotypes stem from the distribution of women and men into social roles. *Journal of Personality and Social Psychology* 46 (4): 735–754.

Eikhof, D.R., C. Warhurst, and A. Haunschild. 2007. Introduction: What work? What life? What balance? *Employer Relations* 29: 325–333.

Epstein, C.F., C. Seron, B. Oglensky, and Saut'e R. 1999. *The part-time paradox: Time norms, professional life, family and gender*. New York: Routledge.

Felstead, A., N. Jewson, A. Phizacklea, and S. Walters. 2002. The option to work at home: Another privilege for the favoured few? *New Technology, Work and Employment* 17: 204–223.

Fried, M. 1998. *Taking time: Parental leave policy and corporate culture*. Philadelphia: Temple University Press.

Frone, M.R., M. Russell, and M.L. Cooper. 1992. Antecedents and outcomes of work-family conflict: Testing a model of the work-family interface. *Journal of Applied Psychology* 77: 65–78.

Galinsky, E., T.D. Bond, and D.E. Friedman. 1996. The role of employers in addressing the needs of employed parents. *Journal of Social Issues* 52: 111–136.

Gerson, K. 1985. *Hard choices: How women decide about work, career, and motherhood*. Berkeley/Los Angeles: University of California Press.

Glass, J.L. 2004. Blessing or curse? Family responsive policies and mothers' wage growth over time. *Work and Occupations* 31: 367–394.

Glass, J.L., and T. Fujimoto. 1995. Organizational characteristics and the provision of family benefits. *Work and Occupations* 22: 380–411.

Glass, J.L., and V. Camarigg. 1992. Gender, parenthood and job-family compatibility. *American Journal of Sociology* 98: 131–151.

Golden, L. 2001. Flexible work schedules: Which workers get them? *American Behavioural Scientist* 44: 1157–1178.

Gregory, A., and S. Milner. 2009. Trade unions and work-life balance: Changing times in France and the UK? *British Journal of Industrial Relations* 47: 122–146.

Hewlett, S.A., and N. Vite-León. 2002. *High-achieving women, 2001*. New York: National Parenting Association.

Hill, E.J., A.J. Hawkins, V. Martinson, and M. Ferris. 2003. Studying "working fathers": Comparing fathers' and mothers' work-family conflict, fit, and adaptive strategies in a global high-tech company. *Fathering* 1: 239–261.

Hochschild, A.R. 1997. *Time bind: When work becomes home and home becomes work*. New York: Metropolitan Books.

Hood, J.C. 1993. *Men, work, and family*. Newbury Park: Sage Publications.

Hope, K. 2016. The millennial generation shaking up the workplace rules. *BBC News*, February 2. http://www.bbc.co.uk/news/business-35460401. Accessed 18 Jan 2017.

Hyde, J.S., M.J. Essex, and F. Horton. 1993. Fathers and parental leave: Attitudes and experiences. *Journal of Family Issues* 14: 616–641.

Kalleberg, A.L., B.F. Reskin, and K. Hudson. 2000. Bad jobs in America: Standard and nonstandard employment relations and job quality in the United States. *American Sociological Review* 65: 256–278.

Kelly, E.L., and A. Kalev. 2006. Managing flexible work arrangements in U.S. organisations: Formalized discretion or "a right to ask". *Socio-Economic Review* 4: 379–416.

Korsell, N. 2008. *The overall situation of lone parent families in Sweden*. Stockholm: Ministry of Health and Social Affairs, Coordination Secretariat.

Kossek, E.E., B. Lautsch, and S.C. Eaton. 2005. Flexibility enactment theory: Relationships between type, boundaries, control, and work-family effectiveness. In *Work and life integration: Organisational, cultural, and individual perspectives*, ed. E. Kossekand and S. Lambert. Mahwah: Lawrence Erlbaum Associates.

Kossek, E.E., S. Lewis, and L.B. Hammer. 2010. Work-life initiatives and organisational change: Overcoming mixed messages to move from the margin to the mainstream. *Human Relations* 63: 3–19.

Lambert, S.J. 2009. Making a difference for hourly employees. In *Work-life policies that make a real difference for individuals, families, and organisations*, ed. A. Booth and A. Crouter. Washington, DC: Urban Institute Press.

Lautsch, B., E. Kossek, and S. Eaton. 2009. Supervisory approaches and paradoxes in managing telecommuting implementation. *Human Relations* 62: 795–827.

Lewis, J. 2001. The decline of the male breadwinner model: Implications for work and care. *Social Politics: International Studies in Gender, State and Society* 8: 152–169.

Maupin, R.J., and C.R. Lehman. 1994. Talking heads. Stereotypes, status, sex-roles and satisfaction of female and male auditors. *Accounting, Organisations, and Society* 19: 427–437.

Mintz, S., and S. Kellog. 1988. *Domestic revolutions: A social history of American life*. New York: Free Press.

Office for National Statistics. 2010. Population estimates by marital status, Mid-2010. http://webarchive.nationalarchives.gov.uk/20160105160709/http://www.ons.gov.uk/ons/dcp171778_244768.pdf. Accessed 18 Jan 2017.

Osterman, P. 1995. Work/family programs and the employment relationship. *Administrative Science Quarterly* 40: 681–700.

Perlow, L.A. 1995. Putting the work back into work/family. *Group and Organisation Management* 20: 227–239.

Pleck, J.H. 1993. Are family-supportive employer policies relevant to men? In *Men, work, and family*, ed. J. Hood, 217–237. Newbury Park: Sage.

———. 1995. The gender role strain paradigm: An update. In *A new psychology of men*, ed. R. Levant and W. Pollack, 11–32. New York: Basic Books.

Poelmans, S., and B. Beham. 2008. The moment of truth: Conceptualizing managerial work–life policy allowance decisions. *Journal of Occupational and Organisational Psychology* 81: 393–400.

Prentice, D.A., and E. Carranza. 2002. What women and men should be, shouldn't be, are allowed to be, and don't have to be: The contents of prescriptive gender stereotypes. *Psychology of Women Quarterly* 26: 269–281.

Reilly, L. 1996. *Women living single: Thirty women share their stories of navigating through a married world*. Boston: Faber and Faber.

Rudman, L.A., and K. Mescher. 2013. Penalizing men who request a family leave: Is flexibility stigma a femininity stigma? *Journal of Social Issues* 69: 322–340.

Ruiz, Y., and A. Walling. 2005. Home-based working using communications technologies. *Labour Market Trends* 113: 417–426.

Ryan, A.M., and E.E. Kossek. 2008. Work–life policy implementation: Breaking down or creating barriers to inclusiveness? *Human Resource Management* 47: 295–310.

Secret, M. 2000. Identifying the family, job, and workplace characteristics of employees who use work–family benefits. *Family Relations* 49: 217–226.

Stone, P. 2007. *Opting out? Why women really quit careers and head home*. Berkeley: University of California Press.

Stone, P., and L.A. Hernandez. 2013. The all-or-nothing workplace: Flexibility stigma and "opting out" among professional-managerial women. *Journal of Social Issues* 69: 235–256.

Thébaud, S. 2010. Masculinity, bargaining, and breadwinning: Understanding men's housework in the context of paid work. *Gender and Society* 24: 330–354.

Thompson, C.A., L.L. Beauvais, and K.S. Lyness. 1999. When work-family benefits are not enough: The influence of work-family culture on benefit utilization, organisational attachment, and work-family conflict. *Journal of Vocational Behaviour* 54: 392–415.

Todd, P., and J. Binns. 2013. Work-life balance: Is it now a problem for management? *Gender, Work and Organisation* 20: 219–231.

Tregaskis, O. 2000. Telework in its national context. In *Managing telework*, ed. K. Daniels, D. Lamond, and P. Standen, 9–20. London: Business Press.

Twenge, J.M. 2010. A review of the empirical evidence on generational differences in work attitudes. *Journal of Business Psychology* 25: 201–210.

Twenge, J.M., and W. Campbell. 2009. *The narcissism epidemic: Living in the age of entitlement*. New York: Free Press.

Van Wanrooy, B., H. Bewley, A. Bryson, F. Forth, S. Freeth, L. Stokes, and S. Wood. 2013. The 2011 workplace employment relations study: First findings. Department for Business, Innovation and Skills. https://www.gov.uk/government/organisations/department-for-business-innovation-skills URN BIS/14/1008 ISBN 978-0-85605-770-0. Accessed 18 Jan 2017.

Vandello, J.A., V.E. Hettinger, J.K. Bosson, and J. Siddiqi. 2013. When equal isn't really equal: The masculine dilemma of seeking work flexibility. *Journal of Social Issues* 69: 303–321.

Wayne, J.H., and B.L. Cordiero. 2003. Who is a good organisational citizen? Social perception of male and female employees who use family leave. *Sex Roles* 49: 233–246.

Wells, S.J. 2007. Are you too family friendly? *HR Magazine*, October, 35–39.

Wharton, A.S., S. Chivers, and M. Blair-Loy. 2008. Use of formal and informal work-family policies on the digital assembly line. *Work and Occupations* 35: 327–350.

Wheatley, D. in press. Employee satisfaction and use of flexible working arrangements. *Work, Employment and Society*. https://doi.org/10.1177/0950017016631447.

Williams, J.C. 2010. *Reshaping the work-family debate: Why men and class matter.* Cambridge, MA: Harvard University Press.

Williams, J.C., M. Blair-Loy, and J.L. Berdahl. 2013. Cultural schemas, social class, and the flexibility stigma. *Journal of Social Issues* 69: 209–234.

Wood, S., L.M. de Menezes, and A. Lasoasa. 2003. Family-friendly management in great Britain: testing various perspectives. *Industrial Relations* 42: 221–250.

Young, M.B. 1996. Career issues for single adults without children. In *The career is dead: Long live the career*, ed. D. Hall, 196–219. San Francisco: Jossey-Bass.

7

LGBT+ Participation in Sports: 'Invisible' Participants, 'Hidden' Spaces of Exclusion

Scott Lawley

7.1 Introduction

This chapter examines the 'hidden' inequalities in sport which lead to the invisibility, exclusion and marginalisation of Lesbian, Gay, Bisexual, Transgender and other non-heterosexual or non-gender binary (LGBT+) participants. In the 2016 Rio Olympic Games, only 56 out of 11,000 competitors (less than half of 1%) identified publicly within the range of LGBT+ identities (Outsports 2016). Furthermore, men's professional football is notable for its lack of any openly gay players in major international leagues, with no such players participating in the 2014 World Cup. This relatively small proportion of visible LGBT+ participants contrasts with society more widely and indeed provides a contradiction with visible, espoused narratives of inclusivity within sport as evidenced in

S. Lawley (✉)
Department of Human Resource Management, Nottingham Business School,
Nottingham Trent University, Nottingham, UK

© The Author(s) 2018
V. Caven, S. Nachmias (eds.), *Hidden Inequalities in the Workplace*,
Palgrave Explorations in Workplace Stigma,
DOI 10.1007/978-3-319-59686-0_7

government charters, inclusivity initiatives by sports governing bodies and policies of individual sports organisations. The chapter argues that these visible narratives of inclusivity stand in contrast with the more 'hidden' dynamics of exclusion which occur in the cultures of sport which themselves take root in individual and, again, 'hidden' spaces of sport. By identifying the 'hidden' dynamics of inequality in sports and the spaces in which they take place, the locations where this inequality might be tackled are also identified.

A chapter about sport may seem unusual in a volume dedicated to 'hidden' inequalities in the workplace; however, this chapter is based in an understanding that sport is made up of a number of organisations, such as grassroots clubs, educational institutions, professional clubs and sports governing bodies. Sports organisations are both workplaces and sites of leisure time consumption and as such stand as an organisational case study in their own right. In that, these organisations are also subject to workplace and goods and services equality legislation but with proportionately different results in terms of LGBT+ visibility; they also serve as an organisational case study of particular interest. The chapter thus draws from both organisational and sports sociology literature, noting common observations around LGBT+ invisibility in both, and drawing on the lessons that each can learn from the other in terms of tackling 'hidden' inequalities.

This crossover reflects the author's background as both an organisation studies' academic with an interest in diversity issues and an activist in the area of LGBT+ inclusion in sport, in the latter case running an LGBT+ community football club and, more recently, being a core member of the international Football v Homophobia campaign.[1] Whilst these remained separate domains of activity for a while, this chapter stems from a realisation that the activist work in sport was dealing with similar issues of culture and attitude change to those dealt with in the management and organisation literature. Furthermore, an examination of the sports sociology literature revealed similar concerns to the management and organisation literature with recent turns to both queer theory and the sociology of space, in particular the ways in which specific masculine, heterosexual gender presentations are manifested in particular (sporting) organisational spaces (e.g. Tyler and Cohen 2010).

The chapter thus examines sport as a set of organisational arrangements whose 'hidden' dynamics marginalise LGBT+ participation and visibility. The chapter begins by examining the more visible structures and regulations of sport which, being organised around a male/female gender divide, can exclude gender non-binary participants. Despite other structures and regulations which promote inclusion in sport, this gender divide serves as the basis for 'hegemonically masculine' (Connell 1995) and 'virile, heterosexual' (Jones and McCarthy 2010) cultures in sport which can marginalise LGBT+ identities either through overt discrimination or through more 'hidden', subtle means.

In a manner similar to the workplace settings discussed in Chap. 9 (Ward and Winstanley 2003), even where LGBT+ participation takes place, the expression of such identity may be 'hidden' and silenced through strategies of covering and passing, thus rendering LGBT+ participants invisible. Such cultures are noted as being 'hidden' in specific sports spaces—behind the walls of the locker room, for example, or within the safety of a crowd in the stadium. Furthermore, these aggressively heterosexist cultures are 'performative' (Butler 1990) in their nature; that is to say they are materialised only within the specific context of these heterogeneous, 'hidden' spaces, thus complicating attempts to tackle such discrimination. The chapter notes that even counter spaces that promote LGBT+ inclusion in sport, such as LGBT+ community sports clubs, can themselves develop 'hidden' normative dynamics of exclusion. The chapter ends with reflections based in the author's own work in LGBT+ sports, drawing out wider issues for 'hidden' inequalities in organisations and arguing for the importance of education and intervention in specific spaces of sport where such inequalities remain 'hidden'.

7.2   The Visible Organisation of Sport

Sport is delivered through organisations which vary in size and scope. There are individual sports clubs which range from informal, small-scale grassroots clubs to high-profile professional clubs. Sport may be delivered within other organisations such as educational institutions, such as schools and universities, or through local government provision through leisure centres and outdoor sports spaces. Individual sports clubs are, more often than not, affiliated and accredited by national governing bodies for their sports and are thus beholden to their rules and regulation which may further stem from international governing bodies. Furthermore, there are sporting organisations such as the Olympic Games which operate across sports at an international level. A common feature of this organisation and regulation is a gender divide in sport which divides competition into male and female categories, thus marginalising participants who do not fit into this 'neatly dualistic two-sexed model underpinning mainstream sport' (Symons 2007, p. 142).

Such a model is enshrined in the visible architecture of sporting spaces, in particular the locker rooms which, in common with similar discussion around toilets in educational and work organisations, are divided between male and female spaces which at once do not recognise transgender participants and can lead to hostility to their presence (Caudwell 2014). It is in this respect that Marlin, a Manchester-based swimming club for transgender participants, has chosen to use a pool with individual changing cubicles around the pool edge rather than gendered communal spaces. Further to that, a report by the UK National Union of Students (2012) recommends that the physical layout of changing facilities should be considered as an area where exclusion might occur.

In addition to the exclusion from the physical space of sporting spaces, transgender athletes also face exclusion based on legislation which often prevents transgender participants from competing alongside their acquired gender (Sykes 2006, p. 7). Such an action often is used on the grounds of imputed physical 'advantages'; for example, UK government guidance (DCMS 2005) initially suggests that transgender participants should be accepted as the gender they present, but later suggests that exclusion can take place on the grounds of ensuring 'fair competition'. Whilst this may, in its own right, serve to exclude transgender participants, further barriers to participation have been created by the enforcement of this divide through procedures such as sex tests and blood tests to monitor hormone levels, with transgender participants having faced a history of being 'regulated and medicalised' (Caudwell 2014, p. 406). In this regard, a video case study presented by the Football v Homophobia campaign highlighted the exclusion of male-to-female transgender football players in the UK for periods of years following transition.[2]

The marginalisation or exclusion of transgender participants on the grounds of competitive advantage is one area where sport does not need to conform to the requirements of the UK Equality Act 2010, where gender identity is one of nine protected characteristics, alongside gender and sexual orientation. In other areas, sport has acted at a legislative level to comply with these requirements. In the UK, a raft of policies and charters have addressed LGBT+ sports participation, for example, in 2007, the English Football Association wrote a ban on homophobic language and behaviour, similar to existing legislation about racist and sexist behaviour, into its ground regulations. In 2011, the UK Government launched a sports charter to increase LGBT+ participation in support, which was signed by individual sports governing bodies and associations.[3] Furthermore, high-profile campaigns, such as Stonewall's Rainbow Laces and the Football v Homophobia month of action have attracted visible support and action from professional football clubs.

In contrast to these high-profile efforts, survey evidence has suggested an ongoing problem with homophobia and transphobia in sport; for example, both international and UK surveys (Out on the Fields 2015; Stonewall 2009) show that spectator stands and team sports environments are perceived as hostile for LGBT+ participants. In youth and educational settings, research undertaken by the National Union of Students (2012) found that 46.8% of respondents experienced sport culture as 'alienating or unwelcoming', whilst a third of LGB young people and 50% of young transgender people aged 16–25 do not feel they can be open about their sexuality or gender identity in a sports club (Youth Chances 2014). It is this latter feeling of being unable to be open about sexuality and/or gender identity, which points to the inequalities in sport being 'hidden' at the cultural rather than structural levels.

7.3 'Hidden' Participants: The Exclusion and Invisibility of LGBT+ Athletes

At the structural level of clubs, organisations, rules and governance, sport has thus adopted a stance of outlawing discrimination and promoting LGBT+ inclusion, but the impact of this on at more 'hidden', cultural levels has been more limited (Elling et al. 2003; Pronger 2000). A similar observation has been made about the limited impact of workplace legislation at a cultural level (McDowell 1995). This section first explores the nature of cultures within sporting organisations, and how they promote a masculine, heteronormative culture which might exclude LGBT+ participants, or which has been observed to operate in more subtle, 'hidden' ways which leaves LGBT+ identities 'hidden' within sport. The chapter then moves on to the nature of culture itself as a 'hidden' entity within organisations, the location of which becomes the focus for LGBT+ inclusivity interventions in sports organisations.

The culture of sporting organisations has traditionally been characterised by an aggressive masculinity from which sexist, homophobic and transphobic behaviours stem. Indeed, Connell (1987, 1995) saw sport as a contributing factor to 'hegemonic masculinity' within society, a form of 'training in masculinity' (Fitzclarence and Hickey 2001, p. 121), with implications for participation and visibility: '…those who are able to participate most effectively adopt an exclusive form of masculinity which draws upon traditional understandings of heterosexual masculinity' (Wellard 2002, p. 237). The athlete is viewed a model of what it is to be a man, the opposite of being feminine or gay (Anderson 2002, 860), an ideal reflected in team sports by 'virile, heterosexual' cultures (Jones and McCarthy 2010, 163), characterised by an atmosphere of competitiveness, masculinity, violence and aggression (Anderson 2002; Pappas et al. 2004; Fitzclarence and Hickey 2001; Pronger 1990).

Similar cultures have been observed in some workplace settings, for example, construction (Chan 2013; Wright 2013), factories (Ackroyd and Crowdy 1990; Collinson 1988), emergency services (Ward and Winstanley 2005; Miller et al. 2003) and the City of London (McDowell 1995; McDowell and Court 1994). Indeed, Gregory (2009) has used the sporting metaphor of the locker room to note the similarities between sporting and workplace cultures as evidenced through behaviours such as banter, teasing and sexualisation of female colleagues, creating dominance over women and gay men, making them a 'potentially hostile arena' (Rumens 2010, p. 137) in which to be openly gay.

Even in less openly hostile workplaces, LGBT+ identities are still marginalised and 'hidden' through more 'subtle means' (Humphrey 1999), such as mundane conversations about private life (Ward and Winstanley

2003, 1268) which silence non-heterosexual identities or characterise them as deviant against an 'assumption of heterosexuality' (Ward and Winstanley 2003, 2005; Bell et al. 2011). Covering and passing strategies are deployed, such as avoiding discussion which may disclose identity (Ward and Winstanley 2003), or faking an identity congruent with the dominant norm (Dejordy 2008). For those people who are 'out of the closet', heteronormative cultures still impact identity management towards being appropriately 'professional' (Bowring and Brewis 2009), avoiding 'flaunting' camp and hedonistic aspects of gay lifestyle and adopting more 'acceptable' heteronormative consumption patterns (Rumens 2011; Rumens and Kerfoot 2009). In other words, even if LGBT+ identity is not completely 'hidden', there are pressures to 'tone down' certain aspects of it.

Similar observations about the effects of masculine, heteronormative cultures upon LGBT+ participants in sport have been made, and again a distinction is drawn between cultures being so hostile that they discourage participation and exclude LGBT+ participants, or whether the effects are more subtle and, rather than resulting in outright exclusion, lead instead to LGBT+ participation but with identities being 'hidden' or managed. A problem with understanding the extent of LGBT+ participation is a lack of empirical data, as noted by Elling and Janssens (2009), and public surveys such as the Sport England Active People survey have only recently begun to include sexual orientation data. Furthermore, the figure for LGBT+ Olympic participation, which began this chapter, can only be an estimate given that such data is not recorded, based on those participants whose LGBT identity is public knowledge, for example through media interviews. It cannot capture those participants whose identity is 'hidden' through the means of silencing discussed in this chapter. Nevertheless, Elling and Janssen's (2009) quantitative study of Dutch sports participation, the most recent Sport England (2012) survey and qualitative case studies detailed in this section of the chapter, all point to trends of gay men preferring individual over team sports, lesbians being more likely to participate in team sports and a relative invisibility of bisexual and transgender participants, echoing their marginalisation even within LGBT+ sports groups, as discussed later in this chapter. Across these ethnographic studies, quantitative studies and public surveys, common effects of silencing and marginalisation on different groups which hide LGBT+ identities in sport are observed.

Gay men's participation in sport is equal to heterosexual men, but steered towards individual rather than team sports (Sport England 2012; Elling and Janssens 2009; Hekma 1998; Symons 2007). Outright homophobic abuse can be a factor in alienation from team sports (Brackenridge et al. 2004), but self-removal is more often a result of discomfort with the macho, heterosexist atmosphere (Jones and McCarthy 2010; Wellard 2002; Hekma 1998), often from school sports onwards (Jones and McCarthy 2010; Carless 2010, 2012; Hekma 1998). If not 'hidden' through outright exclusion, for those remaining in team sports, non-heterosexual identities are silenced (Robertson 2003; Hekma 1998). Against a 'taken for granted' assumption of heterosexuality (Skogvang and Fasting 2013), silencing, passing and covering strategies, for example, by 'faking straightness' (Price and Parker 2003) or using sporting prowess to 'mask' gayness (Wellard 2002) are deployed. For openly gay athletes, aspects of gay identity are 'hidden' or 'toned down', in a similar manner to workplace professionalism, by moderating appearance and behaviour, and not discussing personal life and relationships (Anderson 2002), in Eng's (2006, p. 18) words, 'sexuality is left at home', and is thus 'hidden' from the milieu of team sports.

Lesbians are more likely to participate in mainstream sports teams (Sport England 2012), which can be a haven of community and friendship that does not exist for gay men in mainstream sports (Symons 2007). However, their participation is still marginalised, in the first instance as women, with heteronormativity dictating what counts as acceptable feminine behaviour and appearance (Brackenridge et al. 2004). Participation by women, straight or gay, is deemed to be 'unfeminine' and cast as 'deviant, masculine, homosexual' (Russell 2007). As with gay men, this can lead to pressure to pass as heterosexual (Cox and Thompson 2001), as Caudwell (2002, p. 30) states, 'to be intelligible, that is to be read as a real woman, can often mean staying in the closet'. Out lesbians in mainstream sports can encounter hostility through negative stereotyping, similar to that faced by gay men as sexually deviant or predatory (Norman 2012; Symons 2007; Cox and Thompson 2001). Furthermore, the 'glass closet' (Griffin 1998) exists as a form of 'conditional tolerance', similar to gay men being out but being expected to not 'flaunt' their sexuality (Hekma 1998, Symons 2007). There is pressure to hide authentic identity and present a 'feminine' image, accompanied by silencing of openly political activity, which might challenge governing heteronormative structures in sports (Brackenridge et al. 2004).

7.4 From 'Hidden' Cultures to Spatial Gendered Performances

Whilst cultures may render LGBT+ participants invisible within sport, these cultures in themselves are often 'hidden' and thus difficult to identify and change. King and Lawley (2016) use the metaphor of an iceberg to illustrate the 'hidden' nature of cultures within organisations. Whilst structures and policies might be easily visible above the surface, below the surface the murky depths hide such characteristics as attitudes, cultures and shared values. Cultures are thus not instantly visible, and, even when getting to such 'hidden' depths of the organisation, they can be deeply rooted and obdurate in the face of change. This section examines the nature and location of these cultures within sporting organisations. Noting that cultures are not hegemonically masculine across all sporting locales, the section examines how sporting cultures are heterogeneous, taking root in many different spatially specific manifestations, 'hidden' within specific spaces of sporting organisations such as locker rooms, stadia and pitches. Drawing on queer theory and its use in recent spatial turns in both organisation studies and sports sociology, the cultures are reimagined as gendered presentations which are entirely 'performative' (Butler 1990); that is to say they have lives of their own within specific spaces which do not necessarily reflect the behaviours of the same people outside of those specific spaces. The identification of these specific spaces where performative cultures take place introduces another aspect by which such cultures are 'hidden'.

The heterogeneous nature of sporting cultures and their effect on LGBT+ participation can be noted in two separate trends identified in the sports sociology literature. Firstly, and in contrast to exclusionary and normative pressures for LGBT+ participants previously described, there is evidence of sport liberalising in line with the rest of society (Cashmore and Cleland 2012), reflected in positive media responses to high-profile LGBT+ athletes (McCormack and Anderson 2010; Kian and Anderson 2009). Anderson (2011a, b) suggests a generational shift from hegemonic masculinity to 'inclusive masculinity', with evidence of more positive cultures towards gay athletes in rugby clubs (Anderson and McGuire 2010; McCormack and Anderson 2010) and in association football (Adams et al. 2010). However, there is still evidence that homophobia in sport has not been fully eradicated. Southall et al. (2009) provide survey evidence of a decline in homophobic attitudes amongst male college athletes but with 28% of respondents still demonstrating homophobic behaviours. Norman (2012) critiques the inclusive masculinity approach, suggesting that these improved social attitudes have only been noted in the particular cultures and institutional arrangements of educational institutions. Anderson (2011a) himself notes that, as with the workplace (Dejordy 2008; Miller et al. 2003; Clair et al. 2005; Croteau et al. 2008; Rumens and Broomfield 2012), locale is an important factor in the decision of an athlete to come out, and not all cultures will necessarily be equally supportive. Local and contextual differences suggest that masculine, heteronormative cultures, and how they are experienced by LGBT+ participants, are not uniform across different sporting locales and spaces.

Both organisation studies and sports sociology have recently experienced 'spatial turns' which examine how identities, including heteronormative gendered and sexual identities, are materialised in specific localised spaces and contexts and the power effects that this has on the expression of non-heterosexual identities (Skeggs 1999; Ingram 1997). As Waitt (2003, p. 170) suggests … 'performance in sports cannot be separated from temporally and locational specific terrains of power and discourse'. As such, this approach makes Lefebvre's (1991) concept of 'lived space' the focus of analysis. This is the space that is directly experienced by its users in the midst of social action, as opposed to the more static perceived, 'concrete space' of buildings and architecture and the abstract 'conceived space' of rules, regulations, ideologies and visions which govern sport at both regulatory and cultural levels. Lived space for van Ingen (2003) is where power relations produce gendered, sexualised sports spaces, which can result in them being locations of struggle for marginalised identities and, as lived space, will be generated and experienced in every space where sport takes place. It helps to explain how cultural attitudes to LGBT+ participants differ between different spaces where sport takes place.

Queer theory has been used extensively within organisation studies and sports sociology, and when linked with Lefebvre's lived space, helps to explain how masculine gendered presentations are materialised within the context of specific, material organisational spaces. Queer theory highlights the performative construction and maintenance (Butler 1990) of dominant categories of gender and sexual identity (McDowell and Court 1994) which exist only in their continued repetition and reiteration rather than reflecting any fixed categories of gender (Rumens 2010; Parker 2002). In other words, it shows accepted presentations based around gender and sexuality to be an artifice or a 'performance' that extends to being a parody of itself, but at the same time a performance which gains a seemingly natural life and existence of its own. Phrases such as 'boys don't cry' or associations such as blue for a boy and pink for a girl are arbitrary gendered presentations, but ones that are recognised within society and which impact on expected gendered behaviours. The dominant reference point of such performances is the 'heterosexual matrix' (Butler 1990), which creates an illusion of a hierarchical set of privileged heteronormative behaviours, enabling and making visible those identities 'considered proper' to a heterosexual identity (Sumara and Davis 1999), whilst foreclosing others (Tyler and Cohen 2008).

The spatial turn allows Butler's work to be placed into the specific organisational and lived spaces, where gendered norms are created and experienced, and …'allows us to see that organisational environments serve as contexts for the iteration of whatever is demarcated within such a space, creating and controlling subjectivities and relations amongst them' (Borgerson 2005, p. 69). Organisational symbols, images and objects form the backdrop against which gender norms and subjectivities are not only performed, but are materialised, experienced and embodied in a specific lived organisational space (Hancock and Tyler 2007).

Drawing on Butler's (1993) *Bodies that Matter*, Tyler and Cohen (2010) note the centrality of bodies to this spatial materialisation of norms. Within sports settings, the body is also central to the production of local, spatialised power relations (Caudwell 2007; van Ingen 2003), which Caudwell (2007, 184) suggests are overwhelmingly dominated by men and masculinities. The closeness of bodies in the 'extraordinary setting' (Eng 2006) of the locker room, with an almost 'panic-like' reaction against the possibility of homosexual activity (Eng 2008), is one example of the centrality of bodies and the materialisation of particular gendered norms in specific, localisable spaces. For Fusco (2005), the locker room constructs social relations around a landscape of 'normativity, respectability, cleanliness and purification', which at once privileges certain gendered, racialised and heterosexualised bodily presentations and performances which previously has been seen to exclude non-binary and transgender bodies which do not fit into its norms based around a binary gender divide. Homophobic and (hetero)sexist discourse (Symons 2007) serves to maintain a 'boundary' around acceptable and unacceptable locker-room behaviour (Eng 2008)—a resistance against a gay 'intrusion' into its space (Anderson 2002).

The specific and spatialised nature of heteronormative sports cultures is highlighted in two pieces of research—one ethnographic and one survey based—which demonstrate how homophobic language and behaviours are materialised against the backdrop of specific sporting spaces. It also shows how these behaviours are performed specifically within these spaces, in contrast to an espoused lack of homophobia by the same participants outside of these spaces.

Adams et al. (2010) describe the 'hypermasculine' environment of a semi-professional football team, with coaches using 'masculinity establishing discourses' laced with misogyny and homophobia to motivate the team and similar 'masculinity challenging discourses' which question the players' heterosexuality to chastise poor performance. Players reassert their masculinity with bodily displays, such as punching a locker-room door, and reproduce such language on the field to emasculate opposition players or to berate teammates. However, outside of the football field and locker room a 'relative absence' of homophobia and misogyny amongst the athletes contrasts with its 'relative saturation' in those specific sports spaces (ibid.). Sarcastic comments amongst team members implied that the athletes played along without buying into the coach's 'masculine ideal', suggesting a Butleresque parodic or 'carnivalesque' display of masculinity to meet the required displays of masculinity in that specific sports space. For Adams et al. (293), the 'toxic' behaviour is *just part of the game* rather than part of the people exhibiting it. Materialised in specific spaces, the 'hypermasculine posturing' is *left within the white-lined boundaries of the playing field* (ibid., 292).

Cashmore and Cleland's (2011, 2012) survey evidence found that 93% of fans would accept gay players in their team but, paradoxically, will 'habitually barrage' homophobic abuse at players (2011). Rather than indicating that the person shouting the abuse is homophobic, they suggest the performance happens only within the space of the stadium, and is part of the game as it is materialised in those spaces rather than a property of the individuals themselves. The 'unusual logic' which Cashmore and Cleland suggest underpins this resonates with Adams et al.'s masculinity-challenging discourse. Homophobia is 'too good an opportunity' to exploit a perceived weakness as a means of 'getting into players heads' (2011). It 'reaffirms the macho nature of the sport' and, as such, anything which challenges that masculinity of the players, can be used as an insult. This mismatch reflects the spatially situated nature of homophobia described by Caudwell (2011), who contrasts a 'politics of territory' with 'rhetorical territory' within the stadium setting. The former, similar to Lefebvre's conceived space, is the organisational control of the space, for example, through ground regulations and surveillance technologies. Rhetorical territory, however, is much harder to regulate. As a lived space, it is a more fluid space, one which is experienced and embodied through the sights and sounds of the space, such as homophobic chants and bodily allusions to homosexuality as an indication of 'weakness' against dominant forms of masculinity (Caudwell 2011).

The two cases highlight the performative nature of gendered norms in specific spatial context. Rather than obdurate and enduring cultures, they are seen as being materialised within the moment and within the physical and bodily presence of, for example, the locker room or stadium. This further highlights the 'hidden' nature of much of this behaviour—it is 'hidden' within the inner sanctum of the team locker room, or it is 'hidden' within the crowd behaviour within the stadium. Whilst it might highlight that the behaviour, following Butler, is a parodic iteration of no fixed essence, at the same time, it is behaviour that is experienced by LGBT+ participants as part of a culture that leads to their exclusion and invisibility in sports. However, by pinpointing the grounds within which such behaviours are germinated and manifested, the locations where actions to counter such behaviour and promote LGBT+ visibility within sport can be identified. It is to this that the chapter now turns, first examining the role of LGBT+ sports groups, and then examining interventions in mainstream sport.

7.5   LGBT+ Sports Groups

Recent decades have seen an increase in 'categorical' LGBT+ community sports organisations (Pronger 2000; Elling et al. 2003), as opposed to more 'mainstream' groups, which might be ostensibly open to all but which, as has been seen, operate various mechanisms of exclusion, whereby identities within the LGBT+ spectrum are 'hidden' (Elling et al. 2003). Such groups range from small community clubs based around one sport, through to international multisport tournaments such as the Gay Games. In this respect, they can be viewed as counterpaces, which, in contrast to the 'hidden', spatialised cultures, which contribute to the invisibility of LGBT+ participants, promote both the participation and visibility of such participants. However, the role of such counterpaces in challenging the heteronormative basis of exclusion of LGBT+ participants from sport is far from clear. As this section demonstrates, just as with 'professional' appearances adopted by LGBT+ people in the workplace, there is a tendency for such mainstreaming in LGBT+ sports. Furthermore, the spatially located behaviours, which marginalise LGBT+ participants from mainstream sport, have also been seen to occur with respect to different categories and gender presentations within LGBT+ sports. Identities that are marginalised and 'hidden' in mainstream sport are thus also seen to be 'hidden' within LGBT+-specific sporting environments.

Jones and McCarthy (2010) highlight the role of LGBT+ sports groups in increasing the visibility of LGBT+ participants in their analysis of an LGBT+ football league as …'a form of outward expression of sexuality in and environment where gay men had previously been invisible, an affirmation of gay community and identity in a largely hostile and silencing world' (Symons 2007, p. 148). LGBT+ sport is thus seen to empower social identities, creating 'places of resistance' (Elling and Janssens 2009) where LGBT+ identities are performed as a challenge to heteronormativity (Waitt 2003). Transgression of norms in public spaces is also a theme of large-scale LGBT+ sports events (Book and Eskilsson 2010; Waitt 2003). For Waitt (2003), the Gay Games is a 'queer space' for the way in which it claims backspace against its hegemonic heteronormative understanding. Such groups also adopt cultural and organisational approaches, which seek to minimise the exclusion and invisibility found in mainstream sport. For example, Jones and McCarthy (2010) describe gay football groups in the UK as remaking football with a 'gay sensibility'. This may be through pursuing a non-competitive or less-aggressive ethos, as found in both gay men's and lesbian football teams, for example (Jones and McCarthy 2010; Drury 2011), or with the Gay Games' emphasis on participation over competition (Waitt 2003; Symons 2007). Some groups choose not to affiliate to national governing bodies, allowing them to bypass restrictions on mixed-gender teams or transgender participants. The parodic nature of queer is demonstrated in a drag swimming event at the Gay Games (Symons 2007) or in team names such as 'Brighton Bandits' and 'London Leftfooters' playing with and reclaiming insulting terms for gay men. The importance of visibility within specific spaces is noted with the territory of the football field marked with visible symbols such as flags and banners, a 'temporary dislocation of heterosexual space' (Drury 2011; Caudwell 2002).

The idea that LGBT+ sports spaces create spaces for visibility and engage in radically transformative approaches which aim to disrupt dominant heteronormative structures reflects a radical approach to LGBT+ sports groups (Price and Parker 2003). However, counterarguments suggest that this transformative potential of LGBT+ sports spaces is limited, and the increase in visibility brings with it increasingly mainstream and liberal practices (Pronger 2000) which serve to hide certain behaviours and identities within the LGBT+ spectrum. Liberal approaches (Price and Parker 2003) are concerned with gaining legitimisation though moving towards the mainstream, for example, by participating in mainstream leagues, or gaining accreditation from sports governing bodies and thus complying with their rules and structures, which, as has been demonstrated, can exclude participants on the grounds of gender identity and can legislate against mixed-gender competitive sports.

Mainstreaming tendencies can be viewed in the ethos espoused by the Gay Games to portray gay and lesbian people, through sport, as 'normal' people (Symons 2007; Pronger 2000), challenging stereotypes by showing to mainstream society that gay people can be 'just as skilled' in sports (Stevenson et al. 2005). Such mainstreaming tendencies resonate with workplace discussions of professionalism and the presentation of an acceptable image, and are also reflected in the mainstreaming of LGBT+ urban spaces to present a sanitised, respectable gay identity, where 'seedier' more sexualised elements of gay lifestyle are 'watered down' (Hubbard 2008; Rushbrook 2002). In both cases, there is a toning down of the more flamboyant or sexualised elements of identity. Price and Parker (2003) highlight the liberal agenda of a UK gay men's rugby club to prove the club equal to and as competitive as mainstream teams, which resulted in a presentation of 'normality and respectability' (Price and Parker 2003, p. 121). Top-down management of the club's public image, including management of locker-room behaviour to help present this respectable image, enforced this. Similarly, in the Gay Games, displays of drag and leather are discouraged in a bid to present a more 'wholesome' event (Symons 2007), playing down the more flamboyant, sexualised or 'shameful' (Probyn 2000) aspects of LGBT identity. As Waitt (2003, p. 176) observes: 'the Gay Games became a sportscape in which gay bodies display how they have been taught to perform hegemonically'. The games thus have a 'professional, middle-class' presentation (Symons 2007, 150), evidenced by bid teams in suits at mayoral receptions (Stevenson et al. 2005) or by 'respectable' opening ceremonies (Pronger 2000) that echo those of the Olympic games (Symons 2007). The 'mainstreaming, commodification and depoliticisation' (Bell and Binnie 2004) of the Gay Games means that …'a transformative sports model that questioned the very heteronormative basis of power was not on the agenda' (Symons 2007, p. 149). By assimilating with the mainstream, LGBT+ sports groups offer 'little to challenge' the heterosexist foundation of sports (Price and Parker 2003, 109) and create normative pressures that hide certain aspects of LGBT+ identity and behaviour.

Such normativity within LGBT+ sports groups can also be found at the level of different identities within the LGBT+ spectrum (Elling and Janssens 2009). Homophobic and heteronormative discourses are both resisted and 'inadvertently reproduced' (Drury 2011). Whilst ostensibly 'inclusive' (Drury 2011) or 'progressive' (Sykes 2006), Caudwell (2014) and Ravel and Rail (2007) note that LGBT+ sports teams reflect the marginalisation found on the gay scene, namely that it is overwhelmingly 'LG' to the detriment of bisexual and transgender identities which are seen as 'others' to gay sports culture (Drury 2011). Drury (2011) and Caudwell (2007) have noted a marginalisation of bisexual identities within lesbian football. In one case study, Caudwell further notes how 'butch' gender presentations are privileged over those of a more feminine ('femme') appearance and how, echoing structural marginalisation of transgender athletes, a male-to-female transgender player was perceived to have an 'unfair advantage', and phrases such as 'man on' were used within the team (Caudwell 2007). Sykes (2006) further notes institutional arrangements within LGBT+ sport which marginalise transgender participants. Whilst the Gay Games has attempted to take account of cultural differences in transgender identity, a requirement to produce documentation still, for Sykes, perpetuates an idea of transgender participants being 'untrustworthy' whilst also remaining attached to the gender binaries that underpin mainstream sport.

Alongside the assimilationist and normative arguments, the transformational potential of LGBT+ sport is further questioned by arguments that these groups ghettoise their participants, raising walls and creating isolation from the mainstream (Symons 2007). Such spaces can be seen to reinforce stereotypes and binaries, for example, the friendly and non-competitive atmosphere of LGBT+ sporting events, or the idea of competing separately from heterosexual counterparts can reinforce a stereotype that LGBT+ people are not as good at sport (Drury 2011; Waitt 2003). Drury (2011) further suggests that ghettoisation can in fact minimise visibility and thus risk retrenchment into binaries, through a lack of interaction, awareness and segregation means that straight people are not in any way forced to address their own homophobic beliefs and practices. As Symons (2007) argued, such spaces of visibility can paradoxically contribute to LGBT+ participants being 'hidden' when viewed from the wider perspective of sport as a whole.

The potential for LGBT+ sports spaces to bring about wider change and inclusion within sport thus seems to walk a tightrope between mainstream visibility, which leads to assimilation with heteronormativity, and ghettoisation which leaves it invisible to and thus unable to influence these dominant norms. Whilst LGBT+ sports groups have played an important role in increasing the participation of LGBT+ participants in sport and increasing their visibility, they are not in themselves the solution to a wider problem within mainstream sports, and it is to interventions in this much wider organisational field that the final section of this chapter turns.

7.6   Conclusion and Reflections

This chapter has thus far located the dynamics which marginalise LGBT+ participants in sport and keep their participation 'hidden' are themselves 'hidden' in particular spatial contexts within sporting organisations. Experience from working with the Football v Homophobia campaign suggests that it is to these spaces where the dynamics are created that interventions need to be targeted. This stands in contrast with campaigning, charters and similar initiatives, which, whilst important in setting the background against which sports organisations operate, can be seen to work at a level similar to Lefebvre's abstract notion of conceived space without engaging in the lived spaces where such problematic behaviours occur.

In the case of football stadia, Caudwell (2011) suggests that as the location where this marginalisation occurs, it is in the stadium where a reclamation of the rhetorical territory might take place, using symbols of gay activism such as the colour pink or a rainbow flag. Such a display is a marker of territory, one which uses imagery to 'dislocate heteronormativity' (ibid., p. 134), a type of activism which involves …'the contestation of dominant meanings in the spaces that surround elite men's football' (ibid.). It is thus notable that the fifth anniversary of the Meenzelmänner, the LGBT+ supporters group of FC Mainz in Germany, was marked by a mosaic or 'choreo' where supporters held up coloured cards to create a rainbow flag across a whole stand.[4] More recently, LGBT+ fans' groups and campaigns have focussed their attention on visible displays within the stadium.

Whilst such visible presentations are possible in stadia, especially by engaging with mainstream fans' groups, as was the case with FC Mainz, the enclosed and 'hidden' space of the locker room presents a more difficult challenge, given that it is not so open and that there are so many such spaces each with their own 'hidden' dynamics and cultures. With Football v Homophobia, the role of education has always been emphasised; this requires working across all spaces within sport—locker rooms, board rooms, fans' groups, academies, grassroots clubs, professional clubs, and so on. That space of sport are heterogeneous, with different performative dynamics and different gendered and sexualised norms, means that broad-brush solutions are difficult to implement, and tacking the 'hidden' nature of LGBT+ exclusion from sport means engaging with all of these spaces individually. Schools are particularly important in this, as it is within these spaces that such cultures can take hold and be transmitted to future organisations, but also at this stage, exclusion of LGBT+ participants can begin and set in for life.

By focussing on issues particular to sport, similarities between gendered and heterosexualised performances and cultures in sport, and those more widely in organisational and workplace settings have been noted. Alongside this, sport is a notable case in its own right, on the one hand because the nature of such exclusion is so much more stark, and on the other because the organisational arrangements of sport mean that the possibility to construct counterpaces in the form of LGBT+ sports groups exists in a way that is not generally possible in other workplaces. The chapter is thus presented as a case study of sport in its own right but also as lessons that may be applied to organisations and workplaces more generally.

Notes

1. http://www.footballvhomophobia.com
2. https://www.youtube.com/watch?v=9vrV0sdbMOY
3. https://www.gov.uk/government/publications/sports-charter
4. https://www.youtube.com/watch?v=69kAXVOXIqU

References

Ackroyd, S., and P.A. Crowdy. 1990. Can culture be managed? Working with "raw" material: The case of the English slaughtermen. *Personnel Review* 19: 3–13.

Adams, A., E. Anderson, and M. McCormack. 2010. Establishing and challenging masculinity: The influence of gendered discourses in organized sport. *Journal of language and social psychology* 29: 278–300.

Anderson, E. 2002. Openly gay athletes contesting hegemonic masculinity in a homophobic environment. *Gender and society* 16: 860–877.

———. 2011a. Updating the outcome gay athletes, straight teams, and coming out in educationally based sport teams. *Gender and Society* 25: 250–268.

———. 2011b. Masculinities and sexualities in sport and physical cultures: Three decades of evolving research. *Journal of Homosexuality* 58: 565–578.

Anderson, E., and R. McGuire. 2010. Inclusive masculinity theory and the gendered politics of men's rugby. *Journal of Gender Studies* 19: 249–261.

Bell, D., and J. Binnie. 2004. Authenticating queer space: Citizenship, urbanism and governance. *Urban Studies* 41: 1807–1820.

Bell, M.P., M.F. Özbilgin, T.A. Beauregard, and O. Sürgevil. 2011. Voice, silence, and diversity in 21st century organisations: Strategies for inclusion of gay, lesbian, bisexual, and transgender employees. *Human Resource Management* 50: 131–146.

Book, K., and L. Eskilsson. 2010. Coming out in Copenhagen: Homo sports events in city marketing. *Sport in society* 13: 314–328.

Borgerson, J. 2005. Judith Butler: On organizing subjectivities. *The Sociological Review* 53: 63–79.

Bowring, M.A., and J. Brewis. 2009. Truth and consequences: Managing lesbian and gay identity in the Canadian workplace. *Equal Opportunities International* 28: 361–377.

Brackenridge, C., I. Rivers, B. Gough, and K. Llewellyn. 2004. Driving down participation. Homophobic bullying as a deterrent to doing sport. In *Sport and gender identities: Masculinities, femininities and sexualities*, ed. T. Aitchison and C. Scraton, 122–139. London: Routledge.

Butler, J. 1990. *Gender trouble, feminist theory, and psychoanalytic discourse.* New York: Routledge.

———. 1993. *Bodies that matter: On the discursive limits of sex.* London: Routledge.

Carless, D. 2010. Who the hell was that? Stories, bodies and actions in the world. *Qualitative research in psychology* 7: 332–344.

———. 2012. Negotiating sexuality and masculinity in school sport: An auto-ethnography. *Sport, education and society* 17: 607–625.

Cashmore, E., and J. Cleland. 2011. Glasswing butterflies: Gay professional football players and their culture. *Journal of Sport and Social Issues* 35: 420–436.

———. 2012. Fans, homophobia and masculinities in association football: Evidence of a more inclusive environment. *The British journal of sociology* 63: 370–387.

Caudwell, J. 2002. Women's experiences of sexuality within football contexts: A particular and located footballing epistemology. *Football Studies* 5: 24–45.

———. 2007. Queering the field? The complexities of sexuality within a lesbian-identified football team in England. *Gender, Place and Culture* 14: 183–196.

———. 2011. Does your boyfriend know you're here? The spatiality of homophobia in men's football culture in the UK. *Leisure Studies* 30: 123–138.

———. 2014. [Transgender] young men: Gendered subjectivities and the physically active body. *Sport, Education and Society* 19: 398–414.

Chan, P.W. 2013. Queer eye on a 'straight' life: Deconstructing masculinities in construction. *Construction Management and Economics* 31: 816–831.

Clair, J.A., J.E. Beatty, and T.L. MacLean. 2005. Out of sight but not out of mind: Managing invisible social identities in the workplace. *Academy of Management Review* 30: 78–95.

Collinson, D.L. 1988. Engineering humour: Masculinity, joking and conflict in shop-floor relations. *Organization Studies* 9: 181–199.

Connell, R.W. 1987. *Gender and power: Society, the person and sexual politics.* Cambridge: Polity Press.

———. 1995. *Masculinities.* Cambridge: Polity.

Cox, B., and S. Thompson. 2001. Facing the bogey: Women, football and sexuality. *Football Studies* 4: 7–24.

Croteau, J.M., M.Z. Anderson, and B.L. VanderWal. 2008. Models of workplace sexual identity disclosure and management: Reviewing and extending concepts. *Group and Organization Management* 33: 532–565.

DeJordy, R. 2008. Just passing through: Stigma, passing, and identity decoupling in the work place. *Group and Organization Management* 33: 504–531.

Department for Culture, Media and Sport. 2005. Transexual people and sport: Guidance for sporting bodies. http://www.lgbthistorymonth.org.uk/documents/DCMS%20Guidance%20-%20Transsexual%20People%20and%20Sport%20(1).pdf. Accessed 12 Aug 2016.

Drury, S. 2011. It seems really inclusive in some ways, but... inclusive just for people who identify as lesbian: Discourses of gender and sexuality in a lesbian-identified football club. *Soccer and Society* 12: 421–442.

Elling, A., and J. Janssens. 2009. Sexuality as a structural principle in sport participation: Negotiating sports spaces. *International Review for the Sociology of Sport* 44: 71–86.

Elling, A., P. De Knop, and A. Knoppers. 2003. Gay/lesbian sport clubs and events places of homo-social bonding and cultural resistance? *International Review for the Sociology of Sport* 38: 441–456.

Eng, H. 2006. "We are moving up like a hard-on!": Doing sexuality in sport. *Nordic Journal of Women's Studies* 14: 12–26.

———. 2008. Doing sexuality in sport. *Journal of homosexuality* 54: 103–123.

Fitzclarence, L., and C. Hickey. 2001. Real footballers don't eat quiche old narratives in new times. *Men and Masculinities* 4: 118–139.

Fusco, C. 2005. Cultural landscapes of purification: Sports spaces and discourses of whiteness. *Sociology of Sport Journal* 22: 282–309.

Gregory, M.R. 2009. Inside the locker room: Male homosociability in the advertising industry. *Gender, Work and Organization* 16: 323–347.

Griffin, P. 1998. *Strong women, deep closets: Lesbians and homophobia in sport.* London: Human Kinetics Publishers.

Hancock, P., and M. Tyler. 2007. Undoing gender and the aesthetics of organisational performance. *Gender, Work and Organization* 14: 512–533.

Hekma, G. 1998. As long as they don't make an issue of it... Gay men and lesbians in organized sports in the Netherlands. *Journal of homosexuality* 35: 1–23.

Hubbard, P. 2008. Here, there, everywhere: The ubiquitous geographies of heteronormativity. *Geography Compass* 2: 640–658.

Humphrey, J.C. 1999. Organizing sexualities, organized inequalities: Lesbians and gay men in public service occupations. *Gender, work and organization* 6: 134–151.

Ingram, G.B. 1997. 'Open' space as strategic queer sites. In *Queers in space: Communities/public spaces/sites of resistance*, 95–125. San Francisco: Bay Press.

Jones, L., and M. McCarthy. 2010. Mapping the landscape of gay men's football. *Leisure Studies* 29: 161–173.

Kian, E., and E. Anderson. 2009. John Amaechi: Changing the way sport reporters examine gay athletes. *Journal of Homosexuality* 56: 799–818.

King, D., and S. Lawley. 2016. *Organisational behaviour.* Oxford: Oxford University Press.

Lefebvre, H. 1991. *The production of space.* Oxford: Blackwell.

McCormack, M., and E. Anderson. 2010. The re-production of homosexually-themed discourse in educationally-based organised sport. *Culture, Health and Sexuality* 12: 913–927.

McDowell, L. 1995. Body work: Heterosexual gender performances in city workplaces. In *Mapping desire*, ed. D. Bell and G. Valentine, 75–98. London: Routledge.

McDowell, L., and G. Court. 1994. Missing subjects: Gender, power, and sexuality in merchant banking. *Economic Geography* 70: 229–251.

Miller, S.L., K.B. Forest, and N.C. Jurik. 2003. Diversity in blue lesbian and gay police officers in a masculine occupation. *Men and masculinities* 5: 355–385.

National Union of Students. 2012. Out in sport: LGBT students' experiences of sport. http://www.nus.org.uk/Global/Final%20Out%20in%20Sport_NEW_web.pdf. Accessed 30 Aug 2016.

Norman, L. 2012. Gendered homophobia in sport and coaching: Understanding the everyday experiences of lesbian coaches. *International Review for the Sociology of Sport* 47: 705–723.

Out on the Fields. 2015. Out on the fields: The first international study on homophobia in sport. http://www.outonthefields.com. Accessed 30 Aug 2016.

Outsports. 2016. A record 56 out athletes compete in Rio Olympics. http://www.outsports.com/2016/7/11/12133594/rio-olympics-teams-2016-gay-lgbt-athletes-record. Accessed 30 Aug 2016.

Pappas, N.T., P.C. McKenry, and B.S. Catlett. 2004. Athlete aggression on the rink and off the ice athlete violence and aggression in hockey and interpersonal relationships. *Men and Masculinities* 6: 291–312.

Parker, M. 2002. Queering management and organization. *Gender, Work and Organization* 9: 146–166.

Price, M., and A. Parker. 2003. Sport, sexuality, and the gender order: Amateur rugby union, gay men, and social exclusion. *Sociology of Sport Journal* 20: 108–126.

Probyn, E. 2000. Sporting bodies: Dynamics of shame and pride. *Body & Society* 6: 13–28.

Pronger, B. 1990. *The arena of masculinity: Sports, homosexuality, and the meaning of sex*. New York: St. Martins Press.

———. 2000. Homosexuality and sport: Who's winning? *Research on Men and Masculinities Series* 13: 222–244.

Ravel, B., and G. Rail. 2007. On the limits of "gaie" spaces: Discursive constructions of women's sport in Quebec. *Sociology of Sport Journal* 24: 402–420.

Robertson, S. 2003. 'If I let a goal in, I'll get beat up': Contradictions in masculinity, sport and health. *Health education research* 18: 706–716.

Rumens, N. 2010. Workplace friendships between men: Gay men's perspectives and experiences. *Human Relations* 63: 1541–1562.

———. 2011. Minority support: Friendship and the development of gay and lesbian managerial careers and identities. *Equality, Diversity and Inclusion: An International Journal* 30: 444–462.

Rumens, N., and J. Broomfield. 2012. Gay men in the police: Identity disclosure and management issues. *Human Resource Management Journal* 22: 283–298.

Rumens, N., and D. Kerfoot. 2009. Gay men at work: (Re) constructing the self as professional. *Human Relations* 62: 763–786.

Rushbrook, D. 2002. Cities, queer space, and the cosmopolitan tourist. *A journal of lesbian and gay studies* 8: 183–206.

Russell, K. 2007. Queers, even in netball?': Interpretations of the lesbian label among portswomen. In *Sport and gender identities*, ed. C.C. Aitchison, 104–119. London: Routledge.

Skeggs, B. 1999. Matter out of place: Visibility and sexualities in leisure spaces. *Leisure studies* 18: 213–232.

Skogvang, B.O., and K. Fasting. 2013. Football and sexualities in Norway. *Soccer and Society* 14: 872–886.

Southall, R.M., M.S. Nagel, E. Anderson, F.G. Polite, and C. Southall. 2009. An investigation of male college athletes' attitudes toward sexual-orientation. *Journal of Issues in Intercollegiate Athletics* Special Issue: 62–77.

Sport England. 2012. Sport and sexual orientation. http://funding.sportengland.org/research/key-influences/sexual-orientation/. Assessed 12 Aug 2016.

Stevenson, D., D. Rowe, and K. Markwell. 2005. Explorations in 'event ecology': The case of the International Gay Games. *Social Identities* 11: 447–465.

Stonewall. 2009. Leagues behind: Football's failure to tackle anti-gay abuse. https://www.stonewall.org.uk/resources/leagues-behind-2009. Accessed 30 Aug 2016.

Sumara, D., and B. Davis. 1999. Interrupting heteronormativity: Toward a queer curriculum theory. *Curriculum Inquiry* 29: 191–208.

Sykes, H. 2006. Transsexual and transgender policies in sport. *Women in Sport and Physical Activity Journal* 15: 3–13.

Symons, C. 2007. Challenging homophobia and heterosexism in sport. In *Sport and gender identities: Masculinities, femininities and sexualities*, ed. C.C. Aitchison, 140–159. London: Routledge.

Tyler, M., and L. Cohen. 2008. Management in/as comic relief: Queer theory and gender performativity in the office. *Gender, Work and Organization* 15: 113–132.

————. 2010. Spaces that matter: Gender performativity and organisational space. *Organization Studies* 31: 175–198.

Van Ingen, C. 2003. Geographies of gender, sexuality and race reframing the focus on space in sport sociology. *International Review for the Sociology of Sport* 38: 201–216.

Waitt, G. 2003. Gay Games: Performing 'community' out from the closet of the locker room. *Social and Cultural Geography* 4: 167–183.

Ward, J., and D. Winstanley. 2003. The absent presence: Negative space within discourse and the construction of minority sexual identity in the workplace. *Human Relations* 56: 1255–1280.

————. 2005. Coming out at work: Performativity and the recognition and renegotiation of identity. *The Sociological Review* 53: 447–475.

Wellard, I. 2002. Men, sport, body performance and the maintenance of 'exclusive masculinity'. *Leisure Studies* 21: 235–247.

Wright, T. 2013. Uncovering sexuality and gender: An intersectional examination of women's experience in UK construction. *Construction Management and Economics* 31: 832–844.

Youth Chances. 2014. Youth chances survey of 16–25 year-olds: First reference report. http://www.youthchances.org/wp-content/uploads/2011/03/YouthChancesSurvey-16-25yearOlds_FirstReferenceReport.pdf. Accessed 30 Aug 2016.

8

Gender Differences in Paid and Unpaid Work

Daniel Wheatley, Christopher Lawton, and Irene Hardill

8.1 Introduction

Work comprises a range of activities which can be paid or unpaid (Hardill 2002). In advanced societies, the majority of paid work is undertaken for an employer, although paid work can also be pursued through

D. Wheatley (✉)
Department of Business and Labour Economics, Birmingham Business School, University of Birmingham, Birmingham, UK

C. Lawton
Department of Economics, Nottingham Business School, Nottingham Trent University, Nottingham, UK

I. Hardill
Northumbria Centre for Citizenship and Civil Society, Northumbria University, Newcastle, UK

© The Author(s) 2018
V. Caven, S. Nachmias (eds.), *Hidden Inequalities in the Workplace*,
Palgrave Explorations in Workplace Stigma,
DOI 10.1007/978-3-319-59686-0_8

self-employment. Approximately 15 % of working individuals in the UK are self-employed (ONS 2016). In recent years, there has been a growing flexibilisation of the labour market, including a growth in precarious work, in zero hours, temporary and part-time jobs, which are uncertain, unpredictable and high risk for workers (Kalleberg 2009; Raess and Burgoon 2015). Some of these developments are encapsulated in the term 'gig economy' (Friedman 2014; Harvey et al. 2017). Against this changing economic landscape, patterns of employment and self-employment remain highly gendered, reflecting amongst other factors the persistence of slow-changing social norms, producing a labour market that is both horizontally and vertically gender segregated (Teasdale 2013). One of the primary drivers of this gender segregation is the uneven contribution of men and women to unpaid work. Unpaid work includes a range of activities encapsulated in the term 'social reproduction' (Glucksmann 1995), such as housework and care performed within and away from the home, as well as formal and informal volunteering in the community. Unpaid work remains a key site of gender difference, and one which can act to constrain the ability of women to engage in paid work (Carmichael et al. 2008; Drinkwater 2015). Women still perform the majority of housework, accounting for up to 16 hours of unpaid work among women in part-time paid employment (Wheatley 2017, 88). Many women also remain burdened with the majority of caring responsibilities within and outside of the household, including childcare, grandparental care and care for ill/elderly kin and non-kin (Atkinson and Hall 2009). The uneven contribution of men and women to the household division of labour has important consequences.

Creating space and time to undertake unpaid care within and outside of the home for kin and non-kin results in a number of trade-offs and inequalities with respect to participation in paid work. Those providing lengthier hours of care, and for longer durations, are more likely to reduce their commitment to paid work, through movements to part-time work, by altering the arrangement of work time using flexible working arrangements, or leaving paid employment entirely (Carmichael et al. 2008). Economic inactivity rates vary starkly by gender: in the UK in 2015, the *Annual Population Survey* recorded the economic inactivity rate among men at 17 % in comparison to 28.2 % among women (NOMIS 2016).

Meanwhile, among those who do participate in paid work, estimates from the UK *Labour Force Survey* show that 42.2 % of women reported part-time work in April–June 2015, compared to only 12.9 % of men (ONS 2015a, b). The contrasting impact of unpaid work on the ability of men and women to engage in paid work results in the persistence of significant inequalities in the working lives of men and women throughout the life course.

This chapter explores gendered patterns of paid and unpaid work from a life-course perspective. A life-course approach allows for consideration of an individual's life, encompassing not only the role of chronological age but also experiences throughout the life course, including specific milestones and transitions (Worth and Hardill 2015). In exploring gendered patterns of work, we draw on the *Total Social Organisation of Labour* (TSOL) conceptual framework (Glucksmann 1995; Lyon and Glucksmann 2008; Taylor 2004; Williams 2011), which facilitates the exploration of different forms of work within a continuum, acknowledging the blurred boundaries present between paid and unpaid work (Baines and Hardill 2008). The UK data is extracted from waves 1 to 19 (1992–2009) of the *British Household Panel Survey* (BHPS), waves 2–6 (2010/2011–2014/2015) of *Understanding Society*, the *Annual Population Survey*, the *Annual Survey of Hours and Earnings* (ASHE) and the *Labour Force Survey*. In exploring empirical patterns of paid and unpaid work, this chapter contributes to understanding of the gendered nature of employment, providing insight into the changing experiences of work, both paid and unpaid, encountered by men and women throughout the life course in contemporary advanced societies.

8.2   Work and the Life Course

The life course is central to our understanding of the relationship between paid and unpaid work, which is both complex and highly gendered. A life-course approach to research gives consideration to age, in a broad sense, comprising chronological age, that is, how many years an individual has lived, as well as individual and collective trajectories of experience—in this case, time spent in paid and unpaid work—in space, place and through time as these are shaped by events, roles, memory and retrospection (Worth and Hardill 2015). Age is often conceptualised in life-course research as a social construction, which applies social understanding and significance to chronological age. This is relevant to our chapter as patterns of engagement in paid work, and indeed unpaid work, are closely linked to chronological age including, for example, the age at which an individual finishes their education, or the age at which one retires from paid work. Age boundaries are therefore important to how we understand the life course. Within the extant literature, intergenerationality has largely been explored within the context of the family, including intra-family geographies of parenting, parent-child relations, grandparent-grandchild relations and extra-familial relations (Hardill and Monk 2016, p. 5). A 'transitions' approach to life-course research considers movements during the life course, often contextualised with regard to specific milestones related to age or career, for example, the transition from education to employment. Transitions are seen as dynamic rather than determined (Hardill and Monk 2016). These transitions further extend to the impact of household and familial milestones including having children or a parent requiring care during their old age. Research conducted within this subject area has also sought to explore the 'destandardisation' of the life course including, for example, trends pertaining to deferred retirement (Kim and Moen 2002).

Work is conceptualised, in this chapter, using feminist theorisations of 'work'; in particular, the conceptual framework developed by Miriam Glucksmann (1995; 2000) and others (Taylor 2004; Williams 2011), 'the total social organisation of labour' (TSOL). TSOL encompasses activities that cut across boundaries between paid and unpaid work, market and non-market, and formal and informal sectors (Glucksmann 2000). TSOL proposes a sophisticated model of work that highlights its blurred boundaries, with the existence of activities that can be work or non-work according to context, while it is also argued that work cannot be separated from the social and cultural relationships within which it is conducted. Taylor and, more recently, Williams (Fig. 8.1, 2011) built upon TSOL to situate paid and unpaid work within a continuum of work that can take place in public, institutional or familial settings and can be either paid or unpaid in any of them. This includes acknowledg-

PAID				
1. Formal paid job in private or public sector	2. Formal paid job in voluntary sector	3. Informal employment	4. Reimbursed favours	5. Paid family/household work
Paid care work provided by an organisation under contract to a local authority	*Paid staff who manage/coordinate unpaid volunteers; they enable volunteering*		*Providing paid babysitting*	
FORMAL				**INFORMAL**
Unpaid volunteering at a local hospital	*Volunteering in front-line services and governance roles*	*Recognising unmet need and organising a community group, such as a playgroup*	*The help of family and friends to support a young single mother or housebound relative/neighbour*	*Unpaid domestic work supporting young children or frail partner(sometimes constraining time for volunteering)*
6. Formal unpaid work in private and public sectors	7. Formal unpaid work in voluntary & community sector	8. 'Below the radar' unpaid labour in groups	9. One-to-one unpaid labour	10. Self-provisioning
UNPAID				

Fig. 8.1 Typology of labour practices in TSOL (Source: Reprinted from Hardill and Baines (2011, p. 149), with the permission of Policy Press)

ing how the value attributed to work changes in response to a range of factors including national welfare policies (Lyon and Glucksmann 2008; Taylor 2004). In recognising the neglected dimension of unpaid activity in the public sphere, the TSOL framework facilitates the exploration of different forms of work using this continuum (see Fig. 8.1) from paid work for an employer, to voluntary work for an organisation, to unpaid care within the household, acknowledging the blurred boundaries that exist between what constitutes paid and unpaid work (Baines and Hardill 2008, pp. 308–9). As such, TSOL acknowledges that the gender distribution of labour within the household cannot simply be referred to in the context of a single sphere, but it must instead refer to the organisation of labour across and between boundaries (Glucksmann 1995).

8.3   Paid and Unpaid Work as a Site of Inequity

Since the Industrial Revolution, 'home life' (including unpaid work, such as childcare, cleaning and other household tasks) and 'work' (work for wages, i.e. paid work) have tended to take place in different domains. These domains thus became separated spatially and deeply gendered, with 'home' a largely female domain and 'work' a male domain, with a stereotypical nuclear family comprising a male 'breadwinner' and a female 'homemaker' (Horrell and Humphries 1995; the notion of separate spheres is contested). While traditional models of the household focused on the concept of the male breadwinner, female homemaker, a pure male breadwinner model never existed in practice as women have always engaged in the labour market (Lewis 2001; Pennington and Westover 1989). The incompatibility of the male-breadwinner, female-homemaker model with the lived experiences of men and women in advanced societies has led to a number of alternative models being developed, including transitional models. These include the 'adult-worker model family', often concerned with the 'one and a half worker' model in which men are assumed to work full time and women part time, at least during certain stages of the life course (Lewis 2001), and egalitarian models in which it is recognised that unpaid household work can be shared equally between men and women (Hochschild and Machung 1990).

Despite decades of gender-focused equality policies, and women in the UK becoming more likely than ever to be the household's primary earner (Soobedar 2011), women continue to undertake the majority of household labour. Paid and unpaid care remains deeply gendered; women perform the bulk of housework, and act as care providers for close family members (Garcia et al. 2011) and other kin and non-kin present in the household and in the wider community (Woolvin and Hardill 2013), whether they work full time or part time and regardless of whether they have their own children (Scott and Clery 2013). But providing care impacts significantly on women's labour market participation (Drinkwater 2015; Garcia et al. 2011), and can increase stress levels when juggling paid work with lengthy hours of unpaid housework and care (MacDonald et al. 2005). It has been shown, using a combination of secondary data from the BHPS and primary survey data, that providing lengthier hours of care, and for longer durations, results in a greater propensity to reduce work time, alter the arrangement of paid work including through use of flexible working arrangements, or leave employment entirely (Carmichael et al. 2008). Meanwhile, UK Census data has shown that the demand on individuals to provide care varies throughout the life course, with greater volumes of informal care including grandparenting, for example, being associated with significantly lower levels of labour market participation among older women (Drinkwater 2015). The impact on the ability of a carer to engage in the labour market has also been found to be much greater for those providing care for kin or non-kin present within the same residence than among those providing care to individuals not resident within the home (Heitmueller 2007).

A person's ability to undertake paid work is therefore highly dependent upon the amount of unpaid caring work they have to undertake, as well as how and where this care is being provided, resulting in a trade-off between paid work and unpaid work, including housework, care and voluntary work (Hardill and Wheatley 2017). It has long been argued that family-based care creates and reinforces inequalities within the household (Lewis 2002). But it can marginalise women as subjects in caring relationships which are considered 'other' to masculine ideologies of paid work and the home (Hughes et al. 2005). This unpaid work functions as a social constraint to many women's labour force participation (van Staveren 2010, p. 1130). Women with the economic resources to make choices may, at certain stages in the life course, be able to remain in paid employment by utilising market and non-market, family-based care (Harris et al. 2007). Considering the case of women in Spain using the *Spanish Time Use Survey*, Carrasco and Dominguez (2011, p. 180) find that the provision of care has shifted away from mothers to some extent, but not to fathers, rather to either marketised care or care provided gratis by family members including grandparents. Many women, nevertheless, who are married/co-habiting and have dependent children are often faced with the practical 'choice' of undertaking paid work outside the home alongside significant unpaid work inside the home.

In the post-war period, women have increased their share of employment in virtually all industries and occupations, including the professions in the UK. Writing in 1991, Linda McDowell (1991, p. 417) argued that, *the feminisation of the labour market is amongst the most far-reaching of the [labour market] changes.* This feminisation is largely the consequence of the growth of the service sector (tertiarisation). The growth of the service sector, which requires cognitive and interpersonal skills, alongside the contraction of physically demanding manual occupations, especially in manufacturing, has facilitated increased labour market participation among women (UKCES 2016). Figure 8.2 shows that the employment rate for women increased very significantly between 1971 and 2015, from 53 % to almost 70 %, whilst the male employment rate has declined from 92 % to 79 %. This means that the difference between male and female employment rates has fallen from 40 percentage points at the start of the period to 10 percentage points in the latest estimate. The chart also clearly illustrates the greater impact of economic shocks on male employment, with male-dominated occupations in construction and manufacturing particularly vulnerable to recession, meaning that the long-term convergence in the rates of male and female participation in paid work has accelerated during periods of economic downturn. For example, during

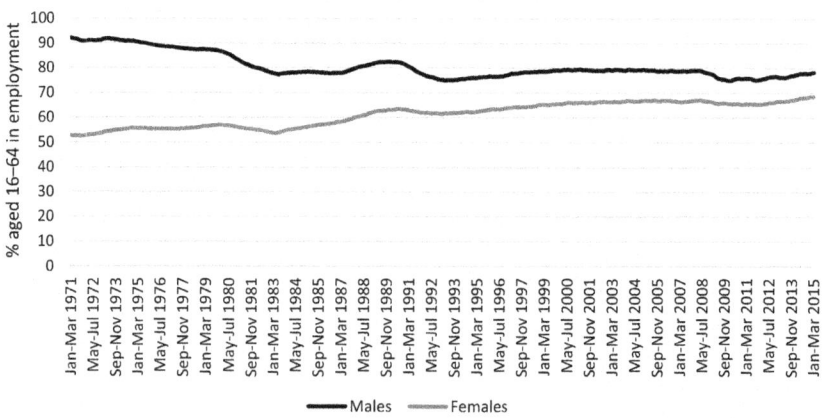

Fig. 8.2 Employment rates for men and women (% aged 16–64)—1971–2015 (Source: Adapted from data from the Office for National Statistics licensed under the Open Government Licence v.3.0—'*Labour Market Statistics*', October 2016, and '*Women in the Labour Market*', 2013)

the early 1990s' recession, male employment fell by 7.4 percentage points between January to March 1990 and February to April 1993, whilst the female employment rate fell by just 1.5 percentage points. In the case of the most recent recession, the male rate of employment fell by 3.3 percentage points between July to September 2008 and January to March 2010, whilst female employment fell by 1.1 percentage points.

Although employment in many service-based, female-dominated occupations has appeared to be more resilient in recent decades, as a result of the uneven distribution of unpaid work, *women predominate in a raft of low-paid jobs, especially part-time, whilst men are better represented in full-time and higher paid jobs* (Kirton and Greene 2016, p. 20). Horizontal and vertical gender segregation by both industry and occupation remains a prominent feature of the labour market in most advanced societies, including the UK (Teasdale 2013). Occupations in UK and international labour market statistics are categorised hierarchically by skill (the Standard Occupational Classifications used in the *Labour Force Survey* are assigned according to the *skill level* and *skill specialisation* of an individual's job), with more highly skilled occupations correlated with higher average wages. Figure 8.3 shows that, in 2015, men were significantly more likely to work as managers, directors and senior officials (12.8 % of male employment compared to 7.5 % of women), the occupational group associated with the highest levels of skill and highest average wages. Although the professional occupations account for a higher share of female employment (particularly due to more gendered professions such as teaching), women are also more likely to work in the intermediate-skilled administrative and secretarial and caring, leisure and other service occupations. In an analysis of the skill level of employment alone (excluding the skill specialisation or manual/cognitive bias of the job), the Office for National Statistics (ONS) estimated that the highest skilled jobs accounted for a similar share of men and women (at 28 % and 25 %, respectively), as did the lowest skilled jobs (at 11 % of both male and female employment). The difference between genders is mainly observed in the intermediate level of the skills hierarchy. Men were very much more likely to be utilising 'upper intermediate' skills (37 % of men compared to 18 % of women), whilst women were over-represented in 'lower intermediate' skilled work (47 % of women and 24 % of men) (ONS 2013).

As a product of these trends, and despite some recorded improvement in the wage gap, pay discrimination still exists (Kilgour 2013). According

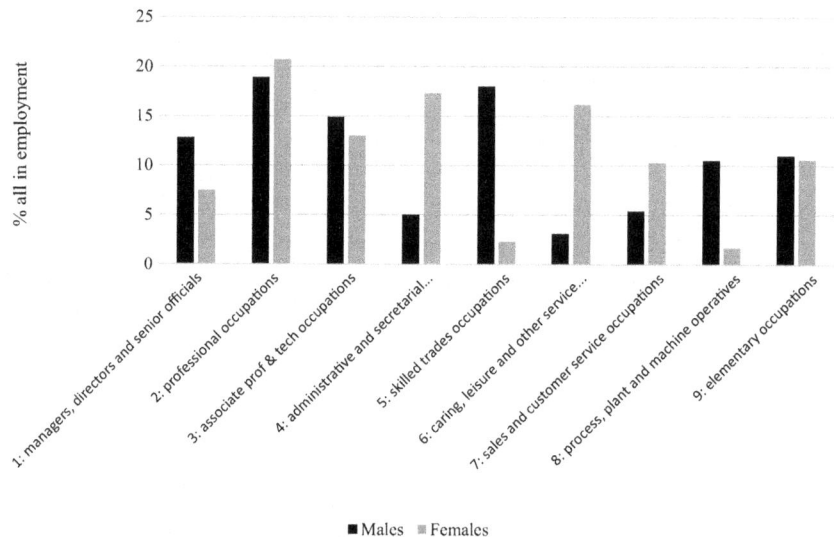

■ Males ■ Females

Fig. 8.3 Occupation of employment (SOC 2010) for men and women (% all in employment)—2015 (Source: Adapted from data from the Office for National Statistics licensed under the Open Government Licence v.3.0—2016 'Annual Population Survey', January–December 2015, from NOMIS [Accessed 30th January, 2017])

to recent data from the *Annual Survey of Hours and Earnings* (ASHE), a gender pay gap of around 10 % is still found among full-time workers, although the 9.4 % gap recorded in 2015 was the lowest recorded since the ASHE survey began in 1997 (ONS 2015b). It should be noted, though, that when women's greater propensity to work part time is incorporated, driven by their greater household contribution, the overall gender pay gap resides at closer to 20 %. The observed gendered patterns of unpaid care also have wider impacts on well-being. For example, using a sample of 14 European Union (EU) countries including the UK, childcare especially for school-age children, has been shown to have potentially negative impacts on satisfaction levels among mothers (Garcia et al. 2007). Meanwhile, evidence from the BHPS suggests that the provision of care for ill or elderly relatives or friends, especially when equating to 20 or more hours per week, can have significant negative effects on satisfaction with leisure among women (Wheatley and Wu 2014, p. 460).

8.4   Paid and Unpaid Work in a Flexibilised Labour Market

Since the latter part of the twentieth century, significant changes have been observed in the labour markets of most advanced societies. In the UK, a period of deindustrialisation was accompanied by equal opportunities and sex discrimination legislation in the 1970s, beginning with the *Equal Pay Act 1970*, which had a focus on reducing inequality present in the labour market and increasing participation among women. By the 1990s, equal pay and comparable worth policies had made notable inroads into reducing sex discrimination in pay (Hakim 2000, pp. 60–1). In the period of the New Labour (1997–2010) government,[1] a number of further changes, summarised in Table 8.1, were enacted following the UK's adoption of the EU Social Chapter, that is, social provisions outlined in the Maastricht and Amsterdam Treaties (Grimshaw and Rubery 2012), which have had significant influence over the labour market, focusing on increasing participation and improving the ability of working parents, and carers, to remain economically active (Smith and Morton 2006; Grimshaw and Rubery 2012).

Table 8.1 Selected UK labour market policy under New Labour, 1997–2010

Legislative act	Details
National Minimum Wage Act 1998	Minimum wage implemented under New Labour in 1999. Rate improved under New Labour relative to median earnings until 2008 (see Grimshaw and Rubery 2012, p. 110)
The Working Time Regulations 1998	1993 *European Working Time Directive* (Council Directive 94/103/EC) introduced through the *Working Time Regulations*, imposing a maximum 48-hour working week averaged over 17 weeks. Also, rules for annual leave, consecutive working hours and employment in specific sectors, for example, agriculture and fishing. In the UK, regulations since inception included an opt-out subject to individual choice
Employment Relations Act 1999	Provision of rights to union recognition (implemented in June 2000 as *Schedule A1 of the Trade Union and Labour Relations (Consolidation) (TULR(C)A) Act 1992*). Later amended under *Employment Relations Act 2004* providing trade unions with greater access to workers Reduction of qualifying period for employees for unfair dismissal rights to 12 months (implemented June 1999)

(continued)

Table 8.1 (continued)

Legislative act	Details
Part-time Workers Regulations 2000	The *Part-time Workers (Prevention of Less Favourable Treatment) Regulations 2000* provided rules for equal treatment of part-time workers with respect to pay, overtime premium payments, annual leave, sickness benefits, redundancy, pensions and a range of bonuses
Employment Act 2002	Range of policy focused on increasing opportunities, including extensions to maternity and paternity leave, increases in statutory maternity pay, dispute resolution within the workplace and equal treatment for fixed-term employees (prevention of pay and pension discrimination)
Flexible Working Regulations 2003	The *Flexible Working (Procedural Requirements) Regulations, SI 2002/3207, and Flexible Working (Eligibility, Complaints and Remedies) SI 2002/3236* are amendments to the *Employment Act 2002*, s. 47, consolidated in the *Employment Rights Act 1996*, ss. 80F–80I (Deakin and Morris 2012, pp. 750–2). Initially, enabling parents of young and disabled children to request alternative working arrangements with their employer. Extended to include carers of certain adults and parents of older children in 2007, and employees with parental responsibility for children under 16 in 2009
Carers (Equal Opportunities) Act 2004 (CEOPA)	Placed a duty on local authorities to provide details to carers of rights and opportunities to access education and training, employment and leisure (see Carmichael et al. 2008, p. 6)

A key feature of the policy enacted during the period of New Labour was a focus on increasing participation among mothers, including single parents, who have since this time been expected to participate in the labour market or be looking for work (Lewis and Campbell 2008). In part, this expectation has been driven by changes to family leave and welfare policies including linking welfare payments and tax credits to labour market participation (McDowell et al. 2005). Since the first term under New Labour, a range of initiatives have been designed to support informal carers in the UK including the Carers (Equal opportunities) Act 2004 (see Carmichael et al. 2008, pp. 6–7). Following the Employment Act 2002, family leave policy, until recently, allowed working women to take up to 26 weeks of paid maternity leave, and a further 26 weeks unpaid, while fathers were able to take up to two weeks paid paternity leave and up to 26 weeks total leave subject to meeting set criteria. Since December 2014, policy has been enacted with an increased focus on providing greater choice to parents in the allocation of caring responsibilities. Shared parental leave and shared parental pay have been introduced through the *Shared parental leave Regulations 2014*. Parents of babies born after 5 April 2015 have since been able to share up to 50 weeks of leave, 37 weeks of which is paid, subject to meeting certain eligibility criteria (Gov.uk 2016). Policy with a central focus on providing greater flexibility over paid work, acknowledging the impacts of unpaid work, was implemented in 2003 through the *Flexible Working Regulations* (see Table 8.1). The *Flexible Working Regulations* have been expanded a number of times since inception, most recently in 2014, to cover all workers following 26 weeks of service.

However, while an array of policy instruments have sought to expand participation and reduce work-life conflict, there has concurrently been a growing flexibilisation of the labour market which has occurred alongside changes in the economic environment in many advanced societies, which has resulted in reductions in public funding for care and related services. It has been argued that freeing up resources through increased investment in formal care provision would enable increases in labour market participation among many carers (Drinkwater 2015). However, this is challenging to enact, given the reductions in funding witnessed since the 2007–2009 global economic crisis. Meanwhile, employer-friendly flexibility in the labour market has resulted in an uncertain employment environment, evidenced in some employers using flexibility predominantly for their own benefit, and creating difficulties for workers in achieving desired work-life balance (Gregory and Milner 2009). This has driven a growth in 'precarious' or 'contingent' work (Kalleberg 2009), including zero hours, an 'on-call' non-guaranteed hours form of paid employment (Mandl et al. 2015; BIS 2014), as well as temporary, seasonal and short-term contracts and work as independent contractors (King 2014). In reaction to concerns surrounding some of these trends, specifically the growth in zero-hours employment, the UK government enacted legislation in 2014 banning exclusivity clauses in zero-hours contracts (BIS 2014). However, the growth of 'gig' work may reflect firms finding an alternative route to flexible labour. A form of on-demand labour or 'piecework' (Alkhatib et al. 2017), gig work is defined as work performed for a firm to complete a particular task or for a defined period of time as an independent contractor or consultant (Friedman 2014; Harvey et al. 2017). The gig economy is a subset of the wider collaborative economy specifically related to the provision of labour, usually facilitated by online and smartphone platforms that provide flexible work, including 'errands' and task sharing (NESTA 2014). The Work Foundation (2016, p. 5) extend this definition to see substantial overlap with more traditional self-employment and micro-business operation, particularly freelancing, where these individuals are *undertaking small and discrete parcels of work through digital technologies that connect providers and customers.* Gig work can enable greater choice over when and where to work and may be used by workers to bargain specific working conditions (Osnowitz and Henson 2016, p. 348), but this may only be possible among those who are more employable, for example, the highly skilled (Green 2011). For the remainder, gig work results in uncertain and insecure employment. The founder of Zipcar, Robin Chase, summed up the impact of the recent changes in the structure of paid work: *My father had one job in his lifetime, I will have six jobs in my lifetime, and my children will have six jobs at the same time* (Robin Chase, cited in Mulcahy 2016, p. 187). Alongside the growth in flexibility in paid work, there is increased acknowledgement of the limitations of current flexible working and work-family policies, which have been criticized for perpetuating gendered social constructs associated with masculinised full-time working routines and often long hours (Lewis and Humbert 2010, p. 242). Meanwhile, women's greater propensity to use flexible working arrangements, including working part time as a result of their greater unpaid work, could render them more at risk of the negative effects of a more flexibilised labour market.

8.5   Patterns of Paid and Unpaid Work Among UK Men and Women

Within life-course research, it is common to combine the collection and analysis of multiple data sources and types. The central premise of combining data sources is that together they should provide a better understanding of a subject than would be generated through exploring a single source. The approach employed in this chapter utilises multiple secondary data sources, providing the analysis with richer insight into patterns of paid and unpaid work, while also enabling some of the limitations of each of the individual data sources, for example, omitted questions in specific surveys, to be effectively mitigated (Lindsey et al. 2015, p. 50). Data is drawn from the UK Annual Population Survey, ASHE, the *Labour Force Survey*, the BHPS and *Understanding Society* to provide insight into gendered patterns of paid and unpaid work.

8.5.1   Gendered Patterns of Paid Work

The analysis of paid work focuses primarily on men and women in employment, although some consideration is given to the self-employed, including the growth in part-time self-employment, associated with the rise of the gig economy. In the *Labour Force Survey*, an individual is defined as 'employed' if they have completed at least one hour of paid work in the period being measured (e.g. over the last month, quarter or year) or are temporarily away from a job, for example, for vacation or sickness absence. In addition to paid work, the official estimates of employment also include individuals working on government-supported workplace training schemes (any form of work, work experience or work-related training) and 'unpaid family workers'. The latter group describes people who *work in a family business who do not receive a formal wage or salary but benefit from the profits of that business* (ONS 2016). Therefore, this excludes people who provide caring services to a relative of friend, unless some or all of that caring is paid. In the *Labour Force Survey*, the individual respondent self-classifies whether or not their employment is 'full-time' or 'part-time', it is not based on a given number of hours per week, although the ONS interviewer will ask several validation questions in certain instances. For example, if, in responses to later questions around hours of work, the respondent states that they usually work fewer than 16 hours per week, their status will be reclassified to part time. This provides some challenges for interpretation, as individuals may classify themselves differently, for example, referring to contracted hours or comparing themselves to colleagues' usual hours of work including unpaid additional hours (Walling 2007). With this caveat in mind, Fig. 8.4 shows that women are significantly more likely than men to be working part time. However, the extent of this difference has decreased in line with the growth in female employment overall and fall in male employment rates shown in Fig. 8.2. Whilst the proportion of women working part time has fluctuated between 42 % and 45 % between 1992 and 2015, the proportion of men working part time has increased from 7 % to almost 13 %. The chart also shows that part-time working is affected by the

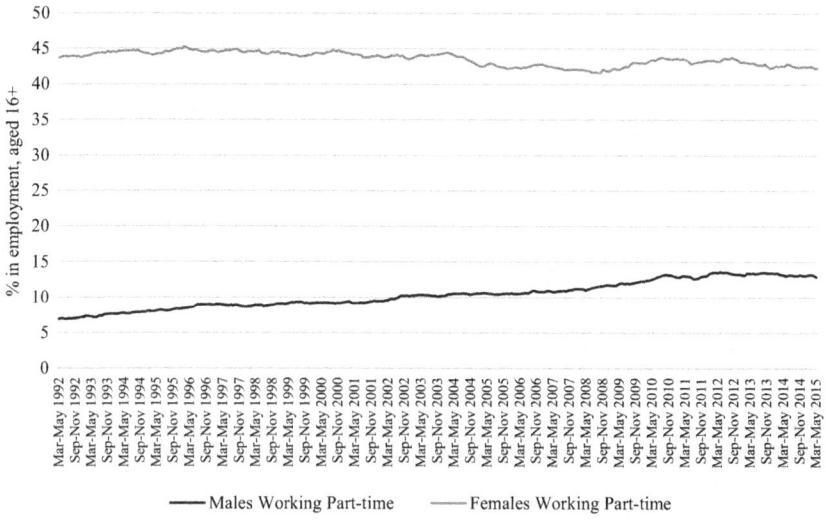

Fig. 8.4 Men and women in paid employment reporting part-time work (% aged 16+)—1992–2015 (Source: Adapted from data from the Office for National Statistics licensed under the Open Government Licence v.3.0. *'Labour Market Statistics'*, October 2016, Table EMP01)

economic cycle, with the proportion of women working part time falling (and working full time increasing) during the period of sustained growth in GDP and overall employment during the early- to mid-2000s, and again during the period of recovery from recession from 2011 to 2012.

Between 2005 and 2015, the number of women working full time has grown more than the number working part time, increasing by 10 % compared to 6 % over the decade. Conversely, the number of men working part time has increased very much more strongly than the number working full time, increasing by 27 % compared to just 3 % since 2005 (ONS 2016). The structure of employment by full-time and part-time working changes over the life course, with differences widening between men and women at certain stages. Part-time work is commonly referred to as being u-shaped, especially among men (Delson 1998; Gregory and Connolly 2008). It is more common among young adults and among those aged over 50, although incidence of part-time work remains present throughout the life course among both men and women, but especially women. For young adults at the start of their working lives, there is a smaller difference between the proportion of men and women working part time (with 21.5 % of 20–24-year-old men working part time compared to 34.3 % of women). However, during the period in which early-to-mid career coincides with peak child-rearing age in advanced societies such as the UK, the difference between men and women widens significantly (with only 7 % of 25–49-year-old men working part time compared to 38.7 % of women). For older workers, aged 50+, the difference between genders becomes smaller again, with both male and female part-time working increasing (to 18.6 % of men and 48 % of women). However, this must be interpreted in the context of the higher rates of employment overall for older men, with 46.3 % of men over 50 in some form of employment in 2015 compared to 35.7 % of women.

With respect to forms of highly flexibilised contingent employment, zero-hours contracts accounted for around 744,000 workers in the UK, approximately 2.4 % of all in employment, in April–June 2015, an increase from 622,000 in April–June 2014. These types of contracts are more prominent earlier in the life course among younger workers: in 2015, around 34 % of those on zero-hours contracts were aged 16–24. Evidence has also been reported of a growth in incidence of involuntary part-time work in the UK, reported in the *Labour Force Survey* in reference to part-time work being undertaken due to a lack of full-time opportunities. In 2015, around 15 % of those working part time reported this form of underemployment—an increase from 10 % in 2008 (Green and Livanos 2015). Meanwhile, employment in temporary roles has risen to 307,000 in April–June 2015. This evidence of contingent work highlights the growth in these forms of employment and also the differing experiences of paid work encountered throughout the life course.

Turning to self-employment, an area of particular relevance in recent years associated with the rise of the 'gig' economy, patterns show significant increases in self-employment overall to around 15 % of all workers, which has been driven equally by both increases in the number of workers reporting full-time and part-time self-employment (Wales and Amankwah 2016). In relative terms, though, this reflects substantial increases in the number reporting part-time self-employment, as summarised in Fig. 8.5. A substantial portion of this growth reflects work in precarious 'gig' self-employment, especially among those returning

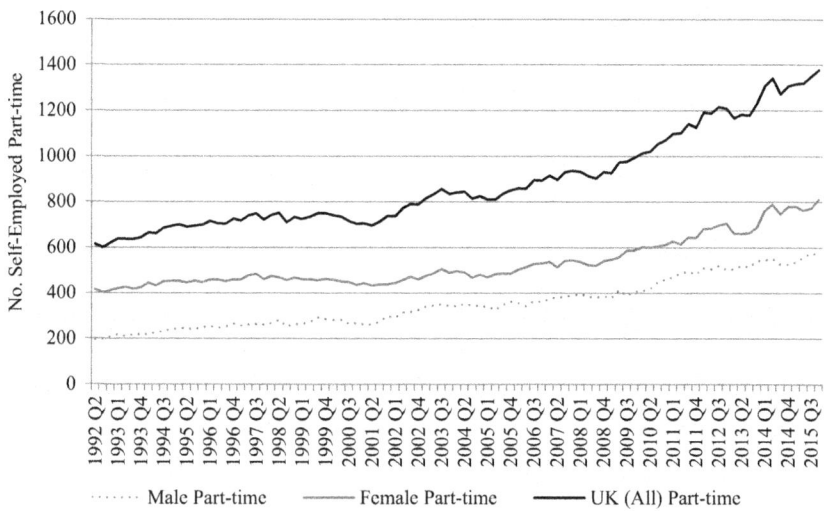

Fig. 8.5 Part-time self-employment among men and women—1992–2015 (Source: Adapted from data from the Office for National Statistics licensed under the Open Government Licence v.3.0. 2016, LFS: Self-employed: Part-time, *'Labour Market Statistics time series dataset (LMS)'*, from ONS [Accessed 10 February, 2017])

to the labour market following unemployment (Wales and Amankwah 2016, p. 28). Part-time self-employment is increasingly evenly split by gender, and is prevalent among workers in their mid-40s and especially among men aged over 60. The over 65s, men and women combined, also accounted for around 22 % of the part-time self-employed in 2015 (Wales and Amankwah 2016, p. 14). These patterns are consistent with some of the suggestions of trading down and bridge employment among some older workers discussed in Chap. 5, and suggest that while labour market flexibility may be affecting younger workers most significantly with regard to zero-hours contracts and some temporary forms of employment, similar flexibilisation is affecting older workers, in particular older men, through increased incidence of part-time self-employment.

Considering the impacts of these patterns of work with respect to earnings, Fig. 8.6 shows that the gender pay gap is principally present in full-time work, with male full-time workers paid a median of £13.97

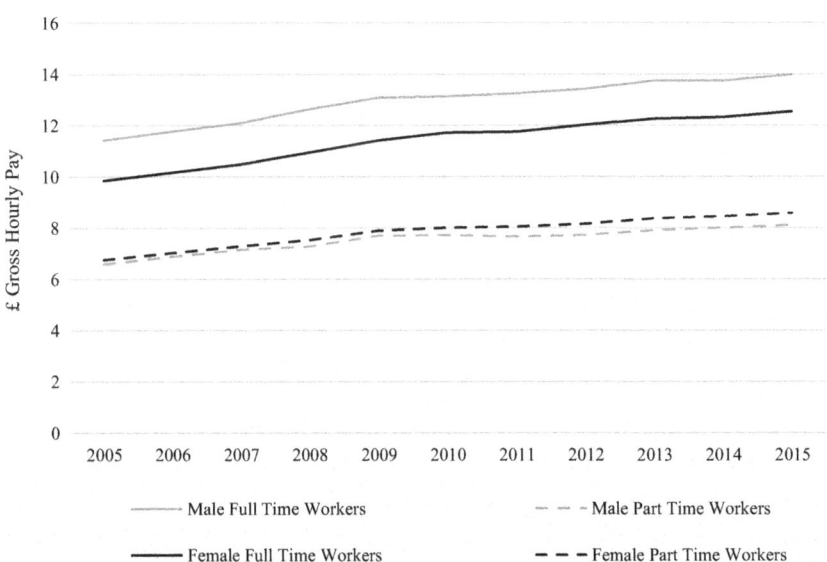

Fig. 8.6 Gross hourly pay for men and women (nominal £ values)—full time and part time (Source: Adapted from data from the Office for National Statistics licensed under the Open Government Licence v.3.0. 'Annual Survey of Hours and Earnings', 2005 to 2015, from NOMIS [Accessed 23rd December, 2016])

an hour—£1.44 more than the median for women full-time workers—whilst there is near parity for part-time workers. However, as a significantly greater proportion of women work part time, it is also important to note that the median hourly earnings for part-time work are much lower than full time. Finally, it is interesting to note that part-time earnings for men have grown more slowly than for women (with median part-time earnings for women slightly exceeding the median for men in 2015), which corresponds with the period of significant increase in male part-time working post-2008 shown in Fig. 8.4. This offers further indication that men have been more likely to 'trade-down' into lower paid part-time employment following the recession, supported by *Labour Force Survey* data that indicates a period of high involuntary part-time employment for men during the initial, uneven stage of recovery in the UK labour market that started in 2011.

8.5.2 Patterns of Unpaid Work Throughout the Life Course

Patterns of paid work remain highly gendered, and this is at least, in part, a product of the gendered distribution of unpaid work including that which takes place within the household (Atkinson and Hall 2009; Garcia et al. 2011). Gendered patterns of unpaid work are captured through the exploration of data from the BHPS and *Understanding Society*, including self-reported patterns of time spent performing housework as well as details surrounding the distribution of tasks within the household, time spent providing care for ill or elderly relatives or friends both within and outside of the household, reported contributions to childcare and time spent in voluntary work. Unpaid work accounts for a substantive use of time among most women; however, this is not the case for men. Patterns of housework are summarised in Fig. 8.7 for the period between 1992 and 2014–2015 using data from the BHPS and *Understanding Society*, reflecting stark differences in the reported household contribution of men and women. Men in work—either employed full time or part time or self-employed—report only around five hours per week spent performing housework, although this has increased to some degree since

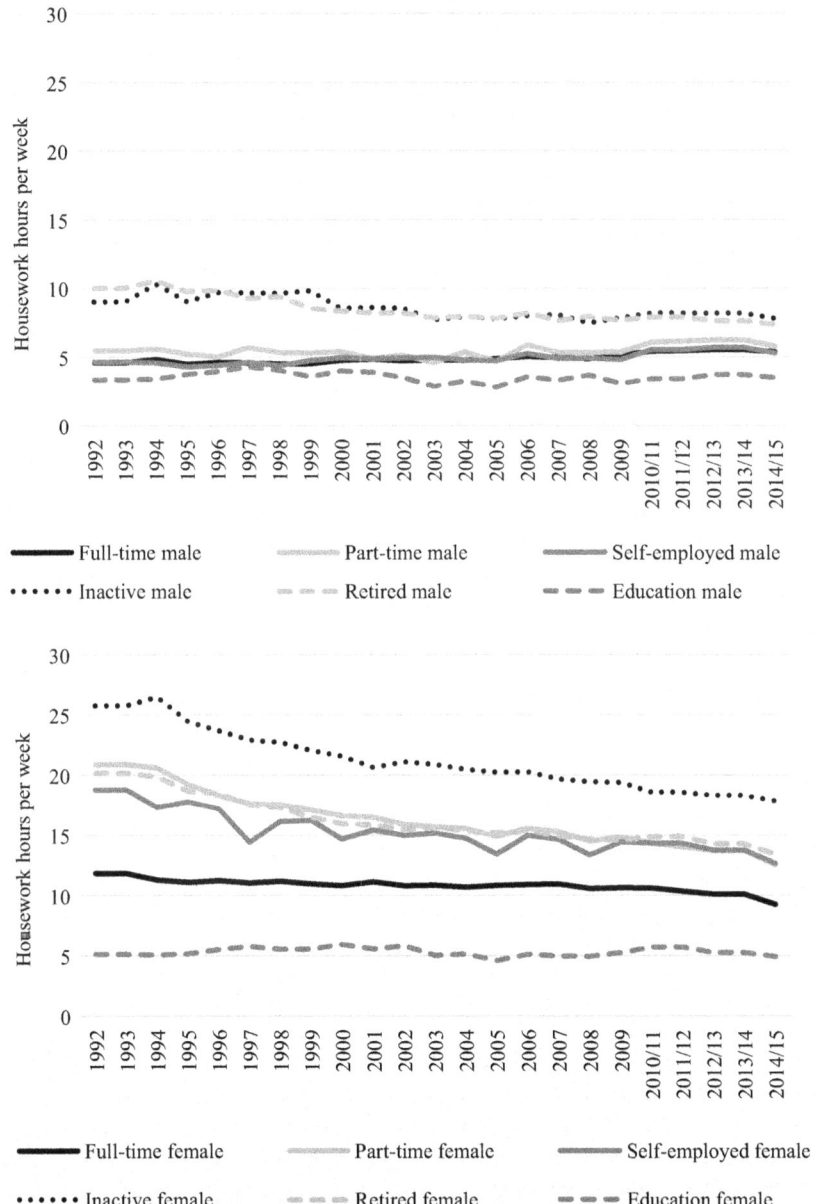

Fig. 8.7 Average housework hours among men and women—1992–2014/2015 (Source: Adapted from *British Household Panel Survey* waves 1–18, 1992–2009; *Understanding Society* wave 2–6 (2010/2011–2014/2015))
Note: Inactive comprises unemployed, long-term sick/disabled, family carers

the early 1990s. Meanwhile, although economically inactive and retired men report a greater household contribution, this has actually decreased significantly in the last two decades from around ten hours per week to around 7.5 hours per week. Women's patterns of housework are much more diverse, although overall their household contribution remains much greater than that of their male counterparts. Importantly, it should be noted that hours of housework reported by women have decreased considerably for all but women employed full-time and women in education, both of which are groups of women who report fewer hours of housework throughout the sample period. Nevertheless, women in full-time employment report lengthy hours of housework which are approximately double that of working men, equal to just under 11 hours per week on average throughout the sample period. Women employed part time and those reporting self-employment report largely similar patterns of lengthy hours of housework, although these have decreased from around 20 hours in the early 1990s to 14 hours since 2010. These patterns are evident of the trade-offs present between paid and unpaid work among those reporting shorter time spent in paid work, and further lend some support to the notion of self-employment being used by women as a method of increasing flexibility at certain points during the life course, including when dependent children are present (Cabrera 2007; Hytti 2010). Women in education, who are predominantly younger women, are the only sub-group to report patterns of housework more consistent to that of men at around four to five hours per week. Finally, economically inactive women report the greatest household contribution but also the greatest reduction from around 21 hours per week in the early 1990s to around 13 hours in more recent years. Overall, these patterns of housework provide initial indication of the significant differences present in unpaid work performed by men and women.

Extending these initial observations to provide a life-course perspective on patterns of unpaid work, Fig. 8.8 summarises patterns of housework, care and voluntary work among men and women in different age groups using recent data from wave 6 (2014–2015) of *Understanding Society*. Gender differences in housework and care provided for ill or elderly relatives or friends are not that stark for those under 25, although they are evident. Men report around 3.5 hours of housework per week compared

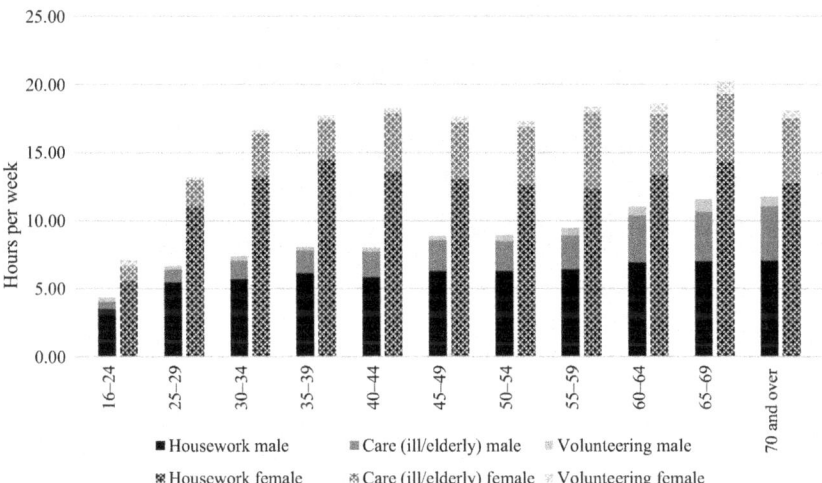

Fig. 8.8 Hours spent in unpaid work by age and gender—2014/2015 (Source: Adapted from *Understanding Society* wave 6 (2014/2015))
Note: Volunteering hours are reported for 'last four weeks' in *Understanding Society*. A weekly estimate has been taken by dividing by four

with 5.5 among women. However, from the age of 25 through to near retirement age, women report a considerably greater household contribution with hours of housework peaking between the age of 35 and 39 at almost 15 hours per week. The provision of care for ill or elderly relatives or friends also falls predominantly on women, consistent with existing evidence on patterns of informal care (Carmichael et al. 2008, p. 26). It becomes a greater demand on time for both men and women from their mid-50s consistent with the presence of, for example, ageing parents or illness of their partner. Gendered patterns are also present in volunteering. Women are more likely to spend a greater amount of time volunteering during the middle part of their lives than men, although as other evidence has shown (see e.g. Hardill and Wheatley 2017), men increase their engagement in voluntary work to similar levels to women as they near and enter retirement.

Patterns of the distribution of household tasks, summarised in Table 8.2, evidence considerable gendered norms present in the allocation of tasks, as well as the continued role of women as primary carers within

Table 8.2 Distribution of unpaid tasks within the household, 2014/2015

	Men (n = 10,914)				Women (n = 12,206)			
Who does the….	Mostly self (%)	Mostly spouse/ partner (%)	Shared (%)	Paid help only (%)	Mostly self (%)	Mostly spouse/ partner (%)	Shared (%)	Paid help only (%)
Grocery shopping?	15.5	40.4	44.0	0.1	50.2	12.0	37.7	0.1
Cooking?	17.1	54.2	28.6	0.1	61.7	13.6	24.6	0.1
Cleaning?	11.6	49.0	35.9	3.6	59.6	8.1	28.3	4.0
Washing/ironing?	8.6	63.1	27.7	0.6	71.6	5.9	21.8	0.7
Gardening?	46.2	19.0	32.0	2.8	24.2	42.4	30.2	3.2
DIY?	74.5	7.3	13.0	5.1	11.3	65.5	16.5	6.7

	Mostly self (%)	Mostly spouse/ partner (%)	Shared (%)	Someone else (%)	Mostly self (%)	Mostly spouse/ partner (%)	Shared (%)	Someone else (%)
Who is mainly responsible for…								
Childcare?	3.7	45.1	49.5	1.8	56.9	3.8	37.8	1.6

Source: Understanding Society, Wave 6 (2014–2015)

most households (Garcia et al. 2011). Respondents in *Understanding Society* are asked to report on the allocation of grocery shopping, cooking, cleaning, washing/ironing, gardening and DIY in response to the question, *I am going to read out some household jobs. Could you please say who mostly does this work here? Is it mostly yourself, or mostly your spouse/partner, or is the work shared equally?* Men report greater contribution to gardening (46.2 % report 'mostly self' as completing this task) and DIY (74.5 %), while women remain greater contributors to grocery shopping (50.2 %), cooking (61.7 %), cleaning (59.6 %) and especially washing/ironing (71.6 %), although it should be noted that grocery shopping is shared by around 40 % of households. Some marketised provision of cleaning, gardening and DIY is also reported, although this only accounts for around 5 % of households. While most social surveys do not ask explicit questions regarding the number of hours spent caring for dependent children, in part as a result of difficulties for parents in quantifying this time-use, *Understanding Society* does include the question, *Who is mainly responsible for looking after the child(ren)?* Responses to this question show that within most households, women remain the primary caregiver: 56.9 % of women reporting being mainly responsible for care for their children, compared to just 3.7 % of men.

Considering the role of the life course offers further insight into the gendered nature of household labour. Around 57 % of younger couples aged up to 24 report sharing grocery shopping. During the middle part of the life course this task becomes the preserve of women, as almost 60 % report mainly completing this task themselves. However, as couples age, they begin to share this task once again. Cooking is a household task which is highly gendered throughout the life course. Over 60 % of women report mainly performing this task regardless of age. Cleaning is similarly gendered throughout the life course, but the use of marketised provision does become more common as couples age, especially between the ages of 35 and 44 (reported by around 5 % of couples) and when aged 70 and over (6 % of couples). In the prior case, this is likely to coincide with both demanding routines of childcare and greater disposable income, while in the latter case, use of marketised services is likely to be a choice made as individuals become less able to perform these tasks themselves. It should be noted that, where marketisation occurs, this often involves women reducing their housework burden through employing other women as cleaners. Washing and ironing is the most gendered of all household tasks measured. In addition, the propensity of women to mainly perform this task increases throughout adulthood from around 60–65 % among younger women and until they reach their mid-30s, to over 80 % among those aged 65 and over. Performing the DIY is, in contrast, a male preserve which is reported by around three quarters of men as mainly performed by themselves. Finally, gardening becomes more evenly shared within the household during the life course. While between the age of 25 and 44 around 50 % of men report mainly performing the gardening, compared to less than 20 % of women, this decreases to under 43 % of men during later life, with over a quarter of women reporting being the main performer of gardening tasks.

Childcare responsibilities mainly fall on women during the earlier part of the life course. Around 65 % of women aged 16–24 report mainly providing childcare, and 61 % aged 25–29. Interestingly, around 5 % of women in these age categories report 'someone else' acting as the main childcare provider, likely reflecting use of both market and non-market, for example, grandparental care provision (Harris et al. 2007). Childcare does appear to become a more shared activity among some households in the middle part of adulthood, coinciding with children in their school-age years. By the time women reach their 40s and early 50s, around 52 % of women report being the main childcare provider. While responsibilities become more commonly shared, as already noted very few men report acting as the main provider of childcare during any part of the life course. The analysis of patterns of unpaid work reaffirms the fact that women remain burdened with the majority of unpaid work in most households (Garcia et al. 2011). This has significant implications for their participation in paid work, as evident in the patterns observed in this chapter, which are consistent with those in the existing literature (Drinkwater 2015, p. 284). Many women, therefore, spend at least part of the life course working reduced hours in part-time employment, or move into self-employment, while some may even leave the labour market entirely, when the demands of unpaid work become more significant, often in the middle part of the life course because of the presence of dependent children.

8.6   Discussion and Summary

This chapter has considered patterns of paid and unpaid work among men and women in the UK, contributing to our understanding of the gendered household division of labour and the gendered nature of employment. Data extracted from a range of UK sources evidences an increased level of participation in paid work among women since the mid-twentieth century, while during the same period men's participation has declined such that levels of engagement are becoming more comparable. Despite a range of policy measures outlined in this chapter, women's labour market participation remains constrained by childcare and other household responsibilities, resulting in the presence of significant inequality in experiences of paid work throughout the life course. While overall participation in paid work may be converging, the majority of men still engage in full-time employment (or self-employment), while over 40 % of women continue to report part-time work. The need to undertake unpaid work acts as a constraint on the participation in paid work among women, including housework, childcare and care for ill or elderly friends or relatives. Moreover, the proportion of grandparents caring for their grandchildren to facilitate the labour market participation of their children, especially daughters, is increasing.

The types of unpaid household tasks undertaken by men and women remain highly gendered. Men garden and perform DIY, while women clean, cook and wash/iron. Grocery shopping is the most commonly shared task, but this still falls predominantly on women. Patterns of unpaid work vary throughout the life course. Men's greatest contribution occurs following retirement from paid employment. Meanwhile, women's patterns of household contribution are consistent with the presence of a trade-off between participation in paid work and levels of unpaid work, which impact women more at certain stages of the life course (Drinkwater 2015). Some women may take on a greater proportion of household labour when labour market engagement is reduced or when they exit the labour market for a period, as a result of unpaid work responsibilities including forms of care. This decision could be consciously made by couples in order to share overall workload (paid plus unpaid work). However, a range of evidence suggests that women remain unevenly burdened with the majority of unpaid work, even where considerable time is also spent in paid work (see e.g. Wheatley and Wu 2014). Women's household contribution, as unpaid work, remains largely 'hidden', but this unpaid work is important to households' successfully managing paid work alongside other responsibilities, while much of this unpaid work can be marketised evidencing the blurred nature of forms of work. Women are also more engaged in voluntary work, but men have similar levels of engagement when paid work is a less significant use of their time, when they are younger (in education) and older (near and after retirement). For working-age adults, both men and women, the ability to undertake unpaid voluntary work is constrained by other time commitments, paid work and caring responsibilities. As was noted in Chap. 5, retirement appears to act as a trigger for older adults to undertake unpaid voluntary work, but the proportion of older adults remaining in paid work is increasing, and this combined with caring for kin could have important implications for their capacity to undertake unpaid voluntary work. This could act to create further societal challenges, given the reductions in social care and welfare budgets witnessed in recent years, and the already constrained resources of voluntary and community sector organisations.

In conclusion, despite a whole raft of social legislation, labour market participation remains highly gendered. For organisations, in all three sectors of the economy, efforts need to be made to reduce those negative associations with respect to reduced hours and other forms of flexible working often used by those with unpaid work obligations. Concern is being raised about the growing numbers in the gig economy and other precarious forms of employment which are low quality and insecure, affecting workers at a range of points throughout the life course, including younger men and women workers (zero hours, temporary work), workers in their 40s (women working reduced hours often as a result of household tasks and part-time self-employed men engaged in gig work) and older workers, especially men reporting part-time self-employment. Employers need to design job tasks so that they are better aligned to non-standard forms of working, and ensure greater equality of opportunity for training and promotion, so that they are not limited to those who are able to follow the full-time model throughout their careers. At the same time, employers should avoid the temptation to focus solely on employer-oriented flexibility, and should instead view flexibility with regard to the potential 'win-win' which can be achieved where flexibility is enacted for the benefit of both employer and employee, for example, providing knowledge workers with the time and space to develop new ideas. Turning to unpaid care work in the home and community, while these individual decisions are determined by negotiations within the home, their impact is felt in the community. New choices and constraints appear to be emerging, especially for older adults, as outlined above, as some continue to undertake paid work beyond state pension age, while others are helping kin through supporting the care of grandchildren or elderly relatives. Welfare budgets will remain tight for the foreseeable future in many advanced societies including the UK, and difficult decisions will be faced regarding the provision of elder care and the level of pensions associated with retirement, and the debate could well test intergenerational solidarity. Finally, the economic and social future within the UK, and to some degree the rest of the EU, is uncertain following the UK's vote to leave in the 2016 UK Referendum on membership of the EU. This uncertainty is likely to result in even greater challenges, at least in the near future, as it casts a cloud over the UK economy for individuals, households and organisations.

Note

1. New Labour refers to the Labour government of 1997–2010 in the UK. New Labour was characterised by a hybrid 'liberal collectivist' model combining the free-market policies of the previous Conservative governments with social support and social investment (Grimshaw and Rubery 2012, p. 106).

References

Alkhatib, A., M. Berstein, and M. Levi. 2017. Examining crowd work and gig work through the historical lens of piecework. Association for Computing Machinery CHI Conference 2017.

Atkinson, C., and L. Hall. 2009. The role of gender in varying forms of flexible working. *Gender, Work and Organisation* 16: 650–666.

Baines, S., and I. Hardill. 2008. 'At least I can do something': The work of volunteering in a community beset by worklessness. *Social Policy and Society* 7: 307–317.

Cabrera, E. 2007. Opting out and opting in: Understanding the complexities of women's career transitions. *Career Development International* 12: 218–237.

Carmichael, F., C. Hulme, S. Sheppard, and G. Connell. 2008. Work-life imbalance: Informal care and paid employment in the UK. *Feminist Economics* 14: 3–35.

Carrasco, C., and M. Domínguez. 2011. Family strategies for meeting care and domestic work needs: Evidence from Spain. *Feminist Economics* 17: 159–188.

Deakin, S., and G. Morris. 2012. *Labour law*. Oxford: Hart.

Delson, L. 1998. Why do men work part time? In *Part-time prospects: An international comparison of part-time work in Europe, North America and the Pacific Rim*, ed. J. O'Reilly and C. Fagan, 57–76. London: Routledge.

Department for Business, Innovation and Skills (BIS). 2014. Zero hours employment contracts. https://www.gov.uk/government/consultations/zero-hours-employment-contracts. Accessed 18 Dec 2016.

Drinkwater, S. 2015. Informal caring and labour markets outcomes within England and Wales. *Regional Studies* 49: 273–286.

Friedman, G. 2014. Workers without employers: Shadow corporations and the rise of the gig economy. *Review of Keynesian Economics* 4: 171–188.

Garcia, I., A. Molina, and M. Navarro. 2007. How satisfied are spouses with their leisure time? Evidence from Europe. *Journal of Family and Economic Issues* 28: 546–565.

Garcia, I., H.A. Molina, and V. Montuenga. 2011. Gender differences in childcare: Time allocation in five European countries. *Feminist Economics* 17: 119–150.

Glucksmann, M. 1995. Why work? Gender and the total social organisation of labour. *Gender, Work and Organisation* 2: 63–75.

Glucksmann, M. 2000. *Cottons and casuals: The gendered organisation of labour in time and space*. Durham: Sociology Press.

Gov.uk. 2016. Shared parental leave. https://www.gov.uk/shared-parental-leave-and-pay-employer-guide/overview. Accessed 18 Dec 2016.

Green, F. 2011. Unpacking the misery multiplier: How employability modifies the impacts of unemployment and job insecurity on life satisfaction and mental health. *Journal of Health Economics* 30: 265–276.

Green, A., and I. Livanos. 2015. Involuntary non-standard employment and the economic crisis: Regional insights from the UK. *Regional Studies* 49: 1223–1235.

Gregory, M., and S. Connolly. 2008. Feature: The price of reconciliation: Part-time work, families and women's satisfaction. *The Economic Journal* 118 (526): F1–F7.

Gregory, A., and S. Milner. 2009. Trade unions and work-life balance: Changing times in France and the UK? *British Journal of Industrial Relations* 47: 122–146.

Grimshaw, D., and J. Rubery. 2012. The end of the UK's liberal collectivist social model? The implications of the coalition government's policy during the austerity crisis. *Cambridge Journal of Economics* 36: 105–126.

Hakim, C. 2000. *Work-lifestyle choices in the 21st century: Preference theory.* New York: Oxford University Press.

Hardill, I. 2002. *Gender, migration and the dual career household,* International studies of women and place series. London: Routledge.

Hardill, I., and S. Baines. 2011. *Enterprising care: Unpaid voluntary action in the 21st century.* Bristol: Policy Press.

Hardill, I., and J. Monk. 2016. Lifecourse methods. In *The Wiley-AAG International Encyclopedia of Geography,* ed. D. Richardson, N. Castree, M. Goodchild, W. Liu, A. Kobayashi, and M. Marston. Hoboken: Association of American Geographers/Wiley-Blackwell.

Hardill, I., and D. Wheatley. 2017. Care and volunteering: The feel good Samaritan? In *Time well spent: Subjective well-being and the work-life balance,* ed. D. Wheatley. London: Rowman and Littlefield International.

Harris, L., C. Foster, and P. Whysall. 2007. Maximising women's potential in the UK's retail sector. *Employee Relations* 29: 492–505.

Harvey, G., C. Rhodes, S. Vachhani, and K. Williams. 2017. Neo-villeiny and the service sector: The case of hyper flexible and precarious work in fitness centres. *Work, Employment and Society* 31: 19–35.

Heitmueller, A. 2007. The chicken or the egg? Endogeneity in labour market participation of informal carers in England. *Journal of Health Economics* 26: 536–559.

Hochschild, A.R., and A. Machung. 1990. *The second shift, working parents and the revolution at home.* London: Piatkus.

Horrell, S., and J. Humphries. 1995. Women's labour force participation and the transition to the male breadwinner family, 1790–1865. *Economic History Review* 48: 89–115.

Hughes, B., L. McKie, D. Hopkins, and N. Watson. 2005. Love's labours lost? Feminism, the disabled people's movement and an ethic of care. *Sociology* 39 (2): 259–275.

Hytti, U. 2010. Contextualizing entrepreneurship in the boundaryless career. *Gender in Management: An International Journal* 25: 64–81.

Kalleberg, A. 2009. Precarious work, insecure workers: Employment relations in transition. *American Sociological Review* 74: 1–22.

Kilgour, J.G. 2013. The pay gap in perspective. *Compensation & Benefits Review* 45: 200–209.

Kim, J.E., and P. Moen. 2002. Retirement transitions, gender, and psychological well-being a life-course, ecological model. *The Journals of Gerontology Series B: Psychological Sciences and Social Sciences* 57: 212–222.

King, M. 2014. Protecting and representing workers in the new gig economy: The case of the freelancers union. In *New labor in New York: Precarious workers and the future of the labour movement*, ed. R. Milkman and E. Ott, 150–170. Ithaca: Cornell University Press.

Kirton, G., and A. Greene. 2016. *The dynamics of managing diversity: A critical approach*. Abingdon: Routledge.

Lewis, J. 2001. The decline of the male breadwinner model: The implications for work and care. *Social Politics* 8 (2): 152–170.

———. 2002. Gender and welfare state change. *European Societies* 4 (4): 331–357.

Lewis, J., and M. Campbell. 2008. What's in a name? 'Work and family' or 'work and life' balance policies in the UK since 1997 and the implications for the pursuit of gender equality. *Social Policy and Administration* 42: 524–541.

Lewis, S., and L. Humbert. 2010. Discourse or reality? Work life balance, flexible working policies and the gendered organization. *Equality, Diversity and Inclusion: An International Journal* 29 (3): 239–254.

Lindsey, R., E. Metcalfe, and R. Edwards. 2015. Time in mixed methods longitudinal research: working across written narratives and large scale panel survey data to investigate attitudes to volunteering. In *Researching the lifecourse: Critical reflections from the social sciences*, ed. N. Worth and I. Hardill, 43–61. Bristol: Policy Press.

Lyon, D., and M. Glucksmann. 2008. Comparative configuration of work across Europe. *Sociology* 42: 101–118.

Mandl, I., M. Curtarelli, S. Riso, O. Vargas, and E. Gerogiannis. 2015. *New forms of employment in Europe*. Dublin: Eurofound.

MacDonald, M., S. Phipps, and L. Lethbridge. 2005. Taking its toll: The influence of paid and unpaid work on women's well-being. *Feminist Economics* 11 (1): 63–94.

McDowell, L. 1991. Life without father and Ford: the new gender order of post Fordism. *Transactions of the Institute of British Geographers* 16: 400–419.

McDowell, L., D. Perrons, C. Fagan, K. Ray, and K. Ward. 2005. The contradictions and intersections of class and gender in a global city: Placing working women's lives on the research agenda. *Environment and Planning A* 37: 441–461.

Mulcahy, D. 2016. *The gig economy: The complete guide to getting better work, taking more time off, and financing the life you want.* New York: American Management Association.

NESTA. 2014. Making sense of the UK collaborative economy. http://www.nesta.org.uk/sites/default/files/making_sense_of_the_uk_collaborative_economy_14.pdf. Accessed 18 Jan 2017.

NOMIS. 2016. Annual population survey 2015: Economic activity and unemployment rates. Office for National Statistics. http://www.nomisweb.co.uk. Accessed 18 Jan 2017.

Office for National Statistics (ONS). 2013. Women in the labour market 2013. https://www.ons.gov.uk/employmentandlabourmarket/peopleinwork/employmentandemployeetypes/articles/womeninthelabourmarket/2013-09-25. Accessed 18 Jan 2017.

———. 2015a. UK labour market. http://www.ons.gov.uk/employmentandlabourmarket/peopleinwork/employmentandemployeetypes/bulletins/uklabourmarket/2015-08-12. Accessed 18 Jan 2017.

———. 2015b. Annual survey of hours and earnings, 2015 provisional results. http://www.ons.gov.uk/ons/dcp171778_385428.pdf. Accessed 18 Jan 2017.

———. 2016. Trends in self-employment in the UK: 2001 to 2015. http://www.ons.gov.uk/employmentandlabourmarket/peopleinwork/employmentandemployeetypes/articles/trendsinselfemploymentintheuk/2001to2015. Accessed 18 Jan 2017.

Osnowitz, D., and K. Henson. 2016. Leveraging limits for contract professionals: Boundary work and control of working time. *Work and Occupations* 43: 326–360.

Pennington, S., and B. Westover. 1989. *A hidden workforce: Homeworkers in England, 1850–1985.* Basingstoke: Macmillan.

Raess, D., and B. Burgoon. 2015. Flexible work and immigration in Europe. *British Journal of Industrial Relations* 53: 94–111.

Scott, J., and E. Clery. 2013. Gender roles: An incomplete revolution? British social attitudes: The 30th report. http://www.bsa.natcen.ac.uk/media/38457/bsa30_gender_roles_final.pdf. Accessed 18 Jan 2017.

Smith, P., and G. Morton. 2006. Nine years of new labour: Neoliberalism and workers' rights. *British Journal of Industrial Relations* 44: 401–420.

Soobedar, Z. 2011. A semi-parametric analysis of the rising breadwinner role of women in the UK. *Review of the Economics of the Household* 9: 415–428.

van Staveren, I. 2010. Post-Keynesianism meets feminist economics. *Cambridge Journal of Economics* 34 (6): 1123–1144.

Taylor, R. 2004. Extending conceptual boundaries: Work, voluntary work and employment. *Work, Employment and Society* 18: 29–49.

Teasdale, N. 2013. Fragmented sisters? The implications of flexible working policies for professional women's workplace relationships. *Gender, Work and Organisation* 20: 397–412.

The Work Foundation. 2016. In search of the gig economy. http://www.theworkfoundation.com/wp-content/uploads/2016/11/407_In-search-of-the-gig-economy_June2016.pdf. Accessed 18 Jan 2017.

Wales, P., and A.A. Amankwah. 2016. Trends in self-employment in the UK: 2001 to 2015. https://www.ons.gov.uk/employmentandlabourmarket/peopleinwork/employmentandemployeetypes/articles/trendsinselfemploymentintheuk/2001to2015/pdf. Accessed 18 Jan 2017.

Walling, A. 2007. Understanding statistics on full-time/part-time employment. *Economic and Labour Market Review* 1: 36–43, in ONS Crown Copyright

Wheatley, D. 2017. Work-time, the quality of work and well-being. In *Time well spent: Subjective well-being and the work-life balance*, ed. D. Wheatley. London: Rowman and Littlefield International.

Wheatley, D., and Z. Wu. 2014. Dual careers, time-use, and satisfaction levels: Evidence from the British household panel survey. *Industrial Relations Journal* 45: 443–464.

Williams, C. 2011. Socio-spatial variations in community self-help: A total organisation of labour perspective. *Social Policy and Society* 10: 365–378.

Wilson, R., N. Sofroniou., R. Beaven, M. May-Gillings, S. Perkins, M. Lee, P. Glover, H. Limmer, and A. Leach, on behalf of the UK Commission for Employment and Skills. 2016. *Working futures 2014–2020, Evidence report 100*. London: UKCES.

Woolvin, M., and I. Hardill. 2013. Localism, voluntarism and devolution: Experiences, opportunities and challenges in a changing policy context. *Local Economy* 28: 273–288.

Worth, N., and I. Hardill. 2015. *Researching the lifecourse: Critical reflections from the social sciences*, 1–22. Bristol: Policy Press.

9

Cognitive Biases in Recruitment, Selection, and Promotion: The Risk of Subconscious Discrimination

Zara Whysall

9.1 Introduction

The topic of workplace diversity has received renewed interest in both the academic literature and popular press in recent years. A growing body of research documented in the academic literature suggests that a diverse workforce provides a number of benefits for meeting the challenges brought about by the modern economic market. Competitive, dynamic, and increasingly global markets demand high levels of adaptability and innovation, which a heterogeneous workforce is better suited to provide, given its broader range of experience and knowledge (see Cox and Blake 1991; Milliken and Martins 1996; Nemeth and Wachtler 1983; Shaw and Barrett-Power 1998; Wright et al. 1995).

Z. Whysall (✉)
Nottingham Business School, Nottingham Trent University, Nottingham, UK

© The Author(s) 2018
V. Caven, S. Nachmias (eds.), *Hidden Inequalities in the Workplace*,
Palgrave Explorations in Workplace Stigma,
DOI 10.1007/978-3-319-59686-0_9

Despite the documented benefits of workplace diversity, however, progress in achieving it has been slow. A recent review of the proportion of women on UK Financial Times Stock Exchange (FTSE) boards, for example, identified that growth has stagnated (Sealy et al. 2016). This is notwithstanding the issue having been a regular topic of debate in the mainstream press and political arenas over recent years. Similarly, statistics suggest a similar pattern in the US, with the proportion of white female managers at US commercial banks having dropped from 39% to 35% between 2003 and 2014 (Dobbin and Kalev 2016), despite the industry having been under the spotlight in terms of gender diversity.

One potential explanation for this apparent disparity is that the gender and race bias which can lead to discrimination in society today is *largely implicit* (Bartlett 2009, p. 1893). It is argued that discrimination has become *invisible, deep, and pervasive* (Bartlett 2009, p. 1895), whilst explicit negative attitudes towards minority groups may have diminished over time (Dovidio 2001). In this case, it is plausible to consider that levels of discrimination in the workplace may not have changed significantly, but the underlying causes of it have simply become less apparent. The implications of such a shift are significant, since the actions required to address discrimination caused by implicit bias are substantially different to those required to address explicit biases on which attention has historically focused. Consistent with the theme of this book, it can be argued that it is now the 'hidden elements' that we must pay greater attention to if we are to make significant improvements in diversity and inclusion. Specifically, this chapter looks at the implicit biases, which can lead to discrimination in the workplace; factors inherent to the decision-making processes affecting employees in the workplace. Therefore, the 'hidden' yet ubiquitous component in this case is the subconscious cognitive processing, which can lead to discrimination, without even the perpetrator or victim's conscious awareness.

Greenwald and Krieger (2006), for example, highlighted that a shift from explicit to implicit discrimination causes a challenge for the legal system since discrimination law and doctrine is based on the assumption that, *barring insanity or mental incompetence, human actors are guided by their avowed (explicit) beliefs, attitudes, and intentions* (Greenwald and Krieger 2006, p. 951). In other words, can someone be held accountable for something they did not realise they were doing? Biancotti et al. (2013) argue that although involuntary behaviour cannot be punished, regulators can *work on debunking the underlying, unconscious assumptions, much in the same spirit of mandating tobacco companies to print health warnings on cigarette packs in order to make smokers more aware of the consequences of their actions* (p. 7).

Further exacerbating the challenge is the belief that the effects of implicit biases (also termed cognitive biases; see Kahneman 2011) are generally not mitigated by awareness of their existence. Given that they operate at an automatic, subconscious level, being made aware that our judgements can be influenced by such biases appears to do little to improve the quality of judgements or decisions at either the individual or the organisational level (Kahneman et al. 2011). Consequently, if lack of diversity is underpinned largely by biases that are implicit, interventions that operate at the level of explicit attitudes and beliefs are likely to be of limited value. This includes traditional diversity training programmes aimed at raising conscious awareness of the importance of avoiding discrimination, about the issues surrounding lack of diversity, or about the benefits brought about by diversity. As articulated by Dobbin and Kalev (2016), *you can't just outlaw bias… The positive effects of diversity training rarely last beyond a day or two, and a number of studies suggest that it can activate bias or spark a backlash. Nonetheless, nearly half of midsize companies use it, as do nearly all the Fortune 500* (p. 4).

Instead, as this chapter outlines, greater attention needs to be paid to the decision-making process itself, in order to unearth the subtler (and potentially job irrelevant) factors that influence selection, recruitment, and promotion decisions. Attention also needs to shift towards addressing the cultural, environmental, or systemic factors which might trigger or maintain implicit biases, and this needs to be not only at the individual level but also team and organisational levels. Organisational culture has been recognised as playing a particularly important role in sustaining implicit, cognitive biases, given the normative influence that culture has on attitudes, beliefs, and behaviours (Pless and Maak 2004; Wallace and Pillans 2016).

This chapter provides an evaluation of the existing academic literature to outline the relevant theories, research, and findings relating to implicit biases; the ways in which they can lead to discrimination; and any emerging evidence regarding how they might be mitigated. The chapter concludes with recommendations for researchers, policymakers, and practitioners.

9.2   What Are Implicit Biases and How Might They Lead to Discrimination?

Implicit cognition suggests that *actors do not always have conscious, intentional control over the processes of social perception, impression formation, and judgment that motivate their actions* (Greenwald and Krieger 2006, p. 946). Also known as heuristics, these 'mental shortcuts' perform an essential role in simplifying everyday human cognitive processing. Kahneman (2011, p. 98) defines a heuristic as *a simple procedure that helps find adequate, though often imperfect, answers to difficult questions.* Given the need to make numerous, rapid decisions during the course of any given day, we adopt heuristics as implicit 'rules of thumb', to avoid being overwhelmed by the vast amounts of data available to our senses. Although typically useful, heuristics can result in oversimplified, inaccurate, and biased decisions or judgements. In the case of diversity, not only have implicit biases been found to predict discriminatory behaviour but implicit bias measures are also significantly more effective than explicit bias measures in predicting behavioural indicators of discrimination (Greenwald and Krieger 2006).

Implicit biases consist of two elements: implicit attitudes and implicit stereotypes. Implicit attitudes are defined as *introspectively unidentified (or inaccurately identified) traces of past experience that mediate favorable or unfavorable feeling, thought, or action toward social objects* (Greenwald and Banaji 1995, p. 8). An example is a voter making their decision based not on an explicit consideration of a particular party's policies and proposals, but instead unconsciously guided by irrelevant factors such as physical similarities to themselves. As highlighted by Greenwald and Banaji, implicit attitudes are particularly interesting (and, indeed problematic) when they differ from the explicit attitudes towards the same object, resulting in a dissociation between implicit and explicit attitudes. Implicit stereotypes, on the other hand, are described as *the introspectively unidentified (or inaccurately identified) traces of past experience that mediate attributions of qualities to members of a social category* (p. 15).

Implicit biases can lead to discrimination in any recruitment, selection, promotion, and reward process, which involves a human judgement or decision-making component. In selection and assessment, for example, implicit biases interfere with the main goal of the process; to evaluate the extent to which a candidate possesses or can demonstrate key characteristics, which are *relevant* for performance in the role being recruited for. Rivera (2012) argues that, in order to understand what is really going on in recruitment procedures, greater attention needs to be paid to the decision-making process itself, to reveal the subtle factors that contribute to employers' decisions. Given that the predictive validity of commonly used selection and assessment methods varies greatly with CVs and assessment centres typically providing predictive validity of around 0.4, approximating to a 40% chance that the selection method will predict subsequent performance on the job (Pilbeam and Corbridge 2006). There remains a large proportion of unexplained variance in many modern selection processes. Furthermore, some of the selection instruments that demonstrate higher predictive validity overall, display considerable ethnic subgroup differences in test performance (De Soete et al. 2012), highlighting the existence of potential discrimination.

9.3 How Do Implicit Biases Typically Manifest in Recruitment, Selection, Promotion, and Reward Decisions?

9.3.1 Stereotyping

One of the most commonly known implicit biases affecting recruitment decisions is stereotyping. Stereotypes are categories that encapsulate what a person believes about, and expects from, other people (Bartlett 2009). Stereotypes not only influence the interpretation and memory of a victim of stereotyping's behaviour but also actual behaviour towards them (Purkiss et al. 2006). The salience of stereotypes is influenced by the context. For example, a black woman's gender will be more salient in a group of men, whilst her race will be more salient in a group of white women (Mitchell et al. 2003). Stereotypes can be problematic because they entail gross assumptions and over extensions, leading to assumptions that members of a particular category are more alike than they really are, and that members of different categories are more dissimilar than they really are. Such is the implicit nature of the bias, research has shown that stereotyping can lead to racial discrimination even when the person making the judgement avows to be completely indifferent to racial stereotypes (Dasgupta et al. 2000).

A simple yet striking example of stereotyping comes from a US study in which researchers sent around 5000 resumes in response to job adverts, each with a randomly assigned a stereotypically African-American- or White-sounding name. Resumes for candidates with stereotypically white-sounding names received 50% more callbacks for interviews, and callbacks are more responsive to resume quality for stereotypically white-sounding names than for African-American ones. This bias persisted regardless of occupation, industry, or employer size (Bertrand and Mullainathan 2004). This phenomenon has been replicated in a host of different contexts, including bias against immigrant applicants (Oreopoulos 2011). Oreopoulos identified discrimination across a variety of occupations towards applicants with foreign experience or those with Indian, Pakistani, Chinese, and Greek names compared with English names. Although recruiters justified their decisions based on language skill concerns, the study demonstrated that listing language fluency, multinational firm experience, or education from highly selective schools did nothing to diminish the effect. Similarly, King et al. (2006) asked 155 white male participants to judge individuals' suitability for jobs based on fictitious resumes, which were designed to be of varying quality. The results revealed that Asian American individuals were evaluated highly for high-status jobs, regardless of resume quality. In contrast, black applicants were evaluated negatively even with a strong resume, a finding that appeared to be underpinned by occupational stereotypes.

A recent study, however, by Deming et al. (2016) found no consistent pattern of differences in callback rates by race, in contrast to the findings of Bertrand and Mullainathan (2004), Oreopoulos (2011), and King et al. (2006). They cite a number of possible reasons, including differing study settings, time periods, labour markets, application processes, employers, and job quality, suggesting that the effect may be more nuanced than initially assumed. Indeed, in their original study, Bertrand and Mullainathan acknowledge that the names used for the resumes may not just evoke race-related stereotypes but may also evoke stereotypes relating to social background and status. However, either way, this reflects discrimination based on factors that are irrelevant to potential job performance.

Illustrating the contextual nature of stereotypes, Booth and Leigh (2010) explored gender discrimination in response to fake CVs for entry-level jobs, but in occupations that are female dominated in Australia, the country research was conducted (these were 'wait-staff', data-entry staff, customer service staff, and sales staff). Averaging across all jobs, they observed substantial discrimination against male candidates, particularly for 'wait-staff' and data entry staff, which were the two occupations with the highest proportion of female employees. As a result, they concluded that the typical male applicant would have to submit 28% more applications in order to receive the same number of callbacks for entry-level jobs that are female dominated. However, in a subsequent meta-analysis of gender stereotypes and bias in experimental simulations of employment decision-making, Koch et al. (2015) identified that men were favoured for male-dominated jobs, whereas no strong preference for either gender was found for female-dominated jobs.

In an applied context, Goldin and Rouse (2000) took advantage of a change in the way symphony orchestras in the US recruit musicians, having moved to blind auditions with a screen to conceal the identity of the candidate from the jury during the 1970s and 1980s. Goldin and Rouse discovered that the screen increases the probability a woman will be advanced out of preliminary rounds by 50%. They estimated the switch to blind auditions as explaining between 30% and 55% of the increase in the proportion of females among new hires since 1970, when less than 5% of all players in top five US symphony orchestras were female, to 25% today.

9.3.2 Stereotype Threat

An additional factor complicating the impact of stereotypes is that stereotypes not only influence outcomes via their impact on decision-makers' judgements but also impact on candidates' actual performance due to the impact of the stereotype threat phenomenon. A concept initially introduced by Steele and Aronson (1995), it acknowledges that certain settings or situations contain subtle reminders of stereotypes that presume certain groups are less capable. As articulated by Schmader (2010), it describes the finding that anyone can exhibit impaired performance when reminded of ways in which they might be negatively stereotyped. This threat in the air (Schmader 2010) can trigger a range of attentional, physiological, cognitive, affective, and motivational processes (see Casad and Merritt 2014), such as inferiority, anxiety, and a concern about confirming these stereotypes, which impairs the individual's ability to perform to their full capability. Stereotype threat has been identified to operate in relation to stereotypes associated with gender, ethnicity, and socioeconomic status, across and in a broad range of settings including academia, athletics, and the workplace (Steele et al. 2002).

Stereotype threat is particularly likely to be triggered in stereotypically masculine fields such as finance and banking, with research demonstrating that stereotype threat among women in management and accounting leads to negative job attitudes and intentions to quit via its effects on identity separation or the perception that one's gender identity is incompatible with one's work identity (Von Hippel et al. 2015). As a result, a catch-22 situation is created, as recognised by the authors: ...*since recruitment and retention of women into fields where they have been historically underrepresented is key to achieving the "critical mass" of women necessary to reduce perceptions of tokenism as well as stereotyping and devaluing of women* (p. 405).

Stereotype threat is also of relevance to promotion and reward decisions since it is a condition for the effect to emerge, that individuals must identify with and care about their performance in the domain (Roberson et al. 2003). Ironically, this means that the motivated and talented may be most vulnerable to stereotype threat (Aronson et al. 1998). Roberson et al. (2003) found that the experience of stereotype threat influenced the way that African American managers in US organisations interpreted and responded to performance feedback. They found that the experience of stereotype threat, the risk of which was increased for individuals who were the only African American in their work group, was associated with increased use of an indirect, monitoring strategy for seeking feedback and a greater degree of feedback discounting. The indirect, monitoring strategy of feedback seeking results in feedback that is more subject to misinterpretation and is less useful than direct inquiry for performance improvements (Ashford and Cummings 1983; Ashford and Tsui 1991; Roberson et al. 2003). Discounting or questioning the veracity of feedback makes it less likely that an individual will act upon it (Cohen et al. 1999; Cohen and Steele 2002), and if employees from minority groups do not use feedback as effectively as non-minority group employees, their chances for advancement and success will be hindered (Crocker et al. 1991). Given the importance of receiving critical feedback for development and career progression, research supports the value of employers being trained in providing 'wise feedback', which aims to remove ambiguity regarding the motive for the feedback so that members of minority groups do not attribute critical feedback to factors relating to their gender or race (Yeager et al. 2014).

In addition, the experience of stereotype threat has been shown to limit an individual's willingness to embrace challenges since any resulting failure could be interpreted as evidence supporting the stereotype (Steele 1997). This may include the type of stretch assignment which might subsequently be used as evidence in cases for a promotion or pay increase. As recognised by Casad and Bryant (2016), repeated experiences of stereotype threat can impact detrimentally on career aspirations, as the experience of threat and perceived incompetence leads individuals to assume that they have reduced chances of success in that environment (Steele 1997; Davies et al. 2005). Again, reduced career aspirations in response to stereotype threat is likely to exacerbate and perpetuate the diversity problems within fields underrepresented by minorities (Murphy et al. 2007; Koenig et al. 2011).

9.3.3 Selective Attention and Confirmation Bias

So pervasive is the impact of stereotypes that they influence what we pay attention to and the information we subsequently process. Where this becomes particularly evident, and problematic, is in the face-to-face selection interview. Although interviews remain the frequently used selection tool in recruitment, evidence denoting their proneness to biases and discrimination is relatively well documented (Barrick et al. 2012; Derous et al. 2016; Purkiss et al. 2006).

As outlined by Derous et al. (2016), implicit biases can influence the interview process at various stages and in different ways. This includes the pre-interview stage, where non-relevant information derived from CVs, for example, can potentially bias all subsequent processing. In other words, the speed at which impressions are formed in interviews suggests that this processing relies on existing heuristics, and is therefore potentially open to implicit biases. For instance, a study by Purkiss et al. (2006) revealed that a candidate's foreign accent and 'ethnic name' activated stereotypes about ethnic minorities, which led these candidates to be viewed less positively by interviewers than the ethnic-named applicant without an accent and non-ethnic-named applicants with and without an accent. This initial impression also affected subsequent ratings of job suitability. The latter finding is consistent with confirmation bias, selective attention, and processing which serves to reinforce the stereotype. Once an initial impression has been formed based on stereotypes, the person making the judgement tends to filter and interpret information in a way that is consistent with the stereotype and disregard any information that counters it (Jonas et al. 2001; Nickerson 1998; Sherman et al. 2005). Anchoring bias (see Tversky and Kahneman 1974) is also likely to be active here, whereby the irrelevant yet salient information noted during the formation of initial impressions subsequently serves as an 'anchor' for final decisions (Derous et al. 2016). We are reluctant to deviate from a given anchor in making judgements (Eroglu and Croxton 2010), something that Derous et al. (2016) consider being a crucial factor impeding post-interview decision-making. There is some evidence that the effects of anchoring bias can be reduced when a situational interviewing technique is adopted (Kataoka et al. 1997).

Interviews are particularly susceptible to bias when conducted in the absence of data relating to valid predictors of job performance, such as ability test scores, which should have the effect of focusing attention on information that is relevant to the job role. For a similar reason, unstructured interviews are more prone to bias and adverse impact than structured interviews (Levashina et al. 2014), due to the exchange of non-job-related information and the fact that interviewers might rely more on their implicit assumptions (Derous et al. 2016). Structuring an interview, for example, by ensuring that all candidates are asked the same questions or by using standardised rating scales to evaluate candidates' responses to each question, is known to enhance the validity of interviews in selection (Campion et al. 1997; Levashina et al. 2014).

Other techniques found to reduce interview bias include allowing interviewers to evaluate candidates after each question during the interview, instead of at the end (Levashina et al. 2014), in addition to building in accountability by asking recruiters to justify their pre-interview impressions (Derous et al. 2016). Derous et al. argue that greater individual accountability for selection decisions might instigate more thorough processing of personalised information and alleviate the impact of implicit biases relating to minority groups. Indeed, there is some evidence to suggest that when white managers are made to feel accountable for their evaluations of applicant pre-interview information such as resumes, they demonstrate less racial bias (Ford et al. 2004).

9.3.4 In-group Bias

In-group bias relates to the implicit tendency to feel a stronger degree of affinity with, and trust of, others who we categorise as similar to ourselves. In other words, *Ingroup bias designates favoritism toward groups to which one belongs* (Greenwald and Krieger 2006, p. 951). As such, in-group bias also provides a reminder that biases can be favourable as well as unfavourable. Also referred to as the 'similar-to-me' bias, in the recruitment context the effect denotes the tendency for interviewers to recruit candidates in their own self-image. As identified by research conducted several decades ago, this effect exerts substantive influence upon their subsequent decision-making process (Rand and Wexley 1975). Research has revealed that raters favour candidates who share similarities with themselves in respect to several different dimensions, including values and habits, beliefs, demographic, and cultural variables such as leisure pursuits, experiences, and self-presentation styles (Bagues and Perez-Villadoniga 2012; Prewett-Livingston et al. 1996; Rivera 2012).

Drawing from 120 interviews, with employers in elite professional service firms, Rivera (2012) discovered that concerns about cultural similarity were highly salient to employers in the selection decision-making process, and often outweighed concerns about absolute productivity. As a result, in-group bias acts to perpetuate homogeneity within organisations, a problem not only due to the potential for discrimination but also given the known advantages of diversity for team and organisational performance. Indeed, research suggests a number of destructive outcomes are associated with selection of managers based on the similar-to-me effect, including increased groupthink and decreased functional conflict (Gholipour et al. 2008).

In-group bias affects cognitive processing in various ways. For instance, raters tend to notice and remember more detailed information about interview candidates similar to themselves, asking more questions to obtain information about 'ingroup' candidates. In contrast, they tend to notice and remember less information about candidates they see as different to themselves, ask questions, and selectively retain information that confirms their existing stereotype about them (Bartlett 2009).

Lin et al. (1992) examined the effects of interviewer and interviewee race and age similarity under two different interview formats: a conventional structured panel interview and a situational panel interview. No age similarity effects were detected with either interview procedure, but same-race effects were evident. Furthermore, analyses revealed stronger same-race effects with the conventional structured interview than with the situational interview.

Once the interview has been completed, implicit bias can still be introduced into the final decision-making effort. As outlined by Linos and Reinhard (2015), final decision-makers are susceptible to a host of biases, including status quo bias, self-serving bias, groupthink, and the availability heuristic, making this a particularly critical part of the interview selection process.

9.3.5 Promotions and Reward Decisions

Research also suggests that in-group bias may also influence promotion and reward decisions, due to the differences observed in relation to attribution bias. Individuals tend to be more generous in their explanations of 'ingroup' persons' behaviour, for instance, more often attributing success of those similar to themselves to internal, dispositional characteristics. In contrast, the achievements of 'outgroup' individuals are more likely to be attributed to external and less-stable characteristics such as chance or fluke (Hewstone 1990). In-group favouritism has also been demonstrated, under experimental conditions, in relation to allocation of rewards (Hung-Ng 1981), and ratings of subordinates' performance, in terms of similarity in demographic characteristics (Tsui and O'Reilly 1989).

Unfortunately, research has historically suggested that promotion decisions tend to be highly subjective. Based on vague or irrelevant criteria, and thereby open to significant bias: *Despite their importance – for both orgs and individuals- we know very little about how any why promotions occur…there has been very little work done on how actual promotion decisions are made* (Ruderman and Ohlott 1994, p. 14). In a review of 64 promotions in three Fortune 500 companies, it was noted that *formally collected data didn't enter into the promotion decision* (p. 14), but promotion decisions were based on *an intuitive, subjective process that concentrated on their personal knowledge of the candidate and opinions of others* (p. 14). In the face of vague or ambiguous criteria, there is a tendency for promotion decision-makers to rely upon perceived similarity to themselves, or the extent to which they feel 'comfortable' with an individual, reasons given more often for promotions involving male employees than females (Ruderman et al. 1995). Other research as demonstrated that the effects of applicant race and gender were only present for promotion decisions made by homogenous (all white male) panels, but were eliminated when diverse panels (mixed gender and/or race) were used (Powell and Butterfield 2002).

More recent research provides a more nuanced understanding of the stage at which discrimination appears more likely to be introduced into the promotion and reward decision-making process. In a large North American service sector organisation known to take pride in offering a diverse work community, for example, Castilla (2008) found no race or sex differences in performance evaluations by managers but significant white male advantages in the size of salary increases awarded in response to these performance evaluations. Castilla believed this differential to be accounted for by two main mechanisms. The first was a lack of accountability on behalf of the decision-maker for ensuring that their decisions are fair. The second was a lack of transparency, allowing bias to go unnoticed at the salary award stage. As argued by Castilla, *the invisibility of salary increase amounts eliminates concrete salary comparisons among employees and thus has the potential to mask unfairness in the performance-compensation link in organisations* (p. 1516). In addition, a study investigating a matched sample of 192 female and male UK executive directors revealed that bonuses awarded to men were larger on average and more sensitive to fluctuations in performance than for female executives suggesting that organisations may be biased to more readily recognise good performance from males (Kulich et al. 2011).

The evidence outlined above illustrates the 'hidden' yet pervasive nature of implicit biases, and as a result, how many existing talent management processes are at risk of causing discrimination as a result. Implicit cognition is an essential and unavoidable part of human information processing, which means that implicit biases, and the potential discrimination that can lead from them, can emerge at any stage of the talent management process; from recruitment and selection, to promotion and development opportunities. So the important question is what can be done about this?

9.4   Recommendations for Practice

The continued lack of diversity in many modern workplaces has been well documented in the popular press over recent years, particularly with regard to gender. Despite attempts to tackle the issue, for instance, through legislation, policy, and interventions such as diversity training, progress has stagnated (Dobbin and Kalev 2016; Sealy et al. 2016). The academic literature has long recognised the importance of subconscious, implicit biases in the act of discrimination (e.g. Greenwald and Banaji 1995), and now a substantial body of evidence suggests that in order to tackle discrimination in the modern workplace, attention must be paid to the more subtle, implicit biases.

Although some employers have recognised the problematic influence of implicit, subconscious bias on organisational decision-making, the development of solutions to mitigate their impact is in its relative infancy. The main barrier would appear to be their invisible nature; since implicit biases operate at an automatic, unconscious level, we are unaware of their existence. Naturally, we do not take action to mitigate something that we are not aware exists. Given that automatic, subconscious processing forms an unavoidable part of human information processing and decision-making, it is probably safe to assume that the decisions taking place in your organisation are exposed to them.

Addressing this issue requires a different approach since rules and legislation will not necessarily be effective in achieving a reduction in discrimination resulting from implicit processes (Bartlett 2009; Dobbin and Kalev 2016). Bartlett argues that not only is *law is an ineffective instrument for eliminating behaviours we cannot readily define or correct* (p. 1899), but it may even be counter-productive. She argues that confrontation about biases which people do not consciously exhibit may inadvertently trigger guilt, subsequently leading to avoidance and resistance, and ultimately to more stereotyping.

Furthermore, some argue that individuals may be able to overcome the automatic reliance on unconscious biases such as stereotypes when encouraged to engage in more effortful impression formation processes, or individuation (Dipboye and Johnson 2013; Fiske 2000). However, others disagree, arguing that awareness or increased deliberative effort is insufficient to overcome subconscious biases, due to the fact that they operate at an automatic, subconscious level (Kahneman et al. 2011). As articulated by Bartlett, *good intentions…are largely ineffective to stop implicit discrimination* (p. 1893).

Perhaps the most obvious way of removing bias from selection, recruitment, and reward decisions is to remove the human from the judgement and decision-making process. Indeed, evidence suggests that digitised job testing is beneficial but only if managers are not given the chance to overrule the test outcome (Hoffman et al. 2015). Aside from removing the human from the equation, the existing evidence points towards two broad areas which offer opportunities for reducing implicit biases in recruitment, selection, and promotion decisions. These are greater focus on the decision-making process itself, and the organisational, cultural, or environment within which these decisions are made. Below, these two areas are explored in terms of implications and recommendations for practice.

9.4.1 The Decision-Making Process

Research has highlighted that greater attention needs to be paid to the decision-making process itself, in order to unearth and address the subtle factors that influence selection and recruitment (and, indeed, reward) decision-making processes (Rivera 2012). As highlighted by Rivera:

> …*even after accounting for measures of applicants' human capital, social capital, and demographic traits, models of employer hiring still exhibit significant unexplained variance. Consequently, much of what drives employer decision-making is still a mystery to scholars.* (p. 1000)

Existing evidence highlights a number of steps that can be taken to reduce implicit bias in the selection, recruitment, and reward decision-making processes. Despite being the most commonly used tool, anti-bias training for assessors involved in the process seems 'weaker than its prevalence would imply' (Linos and Reinhard 2015, p. 17). Some studies have produced positive results (Carnes et al. 2015; Kawakami et al. 2005), but given the nature of the findings and that positive results were only found under specific circumstances, Linos and Reinhard argue that there may be unconscious resistance to anti-bias training. Similarly, Chavez and Weisinger (2008) argue that w*hile few data exist on diversity training effectiveness, there is significant anecdotal evidence that many organisational diversity programs have either failed or brought about less than desired results* (p. 334). Alternatively, evidence does show promise for the following:

Reviewing Applications and CVs

- Screening of resumes and other applicant information should be undertaken 'blind', with any factors irrelevant to job performance omitted, particularly those known to trigger stereotypes such as candidate name, age, gender, and photograph.
- Rather than assessing resumes individually, they should be compared with each other, in batches. Bohnet et al. (2012) found that assessors are more likely to focus on relevant, future job performance when candidates are evaluated jointly rather than separately. When candidates were assessed separately, evaluation tended to focus more on group stereotypes, making joint evaluation not only more effective, less likely to lead to discrimination, but also more cost effective.

Interviews

- Where performance can also be evaluated 'blind' (such as with orchestra auditions, Goldin and Rouse 2000) it should be.
- Interview panels should be diverse.
- Interviews should be structured, situational in nature, and incorporate relevant data where available, to encourage interviewers to focus on relevant factors. As argued by Derous et al. (2016), by structuring an interview in this way, interviewers are likely to gather more comprehensive, standardised, and comparable information about all applicants. As a result, this reduces the likelihood of selection decisions being made based on biases, instead encouraging

interviewers to engage in information that is more conscious processing.

- Whilst it is generally accepted that a 'warm up' conversation is helpful to relax candidates at the start of an interview or other selection process, research shows that it is during this period that irrelevant social information can be introduced, potentially triggering in-group biases. Consideration should be given, therefore, to whether the 'warm up' can be conducted by an individual not involved in the decision-making process.

- Evaluation of candidate responses should take place at the end of each question or interview section rather than at the end of the whole interview. In addition to reducing demand on memory and information-processing capacity, this also ensures that evaluations are specific to the job-related factors identified rather than becoming a generic, global judgement that is not anchored in the relevant data.

- Bias can also be reduced by including people in final decision who have not been involved in assessing candidates since their job is simply to take a balanced overview of the different sources of assessment data. This might also help in ensuring that final 'wash up' decision-making sessions are not reduced to vague, overarching discussions of organisational or cultural 'fit'.

- Use a range of metrics, and before conducting interviews, commit to hire the candidate whose final score is the highest on the relevant metrics. Do not let intuition or liking override the data. As argued by Linos and Reinhard (2015), 'stick to what the scores tell you. It is important not to reduce the predictive power of tests and other scored assessments by introducing partial opinions or post-hoc rationalisation (p. 17).

Promotion and Reward Decisions

- Promotion decisions should also be made by diverse panels and efforts taken to ensure that decisions are based upon clear, formalised, objective criteria.

• Decision-makers should be made accountable for ensuring that their promotion and reward decisions are fair, and transparency should be provided in the monetary awards allocated on the basis of their judgements.

9.4.2 The Environment and Organisational Culture

Factors in the environment and organisational culture can influence both the decision-makers and the performance of the candidates, the latter via stereotype threat. Some research suggests that individual-level interventions to promote identity safety and affirm personal values can mitigate the effects of stereotype threat (Cable et al. 2013; Markus et al. 2000; Sherman and Hartson 2011). However, others argue that due to stereotype threat being a social product, it can only be addressed through broader solutions, which look beyond the individual, to the context. As articulated by Markus et al. (2000) it:

> ...cannot be achieved or maintained by one's self, alone. Identity is a social product and a social process that is interdependent with one's ongoing interactions. It is through engagement with and recognition by others that an individual becomes a person and identities are conferred. (p. 236)

Research has identified several simple environmental cues that can trigger stereotype threat among prospective recruits, even extending to the virtual environment such as the company website. As articulated by Casad and Bryant (2016):

> ...halls decorated with photographs of senior management and executives that represent Caucasian males may trigger doubt that women and minorities can advance in an organisation. Other seemingly benign objects, such as the choice of magazines in a reception area, can affect the perception of the organisation's diversity values (Cohen and Garcia 2008). Do the magazines reflect a diversity of tastes and are they targeted to diverse audiences? Décor that communicates a masculine culture, such as references to geeky pop culture, may signal to women and those who do not identify with these cues that they do not belong.

Consideration must also be given to what is considered and promoted as 'good' in a particular organisational culture, since this will explicitly or implicitly feed into recruitment and promotion processes, yet may or may not relate to factors that actually influence effective job performance. To avoid bias, recruitment and promotion/reward decisions must be based on competencies that have been demonstrated to be predictive of effective job performance, not simply those characterised by the current culture.

In a similar vein, I would argue that careful consideration needs to be given to the weight placed on an individual's 'fit' with the prevailing organisational culture, particularly within recruitment. Which elements of culture are we expecting people to have a good 'fit' with, exactly? Clearly, surface-level elements of culture, such as dress, are likely to be much less relevant to job performance than deeper elements of culture, such as core values. However, the former is much more apparent, and therefore can potentially bias our judgement of fit due to the salience bias (the tendency to use more salient, noticeable, or available sources of information to steer our judgements), even though we may believe we are making our judgement based on other, more relevant criteria. Furthermore, there is also a risk for judgements based on clear, specific, and relevant criteria, to be marred at the final stage, by overriding the objective data with a generic, subjective consideration of fit. Consequently, both HR/recruiters and business leaders have a responsibility to ensure that this consideration is used appropriately. To what extent do we need people to fit with the prevailing culture? Are we simply recruiting people who are similar to ourselves because that is what we are comfortable with? What evidence do you have that homogeneity on any level would be beneficial to organisational performance? These are key questions that HR and business leaders need to address.

In addition, the 'mere exposure' bias (whereby increased exposure to something is misattributed to liking) can also help breakdown stereotypes. For example, women exposed to female leaders in social contexts are less likely to express automatic stereotypical beliefs about women (Dasgupta and Asgari 2004). Research has also shown that just meeting and forming a new connection with a member of a previously devalued outgroup can change implicit attitudes towards that group dramatically and rapidly (Olsson et al. 2005). Similarly, employees of minority groups also demonstrate better attainment when work was organised using teams with less rigid hierarchical job distinctions, and intergroup contact or networking opportunities were increased, which served to reduce stereotypes, increase female, and minority access to managerial positions (Kalev 2009). Consequently, it can be seen how quotas or aspirational targets for achieving a specific representation of minority groups (e.g. women on boards), although controversial, may reduce stereotype bias, and also influence the normative dimension of culture.

9.5   Conclusion

Workplace discrimination, it can be argued, has 'gone underground'. Whilst explicit negative attitudes towards minority groups may have diminished over time (Dovidio 2001), gender and race bias in society today is 'largely implicit' (Bartlett 2009, p. 1893). One of the most pervasive yet 'hidden' elements in this puzzle is the subconscious cognitive processing surrounding almost every decision made regarding people at work—such as whether they are selected to work there in the first place, to whether they are given equal opportunities for promotion once there. Implicit biases present a thorny challenge for equality and diversity because so deep rooted are these biases that not only are they often invisible but the owners of the biases are not consciously aware of their existence either. Consequently, to be successful in achieving diversity, practitioners must pay attention to the 'hidden' biases.

These more subtle, deeper-rooted forms of discrimination require more subtle and deeper-routed interventions. Instead of attempting to 'outlaw' implicit bias, it is important to tackle its motivational underpinning. Bartlett (2009) argues that instead of excessive legal pressure which 'undermines people's sense of autonomy, competence, and relatedness, and thus their commitment to non-discrimination norms' (p. 1894), people need to internalise non-biased attitudes and values. Furthermore, given the normative influence of organisational culture on attitudes and behaviours (and, in turn, the collective influence of employee attitudes and behaviours on shaping organisational culture), it is also important that implicit bias is addressed at the collective, cultural level. Indeed, it is argued that the success of diversity programmes is dependent on organisational situational factors, such as culture, strategy, and operating environments (Jayne and Dipboye 2004), and therefore such initiatives will have limited success unless concepts and actions around diversity and inclusion are embedded into core people processes such as performance management and leadership development.

Finally, it is also important to reflect on the difference between diversity and inclusion. Just because an organisation or community is diverse, it does not mean it is inclusive. As defined by Frost and Kalman (2016), *real inclusion is about bringing those differences together to add value* (p. 49). With this in mind, Chavez and Weisinger (2008) outlined three main objectives, which constitute a strategic approach to organisational diversity, designed to create a more inclusive, culture of diversity:

- Establish a relational culture within which people feel proud of their own uniqueness, while becoming socially integrated into a larger group by celebrating the 'me' within the 'we'.
- Maintain an inclusive culture within which employees are intrinsically motivated to take ownership of the learning experience and to learn from each other so that organisational members can discover and appreciate multiple perspectives.
- Incorporate an organisational strategy that capitalises on the multiple perspectives individuals contribute to creativity, productivity, organisational attractiveness, and employee well-being.

Unfortunately, although it is almost a decade since Chavez and Weisinger's publication, there appears to have been little research carried out to progress this work. For researchers, therefore, there exists a need for research to explore in greater depth, the key features of a culture of diversity, and to identify what steps can be taken in the effort to promote one. In addition, given the significant body of evidence highlighting the range of implicit biases evident in recruitment, selection, and promotion decision-making, a closer look at the decision-making process seems well overdue, to identify the extent to which implicit biases account for the significant unexplained variance in selection and recruitment processes, and subsequent discrimination.

References

Aronson, J., D. Quinn, and S. Spencer. 1998. Stereotype threat and the academic underperformance of women and minorities. In *Stigma: The target's perspective*, ed. J. Swim and C. Stangor, 85–100. New York: Academic.

Ashford, S.J., and L.L. Cummings. 1983. Feedback as an individual resource: Personal strategies of creating information. *Organisational Behavior and Human Performance* 32: 370–339.

Ashford, S.J., and A.S. Tsui. 1991. Self-regulation for managerial effectiveness: The role of active feedback-seeking. *Academy of Management Journal* 34: 251–280.

Bagues, M., and M.J. Perez-Villadoniga. 2012. Do recruiters prefer applicants with similar skills? Evidence from a randomized natural experiment. *Journal of Economic Behavior and Organisation* 82: 12–20.

Barrick, M.R., S.L. Dustin, T.L. Giluk, G.L. Stewart, J.A. Shaffer, and B.W. Swider. 2012. Candidate characteristics driving initial impressions during rapport building: Implications for employment interview validity. *Journal of Occupational and Organisational Psychology* 85: 330–352.

Bartlett, K. 2009. Making good on good intentions: The critical role of motivation in reducing implicit workplace discrimination. *Virginia Law Review* 95: 1893–1972. http://www.jstor.org/stable/27759975?seq=1#page_scan_tab_contents. Accessed 06 Feb 2017.

Bertrand, M., and S. Mullainathan. 2004. Are Emily and Greg more employable than Lakisha and Jamal? A field experiment on labor market discrimination. *American Economic Review* 94: 991–1013.

Biancotti, C., G. Ilardi, and C. Moscatelli. 2013. The glass drop ceiling: Composition effects or implicit discrimination? Occasional papers, number 182 – June 2013, Bank of Italy. http://www.bancaditalia.it/pubblicazioni/qef/2013-0182/QEF_182_ITA.pdf. Accessed 25 Dec 2016.

Bohnet, I., A. van Geen, and M.H. Bazerman. 2012. When performance trumps gender bias: Joint versus separate evaluation. Working paper no 12-083. http://www.hbs.edu/faculty/Publication%20Files/12-083.pdf. Accessed 24 Jan 2017.

Booth, A., and A. Leigh. 2010. Do employers discriminate by gender in female-dominated occupations? Results from a field experiment in female-dominated occupations. CEPR discussion paper no. 7638.

Cable, D.M., F. Gino, and B.R. Staats. 2013. Breaking them in or eliciting their best? Reframing socialization around newcomers' authentic self-expression. *Administration Science Quarterly* 58: 1–36.

Campion, M.A., D.K. Palmer, and J.E. Campion. 1997. A review of structure in the selection interview. *Personnel Psychology* 50: 655–702.

Carnes, M., P.G. Devine, and B. Manwell. 2015. The effect of an intervention to break the gender bias habit for faculty at one institution: A cluster randomized, controlled trial. *Academic Medicine* 90: 221–230.

Casad, B.J., and W.J. Bryant. 2016. Addressing stereotype threat is critical to diversity and inclusion in organisational psychology. *Frontiers in Psychology* 7: 8.

Casad, B.J., and S.M. Merritt. 2014. The importance of stereotype threat mechanisms in workplace outcomes. *Industrial and Organisational Psychology* 7: 413–419.

Castilla, E. 2008. Gender, race, and meritocracy in organisational careers. *American Journal of Sociology* 113: 1479–1526.

Chavez, C.I., and J.Y. Weisinger. 2008. Beyond diversity training: A social infusion for cultural inclusion. *Human Resource Management* 47: 331–350.

Cohen, G.L., and J. Garcia. 2008. Identity, belonging, and achievement: A model, interventions, implications. *Current Directions in Psychological Science* 17: 365–369.

Cohen, G.L., and C.M. Steele. 2002. A barrier of mistrust: How negative stereotypes affect cross-race mentoring. In *Improving academic achievement: Impact of psychological factors on education*, ed. J. Aronson, 303–327. San Diego: Academic Press.

Cohen, G.L., C.M. Steele, and L.D. Ross. 1999. The mentor's dilemma: Providing critical feedback across the racial divide. *Personality and Social Psychology Bulletin* 25: 1302–1318.

Cox, T.H., and S. Blake. 1991. Managing cultural diversity: Implications for organisational competitiveness. *Academy of Management Executive* 5: 45–56.

Crocker, J., K. Voelkl, M. Testa, and B. Major. 1991. Social stigma: The affective consequences of attributional ambiguity. *Journal of Personality and Social Psychology* 60: 218–228.

Dasgupta, N., D.E. McGhee, A.G. Greenwald, and M.R. Banaji. 2000. Automatic preference for White Americans: Ruling out the familiarity effect. *Journal of Experimental Social Psychology* 36: 316–328.

Dasgupta, N., and S. Asgari. 2004. Seeing is believing: Exposure to counter stereotypic women leaders and its effect on the malleability of automatic gender stereotyping. *Journal of Experimental Social Psychology* 40: 642–658.

Davies, P.G., S.J. Spencer, and C.M. Steele. 2005. Clearing the air: Identity safety moderates the effects of stereotype threat on women's leadership aspirations. *Journal of Personality and Social Psychology* 88: 276–287.

De Soete, B., F. Lievens, and C. Druart. 2012. An update on the diversity–validity dilemma in personnel selection: A review. *Psychological Topics* 21: 399–424.

Deming, D.J., N. Yuchtman, A. Abulafi, C. Goldin, and L.F. Katz. 2016. The value of postsecondary credentials in the labor market: An experimental study. *American Economic Review* 106: 778–780.

Derous, E., A. Buijsrogge, N. Roulin, and W. Duyck. 2016. Why your stigma isn't hired: A dual-process framework of interview bias. *Human Resource Management Review* 26: 90–111.

Dipboye, R.L., and S.K. Johnson. 2013. Understanding and improving employee selection interviews. In *APA handbook of testing and assessment in psychology*, ed. K. Geisinger, 479–499. Washington, DC: APA.

Dobbin, F., and A. Kalev. 2016. Why diversity programs fail. *Harvard Business Review* 94: 52–61.

Dovidio, J. 2001. On the nature of contemporary prejudice: The third wave. *Journal of Social Issues* 57: 829–849.

Eroglu, C., and K.L. Croxton. 2010. Biases in judgmental adjustments of statistical forecasts: The role of individual differences. *International Journal of Forecasting* 26: 116–133.

Fiske, S.T. 2000. Stereotyping, prejudice, and discrimination at the seam between the centuries: Evolution, culture, mind and brain. *European Journal of Social Psychology* 30: 299–322.

Ford, T.E., F. Gambino, H. Lee, E. Mayo, and M.A. Ferguson. 2004. The role of accountability in suppressing managers' pre-interview bias against African-American sales job applicants. *Journal of Personal Selling Sales Management* 24: 113–124.

Frost, S., and D. Kalman. 2016. *Inclusive talent management: How business can thrive in an age of diversity.* Croydon: Kogan Page.

Gholipour, A., A. Pourezzat, and A. NikNezhad. 2008. Studying the antecedents of similar-to-me effect in managers' selection. *Iranian Journal of Management Sciences* 3: 7–36.

Goldin, C., and C. Rouse. 2000. Orchestrating impartiality: The impact of "blind" auditions on female musicians. *American Economic Review* 90: 715–741.

Greenwald, A.G., and M.R. Banaji. 1995. Implicit social cognition: Attitudes, self-esteem, and stereotypes. *Psychological Review* 102: 4–27.

Greenwald, A., and L. Krieger. 2006. Implicit bias: Scientific foundations. *California Law Review* 94: 945–968.

Hewstone, M. 1990. The 'ultimate attribution error' a review of the literature on intergroup causal attribution. *European Journal of Social Psychology* 20: 311–335.

Hoffman, M., L.B. Kahn, and D. Li. 2015. *Discretion in hiring* (No. w21709). London: National Bureau of Economic Research.

Hung-Ng, S. 1981. Equity theory and the allocation of rewards between groups. *European Journal of Social Psychology* 11: 439–443.

Jayne, M.E.A., and R.L. Dipboye. 2004. Leveraging diversity to improve business performance: Research findings and recommendations for organisations. *Human Resource Management* 43: 409–424.

Jonas, E., S. Schulz-Hardt, D. Frey, and N. Thelen. 2001. Confirmation bias in sequential information search after preliminary decisions: An expansion of dissonance theoretical research on "selective exposure to information". *Journal of Personality and Social Psychology* 80: 557–571.

Kahneman, D. 2011. *Thinking, fast and slow*. New York: Farrar, Strauss, Giroux.

Kahneman, D., D. Lovallo, and O. Sibony. 2011. Before you make that big decision. *Harvard Business Review*. https://hbr.org/2011/06/the-big-idea-before-you-make-that-big-decision. Accessed 17 Jan 2017.

Kalev, A. 2009. Cracking the glass cages? Restructuring and ascriptive inequality at work. *American Journal of Sociology* 114: 1591–1643.

Kataoka, H.C., G.P. Latham, and G. Whyte. 1997. The relative resistance of the situational, patterned behavior, and conventional structured interviews to anchoring effects. *Human Performance* 10: 47–63.

Kawakami, K., J.F. Dovidio, and S. van Kamp. 2005. Kicking the habit: Effects of nonstereotypic association training and correction processes on hiring decisions. *Journal of Experimental Social Psychology* 41: 68–75.

King, E.B., S.A. Mendoza, J.M. Madera, M.R. Hebl, and J.L. Knight. 2006. What's in a name? A multiracial investigation of the role of occupational stereotypes in selection decisions. *Journal of Applied Social Psychology* 36: 1145–1159.

Koch, A.J., S.D. D'Mello, and P.R. Sackett. 2015. A meta-analysis of gender stereotypes and bias in experimental simulations of employment decision making. *Journal of Applied Psychology* 100: 128–161.

Koenig, A.M., A.H. Eagly, A.A. Mitchell, and T. Ristikari. 2011. Are leader stereotypes masculine? A meta-analysis of three research paradigms. *Psychological Bulletin* 137: 616–642.

Kulich, C., G. Trojanowski, M.K. Ryan, A. Haslam, and L. Renneboog. 2011. Who gets the carrot and who gets the stick? Evidence of gender disparities in executive remuneration. *Strategic Management Journal* 32: 301–321.

Levashina, J., C.J. Hartwell, F.P. Morgeson, and M.A. Campion. 2014. The structured employment interview: Narrative and quantitative review of the research literature. *Personnel Psychology* 67: 241–293.

Lin, T., G. Dobbins, and J. Farh. 1992. A field study of race and age similarity effects on interview ratings in conventional and situational interviews. *Journal of Applied Psychology* 77: 363–371.

Linos, E., and J. Reinhard. 2015. *A head for hiring: The behavioural science of recruitment and selection.* London: Chartered Institute for Professional Development.

Markus, H.R., C. Steele, and D.M. Steele. 2000. Colorblindness as a barrier to inclusion: Assimilation and nonimmigrant minorities. In *The end of tolerance: Engage cultural differences*, ed. R. Shweder, M. Minow, and H. Markus, 233–259. London: Sage.

Milliken, F., and L. Martins. 1996. Searching for common threads: Understanding the multiple effects of diversity in organisational groups. *Academy of Management Review* 21: 402–433.

Mitchell, J.A., B.A. Nosek, and M.R. Banaji. 2003. Contextual variations in implicit evaluation. *Journal of Experimental Psychology* 132: 455–469.

Murphy, M.C., C.M. Steele, and J.J. Gross. 2007. Signaling threat how situational cues affect women in math, science, and engineering settings. *Psychological Science* 18: 879–885.

Nemeth, C.J., and J. Wachtler. 1983. Creative problem solving as a result of majority vs. minority influence. *European Journal of Social Psychology* 13: 45–55.

Nickerson, R.S. 1998. Confirmation bias: A ubiquitous phenomenon in many guises. *Review of General Psychology* 2: 175–220.

Olsson, A., J.P. Ebert, M.R. Banaji, and E.A. Phelps. 2005. The role of social groups in the persistence of learned fear. *Science* 309: 785–787.

Oreopoulos, P. 2011. Why do skilled immigrants struggle in the labor market? A field experiment with six thousand resumes. *American Economic Journal: Economic Policy* 3: 148–171.

Pilbeam, S., and M. Corbridge. 2006. *People resourcing: Contemporary HRM is practice*. Colchester: Prentice Hall.

Pless, N.M., and T. Maak. 2004. Building an inclusive diversity culture: Principles, processes and practice. *Journal of Business Ethics* 54: 129–147.

Powell, G., and D. Butterfield. 2002. Exploring the influence of decision makers' race and gender on actual promotions to top management. *Personnel Psychology* 55: 397–429.

Prewett-Livingston, A.J., H.S. Feild, J.G. Veres III, and P.M. Lewis. 1996. Effects of race on interview ratings in a situational panel interview. *Journal of Applied Psychology* 81: 78–186.

Purkiss, S., P. Perrewé, T. Gillespie, B. Mayesa, and G. Ferris. 2006. Implicit sources of bias in employment interview judgments and decisions. *Organisational Behavior and Human Decision Processes* 101: 152–167.

Rand, T.M., and K.N. Wexley. 1975. Demonstration of the effect, "similar to me," in simulated employment interviews. *Psychological Reports* 36: 535–544.

Rivera, L. 2012. Hiring as cultural matching: The case of Elite professional service firms. *American Sociological Review* 77: 999–1022.

Roberson, L., E.A. Deitch, A.P. Brief, and C.J. Block. 2003. Stereotype threat and feedback seeking in the workplace. *Journal of Vocational Behavior* 62: 176–188.

Ruderman, M.N., and P.J. Ohlott. 1994. *The realities of management promotion*. Greensboro: Center for Creative Leadership.

Ruderman, M.N., P.J. Ohlott, and K.E. Kram. 1995. Promotion decisions as a diversity practice. *Journal of Management Development* 14: 6–23.

Schmader, T. 2010. Stereotype threat deconstructed. Current directions in psychological. *Science* 19: 14–18.

Sealy, R., E. Doldor, and S. Vinnicombe. 2016. The female FTSE board report 2016. Women on boards: Taking stock of where we are. https://www.cranfield.ac.uk/press/news-2016/women-on-boards-ftse-100-company-has-full-gender-balance-for-first-time. Accessed 18 Jan 2017.

Shaw, J., and E. Barrett-Power. 1998. The effects of diversity on small work group processes and performance. *Human Relations* 51: 1307–1325.

Sherman, D.K., and K.A. Hartson. 2011. Reconciling self-protection with self-improvement: Self-affirmation theory. In *The handbook of self-enhancement and self-protection*, ed. M. Alicke and C. Sedikides, 128–151. London: Guilford Press.

Sherman, J.W., S.J. Stroessner, F.R. Conrey, and O. Azam. 2005. Prejudice and stereotype maintenance processes: Attention, attribution, and individuation. *Journal of Personality and Social Psychology* 89: 607–622.

Steele, C.M. 1997. A threat in the air: How stereotypes shape intellectual identity and performance. *American Psychologist* 52: 613–629.

Steele, C.M., and J. Aronson. 1995. Stereotype threat and the intellectual test performance of African Americans. *Journal of Personality and Social Psychology* 69: 797–811.

Steele, C.M., S.J. Spencer, and J. Aronson. 2002. Contending with group image: The psychology of stereotype and social identity threat. In *Advances in experimental social psychology*, ed. M. Zanna, 379–440. New York: Academic Press.

Tsui, A., and C. O'Reilly. 1989. Beyond simple demographic effects: The importance of relational demography in superior-subordinate dyads. *The Academy of Management Journal* 32: 402–423.

Tversky, A., and D. Kahneman. 1974. Judgment under uncertainty: Heuristics and biases. *Science* 185: 1124–1131.

von Hippel, C., D. Sekaquaptewa, and M. McFarlane. 2015. Stereotype threat among women in finance: Negative effects on identity, workplace well-being, and recruiting. *Psychology of Women Quarterly* 39: 405–414.

Wallace, W., and G. Pillans. 2016. *Creating an inclusive culture*. CRF Research Report. Accessed at: http://crforum.co.uk/research-and-resources/crfreport-creating-inclusive-culture/

Wright, P., S.P. Ferris, J.S. Hiller, and M. Kroll. 1995. Competitiveness through management of diversity: Effects on stock price valuations. *Academy of Management Journal* 38: 272–287.

Yeager, D.S., V. Purdie-Vaughns, J. Garcia, N. Apfel, P. BrzustoskiI, A. Master, W.T. Hessert, M.E. Williams, and G.L. Cohen. 2014. Breaking the cycle of mistrust: Wise interventions to provide critical feedback across the racial divide. *Journal of Experimental Psychology: General* 143 (2): 804–824.

10

Men and Gay Identity in the Workplace

Simon Roberts

10.1 Introduction

Arguably, the vast majority of research on sexual minorities in the workplace has focused on the issues surrounding the disclosure/non-disclosure of sexual orientation in the workplace. Furthermore, much of this literature comes from the USA. As Creed and Cooper (2008) have noted, self-disclosure and non-disclosure of a gay identity has been the unifying theme in research on lesbian, gay, bisexual and transgender (LGBT) people. This chapter argues that this research comes under what could be classified as the first wave of studies into the experiences of LGBT employees in the workplace. Centred round the first wave of research are the dilemmas around managing a predominately invisible identity and the consequences in revealing. The vast majority of this literature

S. Roberts (✉)
Department of Leadership, Strategy & Organisations, Bournemouth
University Business School, Bournemouth University, Bournemouth, UK

© The Author(s) 2018
V. Caven, S. Nachmias (eds.), *Hidden Inequalities in the Workplace*,
Palgrave Explorations in Workplace Stigma,
DOI 10.1007/978-3-319-59686-0_10

(Woods and Lucas 1993; King et al. 2008; Chrobot-Mason et al. 2002; Shallenberger 1994; Ward 2008; Ragins et al. 2007; Ragins 2008) has been heavily influenced by Goffman's theoretical work on *Stigmas* (1963, 1968), where the prevailing theme is how gay men might manage a potentially discreditable or stigmatised identity. While the focus of this chapter is gay men, the findings and discussion are equally relevant to other sexual minorities within the LGBT+ arena.

In the UK, as in many western nations, there have been a number of progressive pieces of legislation enacted with the intent to eradicate discrimination on the basis of sexuality in the workplace. At the beginning of this century, there have been five important pieces of legislation with the intent of giving greater protection to LGBT citizens in the UK including the repeal of Local Government Act: Section 28 (2003) and the introduction of the Employment Equality (SO) Regulations (2003), the Civil Partnership Act (2004) and the Equality Act (Sexual Orientation) Regulations (2010), which make it unlawful to discriminate on the grounds of sexual orientation in gaining access to goods, facilities and services and finally the marriage (same-sex couples) Act 2013. The pace and scale of acceptance of gay equality laws have been relatively rapid in recent years. To cite an example, in 2004 gay marriage was only legal in Belgium and Holland, whereas today it is legal in more than ten countries. There have also been significant changes in social attitudes towards homosexuality in the UK in recent years (Ellison and Gunstone 2009; Cowan 2007).

Up until this legislation came into force, the focus of previous research probably unsurprisingly has been predominately around two strands: sexual minorities' experiences of discrimination in the workplace and the issue of disclosure/non-disclosure of a gay identity. There has been little exploration 'beyond the closet', in how gay men manage their identity post anti-discrimination laws combined with more liberal attitudes towards homosexuality. In particular, there has been a paucity of research on the ways gay men challenge, negotiate and conform in the two-way process of managing their identities; this chapter aims to address this gap.

The aim of this chapter is to go beyond solely the issue of disclosure/non-disclosure of sexuality. This chapter explores whether gay men have taken advantage of this new context. In so doing the chapter aims to explore whether gay men feel they can be more assertive or possibly more willing to stamp their identity in the workplace. This is particularly relevant as recent research has indicated that more than two-thirds of gay men in employment in the UK now feel they can be open about their sexual orientation in the workplace (Ellison and Gunstone 2009).

This chapter also highlights the constraints that self-identified gay men experience in the workplace, in particular, how the professionalism demands an asexual employee (Burrell and Hearn 1989) and the downplaying of a gay identity. Professionalism implicitly assumes a heterosexual man (Grey 1998), where others are pressurised to adopt a normalising strategy so as to fit in. What the empirical findings reveal in this chapter is how a significant number of the respondents adopted what Seidman (2002) refers to as the 'good sexual citizen', that is a strategy of assimilation.

This chapter brings to light the pervasiveness of heteronormativity in organisations, where although gay men were able to disclose their sexual orientation, they still had to carefully manage information about their sexuality. The stories below highlight how self-identified gay men had to downplay their 'authentic self' in order to be accepted.

10.2   First-Wave Literature

In this first-wave literature, researchers (Humphrey 1999; Bowen and Blackmon 2003; Creed and Scully 2000; Bernstein 1997; Creed et al. 2010; Day and Schoenrade 1997) have attempted to answer the question as to why sexual minorities decide to disclose their sexual orientation. A common strand among these studies is that sexual minorities may use disclosure as a form of political agency. 'Coming out' is perceived as a powerful means of effecting social change. In fact, Peel (2002) in agreement argues in her study of lesbian and gay educational trainers that 'coming out' and exposure to lesbians and gay men is an efficacious method to bring about social change. Likewise Bowen and Blackmon (2003) argue that disclosure may lead to a reduction in ignorance and prejudice in the workplace. Humphrey (1999) identified three reasons why people choose to 'come out' in the workplace: (1) the personal level, which involves being honest to others and integrity; (2) the professional level, so that individuals can form closer bonds with work colleagues; and (3) the political level, where individuals wish to educate others about a non-heterosexual existence. Humphrey interviewed 23 activists in the UK's largest union, UNISON. They were all employed in public sector occupations. Unlike most previous research, all of Humphrey's respondents were 'out' at work and had been so for a considerable amount of time. Although all her respondents had disclosed their sexual identity, this was not without paying a heavy penalty. Her respondents experienced some of the most blatant forms of discrimination. Humphrey (1999) concluded that being 'out of the closet' was still a hostile place where gays and lesbians had to manage a difficult balancing act *between being out and pursued for their specialist knowledge and out and persecuted for their presumed perversities.* This chapter picks up on this theme to explore whether gay men feel they can push the boundaries in shaping and modifying the labels and meanings ascribed by others in the workplace. Humphrey touches on the way her respondents tried to educate others about a non-heterosexual existence. This chapter explores this idea to see whether gay men feel they can be more assertive and forthright in how they manage their gay identity in light of changes in social attitudes and recent legislation since Humphrey's research.

At around the same time as Humphrey's study, other researchers picked up on this political level, where individuals seek to educate others about a non-heterosexual existence. For example, Creed and Scully (2000) in the USA and Creed, DeJordy and Lok's later study (2010) attempt to theoretically explain why LGBT workers disclose their gay identity. They argue in their study of 66 LGBT employees that there are three main motives for disclosure which they categorise as encounters, educative encounters and advocacy. Encounters, according to Creed and Scully are pivotal moments where LGBT people can effect social change. A claiming encounter requires an LGBT person to state and own a gay identity. This might involve an LGBT employee casually dropping in references to their sexuality in an everyday encounter. An example of this would be where a gay man would talk about his private life, his partner or how he spent his weekend in a casual matter-of-fact way. An educative encounter is where an LGBT person explains to a work colleague some aspect of their identity that they might not have been aware of or might have misunderstood. Educative encounters require LGBT individuals to challenge myths and stereotypes as well as highlighting social injustices around sexual orientation. The main focus of educative encounters is to teach others about sexual minorities' worldview. Finally, an advocacy encounter is one that seems more radical than an educative one. Here the individual highlights and raises a perceived inequity however small and seeks redress through organisational policy or a change in attitudes. In Creed and Scully's work, the distinctions between the different types of encounters are not clearly laid out. In fact, they freely admit that the boundaries between the three kinds of encounters are blurred.

In a similar vein, Bernstein (1997) explores the different strategies that four lesbian and gay campaign groups in the USA use in effecting social change in the workplace. She noted a continuum of identity deployment strategies enacted by her respondents ranging from education to critique. Identity for education draws similarities to Creed and Scully's later study in what they term 'claiming encounters'. This type of identity challenges negative stereotypes about gay people or heteronormative assumptions. The strategy aims to challenge heteronormativity within organisations. However, identity for education, Bernstein argues, focuses on looking for common ground or alikeness with the heterosexual majority. The limitation of this approach is by focusing on issues of sameness and a strategy of normalising a gay identity is that it does not confront dominant norms head on. Identity for education restricts the possibility of problematising the norms and morality of the dominant culture—the source of most discrimination. Identity for critique, on the other hand, is a more radical confrontational approach. This is where individuals or activists do not seek to behave or act in line with mainstream culture, but emphasise and celebrate their difference. The approach is rooted in oppositional cultures confronting head on the practices and values of the dominant culture. The dilemma is finding the right balance between claiming common ground (a sameness approach) to reduce any stigma attached to a gay identity and at the same time highlighting a gay identity's distinctiveness (a difference approach). Bernstein's study explains the motives behind why gays and lesbians choose to reveal their sexuality in the workplace. She argues that the rationale is to change heterosexual people's perspective and at the same time to assert their identity in order to challenge social norms that are the main source of discrimination.

Other researchers (Snape et al. 1995; Wilson and Miller 2002) rather than exploring why sexual minorities choose to reveal their sexual identity in order to effect social change investigate how LGBT people respond to discrimination in the workplace. Parallel studies have been undertaken into response to discrimination in other diversity strands (Boykin and Toms (1985) on race and Hyers (2007) on gender). A common pattern emerging from this literature was that these studies identified coping strategies lying on a continuum ranging from active to passive responses to discrimination. Snape et al. (1995), for example, place responses into two distinct categories: active and passive. A passive response in their research is characterised as someone who would try to ignore discriminatory behaviour in the hope that the perpetrator would tire of harassing. Active personal responses, on the other hand, would be where an individual would reply to verbal abuse or would purposefully make it clear to the discriminator that their behaviour was unacceptable. These respondents in many respects draw similarities to Creed and Scully's concept of 'claiming encounters'. Typically they would make it clear that they had no issue with their sexuality and would thus refuse to be intimidated by others who tried to make it a problem. One of the weaknesses of these studies is that they ignore the social context in which these respondents work. The social and organisational contexts are possibly powerful influential factors in whether an individual is able to choose either a passive or active response to discrimination.

Wilson and Miller (2002) also identified a range of coping strategies in dealing with heterosexism in the workplace. In their study in the USA of 37 African-American gay and bisexual men, they uncovered six management strategies in dealing with discrimination along the active–passive spectrum. They characterised a passive response as one in which an individual would attempt to maintain a quiet and reserved demeanour when listening to homophobic comments made by heterosexual co-workers. Typically these respondents would not challenge the perpetrator choosing instead to suffer in silence. At the other extreme, there were a few individuals in Wilson and Miller's study who stood their ground. These respondents chose to confront discriminatory behaviour directly refusing to back down. In their conclusion, they note that the coping strategies gay and bisexual men used varied along multiple continua. The coping strategies were not mutually exclusive. One of the weaknesses in their study is that they fail to address the motives behind why individuals chose certain coping strategies. As in the case of Creed and Scully's work outlined above, Wilson and Miller seem to ignore the impact of social and organisational context in which these individuals 'chose' how to deal with homophobia.

At the core of this chapter's conceptual framework on gay identity management is Jenkins's (2008, 2014) concept of the *interaction order* from his theoretical study of social identity. Jenkins (2008, 2014) defines the *interaction order* as where our self-identities (internal) meet with the external moment or as the dilemma surrounding the *internal–external dialectic*. The internal moment of the dialectic of identification (defined as the image individuals present of themselves for acceptance by others) meets with the external moment (defined as the reception and response of others of that presentation). According to Jenkins, identities are not unilaterally constructed. Identity construction is a two-way process. For individuals, asserting an identity is not sufficient as identity construction is also dependent on categorisation by others and meanings others we interact with place on such identities. In many respects, how we see ourselves may be very different to how others see us. Just as each of us identifies others, equally others identify us in turn. Consequently, what people think about us is no less significant than what we think about ourselves. It is dialectic due to the fact that the two aspects of identity are contesting and negotiating over the different meanings placed on identities. In this model, Jenkins aims to explain the play-off between the two. In the play-off, the response of others might lead to reflection on the part of the individual. This is where the individual might adapt or edit his identity due to either positive or negative reactions from others. The dilemma faced with the *interaction order*, identified by Jenkins, is that we cannot fully manage or control the outcomes of the presentation we project to others. Even though people have some control over the signals about themselves that they send to others, we are all at a disadvantage in that we cannot ensure either their 'correct' reception or interpretation, or know with certainty how they are received or interpreted (Jenkins 2008,

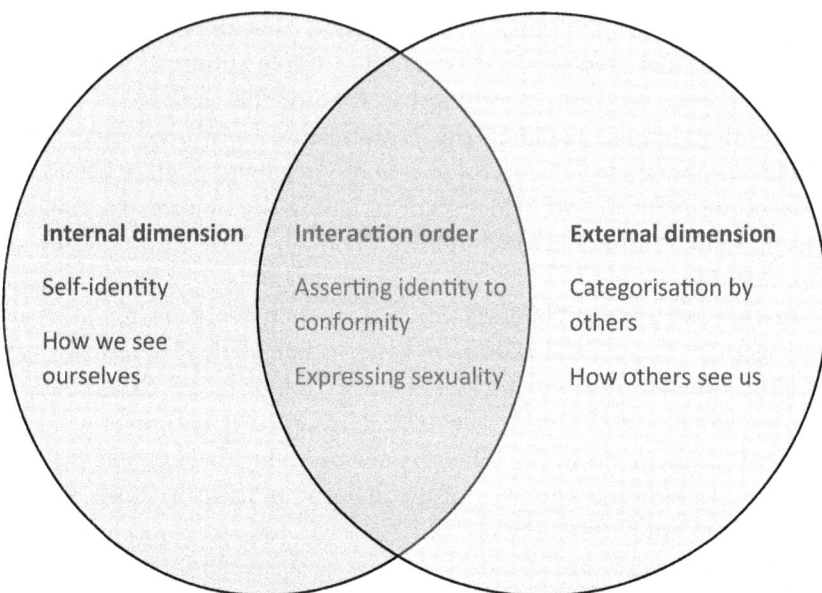

Fig. 10.1 The intersection of internal and external dimensions of identity

p. 42). As Jenkins states, what people think about us is no less significant than what we think about ourselves. Consequently, it is not enough to assert an identity; that assertion must also be validated, or not, by those with whom we have dealings. Figure 10.1 illustrates how this author has developed Jenkins's analytical framework in relation to how gay men construct and manage their gay identity in the workplace.

This chapter focuses on a specific area of Jenkins's *interaction order*, namely, how gay men construct their gay identity at the boundaries. The boundaries are where the internal identities meet the external identities. As illustrated in the Venn diagram above, this is where the internal and external dimensions of social identities intersect. It is here where the boundaries may be pushed between the individual's interpretation of self-identity and that ascribed by others. In many respects, the analytical framework that Jenkins uses to describe the *interaction order* could be interpreted as two shifting plates: one plate the internal dimension and the other the external dimension. This chapter explores the degree to which gay men are, on the one hand, willing to push their interpretation of their self-identity and, on the other, to allow the perceived ascriptions and categorisations by others to prevail.

The diagram also illustrates the ways in which identities are fluid and contextual. These shifting plates are in constant flux. In relation to gay men, the meaning attached to a gay identity may change over time. This fluidity arises because within the *interaction order* identities may be fought over and contested. As Jenkins (2008, p. 45) argues, identification is something over which struggles take place and with which stratagems are advanced. Consequently, this chapter explores the ways in which gay men have contested, fought or conformed to the meanings they perceive as attached to their gay identity.

10.3   Academic and Methodological Considerations

The study data were collected as part of a wider research project exploring how gay men manage their identity in the workplace. The study was conducted in the UK between 2010 and 2012. The sample comprised 45 gay men working in Bournemouth on the South Coast of England. In line with most research on the LGBT population (Martin and Dean 1993; Cooper 2006; Platzer and James 1997; Homfray 2008; Rumens 2008), self-identification or self-definition was used as the primary criterion for participation. As Yip (2008, p. 8) argues, the advantage of self-definition is that it prioritises the participants' standpoint and definition rather than imposing identity labels. The degree of openness about disclosure of their sexuality varied. Seven of the participants chose not to reveal their sexual orientation in the workplace. Participants ranged in age from 29 to 63. Previous research (Colgan et al. 2006) has noted how samples tend to over-represent white-collar middle-class groupings in their studies. Shallenberger (1994) and Woods and Lucas's studies (1993) solely focused on gay professionals, whereas Humphrey (1999) and Colgan et al. (2006) explored the experiences of sexual minorities in the public sector. This sample comprises a much wider range of occupational groupings from skilled manual blue-collar occupations to senior management on the board of directors of large UK corporations. At the time of the interview, 31 respondents worked in white-collar occupations, whereas just under a third (14) were in blue-collar employment. Over two-thirds of respondents worked in the private sector with only 14 in the public sector, including 5 teachers. In order to preserve anonymity and to ensure ethical issues were adhered to, all participants were given pseudonyms. Demographic characteristics of study participants and a brief description of the organisational environment they described are outlined in Table 10.1.

Table 10.1 Profile of participants

Name	Personal details	Occupation sector	Organisational environment
Roy	47, self-defined as gay for 10 years, white, lives with gay partner, was married. Not 'out' in present occupation	Electronic technician Manual Manufacturing Blue collar	Male dominated, small company, 35 employees, age range 17–36 of employees on the shop floor. No diversity policies
Malcolm	45, self-defined as gay for 10 years, white, lives with gay partner, was married, 2 children. 'Out' in present occupation	PCV driving Instructor Transport Blue collar	Male dominated, a large number of gay work colleagues—at least 15. LGBT network but not very active. Diversity awareness courses
Andrew	41, self-defined as gay, white, civil partnered. 'Out' in present occupation	Systems change coordinator Finance White-collar prof	Predominately male, mid- to late 40s, mandatory diversity training. Founder of LGBT group
Mike	32, self-defined as gay, white, single. 'Out' in present occupation	QA software analyst Finance White collar	An entirely male team, small team of five, between the ages of 30 and 50. GLBT network. Mandatory diversity training

(continued)

Table 10.1 (continued)

Name	Personal details	Occupation sector	Organisational environment
Clive	51, self-defined as gay, white, single. Not 'out' in present occupation	Site manager, primary school Blue collar	Traditional, conservative culture, large proportion of elderly staff
Peter	35, self-defined as gay, white, partnered. Not 'out' in present occupation	Electrician Leisure industry Bournemouth Borough council Blue collar	All male, small team of four, diversity training as part of council policy. Aware of other gay men outside his department
Hans	59, self-defined as gay, white, single. 'Out' in present occupation	EFL teacher Education	Mixed gender, not aware of diversity policies
Donald	43, self-defined as gay, white, partnered. 'Out' in present organisation	Gardener Leisure Bournemouth Borough council Blue collar	Male dominated, in small teams, normally work in pairs
Robert	46, self-defined as gay, white, single. 'Out' in present occupation	Team manager Finance	Manager of a small team of 'women of a certain age'. A prominent gay presence. Known as 'Fairy Towers'. Gay senior manager
Neal	27, self-defined as gay, white, single. 'Out' in present organisation	Senior operations supervisor Finance	Managing a team of five ladies. Gay manager. Chair of LGBT group
Alfred	61, self-defined as gay, white, 'out' in present organisation, partnered	Deputy head of primary school	Female dominated, another openly gay younger male teacher. An unsupportive head master

(continued)

Table 10.1 (continued)

Name	Personal details	Occupation sector	Organisational environment
Alex	34, self-defined as gay, white, selectively 'out' but not to subordinate. Partnered	Fencing contractor for ministry of defence Blue collar	Small company working with male boss and a very homophobic labourer
Callum	29, self-defined as gay, white, 'out' in present organisation. Civil partnership	Area manager for a leading retail bank	A significant gay presence in senior management positions. A supportive policy towards sexuality
Dale	36, self-defined as gay, white, 'out' in present organisation, partnered	Receptionist/manager Leisure complex	Female dominated, knows of other gay men who work for the company. Council-run diversity policies in place
George	44, self-defined as gay, white 'out' to everyone, openly expresses his sexuality, single. HIV positive	Bus driver Blue collar	Line manager is bisexual and one of the directors is gay—the only gay bus driver. In previous company there were around 20% of bus drivers who were openly gay
Jenson	40, self-defined as gay, white, 'out', partnered	Finance processing manager	Female dominated, no diversity policies that he is aware of. A large number of gay men
Isaac	41, self-defined as gay, 'out' white, partnered	Finance manager, vice president	Active member of Company LGBT network—the engagement leader. Strong diversity polices—a Stonewall champion

(continued)

Table 10.1 (continued)

Name	Personal details	Occupation sector	Organisational environment
James	45, self-defined as gay, white, 'out', partnered. Civil partnership	Administrator for university	Was a member of LGBT employee network, female-dominated employment
Michael	50, self-defined as gay, white, 'out', single	Regional recruitment manager	Female dominated though works with a heterosexual man who has homophobic views. Large organisation with an international presence
Ron	45, self-defined as gay, white, 'out', living with partner	Sales assistant for retail chain	Female dominated with a strong gay presence
Stuart	41, self-defined as gay, white 'out', partnered	Mental health support worker	A large gay and lesbian presence. Active union and LGBT network though Stuart is not involved
Stefan	40, self-defined as gay, white, not 'out', single	Logistics manager of haulage company Blue collar	Male-dominated industry. Knows of other gay and lesbian employees
Aiden	42, self-defined as gay, white, recently came 'out', partnered	Picture framer/artist	Small company with homophobic director. Worked closely with another gay employee
Daniel	38, self-defined as gay, white, not 'out', single	Market researcher	Company employs 250 people, knows of two other gay guys via Grindr, a strong religious presence, mixed nationalities, mainly male employees

(continued)

Table 10.1 (continued)

Name	Personal details	Occupation sector	Organisational environment
Godfrey	47, self-defined as gay, white, 'out', partnered	Environmental health officer	Small department, mainly middle-aged men. Only gay employee. Council run with diversity training
Kris	30, self-defined as gay, white, 'out' partnered	Taxi driver Blue collar	Male dominated, desk operator is a lesbian, banter around sexuality
Shaun	56, self-defined as gay, white, 'out' to some employees, single	Catering manager	Small family-run café based in a department store
Adam	51, self-defined as gay, white, partnered	IT systems analyst	Mainly men, strong diversity policies, LGBT network though not a member, aware of one other gay employee
Ben	44, self-defined as gay, white, partnered	Deputy ward manager for health care trust	Female dominated, strong diversity policies, LGBT officer for UNISON
Dean	42, self-defined as gay, 'out' white, partnered	Force enquiry officer, LAGLO, special constable	LAGLO Officer, extensive diversity training courses, knows of four other gay employees in call centre
Dec	36, self-defined as gay, 'out', white, civil partnership	Senior contracts administrator for aerospace	50/50 gender mix in offices but not on shop floor, suspect there is one other gay employee who is not 'out', mandatory diversity training but not on sexuality

(continued)

Table 10.1 (continued)

Name	Personal details	Occupation sector	Organisational environment
Greg	45, self-defined as gay, 'out', white, lives with partner	Business manager for life assurance company	Mixed gender, works overseas with Indians, a number of other gay employees
Ivan	43, self-defined as gay, 'out' white, single	Manager (trouble shooter) for glass manufacturer	80 employees, male dominated, family-run business, only gay employee
Jack	34, self-defined as gay, 'out', white, partnered	Company director of gay lifestyle shop	Small gay retailer with mainly gay employees in the centre of the gay community in Bournemouth
Morris	33, self-defined as gay, 'out', white, partnered	Primary school teacher	Female dominated, not aware of diversity polices, sees himself as a pioneer—only gay employee
Nigel	29, self-defined as gay, white, 'out', single	Secondary school head of Science teacher	Mixed gender with 60 staff, union representative, introduced a diversity policy on sexuality, gay deputy head
Phil	31, self-defined as gay, white, partially 'out', single	Manager of a burger bar	Small company, employs one person, a 64-year-old lady
Roland	63, self-defined as gay, white, not 'out', partnered, was married with a son	Property project surveyor for council	Male dominated, a macho environment in building industry, homophobic comments from one of the architect colleagues, knows other gay employees

(continued)

Table 10.1 (continued)

Name	Personal details	Occupation sector	Organisational environment
Sam	46, self-defined as gay, white, 'out' at work, partnered, about to have civil partnership, was married with a son	Installation manager for a gas company	Strong diversity policies on sexuality, male dominated, active member of local Gay Pride group in Bournemouth, aware of other gay men in the organisation
Pablo	31, self-defined as gay, Hispanic, 'out' at work civil partnership	Supply primary school teacher	
Louis	32, self-defined as gay, white, single, 'out' at work, HIV positive	Manager of retail store	Other gay employees, homophobic regional manager
Simon	42, self-defined as gay, white, lives with partner, 'out' at work	Managing director of retail chain	Other gay people high up in organisation

In line with most research on sexual minorities (Yip 2008; Homfray 2008; Cooper 2006; Platzer and James 1997; Rumens and Kerfoot 2009), snowballing was used as one means of recruiting potential volunteers. Indeed, Browne (2005) notes that deploying a snowballing approach is an appropriate method in investigating a 'hidden' or 'invisible' population. Consequently, the author used snowballing techniques through his own personal networks asking friends and acquaintances to be involved. One advantage of deploying snowballing was that those who had already been interviewed could share their experience with other potential volunteers. They could also reassure others about issues of confidentiality and anonymity, trust, interview style and basic information about the interviewer. In one case, after the author had interviewed a junior member of one of the largest organisations in Bournemouth, this contact initiated a further volunteer in a much more senior position as well as access to the company's LGBT group.

Potential volunteers were also recruited at Bourne Free Pride—Bournemouth's Gay Pride Festival in July 2010. In addition, the author visited the gay bars in Bournemouth seeking possible respondents for a later mutually agreed interview. The objective was that this recruitment strategy might bring forward a diverse spread of ages, occupational categories and working environments. Gay Pride Festivals are a common recruitment source as previous research has shown (Martin and Dean 1993; Platzer and James 1997; Yip 2008). There are, however, a number of limitations of employing snowballing as a recruitment strategy. One of the key concerns raised is over the issue of representativeness of the sample. Although not a central concern of this research, a common issue raised with snowballing is the issue of generalisability of the data. This is due to the under-representation of certain sub-groups such as ethnic minorities, disabled and working-class people. Nevertheless, a wide age range and a spread of occupations in both white- and blue-collar occupations were found.

Prior to commencing the interviews, the researcher spoke to the men by phone to explain the nature and purpose of the study. One of the main dilemmas faced was determining how much information should be provided to potential interviewees before the interview. The intention was to be as honest and frank as possible regarding the content of the interview. The aim was to make it clear what the purpose of the research was. Respondents were informed that data drawn from the interview would possibly be used for the researcher's PhD (Doctor of Philosophy) as well as future publications.

The disclosure of the researcher's sexuality as a gay man at either at the recruitment stage or during the interview process seemed appropriate and brought clear benefits as other researchers had observed (Homfray 2008; Cooper 2006; Yip 2008). One major advantage observed was the increased level of trust and rapport achieved through a shared identity. Respondents probably felt more relaxed and forthcoming with a gay identified researcher. Furthermore, the researcher noted how individuals during the recruitment drive were initially reticent to co-operate or allow access to others. For example, access to key individuals beyond initial gatekeepers surrounding Bournemouth Gay Pride was limited until the sexual orientation of the researcher was made known. Previous studies (Yip 2008; Ritchie et al. 2008; Ward and Winstanley 2004) have also noted the benefits of 'insider status' where gate keepers were more disposed to allowing access on the assumption that the researcher was more likely to manage interactions with potential respondents with greater sensitivity and tact.

In order to make participants feel comfortable and at ease discussing their gay identity in the workplace, it seemed appropriate to interview the participants outside the workplace. This meant conducting the research in participants' homes if they requested. As Legard et al. (2008) argue, the choice of venue for in-depth interviews should be left to the participant. However, participants were offered a choice of venues; their workplace, the researcher's workplace or home, their home, another quiet meeting place of their choice, wherever they felt most comfortable as long as the location was quiet enabling the recording of the interview. In fact, the vast majority chose to be interviewed in their home.

The study adopted a qualitative and inductive methodological approach. In line with previous research on sexual minorities (Burke 1993; Ward 2008; Shallenberger 1994), semi-structured interviews were deployed. Interviews lasted between 50 minutes and 1.5 hours. This approach generated rich in-depth responses from participants from which the study findings emerged. Previous researchers have recommended this style of interview especially if the aim is to elicit stories and personal narratives. It also gives greater control and freedom to respondents. An interview guide was created and structured around a number of themes identified from the conceptual framework. These themes included the organisational context, the internal dimensions of identity, the external dimensions of identity and the reactions of others to a gay identity and finally, reflections on how they managed their gay identity throughout their working lives. Only questions pertaining to the two themes addressed in this article are included in the present study; which included questions relating to how they manage their gay identity in the workplace and how they present themselves in their interactions with others.

All of the interviews were digitally recorded and transcribed with consent from the participants. The first stage before analysis could take place was to familiarise oneself with the data (Ritchie et al. 2008). This advice was followed by listening to the audio recordings after each interview. In addition, initial thoughts and reactions about how the interview went were penned down. By doing so, a memo of emerging thoughts and ideas developed. A thematic approach was chosen in order to explore different themes around how gay men saw their gay identity, their interaction with others, and how they believed others in the workplace saw them.

10.4   Findings and Discussion

A key finding drawn from the data was that a variety of strategies were used by the gay men in how they managed their gay identity in the *interaction order*. The approaches adopted ranged from direct confrontational self-assertion strategies (in a minority of cases, eight respondents) to passive acceptance or compliance to the categorisation by others. The strategies have been categorised around three broad themes: normalising a gay identity, a confrontational approach and conformity.

10.4.1   Normalising a Gay Identity

Although none of these strategies were mutually exclusive, rather than challenge stereotypes and labels head on, a preferred, more subtle strategy favoured by a large proportion of respondents (18 respondents) was an attempt to normalise their gay identity. These strategies were not mutually exclusive in the sense that they were dependent on a number of contingency factors such as the work context. Nor were these strategies linear in the sense that an individual did not start at a passive conformist position and move gradually towards an active confrontational position later in their working life. Respondents tried to normalise their gay identity by taking a casual matter-of-fact approach when discussing personal details about themselves. In the cases of Don, Hans and Morris, they felt that just 'being themselves' on a day-to-day basis would allow work colleagues to get to know them and consequently change their assumptions about what gay men are like as well as what it means to be gay. In these cases, the fact that they were 'out' in the workplace meant that they felt able to challenge and change the perceptions and attitudes of what others perceived a gay man to be.

An illustration of this approach was Dean, a police officer, who was the Lesbian and Gay Liaison Officer (LAGLO), who took a liberal assimilationist approach. He felt that sexuality should not be used to mark difference. He felt uncomfortable with the images portrayed on the LAGLO website as it emphasised their difference which he felt did not 'fit in' with the corporate image.

> *I have just taken over our internal website and the first thing that struck me was that an awful lot of it was in pink and there were like rainbow pictures and I was just trying to think about what image that gives within a professional organisation about all our stuff on the internet being different from the corporate blandness if you like. it's for a start doesn't fit in with the corporate template of what things should be and also I think sometimes when we use imagery like that we sort of set ourselves apart as we're different because we're gay. Whereas a lot of my take on things is that we're not different just because we're gay.*

In the quote above, Dean refers to fitting in with the corporate template. Dean's approach seems to be one of conformity. Rather than aspiring to mark difference, he feels that the LAGLO networking website should use the organisational culture as a template to emulate. Of course by adopting this stance, the rules have already been set by others and arguably the heterosexual majority. Implicit in Dean's sentiments is the notion of fitting into heteronormative assumptions of how non-heterosexual people should behave and present themselves.

Nevertheless, the majority of respondents had noticed a shift in attitudes from work colleagues in their perception of gay men and themselves in a positive direction over their working lives. It seems that within the *interaction order*, those who were 'out' were able to push the boundary of their interpretation of their self-identity and as a result seemingly modify the perceptions of others. What seems apparent from the responses of the majority of openly gay respondents was that the issue of disclosure/non-disclosure of sexual identity had moved on to one of normalising homosexuality.

Within the *interaction order*, normalising a gay identity was the most popular strategy adopted by those who were openly gay at work in the workplace. What is revealing is this approach was deemed less threatening as if a more forthright, direct approach would be deemed too confrontational and imposing on the attitudes of others. For example, Nigel, a secondary school teacher, saw limits in the extent to which he felt he could push the boundaries between his self-identity and the attitudes and perceptions of others. A compounding factor in Nigel's case was that he had lived under the shadow of section 28, where he still feared that any discussion around homosexuality within the classroom might lead to concerns being raised by parents or pupils that he was promoting homosexuality. Although Nigel was comfortable with his students knowing his sexuality, he was unwilling to go any further or discuss the issue in the classroom. There seemed to be a fine line between an attempt to normalise a gay identity and pushing the boundaries too far.

Some respondents educated others in the workplace in a traditional way that is a more formal teacher-to-student approach. In this way the respondents took on the role of educator. Neal, 27, employed this strategy. In Neal's case this was probably because of his dual role as manager of a small team in addition to being co-chair of an LGBT group within the bank. He would feel a need on occasion to educate his subordinates. He would correct subordinates when they used the wrong terminology to address gay men or used expected stereotypes. An example of this was where a work colleague asked him who is the man or a woman in a gay relationship.

> *Well, actually it's not the case of being a man or woman. You know, in my mind I'm with a man because I'm gay and which I'm a man in a relationship. You know, that's it. You don't have a man, you have two men ... you're applying a heterosexual relationship and heterosexual make-up into a gay one, which you can't do.*

Here we find Neal tries to assert his difference from his heterosexual colleagues rather than finding commonality. Neal tries to differentiate his gay identity. For Nigel and Neal claiming visibility was not about being trail-blazers on behalf of their identity group, but rather as a means of normalising their homosexuality. Nevertheless, it had unintentionally made them role models in the eyes of their gay subordinates. In the vast majority of these normalising approaches there did not appear to be a political level as identified by Humphrey (1999). Humphrey argued that one motive for 'coming out' was to educate individuals about a non-heterosexual existence to effect social change. Creed and Scully (2000) refer to this approach as an advocacy approach, where individuals seek address through organisational policy or change in attitudes. There did not appear to be such a deliberate strategy to effect social change in these findings. In the case of Humphrey's (1999) study, she conducted her research solely with 23 activists. This might explain why her respondents were more strident and political in their approach. This contrasts with the respondents in this study who in the vast majority of cases were not gay activists. Respondents just wanted to get on with their lives without making a big fuss over their sexuality in the workplace.

10.4.2   Confrontational Approach

In this range of coping strategies, probably the most assertive challenge came from Stuart, 41, a mental health support worker. Stuart's story was probably the most confrontational. This was evident not only in how Stuart expressed his anger through rather strong language, but how the story dominated the interview. Although Stuart's approach was probably atypical among the respondents, his story illustrates the way in which he was determined to push the boundaries within the *interaction order*. Stuart recalled an incident where one day he was cutting up some fruit in the staff kitchen, when another male staff nurse teased him that it must be for 'fruity Stuart'. In light of the fact that the perpetrator, according to Stuart, had a history of making homophobic comments to other members of staff, Stuart wished to take matters further through official channels with the aid of a witness, even though from a third-party perspective, these comments seemed rather innocuous.

I'm a fucking gay man. I immediately think he's making some kind of comment against me. So anyway Liz was like (He shows an open mouthed expression of shock) *stared at him, you know, I'm in the room, like I say, I heard him and then we both made statements* [to management]. Stuart, 41, mental health nurse, *'out' in present organisation.*

This story illustrates the ways in which, according to Jenkins (2008) identification is about struggles and negotiation. In Stuart's case he was able to fight his interpretation of his gay identity so strongly that he managed to have the alleged offender removed from his unit. During the interview he was asked if he still worked with the alleged perpetrator. He responded that the individual was no longer allowed to work on the same ward.

Probably the key issue in Stuart's story centres round power. His story could be very much defined as a struggle to stamp his self-identity in the workplace. Probably due to a number of contextual factors including a supportive union and a large openly gay presence in his organisation, Stuart was able to assert his gay identity and challenge the status quo. Stuart took advantage of the fact that he had these support mechanisms in place giving him the impetus to address any negative comments.

Previous research suggests that those who are in higher incomes tend not to disclose their sexual identity as they have more to lose, never mind challenge homophobic abuse (Schope 2002). These findings seem to be in direct contrast and confirm Brekhus's US findings (2003, p. 132) that those in higher income jobs have more freedom in the management of their gay identity in the workplace. A theme that emerged from the interviews was that there was a strong link between the level of seniority in the organisation and the degree to which an individual was willing to challenge homophobic remarks in an assertive manner. This was the case for Ivan, 43; Isaac, 41; Jenson, 40; Simon, 42; and Sam, 46 all of whom worked in senior management positions. This is in spite of a recent survey where 40% of respondents stated they would be unhappy with an openly gay manager at work (Ellison and Gunstone 2009).

10.4.3 Conformity

As discussed above, a range of approaches were deployed within the *interaction order* from active (direct challenges) to passive (conformity).

A theme that arose from the data was that some respondents were willing to conform to the heterosexual norms and expectations of others in the workplace. Rather than challenge disparaging identity labels imposed by others, there was a degree of acceptance. In many respects they were conforming to the dominant heteronormative discourses[1] by the very fact that they condoned the use of such labelling and accepted low-level homophobic behaviour. In these cases, within the *interaction order*, the contested meaning over a gay identity seemed to lean towards the meanings ascribed by others. The shifting plates within the boundary of the *interaction order* moved towards the meanings ascribed by others. Kris's comments below highlight the typical sentiments obtained from a significant number of respondents.

> *And it's gay friendly, but they rip the piss out of me. They call me faggot, flamer or what have you. But there's no malice behind it.* Kris, 30, taxi driver, 'out' in present organisation.

In Kris's case he did not 'see' the term faggot and flamer as terms of homophobic abuse. This is despite the commonly held assumption that these words are of derogatory nature and are defined as such in most dictionaries.[2]

In George's case, such derogatory terms were inverted and adopted as a label of pride, similar to the way in which the term queer had been embraced by a number of gay activists in the USA in the early 1990s (Jagose 1996, p. 76).

> *Someone will go, someone will turn round to me and say faggot. I say, Miss Faggot to you! Yeah, I always throw something back and it's just banter. They'll come back with something else and I'll come back with something else, but I don't see it as derogatory because it's not meant to be derogatory. They don't mean anything by it.* George, 44, bus driver, 'out' in present organisation

Although there is a degree of compliance by perceiving such labels as not being derogatory, George deploys an assertive strategy reclaiming and embracing these terms ascribed by his co-workers to give them a new meaning as a badge of pride. George refashioned such derogatory terms on his own terms. This is a good example of how the plates are constantly in flux. George's story illustrates the way in which struggles take place over the contested meanings assigned to identities.

A theme identified from respondents (expressed by eight interviewees) was that they did not wish to directly challenge forms of discrimination in the workplace. Neal, 27, for example, while serving customers at a leading supermarket convenience store in 2004, experienced verbal homophobic abuse from work colleagues' children. Eventually, the tirade of abuse over a two month period led to Neal having to take time off work due to stress. It could be argued that by taking time off work, Neal was putting up some form of resistance against the abuse he had received. What is interesting about Neal's case was how organisational context had had a significant impact on his identity management. In this occupation working in a convenience supermarket, Neal was unwilling to articulate a challenge to homophobic remarks. Control and the imposition of identity labels were very much out of his hands. The context was one in which there was little support from work colleagues, all of whom took a blind eye to the torrent of abuse he was receiving. The contrast with his next job could not be more striking. Working in an international bank with a strong culture of diversity, he felt he could be more assertive and challenge identity labels ascribed by others.

A common coping strategy when confronted with homophobic discourse in the workplace was to ignore it in the hope that it would deflect attention away from themselves. These cases illustrate the ways in which some participants were willing to comply or conform to the meanings created by others in the way they managed their gay identity in the workplace. Andrew's story was a good example of this. He was asked whether he had a boyfriend during an interview for an internal post in his present organisation:

I said, 'I hadn't got [a boyfriend] but I'm gay'. And he said, 'Oh, you know, I just thought I needed to double check' and he said, 'Because you will be, you know, working night shifts with a group of lads who you know, the conversation can get a bit blue, unPC, they might rib you a bit and take the piss'. And I said, 'I was fine with that'. Andrew, 41, systems change coordinator in a bank, 'out' at work.

In this example, Andrew was under pressure to conform in how he managed his identity in the workplace if he were to be successful in his application for the internal post. Furthermore, the interviewer had made Andrew's sexuality the problem in fitting in with the other employees rather than the problem being the other work colleagues' values and attitudes towards a sexuality which was different from their own. In addition, the interviewer was condoning the possibility that co-workers might make fun of his sexuality and Andrew was seemingly willing to consent. Andrew's story illustrates the way in which some respondents felt required to conform due to organisational pressure in order to be accepted within the organisation. Roy 47, Alex 34 and Stefan 40 all experienced pressure to conform when faced with displays of hegemonic heterosexual masculinity in the workplace. Alex, for example, working in an all-male environment as a fencing contractor, would feel obliged to join in with the heterosexual male banter in order to conceal his identity.

> *If you were 'out', because they would, every building site does it, you know, they take the mickey out of somebody, and if you were gay I am sure they would take the mickey out for being that … you just take it on the chin. It's just banter. Cos nobody else is going to believe them, you know. I think everyone, I think every site I've worked on they always take the mickey out of someone for being gay and they're not, so who's to say I am and who's to say I am not.* Alex, 34, fencing contractor for Ministry of Defence

The respondents' experiences of working in blue-collar employment seem to concur with Collinson and Collinson's (1989) research, where they noted the powerful pressures to conform to a particular form of male heterosexuality.

10.5   Discussion and Evaluation

The stories discussed in this chapter bring to the fore some of the issues and dilemmas in managing a gay identity in the workplace 'beyond the closet'. Participants deployed a range of strategies in their interactions with others. The data revealed that the approaches ranged from passive conformity to active resistance. However, none of these approaches were exclusive. Nor was it the case that an individual might initially adopt a more compliant approach and as confidence builds moves towards a more assertive stance. There was no linear approach revealed in the data. Although in the majority of cases there was no longer an issue around disclosure of a gay identity, the dominance of heteronormativity in the workplace meant that participants typically took a normalising, sameness approach in how they presented their gay identity. It would seem that this approach was chosen as it would be less threatening and more accepting by others. This chapter has highlighted the dilemma in striking the right balance between claiming common ground (a sameness approach) and at the same time presenting a gay identity's distinctiveness (a difference approach). What is revealing is that a more direct approach would be deemed too confrontational and imposing on the attitudes of others.

The data revealed how participants self-regulated how they presented themselves in order to be accepted in the workplace. In adopting a normalising approach, respondents would downplay their sexuality. 'Normal' would mean emphasising similarities to normative constructions of heterosexuality and at the same time playing down differences. This was particularly the case for those respondents who took on a professional identity or worked in positions that required them to exercise their occupational authority over others. Typically, respondents would modify how they behaved to take on a professional identity sustaining hegemonic forms of heterosexual masculinity.

10.6   Conclusion

This article has brought to attention how gay men manage their identity beyond solely the issue of disclosure/non-disclosure of their sexual orientation. In particular, this study has highlighted the ways gay men challenge, negotiate and conform in the two-way process of managing their identities, an area that has had little academic investigation. Using Jenkins's (2008) concept of the *interaction order*, the chapter draws attention to the ways gay men respond and react at the boundaries between how they present themselves and how they perceived that others react and respond. One of the key contributions of this chapter lies in the richness of the empirical data drawing upon a wide range of workplaces, occupations and experiences. Unlike Humphrey (1999) or Bernstein's (1997) study, the vast majority of participants were not gay activists, but simply wanted to get on with their lives without making a big fuss over their sexuality in the workplace. The research sheds light on the micro-level situational factors that respondents find themselves in, an area that is particularly lacking in previous quantitative research as discussed in the extant literature.

This chapter highlights the impact of top management support in not only assisting with disclosure but also the degree to which gay men were willing to assert their identity in the workplace. In addition, this chapter adds to our understanding of the contextual factors that facilitate both disclosure and identity management strategies.

Interview data from the participants in this sample reveals that although the vast majority of respondents felt that they could reveal their sexual orientation in the workplace, the workplace was still a difficult environment to manage a gay identity. The dominance of heteronormativity made the workplace a difficult place to negotiate, challenge and manage their interactions with others. Although most participants had disclosed their gay identity at work, they would do so by attempting to normalise their gay identity. This meant that participants would self-regulate their behaviour, in how they used their bodies, their clothes and be careful not 'to camp it up'. Normal meant playing down any differences and emphasising normality against heterosexuality as the template to emulate. It would seem that more needs to be done to make organisations a more inclusive place for gay men. The findings in this chapter, it is anticipated, will aid HR practitioners in giving them a better understanding of the dilemmas gay men face in their interactions with others in the workplace.

This chapter has highlighted some of the dilemmas that self-identified gay men experience in managing their gay identity in the workplace. What these findings reveal is that HR practitioners need to take a leading role in making organisations more inclusive. A number of steps could be employed such as initiating diversity awareness programmes, the encouragement of visible gay role models in senior positions, organisational support for gay employee networking groups, organisational policies on

LGBT equality and employee engagement to make organisations more inclusive and welcoming for non-heterosexual employees.

10.7   Limitations and Implications

There are a few shortcomings in this chapter. One of the keys ones is the representativeness of the sample. As with previous research on LGBT people, a concern was that those who would come forward to do the interviews would be a very select type of gay men. Typically, they might be more confident and open about their sexuality. There were problems in finding a representative sample of those who are 'out' and not 'out' at work and the varying degrees of openness in between. The vast majority of respondents identified themselves as being 'out' (38), whereas only a minority (7) claimed that they had not disclosed to anyone in their present workplace. The researcher recognises that the sample composed a number of individuals (9) who might be described as diversity champions particularly as they were active members of in-company LGBT networks or trade union bodies. Nevertheless, it was important to obtain the experiences of those who were actively involved in such bodies particularly as the study aimed to find out whether they were using these networks to be more assertive and forthright in the way they managed their gay identities. Another limitation was that the sample was skewed more towards those in their middle age with a mean age of 41. It would have been interesting to explore whether those in their teens and twenties have a different perspective in how they disclose and manage their identity given that this generation has entered the labour market post recent anti-discriminatory legislation combined with more liberal attitudes towards homosexuality. This certainly could be an area for future research. This chapter also touched upon the impact co-workers and allies had in intervening during critical moments when respondents were faced with adversity. More research is needed in this area to investigate the impact of allies and supportive co-workers on gay identity management, not just among gay men but across the wider LGBT area.

Notes

1. In the context of this chapter, dominant heteronormative discourse is defined from the sexuality in organisations' perspective (Burrell and Hearn 1989; Pringle 1989) where informal interactions among co-workers assume heterosexuality and stigmatise homosexuality.

2. *Faggot*, often shortened to *fag*, is a pejorative term and common homophobic slur used chiefly in North America against homosexual males. Its pejorative use has spread from the USA to varying extents elsewhere in the English-speaking world through mass culture, including movies, music and the internet. *The American Heritage Dictionary of the English Language, Fourth Edition.* Houghton Mifflin (2000).

References

Bernstein, M. 1997. Celebration and suppression: The uses of identity by the lesbian and gay movement. *American Journal of Sociology* 103: 531–565.

Bowen, F., and K. Blackmon. 2003. Spirals of silence: The dynamic effects of diversity on organisational voice. *Journal of Management Studies* 40: 1393–1417.

Boykin, A., and F. Toms. 1985. Black child socialization: A conceptual framework. In *Black children*, ed. H. McAdoo and J. McAdoo, 33–52. Hillsdale: Lawrence Erlbaum.

Brekhus, W. 2003. *Peacocks, chameleons, centaurs. Gay suburbia and the grammar of social identity.* Chicago: University of Chicago Press.

Browne, K. 2005. Snowball sampling: Using social networks to research non-heterosexual women. *International Journal of Social Research Methodology* 8: 47–60.

Burke, M. 1993. *Coming out of the blue.* London: Cassell.

Burrell, G., and J. Hearn. 1989. The sexuality of organisation. In *The sexuality of organisation*, ed. F. Hearn, D. Sheppard, P. Tancred-Sheriff, and G. Burrell, 1–28. London: Sage.

Chrobot-Mason, D., S. Button, and J. DiClementi. 2002. Sexual identity management strategies: An exploration of antecedents and consequences. *Sex Roles* 45: 321–336.

Colgan, F., C. Creegan, T. Wright, and COERC. 2006. *Lesbian, gay and bisexual workers: Equality, diversity and inclusion in the workplace. A qualitative research study.* London: London Metropolitan University.

Collinson, C., and D. Collinson. 1989. Sexuality in the workplace: The domination of men's sexuality. In *The sexuality of organisation*, ed. F. Hearn, D. Sheppard, P. Tancred-Sheriff, and G. Burrell, 91–109. London: Sage.

Cooper, A. 2006. *Identity work: Negotiating gay male identities in a changing world*. London: South Bank University.

Cowan, K. 2007. Living together. British attitudes to lesbian and gay people. Stonewall report. http://www.stonewall.org.uk/documents/living_together_final_web.pdf. Accessed 21 Oct 2016

Creed, D., and E. Cooper. 2008. *'What red light officer?' The grooming of political opportunity in institutional change processes*. USA: University of Rhode Island.

Creed, D., and M. Scully. 2000. Songs of ourselves: Employees' deployment of social identity in workplace encounters. *Journal of Management Inquiry* 9: 391–412.

Creed, D., R. DeJordy, and J. Lok. 2010. Being the change: Resolving institutional contradiction through identity work. *Academy of Management Journal* 53: 1336–1364.

Day, N., and P. Schoenrade. 1997. Staying in the closet versus coming out: Relationship between communication about sexual orientation and work attitudes. *Personnel Psychology* 50: 147–163.

Ellison, G., and B. Gunstone. 2009. *Sexual orientation explored: A study of identity, attraction, behaviour and attitudes in 2009*. EHRC research report no. 35. Manchester: Equality and Human Rights Commission.

Goffman, E. 1963. *Stigma: Notes on the management of spoiled identity*. New York: Prentice Hall.

———. 1968. *Stigma: The management of spoiled identities*. Harmondsworth: Penguin.

Grey, C. 1998. On being a professional in a 'Big Six' firm. *Accounting, Organisations and Society* 23: 569–587.

Homfray, M. 2008. Standpoint, objectivity, and social construction: Reflections from the study of gay and lesbian communities. *Sociological Research Online* 13: 1–7.

Humphrey, J. 1999. Organizing sexualities, organized inequalities: Lesbian and gay men in public service occupations. *Gender, Work and Organisation* 3: 134–151.

Houghton Mifflin Company. 2000. *The American Heritage dictionary of the English language*.

Hyers, L. 2007. Resisting prejudice every day: Exploring women's assertive responses to anti-black racism, anti-semitism, heterosexism, and sexism. *Sex Roles* 56: 1–12.

Jagose, A. 1996. *Queer theory an introduction.* New York: New York University Press.

Jenkins, R. 2008. *Social identity.* London: Routledge.

————. 2014. *Social identity.* London: Routledge.

Legard, R., J. Keegan, and K. Ward. 2008. In depth interviews. In *Qualitative research practice: A guide for social science students and researchers,* ed. J. Richie and J. Lewis, 138–169. London: Sage.

Martin, J., and L. Dean. 1993. Developing a community sample of gay men for an epidemiological study of AIDS. In *Researching sensitive topics,* ed. C. Renzetti and R. Lee, 78–98. London: Sage.

Peel, E. 2002. Lesbian and gay awareness training: Challenging homophobia, liberalism and managing stereotypes. In *Lesbian & gay psychology. New perspectives,* ed. A. Coyle and C. Kitzinger, 255–274. London: Blackwell.

Platzer, H., and T. James. 1997. Methodological issues conducting sensitive research on lesbian and gay men's experience of nursing care. *Journal of Advanced Nursing* 25: 626–633.

Pringle, R. 1989. Bureaucracy, rationality and sexuality: The case of secretaries. In *The sexuality of organisation,* ed. F. Hearn, D. Sheppard, P. Tancred-Sheriff, and G. Burrell, 158–177. London: Sage.

Ragins, B. 2008. Disclosure disconnects: Antecedents and consequences of disclosing invisible stigmas across life domains. *Academy of Management Review* 33: 194–215.

Ragins, B., R. Singh, and J. Cornwell. 2007. Making the invisible visible: Fear and disclosure of sexual orientation at work. *Journal of Applied Psychology* 92: 1103–1118.

Ritchie, J., J. Lewis, and G. Elam. 2008. Designing and selecting samples. In *Qualitative research practice. A guide for social science students and researchers,* ed. J. Ritchie and J. Lewis. London: Sage Publication.

Rumens, N. 2008. Working at intimacy: Gay men's workplace friendships. *Gender, Work and Organisation* 15: 9–30.

Rumens, N., and D. Kerfoot. 2009. Gay men at work: (Re) constructing the self as professional. *Human Relations* 62: 763–786.

King, E., C. Reilly, and M. Hebl. 2008. The best of times, the worst of times. Exploring dual perspectives of 'coming out' in the workplace. *Group Organization Management* 33 (5): 566–601.

Schope, R. 2002. The decision to tell: Factors influencing the disclosure of sexual orientation by gay men. *Journal of Gay & Lesbian Social Services* 14: 1–22.

Seidman, S. 2002. *Beyond the closet: The transformation of gay and lesbian life.* New York: Routledge.

Shallenberger, D. 1994. Professional and openly gay. A narrative study of the experience. *Journal of Management Inquiry* 3: 119–142.

Snape, D., K. Thomson, and M. Chetwynd. 1995. Discrimination against gay men and lesbians. SCPR. http://doc.ukdataservice.ac.uk/doc/3553/mrdoc/pdf/a3553uab.pdf. Accessed 18 Jan 2017.

Ward, J. 2008. *Sexualities, work and organisations*. London: Routledge.

Ward, J., and D. Winstanley. 2004. Sexuality and the city: Exploring the experience of minority sexual identity through storytelling. *Culture and Organisations* 10: 219–236.

Wilson, B., and R. Miller. 2002. Strategies for managing heterosexism used among African American gay and bisexual men. *Journal of Black Psychology* 28: 371–391.

Woods, J., and J. Lucas. 1993. *The corporate closet. The professional lives of gay men in America*. New York: Free Press.

Yip, K. 2008. Researching lesbian, gay and bisexual Christians and Muslims: Some thematic reflections. *Sociological Research Online* 13: 1–45.

11

Examining the Relationship Between Discrimination and Disengagement

Sarah Pass

11.1 Introduction

Employee engagement has long been popular in the public and private sector (see MacLeod and Clarke 2009, 2014) but has only recently become an academic 'hot topic' (Purcell 2014, p. 241). Since MacLeod and Clarke's (2009) report on employee engagement (and subsequent government backing), there has been a flourish of research activity to uncover both what is meant by employee engagement and how we can capture and harvest it. In essence, it has become the (new) Holy Grail. The interest in employee engagement is not surprising, given its ability to improve financial performance and better outcomes (Rayton et al. 2012). Engaged employees are more committed to the organisation, go beyond what is expected of them (commonly known as discretionary effort) and be highly motivated. Yet the antecedents that facilitate engagement are

S. Pass (✉)
Department of Human Resource Management, Nottingham Business School, Nottingham Trent University, Nottingham, UK

© The Author(s) 2018
V. Caven, S. Nachmias (eds.), *Hidden Inequalities in the Workplace*,
Palgrave Explorations in Workplace Stigma,
DOI 10.1007/978-3-319-59686-0_11

still unknown, along with a defined definition of engagement (Purcell 2014). As a result, opinions regarding employee engagement are diverse, and we are left with more questions than answers. With the majority of research focussing on engagement, there is limited research that has focussed on disengagement, specifically the precursors of disengagement. For example, why is one employee engaged and another one disengaged? The following chapter looks at issues of disengagement and proposes that a key antecedent of disengagement is how employees perceive they are treated, especially by their line managers. A specific focus of this chapter is around the impact on engagement of perceived discrimination at work. There is a dearth of research into engagement and discrimination; however, studies that have been conducted highlight a link between the two. For example, there is a relationship between work engagement and perceived gender discrimination (Sia et al. 2015) and age discrimination (Bayl-Smith and Griffin 2014). As emphasised by previous chapters in this book, discrimination is not always in plain sight, but it is often masked, or hidden, only being felt or observed by the target. In addition, discrimination is not always intentional, as highlighted by Caven and Nachmias (2017) (see Chap. 2). Yet the impact of 'hidden' inequalities can have a profound impact on the engagement levels of employees and can be argued to be a contributing factor towards feelings of disengagement.

Line managers' *'act as the interface between the organisation and the employee, and can do much to impact on engagement'* (Alfes et al. 2010, p. 3); however, although they are a fundamental part of the equation, there is limited research on how the behaviour and actions of line managers influence employee engagement (or potentially build disengagement). With line managers experiencing increasing responsibility for the implementation of HR initiatives, it throws into consideration issues of perceived incivility and discrimination. For example, do employees perceive that their line managers act on issues of incivility and discrimination among team members, or is their lack of action a contributing factor? Are line managers' actions contributing to 'hidden' inequalities within the workplace that are contributing (intentionally or unintentionally) to feelings of disengagement? In addition, are line managers more likely to encourage and engage with employees that 'fit' a similar mould to themselves? Exploring these issues, the following chapter reviews the literature on engagement and disengagement. The first part of the chapter briefly outlines what we mean by employee engagement before specifically exploring the relationship between disengagement, incivility and discrimination. The chapter concludes with implications for practitioners, organisations and management.

11.2 Defining Employee Engagement

Employee engagement has captured the attention of business practitioners, academics and the government (Yalabik et al. 2013). Although we know that engagement is crucial, it is not easy to find an acceptable definition. While reviewing issues of engagement in the UK, the MacLeod Review discovered 50 different variations (MacLeod and Clarke 2009). Definitions include:

> *A positive attitude held by the employee towards the organisation and its values. An engaged employee is aware of the business context, and works with colleagues to improve performance within the job for the benefit of the organisation. The organisation must work to develop and nurture engagement, which requires a two-way relationship between employee and employer.* (Robinson et al. 2004, p. 9)

> *a positive, fulfilling, work-related state of mind that is characterised by vigor, dedication, and absorption.* (Schaufeli et al. 2002, p. 74)

> *the behaviours by which people bring in or leave out their personal selves during work role performance.* (Kahn 1990, p. 694)

Although there are several definitions of engagement (Saks 2006), it is evident that it can be distinguishable from workaholics (Taris et al. 2008), job embeddedness (Halbesleben and Wheeler 2008), job involvement and organisational commitment (Hallberg and Schaufeli 2006). Regardless of the variation in definitions, Purcell states that, in essence, they are describing the same thing. He argues that engagement is about *'employees' feelings, beliefs and attitudes concerning their job, their co-workers, the customers, their managers, and concerning the organisation as a whole, and especially the senior management team'* (2012, p. 13). Argued to be multidimensional (Shantz et al. 2013), it is agreed that engagement is '*easy to recognise in practice yet difficult to define*' (Schaufeli 2013, p. 15).

Increasing numbers of studies have shown a positive relationship between employee work engagement and job performance (Demerouti and Cropanzano 2010; Halbesleben and Wheeler 2008; Salanova et al. 2005; Xanthopoulou et al. 2009). Meta-analytic evidence has been found to connect employee engagement with a wide variety of individual performance measures (see Halbesleben 2010; Harrison et al. 2006). For example, links have been discovered between employee engagement and customer loyalty, business growth and profitability (Gallup 2004). Engaged employees are more willing to '*go the extra mile*' (Bakker et al. 2008, p. 194) and are more likely to remain with the organisation for longer (Harter et al. 2002; Schaufeli and Bakker 2004). Research has also shown that increased levels of employee engagement can result in higher levels of business unit performance (Sparrow 2013). However, it is important to note that performance does not necessarily lead to engagement (Riketta 2008). Instead, it is argued that engagement and performance are mutually reinforcing (Winkler et al. 2012). It is from research conducted to date that employee engagement is an important component of organisational success (Kane-Frieder et al. 2013). It is here that we can understand the growing interest in engagement, especially as levels of employee engagement in the UK are described as low. It has been argued that the UK is experiencing an engagement 'deficit', with only one-third of UK workers engaged (Rayton et al. 2012). As a result, it has become a central focus for both practitioners and academics (Macey and Schneider 2008).

11.3 Theoretical Background to Employee Engagement

Kahn (1990) conducted one of the first pieces of academic research on engagement. Conducting ethnographic research, he focused on psychological experiences of work. Concentrating on a need-satisfying approach (see Shuck 2011; Truss et al. 2013), Kahn explored personal engagement and personal disengagement. As a result of his research, Kahn developed a conceptual framework that defined three psychological conditions: meaningfulness, psychological safety and availability. According to Kahn's research, meaningfulness refers to the value of a work goal in relation to an individual's own ideals or standards (May et al. 2004). Meaningfulness explores task and role characteristics and is influenced by the nature of the job. For meaningfulness to occur there needs to be a sense of return on investment of self within the work role (Kahn 1990).

People experience such meaningfulness when they feel worthwhile, useful, and valuable – as though they make a difference and are not taken for granted. (Kahn and Heaphy 2013, p. 83)

To achieve this, tasks need to be challenging, rewarding and provide opportunities to receive rewards and respect (Crawford et al. 2013). If there is a lack of meaning in work, then a negative impact can be experienced, frequently resulting in disengagement (Aktouf 1992). The second psychological condition is described as psychological safety. Kahn refers to psychological safety as employees '*feeling able to show and employ one's self without fear or negative consequences to self-image, status, or career*' (1990, p. 708). The social environment (e.g. social relationships, group dynamics, management style and social norms of behaviour) can have an influence on feelings of psychological safety. If employees have a positive sense of psychological safety at work, where there was no fear of negative consequences, then employees are more likely to be engaged (Kahn 1990). A key element of psychological safety is interpersonal relationships, specifically those that provide support, trust, openness and flexibility. As a result, relationships with line managers, senior management and group dynamics are fundamental. The final psychological condition described by Kahn is the concept of availability. This refers to the availability of an employee's physical, emotional and cognitive resources. Kahn states that for an employee to engage the self at work, they require the use of these three resources. Issues of role overload, work-role conflict and adequate resources can have an impact on the availability of these resources (Crawford et al. 2013). If there is a lack of resources, then an employee's physical and emotional energy can be decreased (Kahn 1990). For example, if an employee faces increasing work pressures due to increasing workload, pressure from (potentially unattainable) targets and a lack of resources (potentially due to financial cuts), then they are likely to become emotionally drained and feel that they do not have the cognitive or physical resources to complete the work required. As a result, they will start to disengage from their organisation and can experience increased levels of stress and anxiety.

Reviewing Kahn's (1990) model of engagement, May et al. (2004) conducted a quantitative study to examine the three psychological components. They found positive links between levels of engagement and meaningfulness. They also discovered connections between levels of engagement, psychological safety and availability, although the relationships were not as strong as the relationship with meaningfulness. Positive relationships were also revealed between meaningfulness and job enrichment, and work-role fit. In addition, May et al. explore relationships with co-workers and supervisors. They found that co-worker and supportive supervisor relations were positively related to safety. However, feelings of psychological safety were negatively related to adherence to co-worker norms. This suggests that pressure to adhere to co-worker norms of behaviour can have a destructive impact on employee engagement. May et al. concluded that all three of Kahn's psychological conditions (i.e. meaningfulness, psychological safety and availability) were important in determining engagement at work, with meaningfulness having the strongest relationship. Consequently, as a result of the research by May et al., there has been a continued focus on Kahn's model of engagement as a model to understand the antecedents of engagement in the hope of harnessing employee engagement levels.

However, many questions still remain, with the concept of engagement remaining a *'catch-all that captures a range of work-related attitudes'* (Truss et al. 2013, p. 2659) and limited research on antecedents of disengagement. As a result, we are unsure *what* employees engaged with, and with whom are they engaging. Instead, there is a fixation on outcomes of engagement (see Rayton et al. 2012) and a need to know more about the antecedents of engagement (Purcell 2014). There are also gaps in our knowledge about the contextual factors that impact on engagement (Jenkins and Delbridge 2013), with studies frequently decontextualising employee engagement from their organisational setting (Jenkins and Delbridge 2013). Another key gap in the research on engagement is around employee perceptions of fairness, justice and trust in management (Purcell 2014), with a need to know more about variations in leadership and supervision, organisational norms and expectations. There is also limited research on why are some employees engaged, while others are actively disengaged. What impact do line managers, co-workers and senior management have in breeding disengagement? Specifically, what impact does discrimination, and 'hidden' inequalities, have on fostering and amplifying disengagement?

11.4 Employee Disengagement

There are a wide range of employee engagement measures available which frequently focus on grouping employees into three categories: highly engaged, unengaged and disengaged (Fletcher and Robinson 2013). While engaged employees create their own resources and perform better, actively disengaged employees are more likely to 'uncouple' themselves from their role (Truss et al. 2013).

> *Disengagement is characterised by the disconnection of individuals from their work roles to protect themselves physically, mentally, and/or emotionally from real or perceived threats.* (Wollard 2011, p. 528)

Although disengaged employees are more inclined to leave the organisation (Hartel et al. 2002; Schaufeli and Bakker 2004), those that did remain have mentally quit. As a result, employees who are disengaged at work but remain in the organisation are likely to be increasingly absent, negative about their organisation and work to rule. Consequently, disengagement has significant implications for the organisation in terms of *'profitability, safety, mental health, turnover, and employee theft'* (Wollard 2011, p. 526). Not only are disengaged employees likely to be unhappy in their work but they are also more inclined to share their unhappiness with others (Gallup 2006). Those experiencing disengagement are more likely to be *'uninvolved and unenthusiastic about their jobs and love to tell others*' how bad things are (Blizzard 2004, paragraph 3). With significant cost implications associated with disengagement (MacLeod and Clarke 2009), it is important to understand how do employees become disengaged. Although we know that disengagement is a process (Kahn 1990), and that it occurs in stages (Macey and Schneider 2008), we do not fully understand the depths and dimensions of employee disengagement. This is due to the limited amount of research on disengagement (Wollard 2011), with the majority of research focussing on engaged employees. Kahn's (1990) original research proposed that when the three proposed psychological conditions of meaningfulness, psychological safety and availability are not met, then the employee will not engage 'the self' in their work and become disengaged. Employee perceptions of discrimination and incivility at work would fall into Kahn's concept of psychological safety, yet we know very little about the connection. Although Kahn's work provides us with an overarching model, more detail and depth is required, especially regarding the role of the line manager in the relationship between discrimination and disengagement.

11.5   The Role of the Line Manager in Fostering (or Impairing) Employee Engagement

Research by Harter et al. (2002) found that there was a strong link between intentions to quit and levels of engagement, with the relationship with the supervisor being a key variant. A central factor was the lack of managerial soft skills which were likely to result in increased disengagement (Towers Perrin 2006). Although there is limited research on the factors that result in disengagement, it is evident that managers, especially line managers, are a key factor (Alfes et al. 2010; MacLeod and Clarke 2009). Research by Kelliher et al. (2013) emphasised the role of line managers in maintaining engagement levels. By examining meanings and antecedents of employee engagement across different national contexts, they found that the role of the line manager was critical, regardless of national context and employee groups.

It was seen as the line manager's role to convert job engagement into employee engagement in other words to ensure that the 'emotional' engagement with the organisation exists alongside the job engagement. (Kelliher et al. 2013, location 5770)

It is easy to see how there is a link between line managers and employee engagement; they provide immediate direction, control and supervision on a day-to-day basis. Line managers are the 'sub-drivers to engagement' (Robinson et al. 2007). Line managers are in *positions representing the first level of management to whom non-managerial employees report* (Hales 2005, p. 473). Line managers have an indispensable part to play in providing and maintaining trust with employees through leadership, enabling employee voice and ensuring meaningfulness (Purcell 2014). This argument is supported by the concept of social exchange theory (see Eisenberger et al. 1986; Robinson et al. 2004; Saks 2006) which proposes that if employees have a trustful relationship and believe line managers support them, then they are likely to respond with positive behaviour, that is, engagement (Rees et al. 2013). In addition, perceived organisational support suggests that employees are more likely to be engaged if they feel supported by their organisation and have a good relationship with their supervisor (Alfes et al. 2013). Ultimately, line managers have an important role as the 'engaging manager' (Robinson and Hayday 2009). Fundamentally, *'the evidence indicates that for [engagement] to be successful, leaders have to champion and line managers have to lead engagement'* (MacLeod and Clarke 2009, p. 114). Although line managers might facilitate and encourage engagement, they can also be a cause of disengagement due to their actions and behaviour.

Research has shown that there is a clear link between the behaviour of managers and the performance of employees (Alfes et al. 2013). However, there is limited research on how employee engagement is influenced by management (Kular et al. 2008) and even fewer on the behaviour of line managers. What we do know is that how practices are intended, implemented (and perceived) varies significantly (Khilji and Wang 2006; Kuvaas 2008). As highlighted by Purcell (Purcell et al. 2009; Purcell et al. 2003), even the best policies and practices are of little value if they are not put into practice as intended. As a result, line managers play a significant role (Purcell and Hutchinson 2007). Although line managers bring policies and practices to life (Purcell and Hutchinson 2007), there is limited research on line managers' perceptions of HR practices (Kuvaas et al. 2014) and engagement initiatives in particular. Although there is an emphasis on line managers putting these practices into operation, many line managers lack the skills and knowledge (or motivation) to do so (Whittaker and Marchington 2003). Research has shown that line managers' perceptions of HR practices are different to the perceptions of HR managers (Wright et al. 2001), which could account for the variation in implementation. Although being theoretically close to the front line, line managers' perceptions of HR practices are also likely to differ from the perceptions of employees (Khilji and Wang 2006). Managing diversity is an example of differing perceptions of HR practices. Trying to manage diversity in practice offers a 'new challenge' (Noon and Ogbonna 2001) for managers. This is highlighted by research conducted by Foster and Harris (2005) who found there were high levels of confusion among line managers in what diversity management is, and how it should be implemented. HR managers' understanding of diversity management varied from line managers, who were confused by the need to provide fair treatment for all, while also ensuring individual differences were met. As a result, it created '*particular dilemmas for line management in terms of how to respond to individual differences, comply with anti-discrimination legislation and promote a general feeling of fair treatment among the workforce*' (Foster and Harris 2005, p. 13). Consequently, inconsistencies in the treatment of employees are frequently evident (Maxwell 2004), but often 'hidden'.

Similar inconsistencies are evident in the research on employee engagement and line managers' implementation. Research has shown that levels of employee engagement vary widely between groups, even within the same company. An issue that has been attributed to the influence line managers have is over the engagement levels of employees. Although there are variations in how line managers implement practices, it is also how these practices are *perceived* by employees that play a significant role in levels of employee engagement A key factor therefore is not only how line managers implement practices but their behaviour and actions while doing so. Perceived line manager's behaviour is an antecedent to employee engagement (Bates 2004; Frank et al. 2004) and can therefore have a damaging impact if it were perceived to be negative. By developing trust, sharing information and providing support (see Settoon et al. 1996), employees feel a positive emotional state, resulting in increased levels of engagement (Avolio et al. 2004). Ultimately, employee levels of engagement are impacted by '*the way they are treated by their line manager*' (Alfes et al. 2013, p. 852). Reflecting on the discussion earlier regarding the management of diversity, line managers are struggling to implement the policy into practice and find a balance between ensuring individual differences are met and maintaining fairness for all. Ensuring the individual needs of one employee are met could be perceived by another employee as being unfair. For example, if an employee has a mental health problem, the organisation is expected to make reasonable adjustments. These could include time to attend mindfulness meetings or clinical appointments. During these periods of absence, it is likely that other members of the team have to cover the workload of the employee (in reality, it is unlikely that an organisation would employ additional resources to cover these periods). Over time, resentment can grow among the employees who are expected to cover the additional work. Growing resentment can fuel uncivil behaviour and discrimination. Feelings of resentment and fairness can be linked to Kahn's (1990) concept of availability (from the perspective of those covering the additional workload) and psychological safety (from the perspective of the employee). Another example of how perceptions of diversity management can be perceived in different lights is evident in the organisational practice of setting recruitment targets. To ensure a diverse workforce, organisations are establishing diversity targets, often referred to as positive action. This usually includes targets on the number of black and minority ethnic (BME) employees, women and employees with disabilities. On the one hand, this has been established to counteract high levels of discrimination in the workplace; however, setting targets can lead to disengagement with the organisation if an employee perceives recruitment to be akin to positive discrimination (which is unlawful in the UK). This can have an impact on both current employees and the newly appointed employee. Current employees may perceive that the appointment was unfair (resulting in emotional disengagement) and result in cognitive disengagement (due to a loss of trust in the manager who made the appointment). If the new employee perceives that they were only appointed to fulfil a target, it could result in emotional disengagement (due to feelings of inferiority). The problem arises in both examples as a result of underlying, or hidden, perceptions of discrimination and incivility. Perceptions (or a belief) in unfairness can fuel negativity, which can then grow from a feeling of disgruntlement into active disengagement. Under the Equality Act 2010, if discrimination was apparent, then the employee could act on the discrimination. However, if the discrimination and uncivil behaviour is masked, it is harder to act on it.

It is evident that poor management skills are a key factor behind feelings of disengagement (MacLeod and Clarke 2009), and there is an emphasis on how poor management skills are perceived by employees. Consequently, attitudes and behaviours are an important element in the engagement/disengagement equation (Allen et al. 2003; Batt 2002). Research by Holbeche and Springett (2003) found that perceptions of 'meaning' were clearly linked to engagement and therefore to performance. However, it is evident that perceptions can vary, with different employees receiving or perceiving information differently (Kular et al. 2008), highlighting the importance of the *perceived* actions of the immediate supervisor (Freeney and Fellenz 2013). It is within the depths of perceptions that further 'hidden' inequality can lie. For example, issues of incivility are on the increase within the workplace (see Yeung and Griffin 2008), with the majority of employees stating that they have experienced uncivil behaviour (Reio and Sanders-Reio 2011). Incivility is described as '*rude, insensitive, disrespectful, and thoughtless behaviour with ambiguous intent to harm*' (Reio and Sanders-Reio 2011, p. 463) and has a direct impact on employee engagement (see Yeung and Griffin 2008). Uncivil behaviour or discrimination can be very subtle: rolling of the eyes, sly comments or in-group sniggering. If it goes unchecked, it can have a prolonged impact on employee engagement manifesting disengagement. As a result, it is linked to Kahn's (1990) concept of availability and psychological safety. A survey by Reio and Sanders-Reio (2011) found that 78% of respondents had experienced supervisor incivility in the past year. Examples of incivility include making fun of others, gossiping, causing embarrassment and ostracising workers (Pearson and Porath 2005) or as described by an employee 'backstabbing and favouritism' (Wollard 2011). How supervisors and line managers handle uncivil behaviour can have a direct impact on perceptions of organisational support. Unfortunately, uncivil behaviour is frequently considered benign by managers and subsequently ignored (Porath and Pearson 2010). However, by ignoring the behaviour, managers are endorsing it. Poor recognition by management contributes to 'hidden' inequalities. This can have a significant impact on the engagement level of the target (or victim). For example, it can result in emotional disengagement (due to increased stress and potential feelings of inferiority and a perceived safety threat), physical or behavioural disengagement (as a direct result of the uncivil behaviour) and cognitive disengagement (due to a loss of trust in their supervisor and organisation, and potential intentions to quit) (see Wollard 2011). Onlookers, perpetrators and targets perceive incivility differently (Pearson et al. 2000). Due to the variations in how uncivil behaviour is perceived, it can easily become 'hidden' in the organisation.

Reasons for uncivil behaviour are evident in workplace discrimination. However, there is limited research on the engagement of discriminated or stigmatised groups (Bayl-Smith and Griffin 2014). For example, there is inadequate research on the links between engagement and race (see Jones and Harter 2005), engagement and workplace bullying (see MacIntosh 2012), engagement and age discrimination (see Bayl-Smith and Griffin 2014) and engagement and religious discrimination (see Messarra 2014). A significant area of research missing is on engagement and discrimination or stigmatisation of employees with mental health issues who are equally likely to experience incivility and discrimination in the workplace. Focussing on research that is available, research by Jones and Harter (2005) showed a link between levels of engagement at work and issues of race. Their research showed connections between race, levels of engagement and intentions to remain in the organisation, and they argued that perceptions of fairness across different racial groups can impact on levels of engagement. Bayl-Smith and Griffin (2014) examined employee engagement and perceived age discrimination. They argued that age discrimination is socially acceptable in the workplace, based upon the stereotype that older workers are less adaptable or willing to learn new skills. Their research showed a negative relationship between perceived age discrimination and levels of employee engagement. Findings by Bayl-Smith and Griffin are supported by research undertaken by Robinson et al. (2004, 2007) who found that the youngest employees had the highest engagement levels compared to all over age groups. However, in contrast, a survey by Blessing White (2008) revealed that younger employees were more likely to be disengaged with their organisation compared to older workers. Although it is clear that there is a relationship between age, discrimination and disengagement, more research in this area is required. Research by Messarra (2014) explored perceptions of employee engagement and perceived religious discrimination. With religious discrimination grievances rising faster than gender or race claims (see Weiss 2008), it has become a new managerial challenge (Messarra 2014). Findings showed that if an employee perceived unfair treatment due to religious discrimination, then there was a negative impact on their emotional state and desire to remain in the organisation. Similar findings are evident in research on gender discrimination and employee engagement. This is not surprising, given the gender inequalities within the workplace, with more women than men experiencing uncivil behaviour (see Reio and Sanders-Reio 2011; Sia et al. 2015). Research by Sia et al. (2015) explored perceived gender discrimination on levels of employee engagement in India. Their findings showed that perceived gender discrimination by female employees had a significant negative relationship with both emotional and cognitive engagement at work. With discrimination being both covert and overt, it is important to remember that '*what matters is how employees perceive discrimination*' (Messarra 2014, p. 61). If an employee feels that their social identity is threatened, then they are more likely to disengage. It is evident from the limited research that there is a connection between incivility, discrimination and levels of employee disengagement, and that perceived organisational and supervisor support is a pivotal factor.

The majority of research conducted, has focussed on managers and leaders being '*genuine in their intentions and behaviour*' (Soane 2013, location 4804). As a result, research predominantly assumes that any negative impacts on engagement of poor management are unintentional. However, Machiavellian behaviour is potentially more widespread than reported. This notion is supported by research on workplace incivility with findings showing a relationship between incivility and power positions (Torkelson et al. 2016). Research by Pearson and Porath (2009) found that 60% of reported issues of workplace incivility were initiated by someone who was in a higher organisational rank than the target of the incivility. A common occurrence of incivility is not praising subordinates or taking credit for other employees' efforts. Giving feedback is positively related to levels of engagement (Shantz et al. 2013); it is not surprising that withdrawing it would result in levels of disengagement.

> *Machiavellian managers could have a direct impact on disengagement through their hard-ball tactics – why would employee engage with their work if it is a constant fight to achieve any recognition or intrinsic reward?* (Soane 2013, location 4805–4806)

However, perceived incivility by those in a higher organisational position were unlikely to be reported; instead, the target is more likely to 'displace' the feelings of fear, sadness and anger (Porath and Pearson 2012), resulting in emotional, behavioural and cognitive disengagement. Perceptions of uncivil behaviour and discrimination can quickly spiral and spread beyond the target and instigator (Pearson and Porath 2005), therefore, having the potential to not only impact the engagement level of the target but also those around them. If unchecked, it could lead to the disengagement of the whole team and/or department.

11.6 Conclusion and Implications

In spite of its popularity in the public and private sector (see MacLeod and Clarke 2009), employee engagement is a relatively recent concept in academic literature (Macey and Schneider 2008). The discrepancy can be largely attributed to academic debate over the concept of engagement. It is understandable that debate exists, given there is a lack of definition and measurement of employee engagement (Masson et al. 2008). However, in more recent years, there has been increasing academic support for the benefits of workforce engagement (Rees et al. 2013). Although there has been increasing interest from academics, there is a call for more critical scrutiny (see Guest 2013; Jenkins and Delbridge 2013; Keenoy 2013; Purcell 2013; Truss et al. 2013). Given the high levels of disengagement in the UK, it is important that future research focuses on contextualising antecedents of engagement, or more specifically disengagement. A key area is the impact of discrimination and incivility in the workplace, and the role line managers play in this equation. Specifically, how their behaviour and actions are perceived by employees and what impact does this have on employee levels of engagement (and potential disengagement). This has significant implications for practitioners, organisations and management.

The above key issues raised by the analysis of the literature highlight the need for greater awareness of the impact of discrimination and incivility on employee disengagement. From an organisational perspective, one of the key issues is around the role of the line manager. Although moving into a line management role might be a standard career path, it does not mean that everyone has the behavioural skills (or the basic training) to fulfil this role. Greater time and attention need to be placed on the line manager's role by organisations, who need to reflect carefully on who they appoint, how they are trained and how they are supported. In terms of training, it is imperative that line managers not only have a good understanding of equality and diversity policy but also how to implement these policies into practice. In order to achieve this, line managers need to be part of the conversation in their development, ensuring that practices are both relevant to practice and can be successfully implemented (rather than considered a tick box). However, although an understanding of policies and practices is important, it is evident from the literature that the behaviour of the line manager has a fundamental impact on employee levels of engagement (and disengagement). Basic line manager training in the transactional aspects of the role is not sufficient, additional training in soft skills is also required. It is evident from the lack of literature that more research is required around issues of incivility and discrimination (specifically age, gender, race and mental health), and the role of the line manager. Greater research on these areas will help our understanding of another key gap in our knowledge of engagement and more specifically the 'hidden' inequalities that can reinforce disengagement.

References

Aktouf, O. 1992. Management and theories of organisations in the 1990s: Toward a critical radical humanism? *The Academy of Management Review* 17: 407.

Alfes, K., C. Truss, E.C. Soane, C. Rees, and M. Gatenby. 2010. Creating an engaged workforce: Findings from the Kingston employee engagement consortium project. http://www2.cipd.co.uk/NR/rdonlyres/DD66E557-DB90-4F07-8198-87C3876F3371/0/Creating_engaged_workforce.pdf. Accessed 9 Dec 2016.

———. 2013. The relationship between line manager behavior, perceived HRM practices, and individual performance: Examining the mediating role of engagement. *Human Resource Management* 52 (6): 839–859.

Allen, D.G., L.M. Shore., and R.W. Griffeth. 2003. The role of perceived organisational support and supportive human resource practices in the turnover process. *Journal of Management* 29: 99–118.

Avolio, B.J., W.L. Gardner, F.O. Walumbwa, F. Luthans, and D.R. May. 2004. Unlocking the mask: A look at the process by which authentic leaders impact follower attitudes and behaviors. *The Leadership Quarterly* 15: 801–823.

Bakker, A., and W. Schaufeli. 2008. Positive organisational behavior: Engaged employees in flourishing organisations. *Journal of Organisational Behavior* 29 (2): 147–154.

Bakker, A.B., W.B. Schaufeli, M. Leiter, and T. Taris. 2008. Work engagement: An emerging concept in occupational health psychology. *Work & Stress* 22: 187–200.

Bates, S. 2004. Getting engaged. *HR Magazine* 49: 44–51.

Batt, R. 2002. Managing customer services: Human resource practices, quit rates, and sales growth. *Academy of Management Journal* 45: 587–597.

Bayl-Smith, P.H., and B. Griffin. 2014. Age discrimination in the workplace: Identifying as a late-career worker and its relationship with engagement and intended retirement age. *Journal of Applied Social Psychology* 44: 588–599.

Blessing White. 2008. *The state of employee engagement – Highlights for UK and Ireland*. Skillman: Blessing White.

Blizzard, R. 2004. Engagement vs satisfaction among hospital teams. *Gallup Poll Tuesday Briefing*. The Gallup Organisation.

Crawford, E.R., B. Rich, B. Buckman, and J. Bergeron. 2013. The antecedents and drivers of employee engagement. In *Employee engagement in theory and practice*, ed. J. Truss, K. Alfes, R. Delbridge, and A. Shantz, 57–81. London: Routledge.

Demerouti, E., and R. Cropanzano. 2010. From thought to action: Employee work engagement and job performance. In *Work engagement: A handbook of essential theory and research*, ed. A. Bakker and M. Leiter, 147–163. New York: Psychology Press.

Eisenberger, R., R. Huntington, S. Hutchinson, and D. Sowa. 1986. Perceived organisational support. *Journal of Applied Psychology* 71: 500–507.

Fletcher, L., and D. Robinson. 2013. Measuring and understanding engagement. In *Employee engagement in theory and practice*, ed. C. Truss, K. Alfes, R. Delbridge, and A. Shantz, 2657–2669. London: Routledge.

Foster, C., and L. Harris. 2005. Easy to say, difficult to do: Diversity management in retail. *Human Resource Management Journal* 15: 4–17.

Frank, F.D., R. Finnegan, and C.R. Taylor. 2004. The race for talent: Retaining and engaging workers in the 21st century. *Human Resource Planning* 27: 12–25.

Freeney, Y., and M. Fellenz. 2013. Work engagement, job design and the role of the social context at work: Exploring antecedents from a relational perspective. *Human Relations* 66: 1427–1445.

Gallup. 2004. *Human sigma: A meta-analysis*. Washington, DC: Gallup. http://www.gallup.com/businessjournal/101956/humansigma-metaanalysisrelationship-between-employee-engag.aspx. Accessed 19 Jan 2017.

Gallup. 2006. Gallup study: Engaged employees inspire company innovation: National survey finds that passionate workers are most likely to drive organisations forward. http://gmj.gallup.com/content/24880/Gallup-Study-Engaged-EmployeesInspire-Company.aspx. Accessed 27 Jan 2017.

Guest, D. 2013. Employee engagement fashionable fad or long-term fixture? In *Employee engagement fashionable fad or long-term fixture?* ed. C. Truss, K. Alfes, R. Delbridge, and A. Shantz, 221–250. London: Routledge.

Halbesleben, J. 2010. A meta-analysis of work engagement: Relationships with burnout, demands, resources and consequences. In *Work engagement: A handbook of essential theory and research*, ed. A. Bakker and M. Leiter, 102–117. New York: Psychology Press.

Halbesleben, J., and A. Wheeler. 2008. The relative roles of engagement and embeddedness in predicting job performance and intention to leave. *Work and Stress* 22: 242–256.

Hales, C. 2005. Rooted in supervision, branching into management: Continuity and change in the role of first-line manager. *Journal of Management Studies* 42: 471–506.

Hallberg, U., and W. Schaufeli. 2006. "Same same" but different? *European Psychologist* 11: 119–127.

Harrison, D.A., D.A. Newman, and P. Roth. 2006. How important are job attitudes? Meta-analytic comparisons of integrative behavioral outcomes and time sequences. *Academy of Management Journal* 49: 305–325.

Harter, J.K., F.L. Schmidt, and T. Hayes. 2002. Business-unit-level relationship between employee satisfaction, employee engagement and business outcomes: A meta-analysis. *Journal of Applied Psychology* 87: 268–279.

Holbeche, L., and N. Springett. 2003. *In search of meaning at work*. 1st ed. Horsham: Roffey Park Institute.

Jenkins, S., and R. Delbridge. 2013. Context matters: Examining 'soft' and 'hard' approaches to employee engagement in two workplaces. *The International Journal of Human Resource Management* 24: 2670–2691.

Jones, J.R., and J. Harter. 2005. Race effects on the employee engagement-turnover intention relationship. *Journal of Leadership & Organisational Studies* 11: 78–88.

Kahn, W. 1990. Psychological conditions of personal engagement and disengagement at work. *The Academy of Management Journal* 33: 692–724.

Kahn, W.A., and E. Heaphy. 2013. Relational contexts of personal engagement at work. In *Employee engagement in theory and practice*, ed. C. Truss, K. Alfes, R. Delbridge, and A. Shantz, 82–96. London: Routledge.

Kane-Frieder, R.E., W.A. Hochwarter, and G.R. Ferris. 2013. Terms of engagement: Political boundaries of work engagement–work outcomes relationships. *Human Relations* 67: 357–382.

Keenoy, T. 2013. Engagement: A murmuration of objects. In *Employee engagement in theory and practice*, ed. C. Truss, K. Alfes, R. Delbridge, and A. Shantz, 197–220. London: Routledge.

Kelliher, C., V. Hope-Hailey, and E. Farndale. 2013. Employee engagement in multi-national organisations. In *Employee engagement in theory and practice*, ed. C. Truss, K. Alfes, R. Delbridge, and A. Shantz, 180–195. London: Routledge.

Khilji, S.E., and X. Wang. 2006. 'Intended' and 'implemented' HRM: The missing linchpin in strategic human resource management research. *The International Journal of Human Resource Management* 17: 1171–1189.

Kular, S., C. Gatenby, C. Rees, E. Soane, and K. Truss. 2008. Employee engagement: A literature review. Kingston University. http://eprints.kingston.ac.uk/4192/1/19wempen.pdf. Accessed 16 Jan 2017.

Kuvaas, B. 2008. An exploration of how the employee? Organisation relationship affects the linkage between perception of developmental human resource practices and employee outcomes. *Journal of Management Studies* 45: 1–25.

Kuvaas, B., A. Dysvik, and R. Buch. 2014. Antecedents and employee outcomes of line managers' perceptions of enabling HR practices. *Journal of Management Studies* 51: 845–868.

Macey, W.H., and P. Schneider. 2008. The meaning of employee engagement. *Industrial and Organisational Psychology* 1: 3–30.

MacIntosh, J. 2012. Workplace bullying influences women's engagement in the workforce. *Issues in Mental Health Nursing* 33: 762–768.

MacLeod, D., and N. Clarke. 2009. *Engaging for success: Enhancing performance through employee engagement a report to government.* http://engageforsuccess. org/wp-content/uploads/2015/08/file52215.pdf. Accessed 19 Jan 2017.

MacLeod, D., and N. Clarke. 2014. *The evidence: Wellbeing and employee engagement.* http://engageforsuccess.org/wp-content/uploads/2015/09/wellbeing-and-engagement-04June2014-Final.pdf. Accessed 19 Jan 2017.

Masson, R., M. Royal, T. Agnew, and S. Fine. 2008. Leveraging employee engagement: The practical implication. *Industrial and Organisational Psychology* 1: 56–59.

Maxwell, G.A. 2004. Minority report. *Employee Relations* 26: 182–202.

May, D., R. Gilson, and L. Harter. 2004. The psychological conditions of meaningfulness, safety and availability and the engagement of the human spirit at work. *Journal of Occupational and Organisational Psychology* 77: 11–37.

Messarra, L.C. 2014. Religious diversity at work: The perceptual effects of religious discrimination on employee engagement and commitment. *Contemporary Management Research* 10: 59–80.

Noon, M., and E. Ogbonna. 2001. *Equality, diversity and disadvantage in employment.* 1st ed. Houndmills: Palgrave.

Pearson, C.M., and C.L. Porath. 2005. On the nature, consequences and remedies of workplace incivility: No time for "nice"? Think again. *Academy of Management Perspectives* 19: 7–18.

———. 2009. *The cost of bad behavior: How incivility damages your business and what you can do about it.* 1st ed. New York: Portfolio.

Pearson, C.M., L.M. Andersson, and C.L. Porath. 2000. Assessing and attacking workplace incivility. *Organisational Dynamics* 29: 123–137.

Porath, C.L., and C.M. Pearson. 2010. The cost of bad behavior. *Organisational Dynamics* 39: 64–71.

Porath, C.L., and C.M. Pearson. 2012. Emotional and behavioral responses to workplace incivility and the impact of hierarchical status. *Journal of Applied Social Psychology* 42: E326–E357.

Purcell, J. 2012. *Voice and participation in the modern workplace: Challenges and prospects.* http://www.acas.org.uk/media/pdf/g/7/Voice_and_Participation_in_the_Modern_Workplace_challenges_and_prospects.pdf. Accessed 19 Jan 2017.

Purcell, J. 2013. Employee voice and engagement. In *Employee engagement in theory and practice*, ed. C. Truss, K. Alfes, R. Delbridge, and A. Shantz, 236–250. London: Routledge.

———. 2014. Disengaging from engagement. *Human Resource Management Journal* 24: 241–254.

Purcell, J., and S. Hutchinson. 2007. Front-line managers as agents in the HRM-performance causal chain: Theory, analysis and evidence. *Human Resource Management Journal* 17: 3–20.

Purcell, J., N. Kinnie, N. Hutchinson, B. Rayton, and J. Swart. 2003. *Understanding the people and performance link: Unlocking the black box.* London: Chartered Institute of Personnel and Development.

Purcell, J., N. Kinnie, J. Swart, B. Rayton, and S. Hutchinson. 2009. *People management and performance.* London: Routledge.

Rayton, B., T. Dodge, and G. D'Analeze. 2012. The evidence: Employee engagement task force "nailing the evidence" work group. Engage for success. http://www.engageforsuccess.org/wp-content/uploads/2012/09/The-Evidence.pdf. Accessed 19 Jan 2017.

Rees, C., K. Alfes, and M. Gatenby. 2013. Employee voice and engagement: Connections and consequences. *The International Journal of Human Resource Management* 24: 2780–2798.

Reio, T.G., and J. Sanders-Reio. 2011. Thinking about workplace engagement: Does supervisor and coworker incivility really matter? *Advances in Developing Human Resources* 13: 462–478.

Riketta, M. 2008. The causal relation between job attitudes and performance: A meta-analysis of panel studies. *Journal of Applied Psychology* 93: 472–481.

Robinson, D., and S. Hayday. 2009. The engaging manager. Institute of Employment Studies. http://www.employment-studies.co.uk/resource/engaging-manager. Accessed 19 Jan 2017.

Robinson, D., P. Perryman, and S. Hayday. 2004. The drivers of employee engagement. Institute of Employment Studies. http://www.employment-studies.co.uk/resource/drivers-employee-engagement. Accessed 19 Jan 2017.

Robinson, D., H. Hooker, and S. Hayday. 2007. Engagement: The continuing story. http://www.employment-studies.co.uk/system/files/resources/files/447.pdf. Accessed 19 Jan 2017.

Saks, A.M. 2006. Antecedents and consequences of employee engagement. *Journal of Managerial Psychology* 21: 600–619.

Salanova, M., S. Agut, and J.M. Peiro. 2005. Linking organisational resources and work engagement to employee performance and customer loyalty: The mediation of service climate. *Journal of Applied Psychology* 90: 1217–1227.

Schaufeli, W.B. 2013. What is engagement? In *Employee engagement in theory and practice*, ed. C. Truss, K. Alfes, R. Delbridge, and A. Shantz, 15–35. London: Routledge.

Schaufeli, W.B., and A.B. Bakker. 2004. Job demands, job resources, and their relationship with burnout and engagement: A multi-sample study. *Journal of Organisational Behavior* 25: 293–315.

Schaufeli, W.B., I.M. Martinez, A. Pinto, M. Salanova, and A. Bakker. 2002. Burnout and engagement in university students: A cross-national study. *Journal of Cross-Cultural Psychology* 33: 464–481.

Settoon, R.P., N. Bennett, and R. Liden. 1996. Social exchange in organisations: Perceived organisational support, leader-member exchange, and employee reciprocity. *Journal of Applied Psychology* 81: 219–227.

Shantz, A., K. Alfes, C. Truss, and E. Soane. 2013. The role of employee engagement in the relationship between job design and task performance, citizenship and deviant behaviours. *The International Journal of Human Resource Management* 24: 2608–2627.

Shuck, B. 2011. Integrative literature review: Four emerging perspectives of employee engagement: An integrative literature review. *Human Resource Development Review* 10: 304–328.

Sia, S.K., B.C. Sahoo, and P. Duari. 2015. Gender discrimination and work engagement: Moderating role of future time perspective. *South Asian Journal of Human Resources Management* 2: 58–84.

Soane, E. 2013. Leadership and employee engagement. In *Employee engagement in theory and practice*, ed. C. Truss, K. Alfes, R. Delbridge, and A. Shantz, 99–115. London: Routledge.

Sparrow, P. 2013. Strategic HRM and employee engagement. In *Employee engagement in theory and practice*, ed. C. Truss, K. Alfes, R. Delbridge, and A. Shantz, 99–115. London: Routledge.

Taris, T.W., S. Geurts, W. Schaufeli, R. Blonk, and S. Lagerveld. 2008. All day and all of the night: The relative contribution of two dimensions of workaholism to well-being in self-employed workers. *Work & Stress* 22: 153–151.

Torkelson, E., K. Holm, and M. Bäckström. 2016. Workplace incivility in a Swedish context. *Nordic Journal of Working Life Studies* 6: 3.

Towers Perrin. 2006. *Ten steps to creating an engaged workforce: Key European findings.* Towers Perrin HR Services. http://wcats.co.za/wpcontent/uploads/2012/03/Ten-steps-to-creating-an-engaged-workforce.pdf. Accessed 17 Jan 2017.

Truss, C., A. Shantz, E. Soane, K. Alfes, and R. Delbridge. 2013. Employee engagement organisational performance and individual well-being: Exploring the evidence, developing the theory. *The International Journal of Human Resource Management* 24: 2657–2669.

Weiss, D.C. 2008. Meatpacker prayer dispute among rising complaints. *American Bar Association Journal.* http://www.abajournal.com/mobile/article/meatpacker_prayer_dispute_among_rising_complaints_of_religious_bias/. Accessed 19 Jan 2017.

Whittaker, S., and M. Marchington. 2003. Devolving HR responsibility to the line. *Employee Relations* 25: 245–261.

Winkler, S., C. König, and M. Kleinmann. 2012. New insights into an old debate: Investigating the temporal sequence of commitment and performance at the business unit level. *Journal of Occupational and Organisational Psychology* 85: 503–522.

Wollard, K.K. 2011. Quiet desperation. *Advances in Developing Human Resources* 13: 526–537.

Wright, P.M., G. McMahan, G. Snell, and B. Gerhart. 2001. Comparing line and HR executives' perceptions of HR effectiveness: Services, roles, and contributions. *Human Resource Management* 40: 111–123.

Xanthopoulou, D., A. Bakker, E. Demerouti, and W. Schaufeli. 2009. Reciprocal relationships between job resources, personal resources, and work engagement. *Journal of Vocational Behavior* 74: 235–244.

Yalabik, Z., P. Popaitoon, J. Chowne, and B. Rayton. 2013. Work engagement as a mediator between employee attitudes and outcomes. *The International Journal of Human Resource Management* 24: 2799–2823.

Yeung, A., and B. Griffin. 2008. Workplace incivility: Does it matter in Asia? *People & Strategy* 31: 14–19.

12

Hidden Inequalities of the Expatriate Workforce

Maranda Ridgway

12.1 Introduction

This chapter explores the notion of 'hidden' inequalities among expatriate workers focussing on those who are outbound from the UK. The discourse surfaces challenges that are faced by both expatriate workers adjusting to life in another country and organisations that are trying to maintain host-country compliance while promoting equality of opportunity for the Expatriate Workforce. According to the International Labour Office (ILO) (2016a), in 2015, there were 243.7 million international migrants, equating to approximately 3% of the world's population. While there is a multitude of different types of migrant worker, and each type faces their own 'hidden' inequalities within the global workplace, the focus of this chapter is on British workers expatriating from the UK

M. Ridgway (✉)
Department of Human Resource Management, Nottingham Business School, Nottingham Trent University, Nottingham, UK

© The Author(s) 2018
V. Caven, S. Nachmias (eds.), *Hidden Inequalities in the Workplace*,
Palgrave Explorations in Workplace Stigma,
DOI 10.1007/978-3-319-59686-0_12

to overseas destinations. The Office for National Statistics (2016) reports that in the period April 2015–March 2016, over 58,000 British citizens emigrated for the primary reason of employment.

The differentiation of expatriation types lacks clarity in contemporary literature. Traditionally, individuals assigned internationally by their employers for a pre-determined period are described as organisational expatriates. More recently, a different group of expatriates has been identified, who relocate for an undefined period to a new opportunity without necessarily having the support of an employer in their country of origin, described as self-initiated expatriates (Suutari and Brewster 2000; Andresen et al. 2014). Organisational expatriates often retain employment protection in the home country, which can cause complexity when the host-country cultural norms are in contrast with the home-country legislative framework, thus presenting a challenge for employers operating in the global arena.

In this chapter, the term 'expatriates' encompasses both organisational expatriates and self-initiated expatriates. While contemporary literature continues to debate the differentiation, Al Ariss (2010) offers the view that expatriate workers tend to originate from developed nations and relocate to developing nations, whereas for their migrant worker counterparts, the mobility pattern is reversed. Indeed, expatriates originating from Western countries are often described as being affluent and privileged (Jamal 2015). This chapter does not explore the 'hidden' inequalities of migrant workers, differentiated from self-initiated expatriates, as those who seek overseas employment from a position of necessity rather than desire; the inequalities at work, both 'hidden' and visible, that migrant workers face are so vast that a dedicated discussion is warranted, hence the decision not to include here. Expatriate workers provide a unique perspective when considering 'hidden' inequalities because their personal characteristics that are protected in the UK through provisions such as the Equality Act 2010 may not be recognised, and they can even be criminalised in different sociocultural contexts. Consequently, such visible inequalities become 'hidden' in the global arena, forming the key argument that this chapter presents.

The Equality Act 2010 was introduced to combine and harmonise previously separate pieces of legislation pertaining to the equality of treatment. The primary purpose of the Equality Act 2010 is to protect people from discrimination in the workplace and wider society. Currently, there are nine characteristics that are protected under the Equality Act 2010, namely Age; Disability; Gender Reassignment; Marriage and Civil Partnership; Pregnancy and Maternity; Race, Religion or Belief; Sex; and Sexual Orientation.

The chapter uses each of the protected characteristics as a sub-heading to explore how each of the nine protected characteristics, which are visible in the UK, may become 'hidden' in an expatriate context. To provide such context, the Gulf Cooperation Council (GCC) is used as a sociocultural setting for discussion and comparison. The GCC is a useful destination to problematise inequalities experienced by expatriate workers for three primary reasons: firstly, 'macro-contextual influences permeate, are enacted in, and are experienced in the micro-context' (Doucerain et al. 2013, p. 687). Secondly, the GCC is a notoriously expatriate-reliant region (Alserhan et al. 2009), as the ILO (2016a) reports that the Arab states host a tenth of the world's migrant workers. Finally, the Equality Act 2010 provides a rigorous equality framework, which governs all aspects of work in the UK. In the GCC, such a framework is lacking, and local norms criminalise some of the characteristics that are protected by the Equality Act 2010, thus presenting an interesting context for illustrating the problematic nature of equality for outbound British expatriate workers.

The legislative framework governing employment differs between each member country of the GCC, a common theme, however, is the lack of regulation to prevent discriminatory practices. While local labour laws exist, the focus is on contractual issues such as working hours, wages and termination; there is also a lack of impartial intermediary and advisory services, such as the UK's Advisory, Conciliation and Arbitration Service (ACAS) to translate legislative requirements into practical application. The nature of employment governance ascribes greater ethical expectations on employers operating in the region (Cooke 2015), particularly to those who also operate in regions with a higher level of governance, such as the UK. As Treviño and Nelson (2011) suggest, managers need support to ensure that their decisions are ethical in ambiguous circumstances; this may mean challenging the need to explore issues beyond local compliance to maintain home-country ethical standards.

It is important to emphasise that the intention of this chapter is not to portray the GCC in a negative light. As the region provides a stark contrast in terms of culture and legislative frameworks, it is a useful comparison to illustrate challenges. For example, social characteristics, such as gender and ethnicity, are a basis on which job allocations are made (Ewers and Dicce 2016). Despite four out of six GCC countries having ratified to eliminate discriminatory practices (ILO 2016b), the inclusion of any anti-discrimination provision in their respective employment law frameworks is vague, superficial or altogether absent. For UK employers managing overseas assignees, this causes conflict between home- and host-country values and the need to balance compliance with contradictory legislative frameworks (Ewers and Dicce 2016). Furthermore, 17% of organisations suggest that compliance issues are the biggest challenge when managing international assignments (Brookfields Global Relocation Services 2016), equal to the challenge of managing assignments' cost. The challenges highlighted are by no means limited to the GCC, but they are encountered frequently by expatriates, and organisations, operating across the world.

Before exploring each characteristic protected by the Equality Act 2010, it is helpful to consider how different sociocultural environments affect interpretations of inequality. Inequality can be described as a social construct that is influenced by an individual's location, attitude and perception of the relative worth of others (Bottero 2005). Alternatively, inequality can be considered as natural, and to reject it is to question that which is divinely ordained (ibid.). It could be argued that equality and diversity are Westernised concepts that originated from the liberal growth of freethinking (Thompson 2011), leading to rational principles replacing superstitious practices with the aim of enabling social progression (Bottero 2005). As a social construct, individual perspectives of inequality are aligned with social norms (Griffin and Pustay 2010), accordingly, the sociocultural context in which an individual is raised and lives influences their understanding of inequality, which could arguably render cross-cultural comparisons pointless (Thomas and Peterson 2014). The development of equality frameworks is complicated further as prejudices arise and are affected by a country's development. As expatriate workers tend to relocate from developed to developing nations (Al Ariss 2010), this presents a clash of cross-cultural notions of inequality. Dimensions of inequality, however, should not be oversimplified, for example, where religious practices are perceived to openly reject equality of sexual orientation (Thompson 2016). The additional complexity arising through the intersectionality of overlapping dimensions of inequality should also be considered. This chapter proceeds by presenting the academic considerations and exploring how each of the protected characteristics, detailed in the Equality Act 2010, become 'hidden' inequalities in an expatriate context.

12.2 Academic Considerations

This chapter is structured using case vignettes to illustrate the complexities that arise in the global arena. Vignettes have gained popularity in a number of disciplines as they provide descriptions of realistic, contextualised and highly complex issues (Leicher and Mulder 2016). The use of vignettes is appropriate in this work as they offer a medium through which socially constructed issues can be understood, particularly, as the nature of the issues raises cross-cultural sensitivities (Bradbury-Jones et al. 2014).

The stories depicted in the vignettes reflect real-life situations that the author has witnessed as an expatriate worker; however, it is not intended that their inclusion be considered empirical research. To ensure the vignettes have face validity, the two-phase process described by Leicher and Mulder (2016) was followed. Firstly, the vignettes were developed based on the author's experiences. Individuals' personal details were changed in the stories to protect anonymity. Stories were chosen that presented extreme scenarios to highlight the complexity but also reflect real-life issues. Secondly, professionals with a similar background to the author were asked to recount some of their experiences and to review the vignettes to ensure the stories matched the reality of issues facing expatriate workers Unlike the work of Leicher and Mulder (2016), however, solutions to the issues were neither sought nor have been presented; the purpose of the vignettes is to surface complex issues, which do not have immediate and present solutions, thus addressing this chapter's primary objective.

12.2.1   Age

The notion of age is a social construction which is influenced by cultural context immediately presenting its potential to become an inequality in the workplace. While the Equality Act 2010 recognises age as a protected characteristic, this is not the case in many host countries to which expatriates may relocate; thus the intersection between ageing populations and migration presents significant issues (King et al. 2016).

Vignette 12.1: Time to Go Home?

Jim has lived in Bahrain for 30 years during which time he has seen significant changes in the country's development and progression in living standards. There have been highs and lows, but Jim and his wife Susan considered Bahrain to be their home. At 61, Jim felt fit, healthy and settled in a long-established successful career and, despite work visas only being issued for a maximum two-year period for expatriates over the age of 60, Jim had every intention to continue living and working in Bahrain. Susan had retired recently and was enjoying volunteering at a nearby animal shelter. Their three children, who had been born and raised in Bahrain, now had their own careers and lived, independently, in different countries around the world.

The time of year arrived for Jim to hand over a cheque for 12 months' advance rental payment on his villa. Although a standard practice, he always experienced fleeting trepidation at such a large payment but soon relaxed in the knowledge that his home was secure.

Shortly afterwards, Jim's boss called him into his office and notified Jim that they had not been able to renew his visa; his notice was served and he had 30 days to leave the country. Jim was shocked, he had received no warning that this might happen and the previous week his colleague, aged 63, had received a renewed visa. Jim's boss tried to make light of the situation and suggested that after all these years, and at Jim's age, shouldn't he think about returning home?

The case Vignette 12.1 demonstrates how age can be a 'hidden' inequality among older expatriate workers. This is compounded in the GCC as, regardless of length of residency, expatriate workers are not able to receive local citizenship and plan to retire in a country that they call home. Consequently, age becomes a determinant of forced retirement and forced repatriation, which presents challenges such as home-country reintegration and reverse culture shock.

Brookfields Global Relocation Services (2016) report that most expatriates are between the ages of 40 and 49, followed by 30 and 39; expatriates aged over 60 or between 20 and 29 are the least represented age groups. Expatriate experience is, however, increasing for younger workers as it is seen to support career development. The actual roles undertaken overseas, and how host-country sociocultural issues and reactions to age affect the experience, however, remain unclear. Subsequently, age, as a 'hidden' inequality, is not exclusive to older expatriate workers. Younger expatriate workers originating from a low power distance context, such as the UK, may face challenges in high power distance contexts, such as the GCC countries. In high power distance contexts, age is often perceived as a determinant of seniority and respect, thus creating potential for conflict in management and teamwork scenarios (Farndale et al. 2015). Age can become a 'hidden' inequality for anyone. For example, the decision to pursue a career change by joining a graduate programme may be prevented if age parameters are exceeded. Furthermore, not conforming to expected social norms by certain ages could be looked upon with pity or disdain (Marsh 2010).

12.2.2 Disability

People with disabilities are already underrepresented in the workplace (Fabian 2013); in a global context, however, the prevailing barriers are amplified due to sociocultural and environmental stigmas (Kronfol 2012).

The Vignette 12.2 depicts an extreme, but not unprecedented, case of an expatriate discovering that he is HIV positive and facing immediate deportation. Many expatriate-reliant countries retain entry restrictions

> **Vignette 12.2: Skin, Blood and Lungs**
>
> Jason arrived in Abu Dhabi ready for a new adventure having secured a five-year assignment as a Programme Director on a prestigious construction project. His wife, Ellen, had given up work and would follow shortly with their two children. The children were both approaching GCSE level at school and while Jason and Ellen were concerned about disrupting their education, the guarantee of schooling in Abu Dhabi reassured them that they had made the right decision.
>
> Jason's employer was highly organised and arranged for his visa formalities within the first week of arrival. After attending government offices for fingerprints and photographs to be taken, he was driven to a designated government medical centre. At the medical centre, he had to provide a blood sample, have his stomach and back inspected and have his lungs X-rayed. It was never explained what the exact purpose of these tests was, but it seemed a necessary part of the visa process.
>
> A few days later, Jason was called back to the hospital under the guise of further testing; upon arrival, however, he was detained and 36 hours later was deported. It was only upon arriving in the UK that Jason learnt he had been diagnosed as HIV positive, and his visa had been denied.

for people living with HIV despite international pressures, and many other countries, having removed such restrictions (Chang et al. 2013). Surprisingly, many organisations do not facilitate pre-testing before departure, and only a concerning few communicate this residence visa requirement to expatriate workers.

Countries, such as those in the GCC, focus healthcare resources on physical disabilities (Kronfol 2012); as Thompson (2011) points out, disability tends to be medically oriented, focussing on how individuals need to be supported and cared for rather than considering social and cultural challenges and how autonomy can be promoted. The social and cultural perspective is particularly relevant in the global arena where social exclusion may be personified, support networks may not be accessible or necessary adjustments not obtainable. While contemporary literature argues the need to make invisible disabilities more visible, Marsh (2010) highlights that many areas within the Middle East demonstrate discomfort, or shame, towards individuals with visible disabilities, which infers that disability remains a 'hidden' inequality.

'Geopolitical, economic, cultural, and religious factors' (Kaladchibachi and Al-Dhafiri 2016, p. 1) render GCC residents relatively more susceptible to mental health disorders and highlight the cultural and social stigmas in the region. Moving home is argued to be one of the most stressful events that individuals face; coupled with a new country and new job, and compounded by a turbulent external environment, it is unsurprising that expatriates experience stress and anxiety (Giorgi et al. 2016). Although mental health issues can be considered synonymous with expatriation, few organisations take proactive steps to mitigate such issues, this is exacerbated as nearly 80% of organisations do not assess the suitability of employees for international assignments resulting in nearly 20% finding it challenging to adjust to the new environment (Brookfields Global Relocation Services 2016).

12.2.3 Gender Reassignment

The global approach to transgenderism is polarised; on the one hand, some countries have legal frameworks that allow individuals to select their gender and undergo gender reassignment, while the other extreme effectively criminalises the existence of transgender people (Ghoshal and Knight 2016). The expatriate transgender population has been identified as an underresearched group (Paisley and Tayar 2016).

Transgender employees already face many barriers in the workplace which are not present for other employees (Ozturk and Tatli 2016). A unique challenge facing transgender expatriates is a host country's approach to gender segregation. As transgenderism is associated with the binary of sex and gender (Paisley and Tayar 2016), this will be influenced strongly by the host country's interpretation of gender norms. Transgender expatriates may find themselves in a position where it is necessary to re-conceal their identity for legal compliance and personal safety during an intentional assignment. This shows how an inequality, which may have once been visible, becomes 'hidden' in the global arena. This is particularly problematic for organisations, as such inability to express gender identity can have a negative impact on an individuals' psychological wellbeing, resulting in a meaningless expatriate experience from both the employee's and employer's perspectives (Paisley and Tayar 2016).

> **Vignette 12.3: Caught Between a Rock and a Hard Place**
>
> Alison had been a computer programmer for many years. She had started her career in the UK and progressed steadily with her UK employer into a senior management role. She felt very loyal to her employer; in no small way, due to the support they had shown her while she went through hormone therapy and gender reassignment surgery and the partnered approach of communicating the transition to her colleagues.
>
> Once Alison felt her gender had been affirmed, she started to explore international work opportunities to satisfy a long-standing career ambition. She applied for an assignment opportunity in Kuwait and was successfully appointed for an initial 18-month period.
>
> Alison settled into her new role quickly and started to make a valuable contribution in her employer's Kuwait City office. In recognition of the positive impact that Alison made, she was asked to take responsibility for coaching and mentoring a group of junior Kuwaiti national employees, as part of the company's efforts to supporting Kuwaiti nationalisation.
>
> Unfortunately, two of the Kuwaiti nationals did not respond well to Alison's guidance. They openly objected to work for a 'man impersonating a woman' despite Alison being able to provide documentation (e.g. her passport and birth certificate) validating her affirmed gender. Alison's employer faced the predicament of repatriating Alison and facing potential discrimination claims or causing conflict with local employees.

Further dilemmas emerge for organisations as they are faced with ensuring that opportunities are equally available to, and accessible by, transgender employees while also maintaining confidentiality and support in line with the Equality Act 2010. Moreover, there is a requirement to maintain a duty of care, as with all employees, to prevent transgender employees coming to any harm through the course of their employment. When operating in the global arena, however, employers must also comply with local customs and laws.

The case Vignette 12.3 shows Alison starting her assignment in her affirmed gender, but this does not prevent unique barriers from emerging leaving both her and her employer in a difficult situation. While some countries are shifting their stance on the matter, for example, according to Human Rights Watch (2015), in Vietnam, gender reassignment surgery and legal recognition for those who have undergone gender reassignment will come into force, the literature is clear that more needs to be done to improve the work lives of transgender individuals; this is also true, if not more so, in the global arena (Ozturk and Tatli 2016).

12.2.4   Marriage and Civil Partnership

Brookfields Global Relocation Services (2016) report that 80% of married international assignees (Marriage and Civil Partnership) relocate globally with their spouse and that the most significant challenge for any married international assignee to overcome is resistance from a spouse.

Vignette 12.4: Should I Stay or Should I Go?

Felicity and James had been married for 12 years, during which time they had lived in (almost) every continent. Felicity's career had gone from strength to strength; she had progressed rapidly as an expert in information systems and technology. Having spent three years in South Africa as a Vice President for a healthcare provider, she was ready for a new challenge. The challenge presented itself as a role as a Chief Technology Officer for a healthcare provider in the United Arab Emirates. Not only would this be the pinnacle of her career, but Felicity and James would be able to 'collect' the final continent.

James worked in hospitality and was content to follow Felicity's career, as he had never struggled to find employment. Abu Dhabi was different; however, he found a job with relative ease, but the treatment and expectations of staff in junior-level roles was unlike his previous experiences, and he soon decided that this wasn't the right region for him, in his line of work. James decided that he would make the most of their new geographic location and pursue his passion for exotic teas with the intent of building a distribution business.

It was only once James had resigned that it became apparent that Felicity would not be able to sponsor him, and he would be without a residence visa. Had their roles been reversed, James could sponsor Felicity without any problems. Not only did James have to exit and re-enter the country every 30 days but he was also unable to take out local medical insurance or obtain a driving licence, among other restrictions.

Despite the opportunity to travel for James, the uncertainty and instability of his living condition became too much and after much soul searching, Felicity decided it was the right thing to resign and move back to the UK.

Despite the high numbers of expatriate workers in the GCC, only women in selected occupations (teachers, engineers and doctors) are occasionally allowed to sponsor their husbands and children. In many cases, this is not clearly communicated, and families uproot and relocate to the GCC only to find on arrival that families where the mother, or wife, is the primary income earner. Other family members cannot secure a residence visa without the father's, or husbands, sponsorship, in which case he must earn a minimum wage before he is able to sponsor family members. This provides a conflict to demographic changes in the UK where the gender pay gap is closing, albeit very slowly. Dual-income earners are on the rise yet, as an expatriate, barriers are reinstated for women with careers. This transforms into an inequality of opportunity, as the rights within marriage are not equal.

An alternative way in which this UK-protected characteristic becomes a 'hidden' inequality is through the requirement for heterosexual couples to be married to cohabit in the GCC. It is not unheard of for couples cohabiting in the UK, as common law partners, to marry purely to meet the requirements to live together in the GCC. This goes beyond the desire to share a home but is required for more generous accommodation allowances, medical insurance and other benefits that are more generous for married employees than their unmarried counterparts. These requirements may reflect why most assignees are married men (49%) followed by single men (22%), according to a report compiled by Brookfields Global Relocation Services (2016); the report also highlighted that single women accounted for only 10% of assignees and married women for 19%.

The same report highlights, however, that family concerns are the most frequently cited reason for international assignment refusal followed by the impact to spouses' careers and the most frequently cited reason for assignment failure. Subsequently, more internationally assignees are choosing to relocate on single status contracts, despite the less favourable remuneration package, due to perceived lack of family support (Brookfields Global Relocation Services 2016).

12.2.5   Pregnancy and Maternity

The traditional expatriate arrangement of the 'trailing spouse' is slowly diminishing, as more dual-career expatriate couples enter the global market (Känsälä et al. 2015). While it is encouraging that the expatriate workplace is slowly diversifying in gender terms, new problems arise as host countries do not have provisions allowing parents, affecting mostly women, the opportunity to raise a family while maintaining a career.

Vignette 12.5: You Can't Have It All

Jean was over the moon to discover that she was pregnant. She and her husband, Carl, had moved to Muscat about 15 months ago. She was enjoying her role as a retail manager, and Carl was settled in his role as a civil engineer. Having established a new home in Muscat, they had discussed the idea of starting a family for the past year and now certainly felt like the right time.

Jean was particularly happy as her medical insurance provided for pregnancy, which was not typical for the region. A friend of hers working for a different company had become pregnant only to realise pregnancy was not covered by medical insurance and had spent a small fortune on antenatal appointments, and scans, not to mention the actual cost of the birth.

The new addition to the family arrived, but after reviewing their finances, Jean and Carl soon realised that it would not be feasible for them to survive on Carl's salary alone, and Jean would need to return to work. Jean's employers refused her request to work part-time, as they had no way to prorate some of her benefits, which would increase the cost of her employment.

With feelings of guilt and trepidation, they hired a live-in maid, Tally, from the Philippines. The power dynamic felt odd, sharing their home and trusting their new baby to a stranger.

Although the number of dual-career couples is increasing (Känsälä et al. 2015), Brookfield Global Relocations Services (2015) report that 48% of expatriate spouses worked prior to being internationally assigned, but not during. As men make up most international assignees, this suggests that women are giving up their own careers to relocate with their spouses and not pursuing an international career as they need to care for children.

The gender pay gap is apparent in most countries around the world as women's career is curtailed due to family responsibilities. This is exacerbated in an expatriate situation, as there are no extended family members to call on for support, and in the GCC, for example, there is no legal provision for part-time or flexible working. Women are faced with the decision to either give up work to raise a family or forced to rely on live-in domestic assistance to continue working, which raises its own challenges (Metcalfe and Rees 2010). The barriers are compounded for non-traditional expatriate families, such as single parents and female breadwinners as they must navigate the same complexity and uncertainty without organisational support, and in some cases, support mechanisms (McNulty 2014).

While recent changes in the UK legislation enable the sharing of parental leave, the GCC, by comparison provides, on average, less than 12 weeks' maternity leave and no paternity leave (except for Saudi Arabia where one day may be taken) (ILO 2014). In 2016, the government in Abu Dhabi announced an extension to the maternity leave provision for government employees, however, as most government employees are Emirati, this emphasises the intersectional 'hidden' inequalities between maternity and nationality. Although progress is being made towards enabling women to have a family and a career, informal traditions and cultural norms render such progress slow (Alhejji et al. 2016).

12.2.6   Race

The 'hidden' inequality of race among the Expatriate Workforce is made visible in many ways, for example, in the GCC, racial inequality can be discerned through the nationalisation agenda and the hierarchisation of privilege.

Vignette 12.6: Navigating the Nationalisation Agenda

Ashima, of Indian ethnicity, was born and raised in Manchester. After school, she undertook a bachelor's degree in HR Management and graduated with honours. She joined the graduate scheme of a prestigious accountancy firm and after two years working in the UK, her rotation took her to Dubai, to gain international experience in the global mobility team.

Ashima thoroughly enjoyed her experience and when an opportunity arose in a locally owned Dubai firm for an Assistant HR Manager, she thought it was a great way to remain overseas while progressing her career quickly. Ashima's new role was a fixed term for two years with the view to train an Emirati employee to take the role in the future. Ashima was fully aware and supportive of the government's Emiratisation programme and was pleased to contribute to the development of the local workforce.

One of Ashima's first tasks was to recruit an HR Administrator. After advertising, and running a selection process, Ashima identified the best candidate for the job, only to be overruled by the HR Director. Ashima was instructed to hire one of the applicants who had a lower-level qualification, no experience and did not perform well during the selection process. The only reason she was given was that this individual happened to be the Finance Director's niece. Despite feeling frustrated that she could not take the decision, she followed the instruction given and made the appointment.

Ashima's frustration only grew as her recruit often arrived late for work, left early and did not show interest in learning how to perform the role. When Ashima attempted to address the issue, her subordinate was surprised and said surely Ashima was 'happy to have a job here as she is Indian'. The HR Director raised the performance issues with Ashima, but instead of supporting her and providing guidance, he informed her that she couldn't initiate any performance management measures and had to find another way for the work to be done, even if it meant doing it herself. To add insult to injury, Ashima discovered that she was being paid 40% less than her subordinate.

Ashima's story exemplifies 'hidden' racial inequality from several different perspectives. Firstly, nationalisation is at the forefront of the governmental agenda for GCC nations with quotas being enforced to increase the number of nationals employed in both public and private sectors (Hertog 2014). The requirement to meet such quotas results in organisations appointing under-qualified or under-experienced staff whose dearth in performance falls on expatriate managers to bear. The gap in salary levels between nationals and expatriate workers only exacerbates this problem and is one of the most notable instances of perceived injustice (Romanowski and Nasser 2014; Al-Waqfi and Al-Faki 2015). Although the nationalisation agenda is transparent and ingrained in the regional labour markets, it is driven through the restriction, or prevention, of some nationalities undertaking specified occupations (Jamal 2015) and shows how treatment of individuals is differentiated based on nationality. It also raises challenges for organisations operating globally, for example, managerial development programmes are often restricted for locals rather than providing equality of opportunity for all employees.

The second problem the case Vignette 12.6 highlights is how the practice of *wasta* can indirectly racially discriminate. The phenomenon of *wasta* is recognised as the 'social network of interpersonal connections, rooted in family and kinship ties, and linked to family affairs as well as work' (Abalkhail and Allan 2015, p. 162). By its very nature, this prevents the inclusion of external participation, reserving opportunities for homogenous groups.

The third issue that is surfaced, although not officially acknowledged, is the hierarchy in privileges afforded to different groups (Jamal 2015). Privilege is manifested through an implicit hierarchal social ordering of racial, national or ethnic stereotypes (Song 2004). In Ashima's story, there is the added complexity of presumptions being made about her nationality, based on her ethnicity, and this saliency affects local's perceptions of expatriate (Sonesh and DeNisi 2016); such perception as an 'out-group' member prevents adjustment and opportunities to socialise.

12.2.7   Religion or Belief

'Religion itself is a socially constructed phenomenon that imposes yet another element of "contradictory yet interrelated" tensions upon individuals, who may carry both a need for spiritual connection and pressure to make work a central activity of their lives' (Khilji et al. 2014, p. 236). Religion is a complex notion as it is the foundation upon which other characteristic perceptions, for example sexuality, are based.

Vignette 12.7: It's Not What You Believe, It's If You Believe

Angela had never been religious. She had an array of friends from different backgrounds and creeds and, thus, had partaken in the celebration of different religious festival. For Angela, however, the importance of such celebrations was time spent with people for whom she cared. She never begrudged anyone his, or her, religious practices, but simply chose not to follow a faith herself.

When presented with an opportunity to spend 12 months in Qatar to support a sport-marketing campaign, Angela jumped at the chance. She was always eager to meet new people from different backgrounds and had heard that so many expatriates from different nationalities currently resided in Qatar.

Usually, Angela didn't particularly feel the need to label herself to fit into a category; however, she was required to declare her religion for visa purposes and noted that there was no box for *atheism* on her visa application form. She wouldn't have given this a second thought had her colleague from the global mobility team highlighted that in Qatar, *atheism* is regarded below any other religion. On reflection, Angela didn't want anything to have a negative impact on her experience and decided to declare herself as a Unitarian Christian.

This was the first time in Angela's life that she had to declare herself as identifying with something that she didn't truly believe.

The case Vignette 12.7 depicts the hierarchisation of different Religions from a GCC perspective and the implied need to confirm to sociocultural expectations. After Islam, Christianity is afforded the next highest status; atheists, agnostics or individuals practising polytheistic faiths are advised to claim Christianity as their Religion to avoid encountering any prejudice (Marsh 2010). As religious pluralism is not embraced in the GCC, implications of the links between intolerance of other Religions and the abuse of migrant workers has been made, although it is important to note that this is not empirically founded (Khashan 2016).

As Borstorff et al. (2012) highlight, it is difficult to separate religious beliefs from the workplace. This presents an issue for expatriate workers whose beliefs are not tolerated in theocratic nations, thus requiring them to hide their beliefs and rendering Religion and belief as a 'hidden' inequality in the expatriate context. In such theocratic countries, religious practices are seen to underpin business management principles such that the employment relations are governed by Religion, as well as physical and psychological contracts (Branine and Pollard 2010). This can cause alienation for expatriate workers when religious beliefs are not shared.

The experience of relocating from a secular society to one where state and Religion are not separated can be a cause of shock and hinder adjustment and acculturation for expatriate workers (Haslberger et al. 2013). Religion is considered to influence and shape a nation's culture (Saroglou and Cohen 2011), thus having a significant impact on the lived experience of expatriate workers regardless of their own faith and beliefs. Furthermore, as assumptions about individuals' religious beliefs are made, based on perceptions of ethnicity, different religious practices and beliefs may also lead to explicit discrimination (Farcas and Gonçalves 2016) or implicit exclusion from integrating with local nationals, as expatriates are perceived as 'the other'.

12.2.8 Sex

Women only account for 25% of employees sent on international assignment by their employers (Brookfields Global Relocation Services 2016); 59% of organisations acknowledge that women face greater challenges than men do.

Vignette 12.8: Should We Send Her There?

Jane works as Regional Head of Marketing for a global consultancy firm. She is divorced and has three children, all of whom have careers and families of their own. She accepted a two-year international assignment, based in Dubai, UAE, with regional responsibility for the firm's offices across the GCC.

During her time in the UAE she travelled regularly, and with relative ease, to the other Gulf States. Challenges arose, however, when she was required to spend time in Riyadh, Saudi Arabia. As a woman, she was not able to travel without a chaperone, requiring the Regional Head of HR, Frank, to accompany her for the trip.

Jane had not received any specific pre-departure training that discussed the detailed nuances of each GCC state. Consequently, several scenarios arose causing Jane to experience embarrassment, confusion and frustration. Firstly, she was required to wear the country's traditional attire for women, an *abaya* (loose-fitting black cloak) and *hijab* (headscarf); she understood the cultural importance placed upon preserving modesty. However, as a woman working in a male-dominated region, coupled with a lack of acclimatisation and the additional clothing layers in the desert heat, Jane began to feel more conscious of her sex. This translated into her feeling that her presence and contribution were tolerated rather than welcomed and valued.

While visiting a client's office, Jane asked to use the lavatory, which caused notable awkwardness among her hosts. It soon became apparent that their facility did not have any provision for women's hygiene. To accommodate Jane, a male member of staff was required to check the men's lavatories to ensure that they were empty and effectively stand guard outside to prevent anyone from entering while Jane occupied the facility. This caused embarrassment for Jane and the male staff member.

On another occasion, Jane and Frank decided to take their evening meal in the hotel's restaurant. Jane and Frank were both taken aback when the waiter approached their table and asked Frank what he would like to order for Jane. Neither Jane nor Frank had anticipated this and both felt quite awkward about the situation.

A seminal study by Adler (1984) identified three reasons causing women's underrepresentation in the Expatriate Workforce. Firstly, women are less motivated to undertake international assignments, which the same study later found to be misrepresentative. Secondly, when relocating, women were offered less organisational support than their male peers were. Finally, and most poignant with the theme of this chapter, the host-country sociocultural environment became an obstacle to women's international assignments.

When moving from an egalitarian-oriented society to a patriarchal regime, the 'hidden' inequality of sex becomes apparent. In a patriarchal regime, expatriate women's identities change and are situation dependent, whereas men's identities are constant (Doan and Portillo 2016). Furthermore, perceptions of host-country prejudice towards female workers actually became a reason deterring organisations from offering international assignments to women (Adler 1984).

Another way in which sex becomes a 'hidden' inequality in the global domains is through exclusion of social events, for example, men and women socialising separately (Wright 2016). Similarly, expectations of expatriate women to dress and behave in a certain way become more apparent in patriarchal societies, such as the GCC, where any deviation from the norm causes complexity (Hutchings et al. 2013; Bonache et al. 2016). Expatriate women are still reported as having achieved successful and varied professional careers in the Middle East region, despite the challenges that have been presented (Harrison and Michailova 2012).

12.2.9 Sexual Orientation

The lesbian, gay and bisexual (sexual minority) population have been identified as an underresearched group in the expatriate field; however, this group's growing representation in talent pools highlights the importance of understanding what prevents them from undertaking expatriate opportunities (McPhail et al. 2016). Brookfield Global Relocation Services (2015) report that women in same-sex relationships accounted for only 1% of international assignments and men in same-sex relationships for 3%.

Vignette 12.9: Looking for Loopholes

Neal had been in Bahrain for three months. Before relocating, he had understood that homosexuality was illegal, but he and his partner Vincent had decided to move anyway. Fortunately, both Neal and Vincent could secure international assignment opportunities from their respective employers and planned to spend the forthcoming three years in Manama.

Neal's employer had been very proactive and adjusted the wording of their international assignment policy; any mention of 'husband' or 'wife' had been replaced with 'spouse' to ensure provision of any benefits could be made without explicitly being in breach of local legislation.

Interestingly, unmarried heterosexual couples are not able to cohabit but same-sex individuals can as homosexuality is criminalised. This emerged as a surprise, as Neal and Vincent each benefitted from an international assignment housing allowance while incurring shared accommodation costs.

Although in a better position financially, and able to cohabit discreetly, Neal often found that he had to mask his personal circumstance at social gatherings and face innocently posed questions about his intention to find a wife. Additionally, when spending time together outside of work and encountering colleagues, Neal felt compelled to introduce Vincent as his housemate rather than reveal the true nature of their relationship.

Interestingly, in countries where homosexuality is criminalised, same-sex relationship socialisation could face fewer barriers, as some public displays of affection (such as holding hands) is normal between same-sex friends (McPhail et al. 2016). As unmarried heterosexual couples are prohibited from cohabiting, it is actually easier for sexual minority couples to cohabit provided their sexuality is closeted, and they portray themselves as heterosexual externally (Marsh 2010). Remarkably, the intersection between being lesbian, gay or bisexual and an expatriate allows for a higher level of tolerance of one's sexual orientation (McPhail et al. 2016), and certain areas within the Middle East host a significant 'underground' sexual minority community; the risk individuals face in countries where homosexuality is criminalised should, however, not be underestimated.

Sexual minority expatriates relocating to tight hostile cultural contexts are forced to address the extent to which they are comfortable expressing their true identity (Paisley and Tayar 2016). The term *global closet* represents the negotiation these groups face when hiding, or masking, their identities to avoid stigmatisation and security issues in a global context (Gedro 2010). The term *glass border* has also been used to describe the restrictions sexual minority expatriates encounter when seeking international career development opportunities (McPhail et al. 2016).

Beyond safety and security considerations, sexual minority expatriates face inequalities through remuneration packages and whether family members, namely same-sex partners, are included. The case Vignette 12.9 implies that same-sex couples may be more affluent and access higher levels of global mobility, reflecting the work of McPhail et al. (2016) if both individuals are working; however, exclusion of same-sex partners from relocation packages leads to inequality (Gedro et al. 2013).

12.3 Conclusion and Implications

This chapter has problematised the nature of inequality, as it is understood from a UK perspective, when it is applied in a global setting and surfaced how visible inequalities become 'hidden', in an expatriate context. Drawing on real-life cases, the chapter presented case vignettes to exemplify how 'hidden' inequalities are amplified in culturally distant and expatriate-reliant regions, such as the GCC. It is important to understand the complexities that organisations face to determine strategies and tactics to contend with, and navigate, local labour markets (Ewers and Dicce 2016). Metcalfe and Rees (2010) succinctly note that that 'the politics of cultural difference obscures inequalities, as many injustices are also a matter of structural inequality' (Metcalfe and Rees 2010).

It is, therefore, inappropriate to assume that the Western notion of equality is correct, particularly as so many characteristics remain outside of the scope of UK equality, such as societal hierarchy, physical appearance and so on. Equality is complex, especially when considered in the global arena and viewed through different sociocultural lens. Even in a society where legal frameworks are in place to ensure equality, it is not always achieved. This raises the question—is it possible to promote and achieve equality where no such governance exists? Maybe it is acceptable and the norm for those who have been raised in such societies, but when the expectations of equality are met with practices of inequality, it is not clear how this should be managed. It can be argued that it is not possible to achieve diversity and inclusivity without equality having firstly been established. The value of diversity is clear, wherein it has 'taken as a western-oriented theory and practice it has been successful in pioneering social change and commitment to individual injustices, by exposing the intersecting dimensions of individual difference, including Sex,

Age, Religion, Ethnicity and so forth' (Metcalfe and Rees 2010, p. 13). Global diversity strategies and initiatives formulated in an organisation's headquarters may not translate to overseas subsidiaries (Lauring 2013), where the local legal framework may prevent equality. In the GCC, there is a stark contrast between nationalisation programmes and global diversity measures, thus presenting a problem for multi-national corporations operating in the region; a similar problem is presented for GCC-owned enterprises operating in other regions, where expectations and frameworks are in place to promote equality of opportunity.

Employers sending individuals on overseas assignments have a duty of care towards those whose protected characteristics may be ostracised in certain regions. The withdrawal of such opportunities, even from a perspective of protection, however, could lead to discrimination in the UK on the very grounds that may cause exclusion in the host country. Yet the requirement remains for the inclusivity of these groups that may not be acknowledged or tolerated in different sociocultural contexts. Preventing opportunities is not the right approach; instead, the duty of care should be manifested through effective communication, which allows individuals to make informed decisions. The hyper-diversity and hybridisation of non-traditional expatriates (McNulty 2015) reinforces the importance of understanding how inequalities become 'hidden' in the global context and the need for organisations to consider how policies will accommodate this growing group. According to a survey completed by Brookfield Global Relocation Services (2015), the second most cited reason for employees undertaking international assignments was to obtain career development to build international management experience. Such career development opportunities are being withheld from groups with inequalities that become 'hidden' in the global context due to emergent sociocultural barriers. Furthermore, the intersection of 'hidden' inequalities adds complexity when trying to understand the lived reality of expatriate experiences.

For UK employees undertaking international assignments, moving one's life coupled with culture shock can lead to challenging and unsettling scenarios (Thomas and Peterson 2014). Despite this, only 38% of organisations provide intercultural training for all international assignees (Brookfield Global Relocation Services 2015), suggesting that employees are not making well-informed decisions. Furthermore, the chapter has surfaced that organisations operating in regions with reduced legislative frameworks often display apathy and inflexibility towards expatriates whose characteristics may be protected in the UK. Although their actions may be compliant with local legislative frameworks, which may not explicitly support expatriate workers, their actions—or lack thereof—may not meet the ethical standards expected in their country of origin.

It is not permissible for organisations to break the law in either home or host nations; however, there is a need for organisations to be more proactive and develop robust communication strategies to support employees and be transparent about the realities of expatriate experiences. Additionally, organisations should explore tactical approaches to facilitate the opportunity for international experience for individuals whose inequalities may become 'hidden', for example, using gender-neutral words for policy purposes, for example, 'spouse' instead of wife. While the intention of this chapter has not been to present solutions, it has highlighted that it is critical that open and honest conversations happen to manage expatriates' expectations and identify mutually agreeable approaches to international opportunities. This chapter has shown that in the global arena, and in the world of expatriate workers, both equalities and inequalities, which are visible in the UK, become 'hidden'.

References

Abalkhail, J.M., and B. Allan. 2015. Women's career advancement: Mentoring and networking in Saudi Arabia and the UK. *Human Resource Development International* 18: 153–168.

Adler, N. 1984. Women do not want international careers: And other myths about international management. *Organisational Dynamics* 13: 66–79.

Al Ariss, A. 2010. Modes of engagement: Migration, self-initiated expatriation, and career development. *Career Development International* 15: 338–358.

Alhejji, H., E. Ng, T. Garavan, and R. Carbery. 2016. The impact of formal and informal distance on gender equality approaches: The case of a British MNC in Saudi Arabia. *Thunderbird International Business Review*. https://doi.org/10.1002/tie.21828

Alserhan, B., I. Forstenlechner, and A. Al-Nakeeb. 2009. Employees' attitudes towards diversity in a non-western context. *Employee Relations* 32: 42–55.

Al-Waqfi, M., and I. Al-Faki. 2015. Gender-based differences in employment conditions of local and expatriate workers in the GCC connect: Empirical evidence from the United Arab Emirates. *International Journal of Manpower* 36: 397–415.

Andresen, M., F. Bergdolt, J. Margenfeld, and M. Dickmann. 2014. Addressing international mobility confusion–developing definitions and differentiations for self-initiated and assigned expatriates as well as migrants. *The International Journal of Human Resource Management* 25: 2295–2318.

Bonache, J., H. Langinier, and C. Zárraga-Oberty. 2016. Antecedents and effects of host country nationals negative stereotyping of corporate expatriates. A social identity analysis. *Human Resource Management Review* 26: 59–68.

Borstorff, P., B. Cunningham, and L. Clark. 2012. The communication and practice of religious accommodation: Employee perceptions. *Journal of Applied Management and Entrepreneurship* 17: 24–37.

Bottero, W. 2005. *Stratification: Social division and inequality*. Oxford: Routledge.

Bradbury-Jones, C., J. Tatlor, and O. Herber. 2014. Vignette development and administration: A framework for protecting research participants. *International Journal of Social Research Methodology* 17: 427–440.

Branine, M., and D. Pollard. 2010. Human resource management with Islamic management principles: A dialectic for a reverse diffusion in management. *Personnel Review* 39: 712–727.

Brookfield Global Relocation Services. 2015. *Global relocation trends survey report*. Woodridge: Brookfield Global Relocation Services.

Brookfields Global Relocation Services. 2016. 2016 global mobility trends. http://globalmobilitytrends.brookfieldgrs.com. Accessed 8 Jan 2017.

Chang, F., H. Prytherch, R. Nesbitt, and A. Wilder-Smith. 2013. HIV-related travel restrictions: Trends and country characteristics. *Global Health Action* 6: 1–8.

Cooke, F. 2015. Corporate social responsibility and sustainability through ethical HRM practices. In *International human resource management*, ed. A. Harzing and A. Pinnington, 87–102. London: Sage.

Doan, A.E., and S. Portillo. 2016. Not a woman, but a soldier: Exploring identity through translocational positionality. *Sex Roles* 76: 1–14.

Doucerain, M., J. Dere, and A. Ryder. 2013. Travels in hyper-diversity: Multiculturalism and contextual assessment of acculturation. *International Journal of Intercultural Relations* 37: 686–699.

Ewers, M., and R. Dicce. 2016. Expatriate labour markets in rapidly globalising cities: Reproducing the migrant division of labour in Abu Dhabi and Dubai. *Journal of Ethnic and Migration Studies* 42: 2448–2467.

Fabian, E. 2013. Work and disability. In *The Oxford handbook of the psychology of working*, ed. F. Blustein, 185–202. Oxford: Oxford University Press.

Farcas, D., and M. Gonçalves. 2016. Do three years make a difference? An updated review and analysis of self-initiated expatriation. *SpringerPlus* 5: 1326.

Farndale, E., M. Biron, D. Briscoe, and S. Raghuram. 2015. A global perspective on diversity and inclusion in work organisations. *The International Journal of Human Resource Management* 26: 677–687.

Gedro, J. 2010. The lavender ceiling atop the global closet: Human resource development and lesbian expatriates. *Human Resource Development Review* 9: 385–404.

Gedro, J., R. Mizzi, T.S. Rocco, and J. van Loo. 2013. Going global: Professional mobility and concerns for LGBT workers. *Human Resource Development* 16: 282–297.

Ghoshal, N., and K. Knight. 2016. Rights in transition: Making legal recognition of transgender people a global priority. Human rights watch world report 2016. http://www.hrw.org. Accessed 13 Nov 2016.

Giorgi, G., F. Montani, J. Fiz-Perez, G. Arcangeli, and N. Mucci. 2016. Expatriates' multiple fears, from terrorism to working conditions: Development of a model. *Frontiers in psychology* 7: 1–11.

Griffin, R., and M. Pustay. 2010. *International business: A managerial perspective.* 6th ed. London: Pearson.

Harrison, E., and S. Michailova. 2012. Working in the Middle East: Western female expatriates' experiences in the United Arab Emirates. *The International Journal of Human Resource Management* 23: 625–644.

Haslberger, A., C. Brewster, and T. Hippler. 2013. The dimensions of expatriate adjustment. *Human Resource Management* 52: 333–351.

Hertog, S. 2014. Arab Gulf states: An assessment of nationalisation policies. http://cadmus.eui.eu. Accessed 8 Jan 2017.

Human Rights Watch. 2015. Vietnam: Positive step for transgender rights. http://www.hrw.org. Accessed 8 Jan 2017.

Hutchings, K., S. Michailova, and E. Harrison. 2013. Neither ghettoed nor cosmopolitan. *Management International Review* 53: 291–318.

International Labour Organisation. 2014. Maternity and paternity at work. http://www.ilo.org. Accessed 4 Aug 2016.

———. 2016a. International labour conference 105th session. http://www.ilo.org. Accessed 4 Aug 2016.

———. 2016b. Ratifications of C111 – Discrimination (employment and occupation) convention, 1958 (No. 111). http://www.ilo.org. Accessed 29 Oct 2016.

Jamal, M. 2015. The "tiering" of citizenship and residency and the "hierarchization" of migrant communities: The United Arab Emirates in historical context. *International Migration Review* 49: 601–632.

Kaladchibachi, S., and A. Al-Dhafiri. 2016. Mental health care in Kuwait: Toward a community-based decentralized approach. *International Social Work*: 1–6. https://doi.org/10.1177/0020872816661403

Känsälä, M., L. Mäkelä, and V. Suutari. 2015. Career coordination strategies among dual career expatriate couples. *The International Journal of Human Resource Management* 26: 2187–2210.

Khashan, H. 2016. Religious intolerance in the Gulf states. http://www.meforum.org. Accessed 8 Jan 2017.

Khilji, S., E. Murphy, R. Greenwood, and B. Mujtaba. 2014. Plurality within contemporary organisations evidence of complexity of value variations and similarities across religions. *Cross Cultural Management* 21: 219–244.

King, R., A. Lulle, D. Sampaio, and J. Vullnetari. 2016. Unpacking the ageing – Migration nexus and challenging the vulnerability trope. *Journal of Ethnic and Migration Studies* 1: 1–17.

Kronfol, N. 2012. Health services to groups with special needs in the Arab world: A review. *Eastern Mediterranean Health Journal* 18: 1247–1253.

Lauring, J. 2013. International diversity management: Global ideals and local responses. *British Journal of Management* 24: 211–224.

Leicher, V., and R. Mulder. 2016. Development of vignettes for learning and professional development. *Gerontology and Geriatrics Education*: 1–17. https://doi.org/10.1080/02701960.2016.1247065

Marsh, D. 2010. *The Middle East unveiled*. London: How To Books Ltd.

McNulty, Y. 2014. Women as female breadwinners in non-traditional expatriate families: Status-reversal marriages, single parents, split families, and lesbian partnerships. In *Research handbook on women in international management*, ed. K. Hutchings and S. Michailova, 332–366. Cheltenham: Edward Elgar Publishing Limited.

————. 2015. Acculturating non-traditional expatriates: A case study of single parent, overseas adoption, split family, and lesbian assignees. *International Journal of Intercultural Relations* 49: 278–293.

McPhail, R., Y. McNulty, and K. Hutchings. 2016. Lesbian and gay expatriation: Opportunities, barriers and challenges for global mobility. *The International Journal of Human Resource Management* 27: 382–406.

Metcalfe, B., and C. Rees. 2010. Gender, globalization and organisation: Exploring power, relations and intersections. *Equality, Diversity and Inclusion: An International Journal* 29: 5–22.

Office for National Statistics. 2016. Short-term international migration annual report: Mid-2014 estimates. http://www.ons.gov.uk. Accessed 31 Oct 2016.

Ozturk, M., and A. Tatli. 2016. Gender identity inclusion in the workplace: Broadening diversity management research and practice through the case of transgender employees in the UK. *The International Journal of Human Resource Management* 27: 781–802.

Paisley, V., and M. Tayar. 2016. Lesbian, gay, bisexual and transgender (LGBT) expatriates: An intersectionality perspective. *The International Journal of Human Resource Management* 27: 766–780.

Romanowski, M., and R. Nasser. 2014. Identity issues: Expatriate professors teaching and researching in Qatar. *The International Journal of Higher Education Research* 69: 653–671.

Saroglou, V., and A.B. Cohen. 2011. Psychology of culture and religion introduction to the JCCP special issue. *Journal of Cross-Cultural Psychology* 42: 1309–1319.

Sonesh, S., and A. DeNisi. 2016. The categorization of expatriates and the support offered by host country nationals. *Journal of Global Mobility* 4: 18–43.

Song, M. 2004. Introduction: Who's at the bottom? Examining claims about racial hierarchy. *Ethnic and Racial Studies* 27: 859–877.

Suutari, V., and C. Brewster. 2000. Making their own way: International experience through self-initiated foreign assignments. *Journal of World Business* 35: 417–436.

Thomas, D., and M. Peterson. 2014. *Cross-cultural management.* 3rd ed. London: Sage.

Thompson, N. 2011. *Promoting equality.* 3rd ed. London: Palgrave.

————. 2016. *Anti-discriminatory practice.* 6th ed. London: Palgrave.

Treviño, L., and K. Nelson. 2011. *Managing business ethics.* 5th ed. New York: Wiley.

Wright, T. 2016. Women's experience of workplace interactions in male-dominated work: The intersections of gender, sexuality and occupational group. *Gender, Work and Organisation* 23: 348–362.

13

Concluding Assessment to Address 'Hidden' Inequalities in the Workplace

Valerie Caven and Stefanos Nachmias

13.1 Concluding Remarks

Throughout this book, we have expounded on the many and intricate ways in which 'hidden' inequalities are entrenched in the workplace. The chapters have drawn on a wide range of sources, including large-scale surveys, interviews, vignettes, focus groups and extended literature reviews to provide a far-reaching insight into the production and reproduction of inequalities. Despite legislation designed to prevent the occurrence of discrimination (cf. Sex Discrimination Act 1975; Equal Pay Act 1970; Equality Act 2010 to name the key ones which affect our area of study), it is clear that 'hidden' inequalities are firmly embedded within organisational practices and even policies. While we acknowledge deficiencies within the legal framework as we discussed in the introduction to this

V. Caven (✉) • S. Nachmias
Department of Human Resource Management, Nottingham Business School, Nottingham Trent University, Nottingham, UK

© The Author(s) 2018
V. Caven, S. Nachmias (eds.), *Hidden Inequalities in the Workplace*,
Palgrave Explorations in Workplace Stigma,
DOI 10.1007/978-3-319-59686-0_13

volume, we reiterate that it is not entirely to blame for the continued existence of unequal treatment at work as it does provide a framework of analysis and mechanism for challenging its perpetuation. Our intended contribution from this collection of chapters is to 'look below the surface' of what is considered accepted practice in employment to examine 'where', 'how' and 'why' inequalities continue despite increased awareness of issues surrounding diversity and inclusion, and the positive steps taken by many organisations in terms of developing an increasingly diverse workforce and the attendant benefits it brings.

Key to the discussions which have taken place in the preceding chapters is the notion of 'cosmetic treatment' of fundamental and underlying principles surrounding diversity issues. We question whether the 'hard' law approach in the UK means that organisations put in place an equality and diversity policy in order to meet the legal requirements, but without a true commitment to integrate true equality for all employees. Without an explicit intention on the part of employers, it cannot become custom and practice. We argue that all too frequently, organisations pay 'lip service' to issues of equality and diversity without any meaningful intention to assimilate them into everyday practices which has been demonstrated by the chapters.

Chapter 1 demonstrates the need to expand our knowledge around 'hidden' inequalities in the workplace and assesses the wider organisational and individual implications. Chapter 2 shows that organisations and managers provide a literal application of the Equality Act 2010 without extending it further to include all employees. It highlights the lack of organisational and managerial understanding about issues of employee dignity and inclusion as well as drawing attention to the liminality of the spheres of public and private aspects of life; here there is the public arena of eating whether it be an everyday lunch or a work-related function as either a celebration or a job-based requirement to entertain clients, for example. The public–private dichotomy/liminality aspect is continued in Chap. 2 with the discussion of neurodiversity. While this is a protected characteristic under the Equality Act 2010, the onus is on the neurodiverse individual to disclose *only if they choose to do so.* The nature of the condition means there is nothing immediately obvious about those with Asperger's to identify them as being on the autistic spectrum; thus individuals may decide not to inform their colleagues or managers (Chap. 3). In other cases, they may request specific adjustments to be made to their working environment; again, there is no requirement to disclose their condition should they choose not to.

A further protected characteristic, that of gender, is explored in Chap. 4. The Police Service is socially constructed as a discriminatory environment where women face serious challenges to becoming accepted, that their development opportunities are restricted and they suffer unequal treatment. The terms of the Equality Act 2010 (and the earlier Sex Discrimination Act of 1975) proscribes such treatment, yet, as this work illustrates, discrimination still occurs demonstrating organisational and institutional reluctance to address areas of inequalities. As Chap. 4 shows the covert nature of discrimination combined with a deeply ingrained sexist culture within the Police Service (England, Wales and Northern Ireland) permits the reproduction and replication of negative behaviours. Chapter 5 turns to the issue of age, again covered by the Equality Act 2010. Following the removal of the Default Retirement Age, employers cannot require employees to retire at a given age, reflecting a policy 'push' encouraging people to work for longer combined with a population who may not be ready to retire. While this is overall a welcome move to provide flexible working patterns, the 'hidden' inequality here is that there are issues in relation to health and wellbeing of older individuals, especially in relation to job quality. The work shows that many older workers are being forced into low-grade jobs or are denied promotion and training opportunities as a result of their age. The theme of denial of opportunities is continued within Chap. 6, which shows that employees who have adopted flexible working patterns are also deprived of chances for advancement or development, as employers and managers' perceptions are that they are somewhat less committed to their work.

Chapter 7 also highlights the role of socially constructed views around lesbians, gays, bisexuals and transgenders+ (LGBT+) in establishing 'hidden' behaviours in sports. The study offers an insightful analysis of the dynamics which marginalise LGBT+ participants in sport and the lack of 'space' to satisfying different sexual orientations. What is more interesting is the current 'culture' of acceptance between gendered and heterosexualised performances in sport, and how the expression of such a culture is often 'hidden' in specific spaces—behind the walls of the locker room or within the safety of the crowd in the stadium. Government bodies and sports governing organisations may have taken actions in raising awareness; nevertheless, there is still need to create interventions to visible and non-visible espoused narratives of inclusivity in sports.

Chapter 8 highlights the existence of 'hidden' gender and age inequalities in paid work, especially in relation to both precarious and gig work but also continues the debate in relation to unpaid and caring work which, in particular, affects many more women than men. Analysis shows that there are differences in employment types in intermediate level jobs where it is a grey area of potential discrimination with men occupying the higher-end intermediate jobs with knock-on effects in perpetuating the gender pay gap. What is more important is the wider career implications associated with the use of flexible working arrangements and reduced participation in paid work. While this chapter looks at the position of those already in employment, Chap. 9 moves to an earlier stage—that of obtaining work or advancement within work and the 'hidden' inequalities generated by cognitive biases in recruitment, selection and promotion. Here, the debates widen to not only examine gender but also to include age and sexuality. In this case, legislation, policy and innervations like diversity training do not tackle the issue of subconscious, implicit biases on organisational decision-making, exposing inherent managerial weaknesses.

The theme of sexuality is continued in Chap. 10 which examines gay men and their identity in the workplace. It shows that stigmatised identity among gay men (the issue of stigmatisation has been also discussed in Chap. 2) has an impact over their ability to perform and integrate in the workplace. Unsurprisingly, the level of management support and organisational accountability of discriminatory behaviours play a vital role in assisting and negotiating disclosure, and the degree to which gay men are willing to assert their identity in the workplace. Organisations have a moral obligation to accommodate disclosure and remove any 'hidden' element of poor management thinking. There is no doubt that a remarkable progress has been made towards the recognition of sexual minority rights in the workplace. However, this chapter shows the need for organisations to take further actions in protecting the identity of sexual minorities. While the preceding chapters have focussed on specific areas of inequality and bias, Chap. 11 provides a much more subjective and increasingly relevant point of view relating to engagement of employees. Each of the issues of 'hidden' inequality from the earlier chapters can contribute towards an employee feeling disempowered and displaying a lack of engagement. The focus turns from that of exclusion due to being stigmatised or experiencing prejudice to the overall impact on the organisation and co-workers of poor levels of employee engagement. Chapter 12 also illustrates an increased layer of complexity which is that of working in a different cultural, national and legal setting. While we have previously examined issues via the national and cultural lens of the UK and within its legal framework, this chapter provides an overview of those people covered by the 'protected characteristics' of the Equality Act 2010 in the UK when they move to a geographical region where there is no level of protection or, more drastically, where to display a protected characteristic carries serious and severe penalties. Using vignettes to provide the reader with 'think points', this chapter does not seek to provide answers rather to ask pertinent questions.

13.2   Future Implications

Our aim at the outset of this book project was to highlight areas of inequalities which fall outside of legal and policy protection, but exist 'under the surface' of organisational life, yet which are very real to those who are subject to the resulting exclusion, bias and discrimination. We believe that this book has brought into the surface the need to enhance awareness among individuals and provide more educational opportunities not only to understand the meaning of differences but also to change individuals' system thinking. We also believe that training is not the answer to all diversity and equality issues in the workplace. Socially constructed views emended in our society and old-fashioned thinking around equality of individuals requires more progressive educational interventions. There is no escape route in dealing with current 'hidden' inequalities as organisational practices should change to address future work trends. The Chartered Institute of Personnel and Development highlights the need for organisations and HR professionals to look beyond 'fads or fashions' around the future of work and ensure employees' voices are heard in a world of increased automation and volatility. In this case, the voices of individuals of all walks of life should be concerned equally.

Reflecting from the contributors insightful arguments, there are three key areas to consider in the future. Firstly, we need to explore and understand how dominant discourses within the literature exert an institutional power on the rhetoric and practice of diversity training, related to the multifaceted social constructs of diversity. Secondly, we have to evaluate whether diversity training could be seen as a possible solution to address discrimination and social differences within the organisation, and how organisation can identify and address 'hidden' inequality in the workplace. Lastly, we need to identify and assess any different training practices that will allow individuals to critically evaluate, debate and assess the impact of their own beliefs, values and prejudices. There is no doubt that various training models and frameworks are available for organisations. Nevertheless, the book demonstrates the need to evaluate further diversity and equality issues as training programmes is a complex web with threads that relate to personal cognitive maps of the knowledge producers.

Index

© The Author(s) 2018
V. Caven, S. Nachmias (eds.), *Hidden Inequalities in the Workplace*,
Palgrave Explorations in Workplace Stigma,
DOI 10.1007/978-3-319-59686-0

Lightning Source UK Ltd.
Milton Keynes UK
UKOW04n2343300817

308261UK00001B/14/P

9 783319 596853